Treasure of Ambedkar Se ies 03

PAKISTAN
OR
THE PARTITION OF INDIA

Treasure of Ambedkar Series 03

PAKISTAN
OR
THE PARTITION OF INDIA

Dr B.R. Ambedkar

KALPAZ

Treasure of Ambedkar Series 03

PAKISTAN OR THE PARTITION OF INDIA

ISBN: 978-93-5128-260-0

First Published 1945

Reprint 2017, in India by
Kalpaz Publications
C-30, Satyawati Nagar,
Delhi – 110052
E-mail: kalpaz@hotmail.com
Ph.: 9212142040

Printed at: G. Print Process, Delhi

TABLE OF CONTENTS

PREFACE TO THE SECOND EDITION

*

The problem of Pakistan has given a headache to everyone, more so to me than to anybody else. I cannot help recalling with regret how much of my time it has consumed when so much of my other literary work of greater importance to me than this is held up for want of it. I therefore hope that this second edition will also be the last. I trust that before it is exhausted either the question will be settled or withdrawn.

There are four respects in which this second edition differs from the first.

The first edition contained many misprints which formed the subject of complaints from many readers as well as reviewers. In preparing this edition, I have taken as much care as is possible to leave no room for complaint on this score. The first edition consisted only of three parts. Part V is an addition. It contains my own views on the various issues involved in the problem of Pakistan. It has been added because of the criticism levelled against the first edition that while I wrote about Pakistan I did not state what views I held on the subject. The present edition differs from the first in another respect. The maps contained in the first edition are retained but the number of appendices have been enlarged. In the first edition there were only eleven appendices. The present edition has twenty-five. To this edition I have also added an index which did not find a place in the first edition.

The book appears to have supplied a real want. I have seen how the thoughts, ideas and arguments contained in it have been pillaged by authors, politicians and editors of newspapers to support their sides. I am sorry they did not observe the decency of acknowledging the source even when they lifted not merely

* In the first edition there unfortunately occurred through oversight in proof correction a discrepancy between the population figures in the different districts of Bengal and the map showing the lay-out of Pakistan as applied to Bengal which had resulted in two districts which should have been included in the Pakistan area being excluded from it. In this edition, this error has been rectified and the map and the figures have been brought into conformity.

the argument but also the language of the book. But that is a matter I do not mind. I am glad that the book has been of service to Indians who are faced with this knotty problem of Pakistan. The fact that Mr. Gandhi and Mr. Jinnah in their recent talks cited the book as an authority on the subject which might be consulted with advantage bespeaks the worth of the book.

The book by its name might appear to deal only with the X. Y. Z. of Pakistan. It does more than that. It is an analytical presentation of Indian history and Indian politics in their communal aspects. As such, it is intended to explain the A. B. C. of Pakistan also. The book is more than a mere treatise on Pakistan. The material relating to Indian history and Indian politics contained in this book is so large and so varied that it might well be called Indian Political What is What.

The book has displeased both Hindus as well as Muslims though the reasons for the dislike of the Hindus are different from the reasons for the dislike of the Muslims. I am not sorry for this reception given to my book. That it is disowned by the Hindus and unowned by the Muslims is to me the best evidence that it has the vices of neither and that from the point of view of independence of thought and fearless presentation of facts the book is not a party production.

Some people are sore because what I have said has hurt them. I have not, I confess, allowed myself to be influenced by fears of wounding either individuals or classes, or shocking opinions however respectable they may be. I have often felt regret in pursuing this course, but remorse never. Those whom I may have offended must forgive me, in consideration of the honesty and disinterestedness of my aim. I do not claim to have written dispassionately though I trust I have written without prejudice. It would be hardly possible—I was going to say decent—for an Indian to be calm when he talks of his country and thinks of the times. In dealing with the question of Pakistan my object has been to draw a perfectly accurate, and, at the same time, a suggestive picture of the situation as I see it. Whatever points of strength and weakness I have discovered on either side I have brought them boldly forward. I have taken pains to throw light on the mischievous effects that are likely to proceed from an obstinate and impracticable course of action.

Preface to the Second Edition

The witness of history regarding the conflict between the forces of the authority of the State and of anti-State nationalism within, has been uncertain, if not equivocal. As Prof. Friedmann* observes:—

> "There is not a single modern State which has not, at one time or another, forced a recalcitrant national group to live under its authority. Scots, Bretons, Catalans, Germans, Poles, Czechs, Finns, all have, at some time or another, been compelled to accept the authority of a more powerful State whether they liked it or not. Often, as in Great Britain or France, force eventually led to co-operation and a co-ordination of State authority and national cohesion. But in many cases, such as those of Germany, Poland, Italy and a host of Central European and Balkan countries, the forces of Nationalism did not rest until they had thrown off the shackles of State Power and formed a State of their own. . . ."

In the last edition, I depicted the experience of countries in which the State engaged itself in senseless suppression of nationalism and weathered away in the attempt. In this edition I have added by way of contrast the experience of other countries to show that given the will to live together it is not impossible for diverse communities and even for diverse nations to live in the bosom of one State. It might be said that in tendering advice to both sides I have used terms more passionate than they need have been. If I have done so it is because I felt that the manner of the physician who tries to surprise the vital principle in each paralyzed organ in order to goad it to action was best suited to stir up the average Indian who is complacent if not somnolent, who is unsuspecting if not ill-informed, to realize what is happening. I hope my effort will have the desired effect.

I cannot close this preface without thanking Prof. Manohar B. Chitnis of the Khalsa College, Bombay, and Mr. K. V. Chitre for their untiring labours to remove all printer's and clerical errors that had crept into the first edition and to see that this edition is free from all such blemishes. I am also very grateful to Prof. Chitnis for the preparation of the Index which has undoubtedly enhanced the utility of the book.

1st January 1945,
22, Prithviraj Road,
New Delhi.

B. R. AMBEDKAR.

---

* *The Crisis of the National State* (1943), p. 4.

PROLOGUE

It can rightly be said that the long introduction with which this treatise opens leaves no excuse for a prologue. But there is an epilogue which is affixed to the treatise. Having done that, I thought of prefixing a prologue, firstly, because an epilogue needs to be balanced by a prologue, and secondly, because the prologue gives me room to state in a few words the origin of this treatise to those who may be curious to know it and to impress upon the readers the importance of the issues raised in it. For the satisfaction of the curious it may be stated that there exists, at any rate in the Bombay Presidency, a political organization called the Independent Labour Party (abbreviated into I.L.P.) for the last three years. It is not an ancient, hoary organization which can claim to have grown grey in politics. The I.L.P. is not in its dotage and is not overtaken by senility, for which second childhood is given as a more agreeable name. Compared with other political organizations, the I.L.P. is a young and fairly active body, not subservient to any clique or interest. Immediately after the passing of the Lahore Resolution on Pakistan by the Muslim League, the Executive Council of the I.L.P. met to consider what attitude it should adopt towards this project of Pakistan. The Executive Council could see that there was underlying Pakistan an idea to which no objection could be taken. Indeed, the Council was attracted to the scheme of Pakistan inasmuch as it meant the creation of ethnic states as a solution of the communal problem. The Council, however, did not feel competent to pronounce at that stage a decided opinion on the issue of Pakistan. The Council, therefore, resolved to appoint a committee to study the question and make a report on it. The committee consisted of myself as the Chairman, and Principal M. V. Donde, B.A., Mr. S. C. Joshi, M.A., LL.B., Advocate (O.S.), M.L.C., Mr. R. R. Bhole, B.Sc., LL.B., M.L.A., Mr. D. G. Jadhav, B.A., LL.B., M.L.A., and Mr. A. V. Chitre, B.A., M.L.A., all belonging to the I.L.P., as members of the committee. Mr. D. V. Pradhan, member, Bombay Municipal Corporation, acted as Secretary to the committee. The committee asked me to prepare a report on Pakistan which I did. The same was submitted to the Executive Council of the I. L. P., which resolved that the report should be published. The treatise now published is that report.

The book is intended to assist the student of Pakistan to come to his own conclusion. With that object in view, I have not only assembled in this volume all the necessary and relevant data but have also added 14 appendices and 3 maps, which, in my judgment, form an important accompaniment to the book.

It is not enough for the reader to go over the material collected in the following pages. He must also reflect over it. Let him take to heart the warning which Carlyle gave to Englishmen of his generation. He said:

> "The Genius of England no longer soars Sunward, world-defiant, like an Eagle through the storms, 'mewing her mighty youth,' . . . . : the Genius of England—much like a greedy Ostrich intent on provender and a whole skin . . . . . ; with its Ostrich-head stuck into . . . . . whatever sheltering Fallacy there may be, and *so* awaits the issue. The issue has been slow; but it now seems to have been inevitable. No Ostrich, intent on gross terrene provender and sticking its head into Fallacies, but will be awakened one day—in a terrible *a posteriori* manner if not otherwise! Awake before it comes to that. Gods and men bid us awake! The Voices of our Fathers, with thousandfold stern monition to one and all, bid us awake."

This warning, I am convinced, applies to Indians in their present circumstances as it once did to Englishmen, and Indians, if they pay no heed to it, will do so at their peril.

Now, a word for those who have helped me in the preparation of this report. Mr. M. G. Tipnis, D.C.E., (Kalabhuwan, Baroda), and Mr. Chhaganlal S. Mody have rendered me great assistance, the former in preparing the maps and the latter in typing the manuscript. I wish to express my gratitude to both for their work which they have done purely as a labour of love. Thanks are also due in a special measure to my friends Mr. B. R. Kadrekar and Mr. K. V. Chitre for their labours in undertaking the most uninteresting and dull task of correcting the proofs and supervising the printing.

28th December, 1940,
'Rajagrah,'
Dadar, Bombay, 14.

B. R. AMBEDKAR.

INTRODUCTION

The Muslim League's Resolution on Pakistan has called forth different reactions. There are some who look upon it as a case of political measles to which a people in the infancy of their conscious unity and power are very liable. Others have taken it as a permanent frame of the Muslim mind and not merely a passing phase and have in consequence been greatly perturbed.

The question is undoubtedly controversial. The issue is vital and there is no argument which has not been used in the controversy by one side to silence the other. Some argue that this demand for partitioning India into two political entities under separate national states staggers their imagination; others are so choked with a sense of righteous indignation at this wanton attempt to break the unity of a country, which, it is claimed, has stood as one for centuries, that their rage prevents them from giving expression to their thoughts. Others think that it need not be taken seriously. They treat it as a trifle and try to destroy it by shooting into it similes and metaphors. "You don't cut your head to cure your headache," "you don't cut a baby into two because two women are engaged in fighting out a claim as to who its mother is," are some of the analogies which are used to prove the absurdity of Pakistan. In a controversy carried on the plane of pure sentiment, there is nothing surprising if a dispassionate student finds more stupefaction and less understanding, more heat and less light, more ridicule and less seriousness.

My position in this behalf is definite, if not singular. I do not think the demand for Pakistan is the result of mere political distemper, which will pass away with the efflux of time. As I read the situation, it seems to me that it is a characteristic in the biological sense of the term, which the Muslim body politic has developed in the same manner as an organism develops a characteristic. Whether it will survive or not, in the process of natural selection, must depend upon the forces that may become operative in the struggle for existence between Hindus and Musalmans. I am not staggered by Pakistan; I am not indignant about it; nor do I believe that it can be smashed by shooting into it similes and metaphors. Those who believe in shooting it by similes should remember that nonsense does not cease to be nonsense because it is put in rhyme, and that a metaphor is no argument though it be sometimes the gunpowder to drive one home and imbed it in memory. I believe that it would be neither wise nor possible to reject summarily a scheme if it has behind it the sentiment, if not the passionate support, of 90 p.c. Muslims of India. I have no doubt that the only proper attitude to Pakistan is to study it in all its aspects, to understand its implications and to form an intelligent judgment about it.

With all this, a reader is sure to ask: Is this book on Pakistan seasonable in the sense that one must read it, as one must eat the fruits of the season to keep oneself in health? If it is seasonable, is it readable? These are natural queries and an author, whose object is to attract readers, may well make use of the introduction to meet them.

As to the seasonableness of the book there can be no doubt. The way of looking at India by Indians themselves must be admitted to have undergone a complete change during the last 20 years. Referring to India Prof. Arnold Toynbee wrote in 1915:—

> "British statesmanship in the nineteenth century regarded India as a 'Sleeping Beauty,' whom Britain had a prescriptive right to woo when she awoke; so it hedged with thorns the garden where she lay, to safeguard her from marauders prowling in the desert without. Now the princess is awake, and is claiming the right to dispose of her own hand, while the marauders have transformed themselves into respectable gentlemen diligently occupied in turning the desert into a garden too, but grievously impeded by the British thorn-hedge. When they politely request us to remove it, we shall do well to consent, for they will not make the demand till they feel themselves strong enough to enforce it, and in the tussle that will follow if we refuse, the sympathies of the Indian princess will not be on our side. Now that she is awake, she wishes to walk abroad among her neighbours; she feels herself capable of rebuffing without our countenance any blandishments or threats they may offer her, and she is becoming as weary as they of the thorn-hedge that confines her to her garden.
>
> "If we treat her with tact, India will never wish to secede from the spiritual brotherhood of the British Empire, but it is

> inevitable that she should lead a more and more independent life of her own, and follow the example of Anglo-Saxon Commonwealths by establishing direct relations with her neighbours. . . ."

Although the writer is an Englishman, the view expressed by him in 1915 was the view commonly held by all Indians irrespective of caste or creed. Now that India the "Sleeping Beauty" of Prof. Toynbee is awake, what is the view of the Indians about her? On this question, there can be no manner of doubt that those who have observed this Sleeping Beauty behave in recent years, feel she is a strange being quite different from the angelic princess that she was supposed to be. She is a mad maiden having a dual personality, half human, half animal, always in convulsions because of her two natures in perpetual conflict. If there is any doubt about her dual personality, it has now been dispelled by the Resolution of the Muslim League demanding the cutting up of India into two, Pakistan and Hindustan, so that these conflicts and convulsions due to a dual personality having been bound in one may cease forever, and so freed from each other, may dwell in separate homes congenial to their respective cultures, Hindu and Muslim.

It is beyond question that Pakistan is a scheme which will have to be taken into account. The Muslims will insist upon the scheme being considered. The British will insist upon some kind of settlement being reached between the Hindus and the Muslims before they consent to any devolution of political power. There is no use blaming the British for insisting upon such a settlement as a condition precedent to the transfer of power. The British cannot consent to settle power upon an aggressive Hindu majority and make it its heir, leaving it to deal with the minorities at its sweet pleasure. That would not be ending imperialism. It would be creating another imperialism. The Hindus, therefore, cannot avoid coming to grips with Pakistan, much as they would like to do.

If the scheme of Pakistan has to be considered, and there is no escape from it, then there are certain points which must be borne in mind.

The first point to note is that the Hindus and Muslims must decide the question themselves. They cannot invoke the aid of anyone else. Certainly, they cannot expect the British to decide it for them. From the point of view of the Empire, it matters very little to the British whether India remains one undivided whole, or is partitioned into two parts, Pakistan and Hindustan, or into twenty linguistic fragments as planned by the Congress, so long as all of them are content to live within the Empire. The British need not interfere for the simple reason that they are not affected by such territorial divisions.

Further, if the Hindus are hoping that the British will use force to put down Pakistan, that is impossible. In the first place, coercion is no remedy. The futility of force and resistance was pointed out by Burke long ago in his speeches relating to the coercion of the American colonies. His memorable words may be quoted not only for the benefit of the Hindu Maha Sabha but also for the benefit of all. This is what he said:

> "The use of force alone is temporary. It may endure a moment but it does not remove the necessity of subduing again: a nation is not governed which is perpetually to be conquered. The next objection to force is its uncertainty. Terror is not always the effect of force, and an armament is not a victory. If you do not succeed you are without resource; for conciliation failing, force remains; but force failing, no further hope of reconciliation is left. Power and Authority are sometimes bought by kindness, but they can never be begged as alms by an impoverished and defeated violence. A further objection to force is that you impair the object by your very endeavours to preserve it. The thing you fought for (to wit the loyalty of the people) is not the thing you recover, but depreciated, sunk, wasted and consumed in the contest."

Coercion, as an alternative to Pakistan, is therefore unthinkable.

Again, the Muslims cannot be deprived of the benefit of the principle of self-determination. The Hindu Nationalists who rely on self-determination and ask how Britain can refuse India what the conscience of the world has conceded to the smallest of the European nations, cannot in the same breath ask the British to deny it to other minorities. The Hindu Nationalist who hopes that Britain will coerce the Muslims into abandoning Pakistan, forgets that the right of nationalism to freedom from an aggressive foreign imperialism and the right of a minority to freedom from an aggressive majority's nationalism are not two

different things; nor does the former stand on a more sacred footing than the latter. They are merely two aspects of the struggle for freedom and as such equal in their moral import. Nationalists, fighting for freedom from aggressive imperialism, cannot well ask the help of the British imperialists to thwart the right of a minority to freedom from the nationalism of an aggressive majority. The matter must, therefore, be decided upon by the Muslims and the Hindus alone. The British cannot decide the issue for them. This is the first important point to note.

The essence of Pakistan is the opposition to the establishment of one Central Government having supremacy over the whole of India. Pakistan contemplates two Central Governments, one for Pakistan and the other for Hindustan. This gives rise to the second important point which Indians must take note of. That point is that the issue of Pakistan shall have to be decided upon before the plans for a new constitution are drawn and its foundations are laid. If there is to be one Central Government for India, the design of the constitutional structure would be different from what it would be if there is to be one Central Government for Hindustan and another for Pakistan. That being so, it will be most unwise to postpone the decision. Either the scheme should be abandoned and another substituted by mutual agreement or it should be decided upon. It will be the greatest folly to suppose that if Pakistan is buried for the moment, it will never raise its head again. I am sure, burying Pakistan is not the same thing as burying the ghost of Pakistan. So long as the hostility to one Central Government for India, which is the ideology underlying Pakistan, persists, the ghost of Pakistan will be there, casting its ominous shadow upon the political future of India. Neither will it be prudent to make some kind of a make-shift arrangement for the time being, leaving the permanent solution to some future day. To do so would be something like curing the symptoms without removing the disease. But, as often happens in such cases, the disease is driven in, thereby making certain its recurrence, perhaps in a more virulent form.

I feel certain that whether India should have one Central Government is not a matter which can be taken as settled; it is a matter in issue and although it may not be a live issue now, some day it will be.

The Muslims have openly declared that they do not want to have any Central Government in India and they have given their reasons in the most unambiguous terms. They have succeeded in bringing into being five provinces which are predominantly Muslim in population. In these provinces, they see the possibility of the Muslims forming a government and they are anxious to see that the independence of the Muslim Governments in these provinces is preserved. Actuated by these considerations, the Central Government is an eye-sore to the Muslims of India. As they visualize the scene, they see their Muslim Provinces made subject to a Central Government predominantly Hindu and endowed with powers of supervision over, and even of interference in, the administration of these Muslim Provinces. The Muslims feel that to accept one Central Government for the whole of India is to consent to place the Muslim Provincial Governments under a Hindu Central Government and to see the gain secured by the creation of Muslim Provinces lost by subjecting them to a Hindu Government at the Centre. The Muslim way of escape from this tyranny of a Hindu Centre is to have no Central Government in India at all.*

Are the Musalmans alone opposed to the existence of a Central Government? What about the Hindus? There seems to be a silent premise underlying all political discussions that are going on among the Hindus that there will always be in India a Central Government as a permanent part of her political constitution. How far such a premise can be taken for granted is more than I can say. I may, however, point out that there are two factors which are dormant for the present but which some day may become dominant and turn the Hindus away from the idea of a Central Government.

The first is the cultural antipathy between the Hindu Provinces. The Hindu Provinces are by no means a happy family. It cannot be pretended that the Sikhs have any tenderness for the Bengalees or the Rajputs or the Madrasis. The Bengalee

* This point of view was put forth by Sir Muhammad Iqbal at the Third Round Table Conference.

loves only himself. The Madrasi is bound by his own world. As to the Mahratta, who does not recall that the Mahrattas, who set out to destroy the Muslim Empire in India, became a menace to the rest of the Hindus whom they harassed and kept under their yoke for nearly a century? The Hindu Provinces have no common traditions and no interests to bind them. On the other hand, the differences of language, race, and the conflicts of the past have been the most powerful forces tending to divide them. It is true that the Hindus are getting together and the spirit moving them to become one united nation is working on them. But it must not be forgotten that they have not yet become a nation. They are in the process of becoming a nation and before the process is completed, there may be a setback which may destroy the work of a whole century.

In the second place, there is the financial factor. It is not sufficiently known what it costs the people of India to maintain the Central Government and the proportionate burden each Province has to bear.

The total revenue of British India comes to Rs. 194,64,17,926 per annum. Of this sum, the amount raised by the Provincial Governments from provincial sources, comes annually to Rs. 73,57,50,125 and that raised by the Central Government from central sources of revenue comes to Rs. 121,06,67,801. This will show what the Central Government costs the people of India. When one considers that the Central Government is concerned only with maintaining peace and does not discharge any functions which have relation to the progress of the people, it should cause no surprise if people begin to ask whether it is necessary that they should pay annually such an enormous price to purchase peace. In this connection, it must be borne in mind that the people in the provinces are literally starving and there is no source left to the provinces to increase their revenue.

This burden of maintaining the Central Government, which the people of India have to bear, is most unevenly distributed over the different provinces. The sources of central revenues are (1) Customs, (2) Excise, (3) Salt, (4) Currency, (5) Posts and Telegraphs, (6) Income Tax and (7) Railways. It is not possible from the accounts published by the Government of India to work out the distribution of the three sources of central revenue, namely Currency, Posts and Telegraphs and Railways. Only the revenue raised from other sources can be worked out province by province. The result is shown in the following table:—

	Provinces.	Revenue raised by Provincial Government from provincial sources.	Revenue raised by Central Government from central sources.
		Rs.	Rs.
1	Madras	16,13,44,520	9,53,26,745
2	Bombay	12,44,59,553	22,53,44,247
3	Bengal	12,76,60,892	23,79,01,583
4	U. P.	12,79,99,851	4,05,53,030
5	Bihar	5,23,83,030	1,54,37,742
6	C. P. & Berar	4,27,41,280	31,42,682
7	Assam	2,58,48,474	1,87,55,967
8	Orissa	1,81,99,823	5,67,346
9	Punjab	11,35,86,355	1,18,01,385
10	N.-W. F. P.	1,80,83,548	9,28,294
11	Sind	3,70,29,354	5,66,46,915

It will be seen from this table that the burden of maintaining the Central Government is not only heavy but falls unequally upon the different provinces. The Bombay Provincial Government raises Rs. 12,44,59,553; as against this, the Central Government raises Rs. 22,53,44,247 from Bombay. The Bengal Government raises Rs. 12,76,60,892; as against this, the Central Government raises Rs. 23,79,01,583 from Bengal. The Sind Government raises Rs. 3,70,29,354; as against this, the Central Government raises Rs. 5,66,46,915 from Sind. The Assam Government raises nearly Rs. 2½ crores; but the Central Government raises nearly Rs. 2 crores from Assam. While such is the burden of the Central Government on these provinces, the rest of the provinces contribute next to nothing to the Central Government. The Punjab raises Rs. 11 crores for itself but contributes only Rs. 1 crore to the Central Government. In the N.-W. F. P. the provincial revenue is Rs. 1,80,83,548; its total contribution to the Central Government however is only Rs. 9,28,294. U.P.

raises Rs. 13 crores but contributes only Rs. 4 crores to the Centre. Bihar collects Rs. 5 crores for itself; she gives only 1½ crores to the Centre. C. P. and Berar levy a total of 4 crores and pay to the Centre 31 lakhs.

This financial factor has so far passed without notice. But time may come when even to the Hindus, who are the strongest supporters of a Central Government in India, the financial considerations may make a greater appeal than what purely patriotic considerations do now. So, it is possible that some day the Muslims, for communal considerations, and the Hindus, for financial considerations, may join hands to abolish the Central Government.

If this were to happen, it is better if it happens before the foundation of a new constitution is laid down. If it happens after the foundation of the new constitution envisaging one Central Government were laid down, it would be the greatest disaster. Out of the general wreck, not only India as an entity will vanish, but it will not be possible to save even the Hindu unity. As I have pointed out, there is not much cement even among the Hindu Provinces, and once that little cement which exists is lost, there will be nothing with which to build up even the unity of the Hindu Provinces. It is because of this that Indians must decide, before preparing the plans and laying the foundations, for whom the constitutional structure is to be raised and whether it is temporary or permanent. After the structure is built as one whole, on one single foundation, with girders running through from one end to the other, if, thereafter, a part is to be severed from the rest, the knocking out of the rivets will shake the whole building and produce cracks in other parts of the structure which are intended to remain as one whole. The danger of cracks is greater, if the cement which binds them is, as in the case of India, of a poor quality. If the new constitution is designed for India as one whole and a structure is raised on that basis, and thereafter the question of separation of Pakistan from Hindustan is raised and the Hindus have to yield, the alterations that may become necessary to give effect to this severance may bring about the collapse of the whole structure. The desire of the Muslim Provinces may easily infect the Hindu Provinces and the spirit of disruption generated by the Muslim Provinces may cause all round disintegration.

History is not wanting in instances of constitutions threatened with disruption. There is the instance of the Southern States of the American Union. Natal has always been anxious to get out from the Union of South Africa and Western Australia recently applied, though unsuccessfully, to secede from the Australian Commonwealth.

In these cases actual disruption has not taken place and where it did, it was soon healed. Indians, however, cannot hope to be so fortunate. Theirs may be the fate of Czechoslovakia. In the first place, it would be futile to entertain the hope that if a disruption of the Indian constitution took place by the Muslim Provinces separating from the Hindu Provinces, it would be possible to win back the seceding provinces as was done in the U.S.A. after the Civil War. Secondly, if the new Indian constitution is a Dominion Constitution, even the British may find themselves powerless to save the constitution from such a disruption, if it takes place after its foundations are laid. It seems to be, therefore, imperative that the issue of Pakistan should be decided upon before the new constitution is devised.

If there can be no doubt that Pakistan is a scheme which Indians will have to resolve upon at the next revision of the constitution and if there is no escape from deciding upon it, then it would be a fatal mistake for the people to approach it without a proper understanding of the question. The ignorance of some of the Indian delegates to the Round Table Conference of constitutional law, I remember, led Mr. Garvin of the *Observer* to remark that it would have been much better if the Simon Commission, instead of writing a report on India, had made a report on constitutional problems of India and how they were met by the constitutions of the different countries of the world. Such a report I know was prepared for the use of the delegates who framed the constitution of South Africa. This is an attempt to make good that deficiency and as such I believe it will be welcomed as a seasonable piece.

So much for the question whether the book is seasonable. As to the second question, whether the book is readable no writer can forget the words of Augustine Birrell when he said :—

> "Cooks, warriors, and authors must be judged by the effects they produce; toothsome dishes, glorious victories, pleasant books, these are our demands. We have nothing to do with ingredients, tactics, or methods. We have no desire to be admitted into the kitchen, the council, or the study. The cook may use her saucepans how she pleases, the warrior place his men as he likes, the author handle his material or weave his plot as best he can; when the dish is served we only ask, Is it good?; when the battle has been fought, Who won?; when the book comes out, Does it read?
>
> "Authors ought not to be above being reminded that it is their first duty to write agreeably. Some very disagreeable men have succeeded in doing so, and there is, therefore, no need for any one to despair. Every author, be he grave or gay, should try to make his book as ingratiating as possible. Reading is not a duty, and has consequently no business to be made disagreeable. Nobody is under any obligation to read any other man's book."

I am fully aware of this. But I am not worried about it. That may well apply to other books but not to a book on Pakistan. Every Indian must read a book on Pakistan, if not this, then some other, if he wants to help his country to steer a clear path.

If any book does not read well, i.e., its taste be not good, the reader will find two things in it which, I am sure, are good.

The first thing he will find is that the ingredients are good. There is in the book material which will be helpful and to gain access to which he will have to labour a great deal. Indeed, the reader will find that the book contains an epitome of India's political and social history during the last twenty years, which it is necessary for every Indian to know.

The second thing he will find is that there is no partisanship. The aim is to expound the scheme of Pakistan in all its aspects and not to advocate it. The aim is to explain and not to convert. It would, however, be a pretence to say that I have no views on Pakistan. Views I have. Some of them are expressed, others may have to be gathered. Two things, however, may well be said about my views. In the first place, wherever they are expressed, they have been reasoned out. Secondly, whatever the views, they have certainly not the fixity of a popular prejudice. They are really thoughts and not views. In other words, I have an open mind, though not an empty mind. A person with an open mind is always the subject of congratulations. While this may be so, it must, at the same time, be realized that an open mind may also be an empty mind and that such an open mind, if it is a happy condition, is also a very dangerous condition for a man to be in. A disaster may easily overtake a man with an empty mind. Such a person is like a ship without ballast and without a rudder. It can have no direction. It may float but may also suffer a shipwreck against a rock for want of direction. While aiming to help the reader by placing before him all the material, relevant and important, the reader will find that I have not sought to impose my views on him. I have placed before him both sides of the question and have left him to form his own opinion.

The reader may complain that I have been provocative in stating the relevant facts. I am conscious that such a charge may be levelled against me. I apologize freely and gladly for the same. My excuse is that I have no intention to hurt. I had only one purpose, that is, to force the attention of the indifferent and casual reader to the issue that is dealt with in the book. I ask the reader to put aside any irritation that he may feel with me and concentrate his thoughts on this tremendous issue: Which is to be, Pakistan or no Pakistan?

PART I

MUSLIM CASE FOR PAKISTAN

The Muslim Case for Pakistan is sought to be justified on the following grounds :—

(*i*) *What the Muslims are asking for is the creation of administrative areas which are ethnically more homogeneous.*

(*ii*) *The Muslims want these homogeneous administrative areas which are predominantly Muslim to be constituted into separate States,*

(*a*) *because the Muslims by themselves constitute a separate nation and desire to have a national home, and*

(*b*) *because experience shows that the Hindus want to use their majority to treat the Muslims as though they were second-class citizens in an alien State.*

This part is devoted to the exposition of these grounds.

CHAPTER I

WHAT DOES THE LEAGUE DEMAND?

I

On the 26th of March 1940, Hindu India was startled to attention as it had never been before. On that day, the Muslim League at its Lahore Session passed the following Resolution :—

"1. While approving and endorsing the action taken by the Council and the Working Committee of the All-India Muslim League as indicated in their resolutions dated the 27th of August, 17th and 18th of September and 22nd of October 1939 and 3rd of February 1940 on the constitutional issue, this Session of the All-India Muslim League emphatically reiterates that the Scheme of Federation embodied in the Government of India Act, 1935, is totally unsuited to, and unworkable in the peculiar conditions of this country and is altogether unacceptable to Muslim India.

"2. It further records its emphatic view that while the declaration dated the 18th of October 1939 made by the Viceroy on behalf of His Majesty's Government is reassuring in as far as it declares that the policy and plan on which the Government of India Act, 1935, is based will be reconsidered in consultation with the various parties, interests and communities in India, Muslim India will not be satisfied unless the whole constitutional plan is reconsidered *de novo* and that no revised plan would be acceptable to the Muslims, unless it is framed with their approval and consent.

"3. Resolved that it is the considered view of this Session of the All-India Muslim League that no constitutional plan would be workable in this country or acceptable to the Muslims unless it is designated on the following basic principle, viz. that geographically contiguous units are demarcated into regions which should be so constituted with such territorial readjustments as may be necessary, that the areas in which the Muslims are numerically in a majority as in the North-Western and Eastern Zones of India should be grouped to constitute "Independent States" in which the Constituent Units shall be autonomous and sovereign;

"4. That adequate, effective and mandatory safeguards should be specifically provided in the constitution for minorities in these units and in the regions for the protection of their religious, cultural, economic, political, administrative and other rights, and interests in consultation with them; and in other parts of India where the Musalmans are in a minority, adequate, effective and mandatory safeguards shall be specifically provided in the constitution for them and other minorities for the protection of their religious, cultural, economic, political, administrative and other rights, and interests in consultation with them.

"5. This Session further authorizes the Working Committee to frame a scheme of Constitution in accordance with these basic principles, providing for the assumption finally by the respective regions of all powers such as defence, external affairs, communication, customs, and such other matters as may be necessary."

What does this Resolution contemplate? A reference to para 3 of the Resolution will show that the Resolution contemplates that the areas in which Muslims predominate shall be incorporated into independent States. In concrete terms, it means that the Punjab, the North-Western Frontier Province, Baluchistan and Sind in the North-West and Bengal in the East instead of remaining as the provinces of British India shall be incorporated as independent States outside of British India. This is the sum and substance of the Resolution of the Muslim League.

Does the Resolution contemplate that these Muslim provinces, after being incorporated into States, will remain each an independent sovereign State or will they be joined together into one constitution as members of a single State, federal or unitary? On this point, the Resolution is rather ambiguous, if not self-contradictory. It speaks of grouping the zones into "Independent States in which the Constituent Units shall be autonomous and sovereign." The use of the terms "Constituent Units" indicates that what is contemplated is a Federation. If that is so, then, the use of the word "sovereign" as an attribute of the Units is out of place. Federation of Units and sovereignty of Units are contradictions. It may be that what is contemplated is a confederation. It is, however, not very material for the moment whether these Independent States are to form into a federation or a confederation. What is important is the basic demand, namely, that these areas are to be separated from India and formed into independent States.

The Resolution is so worded as to give the idea that the scheme adumbrated in it is a new one. But, there can be no doubt that the Resolution merely resuscitates a scheme which was put forth by Sir Mahomed Iqbal in his Presidential address to the Muslim League at its Annual Session held at Lucknow in December 1930. The scheme was not then adopted by the League. It was, however, taken up by one Mr. Rehmat Ali who gave it the name, Pakistan, by which it is known. Mr. Rehmat Ali, M.A., LL.B., founded the Pakistan Movement in 1933. He divided India into two, namely, *Pakistan* and *Hindustan*. His Pakistan included the Punjab, N.-W.F. Province, Kashmir, Sind and Baluchistan. The rest to him was *Hindustan*. His idea was to have an "independent and separate Pakistan" composed of five Muslim provinces in the North as an independent State. The proposal was circulated to the members of the Round Table Conference but never officially put forth. It seems an attempt was made privately to obtain the assent of the British Government, who, however, declined to consider it because they thought that this was a "revival of the old Muslim Empire."*

The League has only enlarged the original scheme of Pakistan. It has sought to create one more Muslim State in the East to include the Muslims in Bengal and Assam. Barring this, it expresses in its essence and general outline the scheme put forth by Sir Mahomed Iqbal and propagated by Mr. Rehmat Ali. There is no name given to this new Muslim State in the East. This has made no difference in the theory and the issues involved in the ideology of Mr. Rehmat Ali. The only difficulty one feels is that the League, while enlarging the facets, has not christened the two Muslims States with short and sweet names as it might have been expected to do. That it did not do and we are left to carry on the discussion with two long jaw-breaking

* Halide Edib — *Inside India*, p. 355.

names of Muslim State in the West and Muslim State in the East. I propose to solve this difficulty by reserving the name Pakistan to express the ideology underlying the two-nation theory and its consequent effect, namely, partition, and by designating the two Muslim States in the North-West and North-East as Western Pakistan and Eastern Pakistan.

The scheme not only called Hindu India to attention but it shocked Hindu India. Now it is natural to ask, what is there that is new or shocking in this scheme?

II

Is the idea of linking up of the provinces in the North-West a shocking idea? If so, let it be remembered that the linking of these provinces is an age-old project put forth by successive Viceroys, Administrators and Generals. Of the Pakistan provinces in the North-West, the Punjab and N.-W.F.P. constituted a single province ever since the Punjab was conquered by the British in 1849. The two continued to be a single province till 1901. It was in 1901 that Lord Curzon broke up their unity and created the present two provinces. As to the linking up of the Punjab with Sind, there can be no doubt that had the conquest of Sind followed and not preceded the conquest of the Punjab, Sind would have been incorporated into the Punjab, for the two are not only contiguous but are connected by a single river which is the most natural tie between them. Although Sind was joined to Bombay, which in the absence of the Punjab was the only base from which it could be governed, the idea of disconnecting Sind from Bombay and joining it to the Punjab was not given up and projects in that behalf were put forth from time to time. It was first put forth during the Governor-Generalship of Lord Dalhousie; but for financial reasons, was not sanctioned by the Court of Directors. After the Mutiny, the question was reconsidered but owing to the backward state of communications along the Indus, Lord Canning refused to give his consent. In 1876, Lord Northbrook was of the opinion that Sind should be joined to the Punjab. In 1877, Lord Lytton, who succeeded Northbrook, sought to create a trans-Indus province, consisting of the six frontier districts of the Punjab and of the trans-Indus districts of Sind. This would have included the six Frontier districts of the Punjab, namely, Hazara, Peshawar, Kohat, Bannu (except the Cis-Indus tracts), Dera Ismail Khan (with the same exception), Dera Ghazi Khan, and trans-Indus Sind (with the exception of Karachi). Lytton also proposed that Bombay should receive the whole or part of the Central Provinces, in order to compensate it for the loss of trans-Indus Sind. These proposals were not acceptable to the Secretary of State. During the Viceroyalty of Lord Lansdowne (1888-94), the same project was revived in its original form, namely, the transfer of Sind to the Punjab, but owing to the formation of the Baluchistan Agency, Sind had ceased to be a Frontier district and the idea which was military in its motive, lost its force and Sind remained without being incorporated in the Punjab. Had the British not acquired Baluchistan and had Lord Curzon not thought of carving out the N.-W.F.P. out of the Punjab, we would have witnessed long ago the creation of Pakistan as an administrative unit.

With regard to the claim for the creation of a national Muslim State in Bengal, again, there is nothing new in it. It will be recalled by many that in 1905, the province of Bengal and Assam was divided by the then Viceroy, Lord Curzon into two provinces: (1) Eastern Bengal and Assam with Dacca as its capital and (2) Western Bengal with Calcutta as its capital. The newly-created province of Eastern Bengal and Assam included Assam and the following districts of the old province of Bengal and Assam: (1) Dacca, (2) Mymensingh, (3) Faridpur, (4) Backergunge, (5) Tippera, (6) Noakhali, (7) Chittagong, (8) Chittagong Hill Tracts, (9) Rajashahi, (10) Dinajpur, (11) Jalpaiguri. (12) Rangpur, (13) Bogra, (14) Pabna and (15) Malda. Western Bengal included the remaining districts of the old Province of Bengal and Assam with the addition of the district of Sambalpur which was transferred from C.P. to Western Bengal.

This division of one province into two, which is known in Indian history as the Partition of Bengal, was an attempt to create a Muslim State in Eastern Bengal, inasmuch as the new province of Eastern Bengal and Assam was, barring parts of Assam, a predominantly Muslim area. But, the partition was abrogated in 1911 by the British who yielded to the Hindus, who were opposed to it and did not care for the wishes of the Muslims, as they were too weak to make themselves felt. If the partition of Bengal had not been annulled, the Muslim State in Eastern Bengal, instead of being a new project, would now have been 39 years old.*

III

Is the idea of separation of Pakistan from Hindustan shocking? If so, let me recall a few facts which are relevant to the issue and which form the basic principles of the Congress policy. It will be remembered that as soon as Mr. Gandhi captured the Congress, he did two things to popularize it. The first thing he did was to introduce Civil Disobedience.

Before Mr. Gandhi's entry into the politics of India, the parties contending for power were the Congress, the Liberals and the Terrorists of Bengal. The Congress and the Liberals were really one party and there was no distinction between them such as divides them today. We can, therefore, safely say that there were only two parties in India, the Liberals and the Terrorists. In both, the conditions for admission were extremely difficult. In the Liberal Party, the condition for admission was not merely education but a high degree of learning. Without first establishing a reputation for study, one could never hope to obtain admission to the Liberal Party. It effectively excluded the uneducated from rising to political power. The Terrorists had prescribed the hardest test conceivable. Only those who were prepared to give their lives for the cause, not in the sense of dedicating them but in the sense of dying for it, could become members of their organization. No knave could, therefore, get an entry into the Terrorists' organization. Civil disobedience does not require learning. It does not call for the shedding of life. It is an easy middle way for that large majority who have no learning and who do not wish to undergo the extreme penalty and at the same time obtain the notoriety of

* Government of India Gazette Notification No. 2832, dated 1st September 1905. The two provinces became separate administrative units from 16th October 1905.

being patriots. It is this middle path which made the Congress more popular than the Liberal Party or the Terrorist Party.

The second thing Mr. Gandhi did was to introduce the principle of Linguistic Provinces. In the constitution that was framed by the Congress under the inspiration and guidance of Mr. Gandhi, India was to be divided into the following Provinces with the language and head-quarters as given below :—

Province.		Language.		Head quarters.
Ajmere-Merwara	...	Hindustani	...	Ajmere.
Andhra	...	Telegu	...	Madras.
Assam	...	Assamese	...	Gauhati.
Bihar	...	Hindustani	...	Patna.
Bengal	...	Bengali	...	Calcutta.
Bombay (City)	...	Marathi-Gujarati	...	Bombay.
Delhi	...	Hindustani	...	Delhi.
Gujarat	...	Gujarati	...	Ahmedabad.
Karnatak	...	Kannada	...	Dharwar.
Kerala	...	Malayalam	...	Calicut.
Mahakosal	...	Hindustani	...	Jubbulpore.
Maharashtra	...	Marathi	...	Poona.
Nagpur	...	Marathi	...	Nagpur.
N.-W. F. P.	...	Pushtu	...	Peshawar.
Punjab	...	Punjabi	...	Lahore.
Sind	...	Sindhi	...	Karachi.
Tamil Nadu	...	Tamil	...	Madras.
United Provinces	...	Hindustani	...	Lucknow.
Utkal	...	Oriya	...	Cuttack.
Vidarbha (Berar)	...	Marathi	...	Akola.

In this distribution no attention was paid to considerations of area, population or revenue. The thought that every administrative unit must be capable of supporting and supplying a minimum standard of civilized life, for which it must have sufficient area, sufficient population and sufficient revenue, had no place in this scheme of distribution of areas for provincial purposes. The determining factor was language. No thought was given to the possibility that it might introduce a disruptive force in the already loose structure of the Indian social life. The scheme was no doubt put forth with the sole object of winning the people to the Congress by appealing to their local patriotism. The idea of linguistic provinces has come to stay and the demand for giving effect to it has become so insistent and irresistible that the Congress, when it came into power, was forced to put it into effect. Orissa has already been separated from Bihar.* Andhra is demanding separation from Madras. Karnatak is asking for separation from Maharashtra.† The only linguistic province that is not demanding separation from Maharashtra is Gujarat. Or rather, Gujarat has given up for the moment the idea of separation. That is probably because Gujarat has realized that union with Maharashtra is, politically as well as commercially, a better investment.

Be that as it may, the fact remains that separation on linguistic basis is now an accepted principle with the Congress. It is no use saying that the separation of Karnatak and Andhra is based on a linguistic difference and that the claim to separation of Pakistan is based on a cultural difference. This is a distinction without difference. Linguistic difference is simply another name for cultural difference.

If there is nothing shocking in the separation of Karnatak and Andhra, what is there to shock in the demand for the separation of Pakistan? If it is disruptive in its effect, it is no more disruptive than the separation of Hindu provinces such as Karnatak from Maharashtra or Andhra from Madras. Pakistan is merely another manifestation of a cultural unit demanding freedom for the growth of its own distinctive culture.

---

* This was done under the Government of India Act, 1935.

† Karnatak also wants some districts from the Madras Presidency.

CHAPTER II

A NATION CALLING FOR A HOME

That there are factors, administrative, linguistic or cultural, which are the predisposing causes behind these demands for separation, is a fact which is admitted and understood by all. Nobody minds these demands and many are prepared to concede them. But, the Hindus say that the Muslims are going beyond the idea of separation and questions, such as what has led them to take this course, why are they asking for partition, for the annulment of the common tie by a legal divorce between Pakistan and Hindustan, are being raised.

The answer is to be found in the declaration made by the Muslim League in its Resolution that the Muslims of India are a separate nation. It is this declaration by the Muslim League, which is both resented and ridiculed by the Hindus.

The Hindu resentment is quite natural. Whether India is a nation or not, has been the subject matter of controversy between the Anglo-Indians and the Hindu politicians ever since the Indian National Congress was founded. The Anglo-Indians were never tired of proclaiming that India was not a nation, that 'Indians' was only another name for the people of India. In the words of one Anglo-Indian "to know India was to forget that there is such a thing as India." The Hindu politicians and patriots have been, on the other hand, equally persistent in their assertion that India is a nation. That the Anglo-Indians were right in their repudiation cannot be gainsaid. Even Dr. Tagore, the national poet of Bengal, agrees with them. But, the Hindus have never yielded on the point even to Dr. Tagore.

This was because of two reasons. Firstly, the Hindu felt ashamed to admit that India was not a nation. In a world where nationality and nationalism were deemed to be special virtues in a people, it was quite natural for the Hindus to feel, to use the language of Mr. H. G. Wells, that it would be as improper for India to be without a nationality as it would be for a man to be without his clothes in a crowded assembly. Secondly, he had realized that nationality had a most intimate connection with the claim for self-government. He knew that by the end of the 19th century, it had become an accepted principle that a people, who constituted a nation, were entitled on that account to self-government and that any patriot, who asked for self-government for his people, had to prove that they were a nation. The Hindu for these reasons never stopped to examine whether India was or was not a nation in fact. He never cared to reason whether nationality was merely a question of *calling* a people a nation or was a question of the people *being* a nation. He knew one thing, namely, that if he was to succeed in his demand for self-government for India, he must maintain, even if he could not prove it, that India was a nation.

In this assertion, he was never contradicted by any Indian. The thesis was so agreeable that even serious Indian students of history came forward to write propagandist literature in support of it, no doubt out of patriotic motives. The Hindu social reformers, who knew that this was a dangerous delusion, could not openly contradict this thesis. For, anyone who questioned it was at once called a tool of the British bureaucracy and enemy of the country. The Hindu politician was able to propagate his view for a long time. His opponent, the Anglo-Indian, had ceased to reply to him. His propaganda had almost succeeded. When it was about to succeed comes this declaration of the Muslim League—this rift in the lute. Just because it does not come from the Anglo-Indian, it is a deadlier blow. It destroys the work which the Hindu politician has done for years. If the Muslims in India are a separate nation, then, of course, India is not a nation. This assertion cuts the whole ground from under the feet of the Hindu politicians. It is natural that they should feel annoyed at it and call it a stab in the back.

But, stab or no stab, the point is, can the Musalmans be said to constitute a nation? Everything else is beside the point. This raises the question: What is a nation? Tomes have been written on the subject. Those who are curious may go through them and study the different basic conceptions as well as the different aspects of it. It is, however, enough to know the core of the subject and that can be set down in a few words. Nationality is a social feeling. It is a feeling of a corporate sentiment of oneness which makes those who are charged with it feel that they are kith and kin. This national feeling is a double edged feeling. It is at once a feeling of fellowship for one's own kith and kin and an anti-fellowship feeling for those who are not one's own kith and kin. It is a feeling of "consciousness of kind" which on the one hand binds together those who have it, so strongly that it over-rides all differences arising out of economic conflicts or social gradations and, on the other, severs them from those who are not of their kind. It is a longing not to belong to any other group. This is the essence of what is called a nationality and national feeling.

Now apply this test to the Muslim claim. Is it or is it not a fact that the Muslims of India are an exclusive group? Is it or is it not a fact that they have a consciousness of kind? Is it or is it not a fact that every Muslim is possessed by a longing to belong to his own group and not to any non-Muslim group?

If the answer to these questions is in the affirmative, then the controversy must end and the Muslim claim that they are a nation must be accepted without cavil.

What the Hindus must show is that notwithstanding some differences, there are enough affinities between Hindus and Musalmans to constitute them into one nation, or, to use plain language, which make Muslims and Hindus long to belong together.

Hindus, who disagree with the Muslim view that the Muslims are a separate nation by themselves, rely upon certain features of Indian social life which seem to form the bonds of integration between Muslim society and Hindu society.

In the first place, it is said that there is no difference of race between the Hindus and the Muslims. That the Punjabi Musalman and the Punjabi Hindu, the U. P. Musalman and the U. P. Hindu, the Bihar Musalman and the Bihar Hindu, the Bengal

Musalman and the Bengal Hindu, the Madras Musalman and the Madras Hindu, and the Bombay Musalman and the Bombay Hindu are racially of one stock. Indeed there is more racial affinity between the Madras Musalman and the Madras Brahmin than there is between the Madras Brahmin and the Punjab Brahmin. In the second place, reliance is placed upon linguistic unity between Hindus and Muslims. It is said that the Musalmans have no common language of their own which can mark them off as a linguistic group separate from the Hindus. On the contrary, there is a complete linguistic unity between the two. In the Punjab, both Hindus and Muslims speak Punjabi. In Sind, both speak Sindhi. In Bengal, both speak Bengali. In Gujarat, both speak Gujarati. In Maharashtra, both speak Marathi. So in every province. It is only in towns that the Musalmans speak Urdu and the Hindus the language of the province. But outside, in the mofussil, there is complete linguistic unity between Hindus and Musalmans. Thirdly, it is pointed out that India is the land which the Hindus and Musalmans have now inhabited together for centuries. It is not exclusively the land of the Hindus, nor is it exclusively the land of the Mahomedans.

Reliance is placed not only upon racial unity but also upon certain common features in the social and cultural life of the two communities. It is pointed out that the social life of many Muslim groups is honeycombed with Hindu customs. For instance, the *Avans* of the Punjab, though they are nearly all Muslims, retain Hindu names and keep their genealogies in the Brahmanic fashion. Hindu surnames are found among Muslims. For instance, the surname Chaudhari is a Hindu surname but is common among the Musalmans of U. P. and Northern India. In the matter of marriage, certain groups of Muslims are Muslims in name only. They either follow the Hindu form of the ceremony alone, or perform the ceremony first by the Hindu rites and then call the Kazi and have it performed in the Muslim form. In some sections of Muslims, the law applied is the Hindu Law in the matter of marriage, guardianship and inheritance. Before the Shariat Act was passed, this was true even in the Punjab and the N.-W. F. P. In the social sphere, the caste system is alleged to be as much a part of Muslim society as it is of Hindu society. In the religious sphere, it is pointed out that many Muslim *pirs* had Hindu disciples; and similarly some Hindu *yogis* have had Muslim *chelas*. Reliance is placed on instances of friendship between saints of the rival creeds. At Girot, in the Punjab, the tombs of two ascetics, Jamali Sultan and Diyal Bhawan, who lived in close amity during the early part of the nineteenth century, stand close to one another, and are reverenced by Hindus and Musalmans alike. Bawa Fathu, a Muslim saint, who lived about 1700 A.D. and whose tomb is at Ranital in the Kangra District, received the title of prophet by the blessing of a Hindu saint, Sodhi Guru Gulab Singh. On the other hand, Baba Shahana, a Hindu saint whose cult is observed in the Jang District, is said to have been the *chela* of a Muslim *pir* who changed the original name (Mihra), of his Hindu follower, into Mir Shah.

All this, no doubt, is true. That a large majority of the Muslims belong to the same race as the Hindus is beyond question. That all Mahomedans do not speak a common tongue, that many speak the same language as the Hindus cannot be denied. That there are certain social customs which are common to both cannot be gainsaid. That certain religious rites and practices are common to both is also a matter of fact. But the question is: can all this support the conclusion that the Hindus and the Mahomedans on account of them constitute one nation or these things have fostered in them a feeling that they long to belong to each other?

There are many flaws in the Hindu argument. In the first place, what are pointed out as common features are not the result of a conscious attempt to adopt and adapt to each other's ways and manners to bring about social fusion. On the other hand, this uniformity is the result of certain purely mechanical causes. They are partly due to incomplete conversions. In a land like India, where the majority of the Muslim population has been recruited from caste and out-caste Hindus, the Muslimization of the convert was neither complete nor effectual, either from fear of revolt or because of the method of persuasion or insufficiency of preaching due to insufficiency of priests.

There is, therefore, little wonder if great sections of the Muslim community here and there reveal their Hindu origin in their religious and social life. Partly it is to be explained as the effect of common environment to which both Hindus and Muslims have been subjected for centuries. A common environment is bound to produce common reactions, and reacting constantly in the same way to the same environment is bound to produce a common type. Partly are these common features to be explained as the remnants of a period of religious amalgamation between the Hindus and the Muslims inaugurated by the Emperor Akbar, the result of a dead past which has no present and no future.

As to the argument based on unity of race, unity of language and inhabiting a common country, the matter stands on a different footing. If these considerations were decisive in making or unmaking a nation, the Hindus would be right in saying that by reason of race, community of language and habitat the Hindus and Musalmans form one nation. As a matter of historical experience, neither race, nor language, nor country has sufficed to mould a people into a nation. The argument is so well put by Renan that it is impossible to improve upon his language. Long ago in his famous essay on Nationality, Renan observed :—

> "that race must not be confounded with nation. The truth is that there is no pure race; and that making politics depend upon ethnographical analysis, is allowing it to be borne upon a chimera .... Racial facts, important as they are in the beginning, have a constant tendency to lose their importance. Human history is essentially different from zoology. Race is not everything, as it is in the sense of rodents and felines."

Speaking about language, Renan points out that :—

> "Language invites re-union; it does not force it. The United States and England, Spanish America and Spain, speak the same languages and do not form single nations. On the contrary, Switzerland which owes her stability to the fact that she was founded by the assent of her several parts counts three or four languages. In man there is something superior to language, —will. The will of Switzerland to be united, in spite of the variety of her languages, is a much more important fact than a similarity of language, often obtained by persecution."

As to common country, Renan argued that:—

> "It is no more the land than the race that makes a nation. The land provides a *substratum*, the field of battle and work; man provides the soul; man is everything in the formation of that sacred thing which is called a people. Nothing of material nature suffices for it."

Having shown that race, language, and country do not suffice to create a nation, Renan raises in a pointed manner the question, what more, then, is necessary to constitute a nation? His answer may be given in his own words:—

> "A nation is a living soul, a spiritual principle. Two things, which in truth are but one, constitute this soul, this spiritual principle. One is in the past, the other in the present. One is the common possession of a rich heritage of memories; the other is the actual consent, the desire to live together, the will to preserve worthily the undivided inheritance which has been handed down. Man does not improvise. The nation, like the individual, is the outcome of a long past of efforts, and sacrifices, and devotion. Ancestor-worship is therefore, all the more legitimate; for our ancestors have made us what we are. A heroic past, great men, glory,—I mean glory of the genuine kind,—these form the social capital, upon which a national idea may be founded. To have common glories in the past, a common will in the present; to have done great things together, to will to do the like again,—such are the essential conditions for the making of a people. We love in proportion to the sacrifices we have consented to make, to the sufferings we have endured. We love the house that we have built, and will hand down to our descendant. The Spartan hymn, 'We are what you were; we shall be what you are,' is in its simplicity the national anthem of every land.
>
> "In the past an inheritance of glory and regrets to be shared, in the future a like ideal to be realised; to have suffered, and rejoiced, and hoped together; all these things are worth more than custom houses in common, and frontiers in accordance with strategical ideas; all these can be understood in spite of diversities of race and language. I said just now, 'to have suffered together' for indeed, suffering in common is a greater bond of union than joy. As regards national memories, mournings are worth more than triumphs; for they impose duties, they demand common effort."

Are there any common historical antecedents which the Hindus and Muslims can be said to share together as matters of pride or as matters of sorrow? That is the crux of the question. That is the question which the Hindus must answer, if they wish to maintain that Hindus and Musalmans together form a nation. So far as this aspect of their relationship is concerned, they have been just two armed battalions warring against each other. There was no common cycle of participation for a common achievement. Their past is a past of mutual destruction—a past of mutual animosities, both in the political as well as in the religious fields. As Bhai Parmanand points out in his pamphlet called "The Hindu National Movement":—"In history the Hindus revere the memory of Prithvi Raj, Partap, Shivaji and Be-ragi Bir who fought for the honour and freedom of this land (against the Muslims), while the Mahomedans look upon the invaders of India, like Muhammad bin Qasim and rulers like Aurangzeb as their national heroes." In the religious field, the Hindus draw their inspiration from the Ramayan, the Mahabharat, and the Geeta. The Musalmans, on the other hand, derive their inspiration from the Quran and the Hadis. Thus, the things that divide are far more vital than the things which unite. In depending upon certain common features of Hindu and Mahomedan social life, in relying upon common language, common race and common country, the Hindu is mistaking what is accidental and superficial for what is essential and fundamental. The political and religious antagonisms divide the Hindus and the Musalmans far more deeply than the so-called common things are able to bind them together. The prospects might perhaps be different if the past of the two communities can be forgotten by both. Renan points out the importance of forgetfulness as a factor in building up a nation:—

> "Forgetfulness, and I shall even say historical error, form an essential factor in the creation of a nation; and thus it is that the progress of historical studies may often be dangerous to the nationality. Historical research, in fact, brings back to light the deeds of violence that have taken place at the commencement of all political formations, even of those the consequences of which have been most beneficial. Unity is ever achieved by brutality. The union of Northern and Southern France was the result of an extermination, and of a reign of terror that lasted for nearly a hundred years. The king of France who was, if I may say so, the ideal type of a secular crystalliser, the king of France who made the most perfect national unity in existence, lost his prestige when seen at too close a distance.

The nation that he had formed cursed him; and today the knowledge of what he was worth, and what he did, belongs only to the cultured.

"It is by contrast that these great laws of the history of Western Europe become apparent. In the undertaking which the king of France, in part by his justice, achieved so admirably, many countries came to disaster. Under the crown of St. Stephen, Magyars and Slavs have remained as distinct as they were eight hundred years ago. Far from combining the different elements in its dominions, the house of Hapsburg has held them apart and often opposed to one another. In Bohemia, the Czech element and the German element are superimposed like oil and water in a glass. The Turkish policy of separation of nationalities according to religion has had much graver results. It has brought about the ruin of the East. Take a town like Smyrna or Salonica; you will find there five or six communities each with its own memories, and possessing among them scarcely anything in common. But the essence of the nation is, that all its individual members should have things in common; and also, that all of them should hold many things in oblivion. No French citizen knows whether he is a Burgundian, an Alan, or a Visigoth; every French citizen ought to have forgotten St. Bartholomew, and the massacres of the South in the thirteenth century. There are not ten families in France able to furnish proof of a French origin; and yet, even if such a proof were given it would be essentially defective, in consequence of a thousand unknown crosses, capable of deranging all genealogical systems."

The pity of it is that the two communities can never forget or obliterate their past. Their past is imbedded in their religion, and for each to give up its past is to give up its religion. To hope for this is to hope in vain.

In the absence of common historical antecedents, the Hindu view that Hindus and Musalmans form one nation falls to the ground. To maintain it is to keep up a hallucination. There is no such longing between the Hindus and the Musalmans to belong together as there is among the Musalmans of India.

It is no use saying that this claim of the Musalmans being a nation is an after-thought of their leaders. As an accusation, it is true. The Muslims were hitherto quite content to call themselves a community. It is only recently that they have begun to style themselves a nation. But an accusation, attacking the motives of a person, does not amount to a refutation of his thesis.

To say that because the Muslims once called themselves a community, they are, therefore, now debarred from calling themselves a nation is to misunderstand the mysterious working of the psychology of national feeling. Such an argument presupposes that wherever there exist a people, who possess the elements that go to the making up of a nation, there *must* be manifested that sentiment of nationality which is their natural consequence and that if they fail to manifest it for some time, then that failure is to be used as evidence showing the unreality of the claim of being a nation, if made afterwards. There is no historical support for such a contention. As Prof. Toynbee points out:—

> "It is impossible to argue *a priori* from the presence of one or even several of these factors to the existence of a nationality; they may have been there for ages and kindled no response and it is impossible to argue from one case to another; precisely the same group of factors may produce nationality here, and there have no effect."

This is probably due to the fact, as pointed out by Prof. Barker, that it is possible for nations to exist and even for centuries, in unreflective silence, although there exists that spiritual essence of a national life of which many of its members are not aware. Some such thing has no doubt happened in the case of the Musalmans. They were not aware of the fact that there existed for them the spiritual essence of a national life. This explains why their claim to separate nationality was made by them so late. But, it does not mean that the spiritual essence of a national life had no existence at all.

It is no use contending that there are cases where a sense of nationality exists but there is no desire for a separate national existence. Cases of the French in Canada and of the English in South Africa, may be cited as cases in point. It must be admitted that there do exist cases, where people are aware of their nationality, but this awareness does not produce in them that passion which is called nationalism. In other words, there may be nations conscious of themselves without being charged with nationalism. On the basis of this reasoning, it may be argued that the Musalmans may hold that they are a nation but they need not on that account demand a separate national existence; why can they not be content with the position which the French occupy in Canada and the English occupy in South Africa? Such a position is quite a sound position. It must, however, be remembered that such a position can only be taken by way of pleading with the Muslims not to insist on partition. It is no argument against their claim for partition, if they insist upon it.

Lest pleading should be mistaken for refutation, it is necessary to draw attention to two things. First, there is a difference between nationality and nationalism. They are two different psychological states of the human mind. Nationality means "consciousness of kind, awareness of the existence of that tie of kinship." Nationalism means "the desire for a separate national existence for those who are bound by this tie of kinship." Secondly, it is true that there cannot be nationalism without the feeling of nationality being in existence. But, it is important to bear in mind that the converse is not always true. The feeling of nationality may be present and yet the feeling of nationalism may be quite absent. That is to say, nationality does not in all cases produce nationalism. For nationality to flame into nationalism two conditions must exist. First, there must arise the "will to live as a nation." Nationalism is the dynamic expression of that desire. Secondly, there must be a territory which nationalism could occupy and make it a state, as well as a cultural home of the nation. Without such a territory, nationalism, to use Lord Acton's phrase, would be a "soul as it were wandering in search of a body in which to begin life over again and dies out finding none." The Muslims have developed a "will to live as a nation." For them nature has found a territory which they can occupy and make it a state as well as a cultural home for the new-born Muslim nation. Given these favourable conditions, there should be no wonder, if the Muslims say that they are not content to occupy the position which the French choose to occupy in Canada or the English choose to occupy in South Africa, and that they shall have a national home which they can call their own.

CHAPTER III

ESCAPE FROM DEGRADATION

"What justification have the Musalmans of India for demanding the partition of India and the establishment of separate Muslim States? Why this insurrection? What grievances have they?"—ask the Hindus in a spirit of righteous indignation.

Anyone, who knows history, will not fail to realize that it has now been a well established principle that nationalism is a sufficient justification for the creation of a national state. As the great historian Lord Acton points out:—

> "In the old European system, the rights of nationalities were neither recognized by governments nor asserted by the people. The interest of the reigning families, not those of the nations, regulated the frontiers, and the administration was conducted generally without any reference to popular desires. Where all liberties were suppressed, the claims of national independence were necessarily ignored, and a princess, in the words of Fenelon, carried a monarchy in her wedding portion."

Nationalities were at first listless. When they became conscious—

> "They first rose against their conquerors in defence of their legitimate rulers. They refused to be governed by usurpers. Next came a time when they revolted because of the wrongs inflicted upon them by their rulers. The insurrections were provoked by particular grievances justified by definite complaints. Then came the French Revolution which effected a complete change. It taught the people to regard their wishes and wants as the supreme criterion of their right to do what they liked to do with themselves. It proclaimed the idea of the sovereignty of the people uncontrolled by the past and uncontrolled by the existing state. This text taught by the French Revolution became an accepted dogma of all liberal thinkers. Mill gave it his support. 'One hardly knows,' says Mill, 'what any division of the human race should be free to do, if not to determine with which of the various collective bodies of human beings they choose to associate themselves.'"

He even went so far as to hold that—

> "It is in general a necessary condition of free institutions that the boundaries of governments should coincide in the main with those of nationalities."

Thus history shows that the theory of nationality is imbedded in the democratic theory of the sovereignty of the will of a people. This means that the demand by a nationality for a national state does not require to be supported by any list of grievances. The will of the people is enough to justify it.

But, if grievances must be cited in support of their claim, the Muslims say that they have them in plenty. They may be summed up in one sentence, that constitutional safeguards have failed to save them from the tyranny of the Hindu majority.

At the Round Table Conference, the Muslims presented their list of safeguards, which were formulated in the well-known fourteen points. The Hindu representatives at the Round Table Conference would not consent to them. There was an impasse. The British Government intervened and gave what is known as "the Communal decision." By that decision, the Muslims got all their fourteen points. There was much bitterness amongst the Hindus against the Communal Award. But, the Congress did not take part in the hostility that was displayed by the Hindus generally towards it, although it did retain the right to describe it as anti-national and to get it changed with the consent of the Muslims. So careful was the Congress not to wound the feelings of the Muslims that when the Resolution was moved in the Central Assembly condemning the Communal Award, the Congress, though it did not bless it, remained neutral, neither opposing nor supporting it. The Mahomedans were well justified in looking upon this Congress attitude as a friendly gesture.

The victory of the Congress at the polls in the provinces, where the Hindus are in a majority, did not disturb the tranquillity of the Musalmans. They felt they had nothing to fear from the Congress and the prospects were that the Congress and the Muslim League would work the constitution in partnership. But, two years and three months of the Congress Government in the Hindu Provinces have completely disillusioned them and have made them the bitterest enemies of the Congress. The Deliverance Day celebration held on the 22nd December 1939 shows the depth of their resentment. What is worse, their bitterness is not confined to the Congress. The Musalmans, who at the Round Table Conference joined in the demand for Swaraj, are today the most ruthless opponents of Swaraj.

What has the Congress done to annoy the Muslims so much? The Muslim League has asserted that under the Congress regime the Muslims were actually tyrannized and oppressed. Two committees appointed by the League are said to have investigated and reported on the matter. But apart from these matters which require to be examined by an impartial tribunal, there are undoubtedly two things which have produced the clash: (1) the refusal by the Congress to recognize the Muslim League as the only representative body of the Muslims, (2) the refusal by the Congress to form Coalition Ministries in the Congress Provinces.

On the first question, both the Congress and the League are adamant. The Congress is prepared to accept the Muslim League as one of the many Muslim political organizations, such as the Ahrars, the National Muslims and the Jamiat-ul-Ulema. But it will not accept the Muslim League as the only representative body of the Muslims. The Muslim League, on the other hand, is not prepared to enter into any talk unless the Congress accepts it as the only representative body of the Musalmans of India. The Hindus stigmatize the claim of the League as an extravagant one and try to ridicule it. The Muslims may say that if the Hindus would only stop to inquire how treaties between nations are made, they would realize the stupidity of their view. It may be argued that when a nation proceeds to make a treaty with another nation, it recognizes the Government of the latter as fully representing it. In no country does the Government of the day represent the whole body of people. Everywhere it represents only a majority. But nations do not refuse to settle their disputes because the Governments, which represent them, do not represent the whole people. It is enough if each Government represents a majority of its citizens. This analogy, the Muslims may contend, must apply to the

Congress-League quarrel on this issue. The League may not represent the whole body of the Muslims but if it represents a majority of them, the Congress should have no compunction to deal with it for the purpose of effecting a settlement of the Hindu-Muslim question. Of course, it is open to the Government of a country not to recognize the Government of another country where there is more than one body claiming to be the Government. Similarly, the Congress may not recognize the League. It must, however, recognize either the National Muslims or the Ahrars or the Jamiat-ul-Ulema and fix the terms of settlement between the two communities. Of course, it must act with the full knowledge as to which is more likely to be repudiated by the Muslims—an agreement with the League or an agreement with the other Muslim parties. The Congress must deal with one or the other. To deal with neither is not only stupid but mischievous. This attitude of the Congress only serves to annoy the Muslims and to exasperate them. The Muslims rightly interpret this attitude of the Congress as an attempt to create divisions among them with a view to cause confusion in their ranks and weaken their front.

On the second issue, the Muslim demand has been that in the cabinets there shall be included Muslim Ministers who have the confidence of the Muslim members in the Legislature. They expected that this demand of theirs would be met by the Congress if it came in power. But, they were sorely disappointed. With regard to this demand, the Congress took a legalistic attitude. The Congress agreed to include Muslims in their cabinets, provided they resigned from their parties, joined the Congress and signed the Congress pledge. This was resented by the Muslims on three grounds.

In the first place, they regarded it as a breach of faith. The Muslims say that this demand of theirs is in accordance with the spirit of the Constitution. At the Round Table Conference, it was agreed that the cabinets shall include representatives of the minority communities. The minorities insisted that a provision to that effect should be made a part of the statute. The Hindus, on the other hand, desired that the matter should be left to be regulated by convention. A *via media* was found. It was agreed that the provision should find a place in the Instrument of Instructions to the Governors of the provinces and an obligation should be imposed upon them to see that effect was given to the convention in the formation of the cabinets. The Musalmans did not insist upon making this provision a part of the statute because they depended upon the good faith of the Hindus. This agreement was broken by a party which had given the Muslims to understand that towards them its attitude would be not only correct but considerate.

In the second place, the Muslims felt that the Congress view was a perversion of the real scope of the convention. They rely upon the text of the clause* in the Instrument of Instructions and argue that the words "member of a minority community" in it can have only one meaning, namely, a person having the confidence of the community. The position taken by the Congress is in direct contradiction with the meaning of this clause and is indeed a covert attempt to break all other parties in the country and to make the Congress the only political party in the country. The demand for signing the Congress pledge can have no other intention. This attempt to establish a totalitarian state may be welcome to the Hindus, but it meant the political death of the Muslims as a free people.

This resentment of the Muslims was considerably aggravated when they found the Governors, on whom the obligation was imposed to see that effect was given to the convention, declining to act. Some Governors declined, because they were helpless by reason of the fact that the Congress was the only majority party which could produce a stable government, that a Congress Government was the only government possible and that there was no alternative to it except suspending the constitution. Other Governors declined, because they became active supporters

* "In making appointments to his Council of Ministers, our Governor shall use his best endeavours to select his Ministers in the following manner, that is to say, to appoint in consultation with the person who in his judgment is most likely to command a stable majority in the Legislature, those persons (including so far as practicable, members of important minority communities) who will best be in a position collectively to command the confidence of the Legislature. In so acting, he shall bear constantly in mind the need for fostering a sense of joint responsibility among his Ministers."

of the Congress Government and showed their partisanship by praising the Congress or by wearing Khadi which is the official party dress of the Congress. Whatever be the reasons, the Muslims discovered that an important safeguard had failed to save them.

The Congress reply to these accusations by the Muslims is twofold. In the first place, they say that coalition cabinets are inconsistent with collective responsibility of the cabinets. This, the Musalmans refuse to accept as an honest plea. The English people were the first and the only people, who made it a principle of their system of government. But, even there it has been abandoned since. The English Parliament debated* the issue and came to the conclusion that it was not so sacrosanct as it was once held and that a departure from it need not necessarily affect the efficiency or smooth working of the governmental machine. Secondly, as a matter of fact, there was no collective responsibility in the Congress Government. It was a government by departments. Each Minister was independent of the other and the Prime Minister was just a Minister. For the Congress to talk about collective responsibility was really impertinent. The plea was even dishonest, because it is a fact that in the provinces where the Congress was in a minority, they did form Coalition Ministries without asking the Ministers from other parties to sign the Congress pledge. The Muslims are entitled to ask 'if coalition is bad, how can it be good in one place and bad in another?'

The second reply of the Congress is that even if they take Muslim Ministers in their cabinet who have not the confidence of the majority of the Muslims, they have not failed to protect their interests. Indeed, they have done everything to advance the interests of the Muslims. This no doubt rests on the view Pope held of government when he said—

> "For forms of government let fools contest;
> What is best administered is best."

In making this reply, the Congress High Command seem to

* See the announcement of 22nd January 1932 by the British Prime Minister on the decision of the cabinet to agree to differ on the Tariff Question and the debate on it in Parliament.

have misunderstood what the main contention of the Muslims and the minorities has been. Their quarrel is not on the issue whether the Congress has or has not done any good to the Muslims and the minorities. Their quarrel is on an issue which is totally different. Are the Hindus to be a ruling race and the Muslims and other minorities to be subject races under Swaraj? That is the issue involved in the demand for coalition ministries. On that, the Muslims and other minorities have taken a definite stand. They are not prepared to accept the position of subject races.

That the ruling community has done good to the ruled is quite beside the point and is no answer to the contention of the minority communities that they refuse to be treated as a subject people. The British have done many good things in India for the Indians. They have improved their roads, constructed canals on more scientific principles, effected their transport by rail, carried their letters by penny post, flashed their messages by lightning, improved their currency, regulated their weights and measures, corrected their notions of geography, astronomy and medicine, and stopped their internal quarrels and effected some advancement in their material conditions. Because of these acts of good government, did anybody ask the Indian people to remain grateful to the British and give up their agitation for self-government? Or because of these acts of social uplift, did the Indians give up their protest against being treated as a subject race by the British? The Indians did nothing of the kind. They refused to be satisfied with these good deeds and continued to agitate for their right to rule themselves. This is as it should be. For, as was said by Curran, the Irish patriot, no man can be grateful at the cost of his self-respect, no woman can be grateful at the cost of her chastity and no nation can be grateful at the cost of its honour. To do otherwise is to show that one's philosophy of life is just what Carlyle called 'pig philosophy.' The Congress High Command does not seem to realize that the Muslims and other minorities care more for the recognition of their self-respect at the hand of the Congress than for mere good deeds on the part of the Congress. Men, who are conscious of their being, are not pigs who care only for fattening food. They have their pride which they will not yield even for gold. In short "life is more than the meat."

It is no use saying that the Congress is not a Hindu body. A body which is Hindu in its composition is bound to reflect the Hindu mind and support Hindu aspirations. The only difference between the Congress and the Hindu Maha Sabha is that the latter is crude in its utterances and brutal in its actions while the Congress is politic and polite. Apart from this difference of fact, there is no other difference between the Congress and the Hindu Maha Sabha.

Similarly, it is no use saying that the Congress does not recognize the distinction between the ruler and the ruled. If this is so, the Congress must prove its *bona fides* by showing its readiness to recognize the other communities as free and equal partners. What is the test of such recognition? It seems to me that there can be only one—namely, agreeing to share power with the *effective* representatives of the minority communities. Is the Congress prepared for it? Everyone knows the answer. The Congress is not prepared to share power with a member of a community who does not owe allegiance to the Congress. Allegiance to the Congress is a condition precedent to sharing power. It seems to be a rule with the Congress that if allegiance to the Congress is not forthcoming from a community, that community must be excluded from political power.

Exclusion from political power is the essence of the distinction between a ruling race and a subject race; and inasmuch as the Congress maintained this principle, it must be said that this distinction was enforced by the Congress while it was in the saddle. The Musalmans may well complain that they have already suffered enough and that this reduction to the position of a subject race is like the proverbial last straw. Their decline and fall in India began ever since the British occupation of the country. Every change, executive, administrative, or legal, introduced by the British, has inflicted a series of blows upon the Muslim community. The Muslim rulers of India had allowed the Hindus to retain their law in civil matters. But, they abrogated the Hindu criminal law and made the Muslim criminal law the law of the state, applicable to all Hindus as well as Muslims. The first thing the British did was to displace gradually the Muslim criminal law by another of their making, until the process was finally completed by the enactment of Macaulay's Penal Code. This was the first blow to the prestige and position of the Muslim community in India. This was followed by the abridgment of the field of application of the Shariat or the Muslim Civil Law. Its application was restricted to matters concerning personal relations, such as marriage and inheritance, and then only to the extent permitted by the British. Side by side came the abolition, in 1837, of Persian as the official language of the Court and of general administration and the substitution of English and the vernaculars in place of Persian. Then came the abolition of the Qazis, who, during the Muslim rule, administered the Shariat. In their places, were appointed law officers and judges, who might be of any religion but who got the right of interpreting Muslim law and whose decisions became binding on Muslims. These were severe blows to the Muslims. As a result, the Muslims found their prestige gone, their laws replaced, their language shelved and their education shorn of its monetary value. Along with these came more palpable blows in the shape of annexation of Sind and Oudh and the Mutiny. The last, particularly, affected the higher classes of Muslims, who suffered enormously by the extensive confiscation of property inflicted upon them by the British, as a punishment for their suspected complicity in the Mutiny. By the end of the Mutiny, the Musalmans, high and low, were brought down by these series of events to the lowest depths of broken pride, black despair and general penury. Without prestige, without education and without resources, the Muslims were left to face the Hindus. The British, pledged to neutrality, were indifferent to the result of the struggle between the two communities. The result was that the Musalmans were completely worsened in the struggle. The British conquest of India brought about a complete political revolution in the relative position of the two communities. For six hundred years, the Musalmans had been the masters of the Hindus. The British occupation brought them down to the level of the Hindus. From masters to fellow subjects was degradation enough, but a change from the status of fellow subjects to that of subjects of the Hindus is really humiliation. Is, it unnatural, ask the Muslims, if they seek an escape from so intolerable a position by the creation of separate national States, in which the Muslims can find a peaceful home and in which the conflicts between a ruling race and a subject race can find no place to plague their lives?

PART II

HINDU CASE AGAINST PAKISTAN

There seem to be three reasons present to the mind of the Hindus who are opposing this scheme of Pakistan. They object to the scheme:—

1. *Because it involves the breaking-up of the unity of India.*

2. *Because it weakens the defence of India.*

3. *Because it fails to solve the communal problem.*

Is there any substance in these objections? This Part is concerned with an examination of the validity of these objections.

CHAPTER IV

BREAK-UP OF UNITY

I

Before the Hindus complain of the destruction of the unity of India, let them make certain that the unity they are harping upon does exist. What unity is there between Pakistan and Hindustan?

Those Hindus, who maintain the affirmative, rely chiefly upon the fact that the areas which the Muslims want to be separated from India have always been a part of India. Historically this is, no doubt, true. This area was a part of India when Chandragupta was the ruler; it continued to be a part of India when Hsuan Tsang, the Chinese pilgrim, visited India in the 7th century A. D. In his diary, Hsuan Tsang has recorded that India was divided into five divisions or to use his language, there were 'five Indies'*: (1) Northern India, (2) Western India, (3) Central India, (4) Eastern India and (5) Southern India and that these five divisions contained 80 kingdoms. According to Hsuan Tsang, Northern India comprised the Punjab proper, including Kashmir and the adjoining hill states with the whole of Eastern Afghanistan beyond the Indus, and the present Cis-Satlej States to the west of the Sarasvati river. Thus, in Northern India there were included the districts of Kabul, Jallalabad, Peshawar, Ghazni and Bannu, which were all subject to the ruler of Kapisa, who was a Hindu Kshatriya and whose capital was most probably at Charikar, 27 miles from Kabul. In the Punjab proper, the hilly districts of Taxila, Singhapura, Urasa Punch and Rajaori, were subject to the Raja of Kashmir; while the whole of the plains, including Multan and Shorkot, were dependent

* Cunningham's *Ancient Geography of India* (Ed. Majumdar), pp. 13-14. The writers of the Puranas divided India into nine divisions.

on the ruler of Taki or Sangala, near Lahore. Such was the extent of the northern boundary of India at the time when Hsuan Tsang came on his pilgrimage. But as Prof. Toynbee points out—

> "We must be on our guard against 'historical sentiment', that is, against arguments taken from conditions which once existed or were supposed to exist, but which are no longer real at the present moment. They are most easily illustrated by extreme examples. Italian newspapers have described the annexation of Tripoli as recovering the soil of the Fatherland because it was once a province of the Roman Empire; and the entire region of Macedonia is claimed by Greek Chauvinists on the one hand, because it contains the site of Pella, the cradle of Alexander the Great in the fourth century B. C. and by Bulgarians on the other, because Ochrida, in the opposite corner, was the capital of the Bulgarian Tzardom in the tenth century A. D., though the drift of time has buried the tradition of the latter almost as deep as the achievements of the 'Emathian Conqueror' on which the modern Greek nationalists insist so strongly."

The same logic applies here. Here also arguments are taken from conditions which once existed but which are no longer real and which omit to take into consideration later facts which history has to record during practically one thousand years—after the return of Hsuan Tsang.

It is true that when Hsuan Tsang came, not only the Punjab but what is now Afghanistan was part of India and further, the people of the Punjab and Afghanistan were either Vedic or Buddhist by religion. But what has happened since Hsuan Tsang left India?

The most important thing that has happened is the invasion of India by the Muslim hordes from the north-west. The first Muslim invasion of India was by the Arabs who were led by Mahommad bin Qasim. It took place in 711 A. D. and resulted in the conquest of Sind. This first Muslim invasion did not result in a permanent occupation of the country because the Caliphate of Baghdad, by whose order and command the invasion had taken place, was obliged by the middle of the 9th century A. D. to withdraw* its direct control from this distant province of

* Sind was reoccupied by Mahommed Ghori.

Sind. Soon after this withdrawal, there began a series of terrible invasions by Muhammad of Ghazni in 1001 A.D. Muhammad died in 1030 A. D., but within the short span of 30 years, he invaded India 17 times. He was followed by Mahommed Ghori who began his career as an invader in 1173. He was killed in 1206. For thirty years had Muhammad of Ghazni ravaged India and for thirty years Mahommed Ghori harried the same country in the same way. Then followed the incursions of the Moghul hordes of Chenghiz Khan. They first came in 1221. They then only wintered on the border of India but did not enter it. Twenty years after, they marched on Lahore and sacked it. Of their inroads, the most terrible was under Taimur in 1398. Then comes on the scene a new invader in the person of Babar who invaded India in 1526. The invasions of India did not stop with that of Babar. There occurred two more invasions. In 1738 Nadirshah's invading host swept over the Punjab like a flooded river "furious as the ocean". He was followed by Ahmadshah Abdalli who invaded India in 1761, smashed the forces of the Mahrattas at Panipat and crushed for ever the attempt of the Hindus to gain the ground which they had lost to their Muslim invaders.

These Muslim invasions were not undertaken merely out of lust for loot or conquest. There was another object behind them. The expedition against Sind by Mahommad bin Qasim was of a punitive character and was undertaken to punish Raja Dahir of Sind who had refused to make restitution for the seizure of an Arab ship at Debul, one of the sea-port towns of Sind. But, there is no doubt that striking a blow at the idolatry and polytheism of Hindus and establishing Islam in India was also one of the aims of this expedition. In one of his despatches to Hajjaj, Mahommad bin Qasim is quoted to have said :—

> "The nephew of Raja Dahir, his warriors and principal officers have been dispatched, and the infidels converted to Islam or destroyed. Instead of idol-temples, mosques and other places of worship have been created, the Kutbah is read, the call to prayers is raised, so that devotions are performed at stated hours. The Takbir and praise to the Almighty God are offered every morning and evening."*

* *Indian Islam* by Dr. Titus, p. 10.

After receiving the above despatch, which had been forwarded with the head of the Raja, Hajjaj sent the following reply to his general:—

> "Except that you give protection to all, great and small alike, make no difference between enemy and friend. God says, 'Give no quarter to infidels but cut their throats.' Then know that this is the command of the great God. You shall not be too ready to grant protection, because it will prolong your work. After this give no quarter to any enemy except those who are of rank."*

Muhammad of Ghazni also looked upon his numerous invasions of India as the waging of a holy war. Al' Utbi, the historian of Muhammad, describing his raids writes:—

> "He demolished idol temples and established Islam. He captured .... cities, killed the polluted wretches, destroying the idolators, and gratifying Muslims. 'He then returned home and promulgated accounts of the victories obtained for Islam .... and vowed that every year he would undertake a holy war aginst Hind.'"†

Mahommed Ghori was actuated by the same holy zeal in his invasions of India. Hasan Nizami, the historian, describes his work in the following terms:—

> "He purged by his sword the land of Hind from the filth of infidelity and vice, and freed the whole of that country from the thorn of God-plurality and the impurity of idol-worship, and by his royal vigour and intrepidity left not one temple standing."‡

Taimur has in his Memoir explained what led him to invade India. He says:—

> "My object in the invasions of Hindustan is to lead a campaign against the infidels, to convert them to the true faith according to the command of Muhammad (on whom and his family be the blessing and peace of God), to purify the land from the defilement of misbelief and polytheism, and overthrow the temples and idols, whereby we shall be *Ghazis* and *Mujahids*, companions and soldiers of the faith before God."¶

These invasions of India by Muslims were as much invasions of India as they were wars among the Muslims themselves.

* Quoted by Dr. Titus—Ibid., p. 10.
† Ibid., p. 11.
‡ Ibid., p. 11.
¶ Quoted by Lane Poole in *Medieval India*, p. 155.

This fact has remained hidden because the invaders are all lumped together as Muslims without distinction. But as a matter of fact, they were Tartars, Afghans and Mongols. Muhammad of Ghazni was a Tartar, Mahommed of Ghori was an Afghan, Taimur was a Mongol, Babar was a Tartar, while Nadirshah and Ahmadshah Abdalli were Afghans. In invading India, the Afghan was out to destroy the Tartar and the Mongol was out to destroy the Tartar as well as the Afghan. They were not a loving family cemented by the feeling of Islamic brotherhood. They were deadly rivals of one another and their wars were often wars of mutual extermination. What is, however, important to bear in mind is that with all their internecine conflicts they were all united by one common objective and that was to destroy the Hindu faith.

The methods adopted by the Muslim invaders of India are not less significant for the subsequent history of India than the object of their invasions.

Mahommad bin Qasim's first act of religious zeal was forcibly to circumcise the Brahmins of the captured city of Debul; but on discovering that they objected to this sort of conversion, he proceeded to put all above the age of 17 to death, and to order all others, with women and children, to be led into slavery. The temple of the Hindus was looted, and the rich booty was divided equally among the soldiers, after one-fifth, the legal portion for the government, had been set aside.

Muhammad of Ghazni from the first adopted those plans that would strike terror into the hearts of the Hindus. After the defeat of Raja Jaipal in A. D. 1001, Muhammad ordered that Jaipal "be paraded about in the streets so that his sons and chieftains might see him in that condition of shame, bonds and disgrace; and that fear of Islam might fly abroad through the country of the infidels."

"The slaughtering of 'infidels' seemed to be one thing that gave Muhammad particular pleasure. In one attack on Chand Rai, in A. D. 1019, many infidels were slain or taken prisoners, and the Muslims paid no regard to booty until they had satiated themselves with the slaughter of the infidels and worshippers of the sun and fire. The historian naively adds that the elephants of

> the Hindu armies came to Muhammad of their own accord, leaving idols, preferring the service of the religion of Islam."*

Not infrequently, the slaughter of the Hindus gave a great setback to the indigenous culture of the Hindus, as in the conquest of Bihar by Muhammad Bakhtyar Khilji. When he took Nuddea (Bihar) the Tabaquat-i-Nasiri informs us that

> "great plunder fell into the hands of the victors. Most of the inhabitants were Brahmins with shaven heads. They were put to death. Large numbers of books were found. .....but none could explain their contents as all the men had been killed, the whole fort and city being a place of study."†

Summing up the evidence on the point, Dr. Titus concludes :

> "Of the destruction of temples and the desecration of idols we have an abundance of evidence. Mahommad bin Qasim carried out his plan of destruction systematically in Sind, we have seen, but he made an exception of the famous temple at Multan for purposes of revenue, as this temple was a place of resort for pilgrims, who made large gifts to the idol. Nevertheless, while he thus satisfied his avarice by letting the temple stand, he gave vent to his malignity by having a piece of cow's flesh tied around the neck of the idol.
>
> "Minhaj-as-Siraj further tells how Mahommad became widely known for having destroyed as many as a thousand temples, and of his great feat in destroying the temple of Somnath and carrying off its idol, which he asserts was broken into four parts. One part he deposited in the Jami Masjid of Ghazni, one he placed at the entrance of the royal palace, the third he sent to Mecca, and the fourth to Medina."‡

It is said by Lane Poole that Muhammad of Ghazni "who had vowed that every year should see him wage a holy war against the infidels of Hindustan" could not rest from his idol-breaking campaign so long as the temple of Somnath remained inviolate. It was for this specific purpose that he, at the very close of his career, undertook his arduous march across the desert from Multan to Anhalwara on the coast, fighting as he went, until he saw at last the famous temple.

* Dr. Titus—Ibid., p. 22.

† Ibid., p. 22.

‡ Ibid., pp. 22-23.

"There a hundred thousand pilgrims were wont to assemble, a thousand Brahmins served the temple and guarded its treasures, and hundreds of dancers and singers played before its gates. Within stood the famous linga, a rude pillar stone adorned with gems and lighted by jewelled candelebra which were reflected in rich hangings, embroidered with precious stones like stars, that decked the shrine...... Its ramparts were swarmed with incredulous Brahmins, mocking the vain arrogance of foreign infidels whom the God of Somnath would assuredly consume. The foreigners, nothing daunted, scaled the walls; the God remained dumb to the urgent appeals of his servants; fifty thousand Hindus suffered for their faith and the sacred shrine was sacked to the joy of the true believers. The great stone was cast down and its fragments were carried off to grace the conqueror's palace. The temple gates were set up at Ghazni and a million pounds worth of treasure rewarded the iconoclast." *

The work done by Muhammad of Ghazni became a pious tradition and was faithfully followed by those who came after him. In the words of Dr. Titus †

"Mahommed Ghori, one of the enthusiastic successors of Muhammad of Ghazni, in his conquest of Ajmir destroyed pillars and foundations of the idol-temples, and built in their stead mosques and colleges, and the precepts of Islam and the customs of the law were divulged and established. At Delhi, the city and its vicinity were freed from idols and idol worship, and in the sanctuaries of the images of the gods mosques were raised by the worshippers of the one God.

"Qutb-ud-Din Aybak also is said to have destroyed nearly a thousand temples, and then raised mosques on their foundations. The same author states that he built the Jami Masjid, Delhi, and adorned it with the stones and gold obtained from the temples which had been demolished by elephants, and covered it with inscriptions (from the Quran) containing the divine commands. We have further evidence of this harrowing process having been systematically employed from the inscription extant over the eastern gateway of this same mosque at Delhi, which relates that the materials of 27 idol temples were used in its construction.

"Ala-ud-Din, in his zeal to build a second Minar to the Jami Masjid, to rival the one built by Qutb-ud-Din, is said by Amir Khusru not only to have dug stones out of the hills, but to have demolished temples of the infidels to furnish a supply. In his

* *Medieval India*, p. 26.

† Ibid., pp. 23-24.

conquests of South India the destruction of temples was carried out by Ala-ud-Din as it had been in the north by his predecessors.

"The Sultan Firoz Shah, in his Futuhat, graphically relates how he treated Hindus who had dared to build new temples. 'When they did this in the city (Delhi) and the environs, in opposition to the law of the Prophet, which declares that such are not to be tolerated, under Divine guidance I destroyed these edifices, I killed these leaders of infidelity and punished others with stripes, until this abuse was entirely abolished and where infidels and idolaters worshipped idols, Musalmans now by God's mercy perform their devotions to the true God."

Even in the reign of Shah Jahan, we read of the destruction of the temples that the Hindus had started to rebuild, and the account of this direct attack on the piety of the Hindus is thus solemnly recorded in the Badshah-namah:

"It had been brought to the notice of His Majesty, says the historian, that during the late reign (of Akbar) many idol-temples had been begun but remained unfinished at Benares, the great stronghold of infidelity. The infidels were now desirous of completing them. His Majesty, the defender of the faith, gave orders that at Benares and throughout all his dominions in every place all temples that had been begun should be cast down. It was reported from the Province of Allahabad that 76 temples had been destroyed in the district of Benares." *

It was left to Aurangzeb to make a final attempt to overthrow idolatry. The author of '*Ma' athir i-Alamgiri* dilates upon his efforts to put down Hindu teaching, and his destruction of temples in the following terms:—

"In April, A. D. 1669, Aurangzib learned that in the provinces of Thatta, Multan and Benares, but especially in the latter, foolish Brahmins were in the habit of expounding frivolous books in their schools, and that learners, Muslims as well as Hindus, went there from long distances...... The 'Director of the Faith' consequently issued orders to all the governors of provinces to destroy with a willing hand the schools and temples of the infidels; and they were enjoined to put an entire stop to the teaching and practising of idolatrous worship...... Later it was reported to his religious Majesty that the Government officers had destroyed the temple of Bishnath at Benares." †

* Dr. Titus—Ibid., p. 24.

† Ibid., p. 22.

As Dr. Titus observes*—

> "Such invaders as Muhammad and Timur seem to have been more concerned with iconoclasm, the collection of booty, the enslaving of captives, and the sending of infidels to hell with the 'proselytizing sword' than they were with the conversion of them even by force. But when rulers were permanently established the winning of converts became a matter of supreme urgency. It was a part of the state policy to establish Islam as the religion of the whole land.
>
> "Qutb-ud-Din, whose reputation for destroying temples was almost as great as that of Muhammad, in the latter part of the twelfth century and early years of the thirteenth, must have frequently resorted to force as an incentive to conversion. One instance may be noted: when he approached Koil (Aligarh) in A. D. 1194, 'those of the garrison who were wise and acute were converted to Islam, but the others were slain with the sword'.
>
> "Further examples of extreme measures employed to effect a change of faith are all too numerous. One pathetic case is mentioned in the time of the reign of Firoz Shah (A. D. 1351-1388). An old Brahmin of Delhi had been accused of worshipping idols in his house, and of even leading Muslim women to become infidels. He was sent for and his case placed before the judges, doctors, elders and lawyers. Their reply was that the provisions of the law were clear. The Brahmin must either become a Muslim or be burned. The true faith was declared to him and the right course pointed out, but he refused to accept it. Consequently he was burned by the order of the Sultan, and the commentator adds, 'Behold the Sultan's strict adherence to law and rectitude, how he would not deviate in the least from its decrees.'"

Muhammad not only destroyed temples but made it a policy to make slaves of the Hindus he conquered. In the words of Dr. Titus—

> "Not only was slaughter of the infidels and the destruction of their temples resorted to in earlier period of Islam's contact with India, but as we have seen, many of the vanquished were led into slavery. The dividing up of booty was one of the special attractions, to the leaders as well as to the common soldiers in these expeditions. Muhammad seems to have made the slaughter of infidels, the destruction of their temples, the capturing of slaves, and the plundering of the wealth of the people, particularly of the temples and the priests, the main object of his raids. On the occasion of his first raid he is said to have taken much booty;

* Dr. Titus—Ibid., pp. 31-32.

and half a million Hindus, 'beautiful men and women', were reduced to slavery and taken back to Ghazni."*

When Muhammad later took Kanauj, in A. D. 1017, he took so much booty and so many prisoners that 'the fingers of those who counted them would have tired'. Describing how common Indian slaves had become in Ghazni and Central Asia after the campaign of A. D. 1019, the historian of the times says †:

> "The number of prisoners may be conceived from the fact that each was sold for from two to ten dirhams. These were afterwards taken to Ghazni, and merchants came from far distant cities to purchase them; ...... and the fair and the dark, the rich and the poor were commingled in one common slavery.
>
> "In the year A.D. 1202, when Qutb-ud-Din captured Kalinjar, after the temples had been converted into mosques, and the very name of idolatry was annihilated, fifty thousand men came under the collar of slavery and the plain became black as pitch with Hindus."

Slavery was the fate of those Hindus who were captured in the holy war. But, when there was no war the systematic abasement of the Hindus played no unimportant part in the methods adopted by the Muslim invaders. In the days of Ala-ud-Din, at the beginning of the fourteenth century, the Hindus had in certain parts given the Sultan much trouble. So, he determined to impose such taxes on them that they would be prevented from rising in rebellion.

> "The Hindu was to be left unable to keep a horse to ride on, to carry arms, to wear fine clothes, or to enjoy any of the luxuries of life." ‡

Speaking of the levy of Jizyah Dr. Titus says¶:

> "The payment of the Jizyah by the Hindus continued throughout the dominions of the sultans, emperors, and kings in various parts of India with more or less regularity, though often, the law was in force in theory only; since it depended entirely on the ability of the sovereign to enforce his demands. But, finally, it was abolished throughout the Moghul Empire in the ninth year of the enlightened Akbar's reign (A.D. 1665), after

* Ibid., p. 24.
† Quoted by Dr. Titus—Ibid., p. 26.
‡ Ibid., p. 29.
¶ Ibid., p. 30.

it had been accepted as a fundamental part of Muslim government policy in India for a period of more than eight centuries."

Lane Poole says that

> "the Hindu was taxed to the extent of half the produce of his land, and had to pay duties on all his buffaloes, goats, and other milch-cattle. The taxes were to be levied equally on rich and poor, at so much per acre, so much per animal. Any collectors or officers taking bribes were summarily dismissed and heavily punished with sticks, pincers, the rack, imprisonment and chains. The new rules were strictly carried out, so that one revenue officer would string together 20 Hindu notables and enforce payment by blows. No gold or silver, not even the betel-nut, so cheering and stimulative to pleasure, was to be seen in a Hindu house, and the wives of the impoverished native officials were reduced to taking service in Muslim families. Revenue officers came to be regarded as more deadly than the plague; and to be a government clerk was disgrace worse than death, in so much that no Hindu would marry his daughter to such a man."*

These edicts, says the historian of the period,

> "were so strictly carried out that the *chaukidars* and *khuts* and *muqaddims* were not able to ride on horseback, to find weapon, to wear fine clothes, or to indulge in betel...... No Hindu could hold up his head...... Blows, confinement in the stocks, imprisonment and chains were all employed to enforce payment."

All this was not the result of mere caprice or moral perversion. On the other hand, what was done was in accordance with the ruling ideas of the leaders of Islam in the broadest aspects. These ideas were well expressed by the Kazi in reply to a question put by Sultan Ala-ud-Din wanting to know the legal position of the Hindus under Muslim law. The Kazi said:—

> "They are called payers of tribute, and when the revenue officer demands silver from them they should without question, and with all humility and respect, tender gold. If the officer throws dirt in their mouths, they must without reluctance open their mouths wide to receive it.... The due subordination of the Dhimmi is exhibited in this humble payment, and by this throwing of dirt into their mouths. The glorification of Islam is a

* *Medieval India*, p. 104.

> duty, and contempt for religion is vain. God holds them in contempt, for he says, 'Keep them in subjection.' To keep the Hindus in abasement is especially a religious duty, because they are the most inveterate enemies of the Prophet, and because the Prophet has commanded us to slay them, plunder them, and make them captive, saying, 'Convert them to Islam or kill them, and make them slaves, and spoil their wealth and property'. No doctor but the great doctor (Hanifah), to whose school we belong, has assented to the imposition of jizya on Hindus; doctors of other schools allow no other alternative but 'Death or Islam'."*

Such is the story of this period of 762 years which elapsed between the advent of Muhammad of Ghazni and the return of Ahmadshah Abdalli.

How far is it open to the Hindus to say that Northern India is part of Aryavarta? How far is it open to the Hindus to say because once it belonged to them, therefore, it must remain for ever an integral part of India? Those who oppose separation and hold to the 'historic sentiment' arising out of an ancient fact that Northern India including Afghanistan was once part of India and that the people of that area were either Buddhist or Hindus, must be asked whether the events of these 762 years of incessant Muslim invasions, the object with which they were launched and the methods adopted by these invaders to give effect to their object are to be treated as though they were matters of no account?

Apart from other consequences which have flowed from them these invasions have, in my opinion, so profoundly altered the culture and character of the northern areas, which it is now proposed to be included in a Pakistan, that there is not only no unity between that area and the rest of India but that there is as a matter of fact a real antipathy between the two.

The first consequence of these invasions was the breaking up of the unity of Northern India with the rest of India. After his conquest of Northern India, Muhammad of Ghazni detached it from India and ruled it from Ghazni. When Mahommed Ghori came in the field as a conqueror, he again attached it to India and ruled it from Lahore and then from Delhi. Hakim,

* Quoted by Dr. Titus—Ibid., p. 29.

the brother of Akbar, detached Kabul and Kandahar from Northern India. Akbar again attached it to Northern India. They were again detached by Nadirshah in 1738 and the whole of Northern India would have been severed from India had it not been for the check provided by the rise of the Sikhs. Northern India, therefore, has been like a wagon in a train, which can be coupled or uncoupled according to the circumstances of the moment. If analogy is wanted, the case of Alsace-Lorraine could be cited. Alsace-Lorraine was originally part of Germany, like the rest of Switzerland and the Low Countries. It continued to be so till 1680, when it was taken by France and incorporated into French territory. It belonged to France till 1871, when it was detached by Germany and made part of her territory. In 1918, it was again detached from Germany and made part of France. In 1940, it was detached from France and made part of Germany.

The methods adopted by the invaders have left behind them their aftermath. One aftermath is the bitterness between the Hindus and the Muslims which they have caused. This bitterness, between the two, is so deep-seated that a century of political life has neither succeeded in assuaging it, nor in making people forget it. As the invasions were accompanied with destruction of temples and forced conversions, with spoliation of property, with slaughter, enslavement and abasement of men, women and children, what wonder if the memory of these invasions has ever remained green, as a source of pride to the Muslims and as a source of shame to the Hindus? But these things apart, this north-west corner of India has been a theatre in which a stern drama has been played. Muslim hordes, in wave after wave, have surged down into this area and from thence scattered themselves in spray over the rest of India. These reached the rest of India in thin currents. In time, they also receded from their farthest limits; while they lasted, they left a deep deposit of Islamic culture over the original Aryan culture in this north-west corner of India which has given it a totally different colour, both in religious and political outlook. The Muslim invaders, no doubt, came to India singing a hymn of hate against the Hindus. But, they did not merely sing their hymn of hate and go back burning a few temples on the way. That would have been a blessing. They were not content with so negative a result. They did a positive act, namely, to plant the seed of Islam. The growth of this plant is remarkable. It is not a summer sapling. It is as great and as strong as an oak. Its growth is the thickest in Northern India. The successive invasions have deposited their 'silt' more there than anywhere else, and have served as watering exercises of devoted gardeners. Its growth is so thick in Northern India that the remnants of Hindu and Buddhist culture are just shrubs. Even the Sikh axe could not fell this oak. Sikhs, no doubt, became the political masters of Northern India, but they did not gain back Northern India to that spiritual and cultural unity by which it was bound to the rest of India before Hsuan Tsang. The Sikhs coupled it back to India. Still, it remains like Alsace-Lorraine politically detachable and spiritually alien so far as the rest of India is concerned. It is only an unimaginative person who could fail to take notice of these facts or insist in the face of them that Pakistan means breaking up into two what is one whole.

What is the unity the Hindu sees between Pakistan and Hindustan? If it is geographical unity, then that is no unity. Geographical unity is unity intended by nature. In building up a nationality on geographical unity, it must be remembered that it is a case where Nature proposes and Man disposes. If it is unity in external things, such as ways and habits of life, that is no unity. Such unity is the result of exposure to a common environment. If it is administrative unity, that again is no unity. The instance of Burma is in point. Arakan and Tenasserim were annexed in 1826 by the treaty of Yendabu. Pegu and Martaban were annexed in 1852. Upper Burma was annexed in 1886. The administrative unity between India and Burma was forged in 1826. For over 110 years that administrative unity continued to exist. In 1937, the knot that tied the two together was cut asunder and nobody shed a tear over it. The unity between India and Burma was not less fundamental. If unity is to be of an abiding character, it must be founded on a sense of kinship, in the feeling of being kindred. In short, it must be spiritual. Judged in the light of these considerations, the unity between Pakistan and Hindustan is a myth. Indeed, there is more spiritual unity between Hindustan and Burma than there is between Pakistan and Hindustan. And if the Hindus did not object to the severance of Burma from India, it is difficult to understand how the Hindus can object to the severance of an area like Pakistan, which, to repeat, is politically detachable from, socially hostile and spiritually alien to, the rest of India.

CHAPTER V

WEAKENING OF THE DEFENCES

How will the creation of Pakistan affect the question of the Defence of Hindustan? The question is not a very urgent one. For, there is no reason to suppose that Pakistan will be at war with Hindustan immediately it is brought into being. Nevertheless, as the question is sure to be raised, it is better to deal with it.

The question may be considered under three heads: (1) Question of Frontiers, (2) Question of Resources and (3) Question of Armed Forces.

I

QUESTION OF FRONTIERS

It is sure to be urged by the Hindus that Pakistan leaves Hindustan without a scientific frontier. The obvious reply, of course, is that the Musalmans cannot be asked to give up their right to Pakistan, because it adversely affects the Hindus in the matter of their boundaries. But banter apart, there are really two considerations, which, if taken into account, will show that the apprehensions of the Hindus in this matter are quite uncalled for.

In the first place, can any country hope to have a frontier which may be called scientific? As Mr. Davies, the author of *North-West Frontier*, observes:—

> "It would be impossible to demarcate on the North-West of our Indian Empire a frontier which would satisfy ethnological, political and military requirements. To seek for a zone which traverses easily definable geographical features; which does not

> violate ethnic considerations by cutting through the territories of closely related tribes; and which at the same time serves as a political boundary, is utopian."

As a matter of history, there has been no one scientific boundary for India and different persons have advocated different boundaries for India. The question of boundaries has given rise to two policies, the "Forward" Policy and the "Back to the Indus" Policy. The "Forward" Policy had a greater and a lesser intent, to use the language of Sir George Macmunn. In its greater intent, it meant active control in the affairs of Afghanistan as an *Etat Tampion* to India and the extension of Indian influence upto the Oxus. In its lesser intent, it was confined to the absorption of the tribal hills between the administered territory (i.e. the Province of N.-W. F.) and Afghanistan as defined by the Durand Line and the exercise of British control right up to that line. The greater intent of the Forward Policy, as a basis for a safe boundary for India, has long been abandoned. Consequently, there remain three possible boundary lines to choose from: (1) the Indus River, (2) the present administrative boundary of the N.-W. F. P. and (3) the Durand Line. Pakistan will no doubt bring the boundary of Hindustan Back to the Indus, indeed behind the Indus, to the Sutlej. But this "Back to the Indus" policy was not without its advocates. The greatest exponent of the Indus boundary was Lord Lawrence, who was strongly opposed to any forward move beyond the trans-Indus foot hills. He advocated meeting any invader in the valley of the Indus. In his opinion, it would be an act of folly and weakness to give battle at any great distance from the Indus base; and the longer the distance an invading army has to march through Afghanistan and the tribal country, the more harassed it would be. Others, no doubt, have pointed out that a river is a weak line of defence. But the principal reason for not retiring to the Indus boundary seems to lie elsewhere. Mr. Davies gives the real reason when he says that the—

> "'Back to Indus' cry becomes absurd when it is examined from the point of view of the inhabitants of the modern North-West Frontier Province. Not only would withdrawal mean loss of prestige, but it would also be a gross betrayal of those peoples to whom we have extended our beneficent rule."

In fact, it is no use insisting that any particular boundary is the safest, for the simple reason that geographical conditions are not decisive in the world to-day and modern technique has robbed natural frontiers of much of their former importance, even where they are mighty mountains, the broadest streams, widest seas or far stretching deserts.

In the second place, it is always possible for nations with no natural boundaries to make good this defect. Countries are not wanting which have no natural boundaries. Yet, all have made good the deficiencies of nature, by creating artificial fortifications as barriers, which can be far more impregnable than natural barriers. There is no reason to suppose that the Hindus will not be able to accomplish what other countries similarly situated have done. Given the resources, Hindus need have no fear for want of a naturally safe frontier.

II

QUESTION OF RESOURCES

More important than the question of a scientific frontier, is the question of resources. If resources are ample for the necessary equipment, then it is always possible to overcome the difficulties created by an unscientific or a weak frontier. We must, therefore, consider the comparative resources of Pakistan and Hindustan. The following figures are intended to convey an idea of their comparative resources :—

Resources of Pakistan.

Provinces.	Area.	Population.	Revenues.* Rs.
N.-W. F. P. ...	13,518	2,425,003	1,90,11,842
Punjab ...	91,919	23,551,210	12,53,87,730
Sind ...	46,378	3,887,070	9,56,76,269
Baluchistan ...	54,228	420,648	......
Bengal ...	82,955	50,000,000	36,55,62,485
Total ...	288,998	80,283,931	60,56,38,326

Resources of Hindustan.

Provinces.	Area.	Population.	Revenues.* Rs.
Ajmer-Merwara	2,711	560,292	21,00,000
Assam	55,014	8,622,251	4,46,04,441
Bihar	69,348	32,371,434	6,78,21,588
Bombay	77,271	18,000,000	34,98,03,800
C. P. & Berar	99,957	15,507,723	4,58,83,962
Coorg	1,593	163,327	11,00,000
Delhi	573	636,246	70,00,000
Madras	142,277	46,000,000	25,66,71,265
Orissa	32,695	8,043,681	87,67,269
U. P.	206,248	48,408,763	16,85,52,881
Total	607,657	178,513,919	96,24,05,206

These are gross figures. They are subject to certain additions and deductions. Revenues derived by the Central Government from Railways, Currency and Post and Telegraphs are not included in these figures, as it is not possible to ascertain how much is raised from each Province. When it is done, certain additions will have to be made to the figures under revenue. There can be no doubt that the share from these heads of revenue that will come to Hindustan, will be much larger than the share that will go to Pakistan. Just as additions will have to be made to these figures, so also deductions will have to be made from them. Most of these deductions will, of course, fall to the lot of Pakistan. As will be shown later, some portion of the Punjab will have to be excluded from the scheme of Western Pakistan. Similarly, some portion of Bengal will have to be excluded from the proposed Eastern Pakistan, although a district from Assam will have to be added to it. According to me, fifteen districts will have to be excluded from Bengal and thirteen districts shall have to be excluded from the Punjab. Sufficient

* Revenues include revenue raised both by Provincial Governments in the Provinces from provincial sources and by the Central Government from Central revenues.

data are not available to enable any one to give an exact idea of what would be the reduction in the area, population and revenue, that would result from the exclusion of these districts. One may, however, hazard the guess that so far as the Punjab and Bengal are concerned, their revenues would be halved. What is lost by Pakistan by this exclusion, will of course be gained by Hindustan. To put it in concrete terms, while the revenues of Western and Eastern Pakistan will be 60 crores *minus* 24 crores, i.e. 36 crores, the revenues of Hindustan will be about 96 crores *plus* 24 crores, i.e. 120 crores.

The study of these figures, in the light of the observations I have made, will show that the resources of Hindustan are far greater than the resources of Pakistan, whether one considers the question in terms of area, population or revenue. There need, therefore, be no apprehension on the score of resources. For, the creation of Pakistan will not leave Hindustan in a weakened condition.

III

QUESTION OF ARMED FORCES

The defence of a country does not depend so much upon its scientific frontier as it does upon its resources. But more than resources does it depend upon the fighting forces available to it.

What are the fighting forces available to Pakistan and to Hindustan?

The Simon Commission pointed out, as a special feature of the Indian Defence Problem, that there were special areas which alone offered recruits to the Indian Army and that there were other areas which offered none or if at all, very few. The facts revealed in the following table, taken from the Report of the Commission, undoubtedly will come as a most disagreeable surprise to many Indians, who think and care about the defence of India.

	Areas of Recruitment.		Number of Recruits drawn.
1	N.-W. Frontier Province	...	5,600
2	Kashmir	...	6,500
3	Punjab	...	86,000
4	Baluchistan	...	300
5	Nepal	...	19,000
6	United Provinces	...	16,500
7	Rajputana	...	7,000
8	Central India	...	200
9	Bombay	...	7,000
10	Central Provinces	...	100
11	Bihar & Orissa	...	300
12	Bengal	...	Nil
13	Assam	...	Nil
14	Burma	...	3,000
15	Hyderabad	...	700
16	Mysore	...	100
17	Madras	...	4,000
18	Miscellaneous	...	1,900
	Total	...	158,200

The Simon Commission found that this state of affairs was natural to India, and in support of it, cited the following figures of recruitment from the different Provinces of India during the Great War especially because "it cannot be suggested that any discouragement was offered to recruitment in any area":—

Province.		Combatant Recruits Enlisted.	Non-combatant Recruits Enlisted.	Total.
Madras	...	51,223	41,117	92,340
Bombay	...	41,272	30,211	71,483
Bengal	...	7,117	51,935	59,052
United Provinces	...	163,578	117,565	281,143
Punjab	...	349,688	97,288	446,976
North-West Frontier	...	32,181	13,050	45,231
Baluchistan	...	1,761	327	2,088
Burma	...	14,094	4,579	18,673
Bihar & Orissa	...	8,576	32,976	41,552
Central Provinces	...	5,376	9,631	15,007
Assam	...	942	14,182	15,124
Ajmer-Merwara	...	7,341	1,632	8,973
Nepal	...	58,904	...	58,904
Total	...	742,053	414,493	1,156,546

These data reveal in a striking manner that the fighting forces available for the defence of India mostly come from areas which are to be included in Pakistan. From this it may be argued, that without Pakistan, Hindustan cannot defend itself.

The facts brought out by the Simon Commission are, of course, beyond question. But they cannot be made the basis of a conclusion, such as is suggested by the Simon Commission, namely, that only Pakistan can produce soldiers and that Hindustan cannot. That such a conclusion is quite untenable will be seen from the following considerations.

In the first place, what is regarded by the Simon Commission as something peculiar to India is not quite so peculiar. What appears to be peculiar is not due to any inherent defect in the people. The peculiarity arises because of the policy of recruitment followed by the British Government for years past. The official explanation of this predominance in the Indian Army of the men of the North-West is that they belong to the Martial Classes. But Mr. Chaudhari* has demonstrated, by unimpeachable data, that this explanation is far from being true. He has shown that the predominance in the Army of the men of the North-West took place as early as the Mutiny of 1857, some 20 years before the theory of Martial and Non-martial Classes was projected in an indistinct form for the first time in 1879 by the Special Army Committee† appointed in that year, and that their predominance had nothing to do with their alleged fighting qualities but was due to the fact, that they helped the British to suppress the Mutiny in which the Bengal Army was so completely involved. To quote Mr. Chaudhari:—

> "The pre-Mutiny army of Bengal was essentially a Brahmin and Kshatriya army of the Ganges basin. All the three Presidency Armies of those days, as we have stated in the first part of this article, were in a sense quite representative of the military

* See his series of articles on "The Martial Races of India" published in the *Modern Review* for July 1930, September 1930, January 1931 and February 1931.

† The Questionnaire circulated by the Committee included the following question: "If an efficient and available reserve of the Indian Army be considered necessary for the safety of the Empire, should it not be recruited and maintained from those parts of the country which give us best soldiers, rather than amongst the weakest and least warlike races of India?"......

potentialities of the areas to which they belonged, though none of them could, strictly speaking, be correctly described as national armies of the provinces concerned, as there was no attempt to draw upon any but the traditional martial elements of the population. But they all got their recruits mainly from their natural areas of recruitment, viz., the Madras Army from the Tamil and Telugu countries, the Bombay Army from Western India, and the Bengal Army from Bihar and U. P. and to a very limited extent from Bengal. There was no official restriction on the enrolment of men of any particular tribe or caste or region, provided they were otherwise eligible. Leaving aside for the moment the practice of the Bombay and the Madras Armies, the only exception to this general rule in the Bengal Army was that which applied to the Punjabis and Sikhs, who, inspite of their magnificent military traditions, were not given a fair representation in the Army of Northern India. Their recruitment, on the contrary, was placed under severe restrictions by an order of the Government, which laid down that 'the number of Punjabis in a regiment is never to exceed 200, nor are more than 100 of them to be Sikhs'. It was only the revolt of the Hindustani regiments of the Bengal Army that gave an opportunity to the Punjabis to rehabilitate themselves in the eyes of the British authorities. Till then, they remained suspect and under a ban, and the Bengal Army on the eve of the Mutiny was mainly recruited from Oudh, North and South Bihar, especially the latter, principally Shahabad and Bhojpur, the Doab of the Ganges and Jumna and Rohilkhund. The soldiers recruited from these areas were mostly high-caste men, Brahmins of all denominations, Kshatriyas, Rajputs and Ahirs. The average proportion in which these classes were enrolled in a regiment was: (1) Brahmin 7/24, (2) Rajputs 1/4, (3) Inferior Hindus 1/6, (4) Musalmans 1/6, (5) Punjabis 1/8.

"To this army, the area which now-a-days furnishes the greatest number of soldiers—the Punjab, Nepal, N.-W. F. Province, the hill tracts of Kumaon and Garhwal, Rajputana,—furnished very few recruits or none at all. There was practical exclusion in it of all the famous fighting castes of India,—Sikhs, Gurkhas, Punjabi Musalmans, Dogras, Jats, Pathans, Garhwalis, Rajputana Rajputs, Kumaonis, Gujaras, all the tribes and sects, in fact, which are looked upon today as a tower of strength of the Indian Army. A single year and a single rebellion was, however, to change all thi . The Mutiny, which broke out in 1857, blew up the old Benga Army and brought into existence a Punjabized and barbarized army, resembling the Indian Army of today in broad lines and general proportions of its composition.

"The gaps created by the revolt of the Hindustani regiments (of the Bengal Army) were at once filled up by Sikhs and other Punjabis, and hillmen eager for revenge and for the loot of the cities of Hindustan. They had all been conquered and subjugated by the British with the help of the Hindustani soldiers, and in their ignorance, they regarded the Hindustanis, rather the handful of British, as their real enemies. This enmity was magnificently exploited by the British authorities in suppressing the Mutiny. When the news of the enlistment of Gurkhas reached Lord Dalhousie in England he expressed great satisfaction and wrote to a friend: 'Against the Oude Sepoys they may confidently be expected to fight like devils'. And after the Mutiny, General Mansfield, the Chief of the Staff of the Indian Army, wrote about the Sikhs: 'It was not because they loved us, but because they hated Hindustan and hated the Bengal Army that the Sikhs had flocked to our standard instead of seeking the opportunity to strike again for their freedom. They wanted to revenge themselves and to gain riches by the plunder of Hindustani cities. They were not attracted by mere daily pay, it was rather the prospect of wholesale plunder and stamping on the heads of their enemies. In short, we turned to profit the *esprit de corps* of the old Khalsa Army of Ranjit Singh, in the manner which for a time would most effectually bind the Sikhs to us as long as the active service against their old enemies may last'.

"The relations thus established were in fact to last much longer. The services rendered by the Sikhs and Gurkhas during the Mutiny were not forgotten and henceforward the Punjab and Nepal had the place of honour in the Indian Army."

That Mr. Chaudhari is right when he says that it was the Mutiny of 1857 which was the real cause of the preponderance in the Indian Army of the men of the North-West is beyond the possibility of doubt. Equally incontrovertible is the view of Mr. Chaudhari that this preponderance of the men of the North-West is not due to their native superiority in fighting qualities, as the same is amply borne out by the figures which he has collected, showing the changes in the composition of the Indian Infantry before and after the Mutiny.

CHANGES IN THE COMPOSITION OF THE INDIAN INFANTRY

Percentage of men from different Parts

Year.	North-West India.		North-East India U.P., Bihar.	South India.	Burma.
	Punjab, N.-W. F., Kashmir.	Nepal, Garhwal, Kumaon.			
1856	Less than 10	Negligible.	Not less than 90	...	Nil
1858	47	6	47	...	,,
1883	48	17	35	...	,,
1893	53	24	23	...	,,
1905	47	15	22	16	,,
1919	46	14.8	25.5	12	1.7
1930	58.5	22	11.0	5.5	3

These figures show that in 1856, one year before the Mutiny, the men from the North-West were a negligible factor in the Indian Army. But in 1858, one year after the Mutiny, they had acquired a dominant position which has never received a set-back.

It will thus be seen that the distinction between Martial and Non-martial Classes, which was put forth for the first time in 1879, as a matter of principle, which was later on insisted upon as a matter of serious consideration by Lord Roberts* and which was subsequently recognised by Lord Kitchener as a principle governing recruitment to the Indian Army, had nothing to do

* In his *Forty-One Years* he wrote: "Each cold season, I made long tours in order to acquaint myself with the needs and capabilities of the men of the Madras Army. I tried hard to discover in them those fighting qualities which had distinguished their forefathers during the wars of the last and the beginning of the present century . . . And I was forced to the conclusion that the ancient military spirit had died in them, as it had died in the ordinary Hindustani of Bengal and the Mahratta of Bombay, and that they could no longer with safety be pitted against warlike races, or employed outside the limit of Southern India."

with the origin of this preponderance of the men of the North-West in the Indian Army. No doubt, the accident that the people from North-West India had the good luck of being declared by the Government as belonging to the Martial Class, while most of the classes coming from the rest of India had the ill-luck of being declared Non-martial Classes had important consequences. Being regularly employed in the Army, the people of North-West India came to look upon service in the Army as an occupation with a security and a career which was denied to men from the rest of India. The large number of recruits drawn from North-West India, therefore, indicates nothing more than this—namely, owing to the policy of the British Government, service in the Army has become their occupation and if people in other parts of India do not readily come forth to enlist in the Army, the reason is that Government did not employ them in the Army. People follow their ancestral occupations whether they like it or not. When a people do not take to a new occupation it does not necessarily mean that they are not fit for it. It only means that it is not their ancestral occupation.

This division between Martial and Non-martial Classes is, of course, a purely arbitrary and artificial distinction. It is as foolish as the Hindu theory of caste, making birth instead of worth, the basis for recognition. At one time, the Government insisted that the distinction they had adopted was a real distinction and that in terms of fighting qualities, it meant so much fighting value. In fact, this was their justification for recruiting more men from the North-West of India. That this distinction has nothing to do with any difference in fighting qualities has now been admitted. Sir Phillip Chetwode,* late Commander-in-Chief of India, broadcasting from London on the constitution of the Indian Army, took pains to explain that the recruitment of a larger proportion of it from the Punjab, did not mean that the people of the Peninsula were without martial qualities. Sir Phillip Chetwode explained that the reason why men of the North were largely recruited for the Indian Army was chiefly climatic, as the men from the South cannot stand the extremes of heat and cold of North India. No race can be permanently

* *Indian Social Reformer*, January 27th, 1940.

without martial spirit. Martial spirit is not a matter of native instinct. It is a matter of training and anybody can be trained to it.

But apart from this, there is enough fighting material in Hindustan, besides what might be produced by special training. There are the Sikhs, about whose fighting qualities nothing need be said. There are the Rajputs who are even now included in the category of Martial Classes. In addition to these, there are the Mahrattas who proved their calibre as a fighting race during the last European War. Even the people of the Madras Presidency can be depended upon for military purposes. Speaking of the Madrasis as soldiers, General Sir Frederick P. Haines, at one time Commander-in-Chief in India, observed :—

> "It has been customary to declare that the Madras Army is composed of men physically inferior to those of the Bengal Army, and if stature alone be taken into consideration, this is true. It is also said that by the force of circumstances the martial feeling and the characteristics necessary to the real soldier are no longer to be found in its ranks. I feel bound to reject the above assertions and others which ascribe comparative inefficiency to Madras troops. It is true that in recent years they have seen but little service ; for, with the exception of the sappers, they have been specially excluded from all participation in work in the field. I cannot admit for one moment that anything has occurred to disclose the fact that the Madras Sepoy is inferior as a fighting man. The facts of history warrant us in assuming the contrary. In drill training and discipline, the Madras Sepoy is inferior to none ; while in point of health, as exhibited by returns, he compares favourably with his neighbours. This has been manifested by the sappers and their followers in the Khyber ; and the sappers are of the same race as the sepoys."

Hindustan need, therefore, have no apprehension regarding the supply of an adequate fighting force from among its own people. The separation of Pakistan cannot weaken her in that respect.

The Simon Commission drew attention to three features of the Indian Army, which struck them as being special and peculiar to India. It pointed out that the duty of the Army in India was two-fold; firstly, to prevent the independent tribes on the Indian side of the Afghan frontier from raiding the peaceful inhabitants of the plains below. Secondly, to protect India against invasion by countries lying behind and beyond this belt of unorganized territories. The Commission took note of the fact that from 1850 to 1922, there were 72 expeditions against the independent tribes, an average of one a year, and also of the fact that in the countries behind and beyond this belt of unorganized territory, lies the direction from which, throughout the ages, the danger to India's territorial integrity has come. This quarter is occupied by "States which according to the Commission are not members of the League of Nations" and is, therefore, a greater danger to India now than before. The Commission insisted on emphasizing that these two facts constituted a peculiar feature of the problem of military defence in India and so far as the urgency and extent of the problem is concerned, they are "without parallel elsewhere in the Empire, and constituted a difficulty in developing self-government which never arose in any comparable degree in the case of the self-governing Dominions."

As a second unique feature of the Indian Army, the Commission observed :—

> "The Army in India is not only provided and organized to ensure against external dangers of a wholly exceptional character: it is also distributed and habitually used throughout India for the purpose of maintaining or restoring internal peace. In all countries .... the military is not normally employed in this way, and certainly is not organized for this purpose. But the case of India is entirely different. Troops are employed many times a year to prevent internal disorder and, if necessary, to quell it. Police forces, admirably organized as they are, cannot be expected in all cases to cope with the sudden and violent outburst of a mob driven frantic by religious frenzy. It is, therefore, well understood in India both by the police and by the military — and, what is even more to the point, by the public at large — that the soldiers may have to be sent for... This use of the Army for the purpose of maintaining or restoring internal order was increasing rather than diminishing, and that on these occasions the practically universal request was for British troops. The proportion of the British to Indian troops allotted to this duty has in fact risen in the last quarter of a century. The reason, of course, is that the British soldier is a neutral, and is under no suspicion of favouring Hindus against Mahomedans or Mahomedans against Hindus ...... Inasmuch as the vast majority of the disturbances which call for the intervention of the military have a communal

or religious complexion, it is natural and inevitable that the intervention which is most likely to be authoritative should be that which has no bias, real or suspected, to either side. It is a striking fact in this connection that, while in regular units of the Army in India as a whole British soldiers are in a minority of about 1 to 2½, in the troops allotted for internal security the preponderance is reversed, and for this purpose a majority of British troops is employed — in the troops ear-marked for internal security the proportion is about eight British to seven Indian soldiers."

Commenting upon this feature of the Indian Army the Commission said:—

> "When, therefore, one contemplates a future for India in which, in place of the existing Army organization, the country is defended and pacified by exclusively Indian units, just as Canada relies on Canadian troops and Ireland on Irish troops, it is essential to realize and bear in mind the dimensions and character of the Indian problem of internal order and the part which the British soldier at present plays (to the general satisfaction of the country-side) in supporting peaceful government."

The third unique feature of the Indian Army, which was pointed out by the Simon Commission, is the preponderance in it of the men from the North-West. The origin of this preponderance and the reasons underlying the official explanation given therefor have already been examined.

But, there is one more special feature of the Indian Army to which the Commission made no reference at all. The Commission either ignored it or was not aware of it. It is such an important feature that it overshadows all the three features to which the Commission refers, in its importance and in its social and political consequences.

It is a feature which, if widely known, will set many people to think furiously. It is sure to raise questions which may prove insoluble and which may easily block the path of India's political progress — questions of far greater importance and complexity than those relating to Indianization of the Army.

This neglected feature relates to the communal composition of the Indian Army. Mr. Chaudhari has collected the relevant data in his articles, already referred to, which throws a flood of light on this aspect of the Indian Army. The following table

shows the proportion of soldiers serving in the Indian Infantry, **according to the area** and the community from which they are **drawn :—**

CHANGES IN THE COMMUNAL COMPOSITION OF THE INDIAN ARMY

Area and Communities.	Percentage in 1914.	Percentage in 1918.	Percentage in 1919.	Percentage in 1930.
I The Punjab, N.-W. F. P. and Kashmir ..	47	46·5	46	58·5
1 Sikhs ..	19·2	17·4	15·4	13·58
2 Punjabi Musalmans ..	11·1	11·3	12·4	22·6
3 Pathans ..	6·2	5·42	4·54	6·35
II Nepal, Kumaon, Garhwal	15	18·9	14·9	22·0
1 Gurkhas ..	13·1	16·6	12·2	16·4
III Upper India ..	22	22·7	25·5	11·0
1 U.P. Rajputs ..	6·4	6·8	7·7	2·55
2 Hindustani Musalmans	4·1	3·42	4·45	Nil.
3 Brahmins ..	1·8	1·86	2·5	Nil.
IV South India ..	16	11·9	12	5·5
1 Mahrattas ..	4·9	3·85	3·7	5·33
2 Madrasi Musalmans ..	3·5	2·71	2·13	Nil.
3 Tamils ..	2·5	2·0	1·67	Nil.
V. Burma				
1 Burmans	Nil.	Negligible	1·7	3·0

This table brings out in an unmistakable manner the profound changes which have been going on in the communal composition of the Indian Army particularly after 1919. They are (1) a phenomenal rise in the strength of the Punjabi Musalman and the Pathan, (2) a substantial reduction in the position of Sikhs from first to third, (3) the degradation of the Rajputs to the fourth place, and (4) the shutting out of the U. P. Brahmins, the Madrasi Musalmans, and the Tamilians, both Brahmins and Non-Brahmins.

A further analysis of the figures for 1930, which discloses the communal composition of the Indian Infantry and Indian Cavalry, has been made by Mr. Chaudhari in the following table.*

COMMUNAL COMPOSITION OF THE INDIAN ARMY IN 1930

	Class.	Areas.	Percentage in Infantry.		Percentage in Cavalry.
			Excluding Gurkhas.	Including Gurkhas.	
1	Punjabi Musalman	Punjab	27	22·6	14·28
2	Gurkhas	Nepal	...	16·4	...
3	Sikhs	Punjab	16·24	13·58	23·81
4	Dogras	North Punjab and Kashmir	11·4	9·54	9·53
5	Jats	Rajputana, U. P., Punjab	9·5	7·94	19·06
6	Pathans	N.-W. F. Province	7·57	6·35	4·76
7	Mahrattas	Konkan	6·34	5·33	...
8	Garhwalis	Garhwal	4·53	3·63	...
9	U. P. Rajputs	U. P.	3·04	2·54	...
10	Rajputana Rajputs	Rajputana	2·8	2·35	...
11	Kumaonis	Kumaon	2·44	2·05	...
12	Gujars	N. E. Rajputana	1·52	1·28	...
13	Punjabi Hindus	Punjab	1·52	1·28	...
14	Ahirs	Do.	1·22	1·024	...
15	Musalmans, Rajputs Ranghars.	Neighbourhood of Delhi	1·22	1·024	7·14
16	Kaimkhanis	Rajputana	...	...	4·76
17	Kachins	Burma	1·22	1·024	...
18	Chins	Do.	1·22	1·024	...
19	Karens	Do.	1·22	1·024	...
20	Dekhani Musalmans	Deccan	...	...	4·76
21	Hindustani Musalmans	U. P.	...	...	2·38

* This table shows the percentage of men of each eligible class in the Indian Infantry (82 active and 18 training battalions), the Indian Cavalry (21 regiments), and the 20 battalions of the Gurkha Infantry. This table does not include the Indian personnel of (a) the 19 batteries of Indian Mountain Artillery, and (b) 3 regiments of Sappers and Miners, (c) the Indian Signal Corps, and (d) the Corps of Indian Pioneers, all of which are composed of different proportions of the Punjabi Musalmans, Sikhs, Pathans, Hindustani Hindus and Musalmans, Madrasis of all classes and Hazra Afghans, either in class units or class companies. Except that some units in these arms of the service are composed of the Madrasis and Hazras, now enrolled in other units of the Indian Army, the class composition of these units does not materially alter the proportion of the classes as given in the table. This table does not also include the Indian personnel attached to the British Infantry and Artillery units.

Reducing these figures in terms of communities, we get the following percentage as it stood in 1930:—

Communities.	Percentage in Infantry.		Percentage in Cavalry.
	Including Gurkhas.	Excluding Gurkhas.	
1 Hindus and Sikhs	60·55	50·554	61·92
2 Gurkhas	......	16·4	......
3 Muhammadans	35·79	29·974	30·08
4 Burmans	3·66	3·072	......

These figures show the communal composition of the Indian Army. The Musalmans according to Mr. Chaudhari formed 36% of the Indian Infantry and 30% of the Indian Cavalry.

These figures relate to the year 1930. We must now find out what changes have taken place since then in this proportion.

It is one of the most intriguing things in the Military history of India that no information is available on this point after 1930. It is impossible to know what the proportion of the Muslims in the Indian Army at present is. There is no Government publication from which such information can be gathered. In the past, there was no dearth of publications giving this information. It is very surprising that they should have now disappeared, or if they do appear, that they should cease to contain this information. Not only is there no Government publication containing information on this point, but Government has refused to give any information on the point when asked by members of the Central Legislative Assembly. The following questions and answers taken from the proceedings of the Central Legislative Assembly show how Government has been strenuously combating every attempt to obtain information on the point:—

There was an interpellation on 15th September 1938, when the following questions were asked and replies as stated below were given:—

*Arrangements for the Defence of India.**

* Legislative Assembly Debates, 1938 Vol. VI, page 2462.

Q. 1360 : *Mr. Badri Dutt Pande* (on behalf of Mr. Amarendra Nath Chattopadhya).

(*a*) x x x x

(*b*) x x x x

(*c*) x x x x

(*d*) How many Indians have been recruited during 1937 and 1938 as soldiers and officers during 1937-38 for the Infantry and Cavalry respectively? Amongst the soldiers and officers recruited, how many are Punjabi Sikhs, Pathans, Garhwalis, Mahrattas, Madrasis, Biharis, Bengalis and Hindustanis of the United Provinces and Gurkhas?

(*e*) If none but the Punjabi Sikhs, Pathans and Garhwalis have been recruited, is it in contemplation of the Honourable Member to recruit from all the Provinces for the defence of India and give them proper military training?

(*f*) Will the Defence Secretary be pleased to state if Provincial Governments will be asked to raise Provincial Regiments, trained and fully mechanised, for the defence of India? If not, what is his plan of raising an efficient army for the defence of India?

Mr. C. M. G. Ogilvie :—

(*a*) The Honourable Member will appreciate that it is not in the public interest to disclose the details of such arrangements.

(*b*) 5 cadets and 33 Indian apprentices were recruited for the Indian Air Force during 1937-38.

(*c*) During 1937-38, 5 Indians have already been recruited to commissioned ranks in the Royal Indian Navy, 4 will be taken by competitive examination in October 1938, and 3 more by special examination of "Dufferin" cadets only. During the same period, 314 Indians were recruited to different non-commissioned categories in the Royal Indian Navy.

(*d*) During the year ending the 31st March 1938, 54 Indians were commissioned as Indian Commissioned Officers. They are now attached to British units for training, and it is not yet possible to say what proportion will be posted to infantry, and cavalry respectively. During the same period, 961 Indian soldiers were recruited for cavalry, and 7,970 for infantry. Their details by classes are not available at Army Headquarters and to call for them from the recruiting officers all over India would not justify the expenditure of time and labour involved.

(*e*) No.

(*f*) The reply to the first portion is in the negative. The reply to the second portion is that India already possesses an efficient army and so far as finances permit, every effort is made to keep it up-to-date in all respects.

Mr. S. Satyamurti: With reference to the answers to clauses (*d*) and (*e*) of the question taken together, may I know whether the attention of Government has been drawn to statements made by many public men that the bulk of the army is from the Punjab and from one community? Have Government considered those facts and will Government also consider the desirability of making the army truly national by extending recruitment to all provinces and communities, so as to avoid the danger present in all countries of a military dictatorship seizing political power?

Mr. C. M. G. Ogilvie: I am not sure how that arises from this question, but I am prepared to say that provincial boundaries do not enter into Government's calculations at all. The best soldiers are chosen to provide the best army for India and not for any province, and in this matter national considerations must come above provincial considerations. Where the bulk of best military material is found, there we will go to get it, and not elsewhere.

Mr. S. Satyamurti: May I know whether the bulk of the army is from the Punjab and whether the Government have forgotten the experience of the brave exploits of men from my province not very long ago in the Indian Army, and may I know if Madrasis are practically kept out and many other provinces are kept out of the army altogether?

Mr. C. M. G. Ogilvie: Madras is not practically kept out of the army. Government gladly acknowledge the gallant services of the Madrasis in the army and they are now recruited to those Units where experience has proved them to be best. There are some 4,500 serving chiefly in the Sappers and Miners and Artillery.

Mr. S. Satyamurti: Out of a total of 120,000?

Mr. C. M. G. Ogilvie: About that.

Mr. S. Satyamurti: May I take it, that, that is a proper proportion, considering the population of Madras, the revenue that Madras pays to the Central exchequer, and the necessity of having a national army recruited from all the provinces?

Mr. C. M. G. Ogilvie: The only necessity we recognise is to obtain the best possible army.

Mr. S. Satyamurti: May I know by what tests Government have come to the conclusion that provinces other than the Punjab cannot supply the best elements in the Indian Army?

Mr. Ogilvie: By experience.

Dr. Sir Ziauddin Ahmed: May I ask if it is not a fact that all branches of Accounts Department are monopolised by the Madrasis and will Government immediately reduce the number in proportion to their numerical strength in India?

Mr. Ogilvie: I do not see how that arises from this question either, but the Government are again not prepared to sacrifice efficiency for any provincial cause.

*Indian Regiment consisting of Indians belonging to Different Castes.**

* Legislative Assembly Debates, 1938, Vol. VI, page 2478.

Weakening of the Defences

Q. 1078: *Mr. M. Anantasayanam Ayyangar* (on behalf of Mr. Manu Subedar):

(*a*) Will the Defence Secretary state whether any experiment has ever been made under British rule of having an Indian regiment consisting of Indians recruited from different provinces and belonging to the different castes and sections, such as Sikhs, Mahrattas, Rajputs, Brahmins and Muslims?

(*b*) If the reply to part (*a*) be in the negative, can a statement of Government's policy in this regard be made giving reasons why it has not been considered proper to take such action?

(*c*) Is His Excellency the Commander-in-Chief prepared to take up this matter with His Majesty's Government?

(*d*) Are Government aware that in the University Corps and in the Bombay Scout Movement, and in the Police Forces of the country, there is no separation by caste or creed?

Mr. C. M. G. Ogilvie:

(*a*) No.

(*b*) Government regard it as a fundamental principle of organization that Military Sub-Units, such as companies and squadrons, must be homogeneous.

(*c*) No, for the reason just mentioned.

(*d*) Yes.

Mr. S. Satyamurti: May I know the meaning which Government attach to the word "homogeneous"? Does it mean from the same province or the same community?

Mr. C. M. G. Ogilvie: It means that they must belong to the same class of persons.

Mr. S. Satyamurti: May I ask for some elucidation of this point? Do they make distinction between one class and another?

Mr. C. M. G. Ogilvie: Certainly.

Mr. S. Satyamurti: On what basis? Is it religious class or racial class or provincial class?

Mr. C. M. G. Ogilvie: Neither. It is largely racial class.

Mr. S. Satyamurti: Which races are preferred and which are not preferred?

Mr. C. M. G. Ogilvie: I refer the Honourable Member to the Army List.

*Recruitment to the Indian Army.**

Q. 1162 : *Mr. Brojendra Narayan Chaudhary:* Will the Defence Secretary please state:—

(*a*) Whether the attention of Government has been drawn to the address of the Punjab's Premier, the Hon'ble Sir Sikander Hyat Khan to his brother soldiers, in these words: "No patriotic Punjabi would wish to impair Punjab's position of supremacy in the Army," as reported by the Associated Press of India in the *Hindustan Times* of the 5th September 1938; and

(*b*) Whether it is the policy of Government to maintain the supremacy of Punjabis in the army by continuing to recruit the major portion from the Punjab; or to attempt recruitment of the Army from all the provinces without racial or provincial considerations?

Mr. C. M. G. Ogilvie:

(*a*) Yes.

(*b*) I refer the Honourable Member to replies I gave to the supplementary questions arising from starred question No. 1060 asked by Mr. Amarendra Nath Chattopadhyaya on 15th September 1938.

* Legislative Assembly Debates, 1938, Vol. VI, page 2754.

Mr. S. Satyamurti: With reference to the answer to part (*a*) of the question, my Honourable friend referred to previous answers. As far as I remember, they were not given after this statement was brought before this House. May I know if the Government of India have examined this statement of the Punjab Premier, "No patriotic Punjabi would wish to impair Punjab's position of supremacy in the Army"? May I know whether Government have considered the dangerous implications of this statement and will they take steps to prevent a responsible Minister going about and claiming provincial or communal supremacy in the Indian Army, which ought to remain Indian first and Indian last?

Mr. C. M. G. Ogilvie: I can only answer in exactly the same words as I answered to a precisely similar question of the Hon'ble Member on the 15th September last. The policy of Government with regard to the recruitment has been repeatedly stated and is perfectly clear.

Mr. S. Satyamurti: That policy is to get the best material and I am specifically asking my Honourable friend I hope he realises the implications of that statement of the Punjab Premier. I want to know whether the Government have examined the dangerous implications of any provincial Premier claiming provincial supremacy in the Indian Army and whether they propose to take any steps to correct this dangerous misapprehension?

Mr. C. M. G. Ogilvie: Government consider that there are no dangerous implications whatever but rather the reverse.

Mr. Satyamurti: Do Government accept the supremacy of any province or any community as desirable consideration, even if it is a fact, to be uttered by responsible public men and do not the Government consider that this will give rise to communal and provincial quarrels and jealousies inside the army and possibly a military dictatorship in this country?

Mr. C. M. G. Ogilvie: Government consider that none of these forebodings have any justification at all.

Mr. M. S. Aney: Do the Government subscribe to the policy implied in the statement of Sir Sikander Hyat Khan?

Mr. C. M. G. Ogilvie: Government's policy has been repeatedly stated and made clear.

Mr. M. S. Aney: Is it the policy that the Punjab should have its supremacy in the Army?

Mr. C. M. G. Ogilvie: The policy is that the best material should be recruited for the Army.

Mr. M. S. Aney: I again repeat the question. Is it the policy of Government that Punjab should have supremacy in the Army?

Mr. C. M. G. Ogilvie: I have repeatedly answered that question. The policy is that the Army should get the best material from all provinces and Government are quite satisfied that it has the best material at present.

Mr. M. S. Aney: Is it not, therefore, necessary that Government should make a statement modifying the policy suggested by Sir Sikander Hyat Khan?

Mr. C. M. G. Ogilvie: Government have no intention whatever of changing their policy in particular.

Another interpellation took place on 23rd November 1938 when the question stated below was asked :—

*Recruitment to the Indian Army from the Central Provinces & Berar.**

Q. 1402: *Mr. Govind V. Deshmukh:* Will the Defence Secretary please state :—

(*a*) The centres in the Central Provinces and Berar for recruiting men for the Indian Army;

(*b*) The classes from which such men are recruited;

(*c*) The proportion of the men from the C. P. & Berar in the Army to the total strength of the Army, as well as to the population of these provinces; and

* Legislative Assembly Debates, 1938, Vol. VII, page 3313.

(*d*) The present policy of recruitment, and if it is going to be revised; if not, why not?

Mr. C. M. G. Ogilvie:

(*a*) There are no recruiting centres in the C. P. or Berar. Men residing in the C. P. are in the area of the Recruiting Officer, Delhi, and those of Berar in the area of the Recruiting Officer, Poona.

(*b*) Mahrattas of Berar are recruited as a separate class. Other Hindus and Mussalmans who are recruited from the C. P. and Berar are classified as "Hindus" or "Musalmans", and are not entered under any class denomination.

(*c*) The proportion to the total strength of the Army is .03 per cent. and the proportion to the total male population of these provinces is .0004 per cent.

(*d*) There is at present no intention of revising the present policy, the reasons for which were stated in my reply to a supplementary question arising out of Mr. Satyamurti's starred question No. 1060, on the 15th September 1938, and in answer to part (*a*) of starred question No. 1086 asked by Mian Ghulam Kadir Muhammad Shahban on the same date, and in the reply of His Excellency the Commander-in-Chief to the debates in the Council of State on the Honourable Mr. Sushil Kumar Roy Chaudhary's Resolution regarding military training for Indians on the 21st February 1938 and on the Honourable Mr. P. N. Sapru's Resolution on the recruitment of all classes to the Indian Army in April 1935.

This was followed by an interpellation on 6th February 1939, when the below mentioned question was asked:—

*Recruitment to the Indian Army.**

Q. 129: *Mr. S. Satyamurti:* Will the Defence Secretary be pleased to state:

* Legislative Assembly Debates, 1939, Vol. I, page 253.

(*a*) Whether Government have since the last answer on this question reconsidered the question of recruiting to the Indian Army from all provinces and from all castes and communities;

(*b*) Whether they have come to any conclusion;

(*c*) Whether Government will categorically state the reasons as to why other provinces and communities are not allowed to serve in the army; and

(*d*) What are the tests by which they have come to the conclusion that other provinces and other communities than those from whom recruitment is made to the Indian Army to-day cannot come up to the standard of efficiency required of the Indian Army?

Mr. C. M. G. Ogilvie:

(*a*) No.

(*b*) Does not arise.

(*c*) and (*d*) The reasons have been categorically stated in my replies to starred questions Nos. 1060 and 1086 of 15th September 1938, No. 1162 of 20th September 1938 and No. 1402 of 23rd November 1938 and also in the replies of His Excellency the Commander-in-Chief in the Council of State to the debates on the Honourable Mr. P. N. Sapru's Resolution regarding recruitment of all classes to the Indian Army and the Honourable Mr. Sushil Kumar Roy Chaudhary's Resolution regarding Military training for Indians, on the 13th March 1935 and 21st February 1938 respectively.

This conspiracy of silence on the part of the Government of India, was quite recently broken by the Secretary of State for India, who came forward to give the fullest information on this most vital and most exciting subject, in answer to a question in the House of Commons. From his answer given on 8th July

1943 we know the existing communal and provincial composition of the Indian Army to be as follows :—

I. PROVINCIAL COMPOSITION OF THE INDIAN ARMY

Province.	Percentage.	Province.	Percentage.
1. Punjab	50	7. Bengal Presidency	2
2. U. P.	15	8. C. P. & Berar	
3. Madras Presidency	10	9. Assam	5
4. Bombay Presidency	10	10. Bihar	
5. N.-W. F. Province	5	11. Orissa	
6. Ajmere & Merwara	3	12. Nepal	8

II. COMMUNAL COMPOSITION OF THE INDIAN ARMY

1.	Muslims	34 p.c.
2.	Hindus & Gurkhas	50 p.c.
3.	Sikhs	10 p.c.
4.	Christians & The Rest	6 p.c.

The information given by the Secretary of State is indeed very welcome. But, this is the war-time composition of the Indian Army. The peace-time composition must be very different. It rested on the well-known distinction between the Martial and Non-Martial Races. That distinction was abolished during the War. There is, however, no certainty that it will not be revived now that peace has returned. What we want to know is the peace-time communal composition of the Indian Army. That still remains an unknown fact and a subject of speculation.

Some say that the normal pre-war proportion of Muslims was between 60 and 70 p.c. Others say that it is somewhere in the neighbourhood of 50 p.c. In the absence of exact information, one could well adopt the latter figure as disclosing the true situation especially, when on inquiry, it happens to be confirmed by those who are in a position to form some idea on the matter. Even if the proportion be 50% it is high enough to cause alarm to the Hindus. If this is true, it is a flagrant violation of well established principles of British Army policy in India, adopted after the Mutiny.

After the Mutiny, the British Government ordered two investigations into the organization of the Indian Army. The first investigation was carried out by the Peel Commission which was appointed in 1859. The second investigation was undertaken by a body, called the Special Army Committee, appointed in 1879 to which reference has already been made.

The principal question considered by the Peel Commission was to find out the weaknesses in the Bengal Army, which led to the Mutiny of 1857. The Peel Commission was told by witness after witness that the principal weakness in the Bengal Army which mutinied was that

> "In the ranks of the regular Army men stood mixed up as chance might befall. There was no separating by class and clan into companies....... In the lines, Hindu and Mahomedan, Sikh and Poorbeah were mixed up, so that each and all lost to some extent their racial prejudice and became inspired with one common sentiment."*

It was, therefore, proposed by Sir John Lawrence that in organizing the Indian Army care should be taken "to preserve that distinctiveness which is so valuable, and, while it lasts, makes the Mahomedan of one country despise, fear or dislike the Mahomedan of another; Corps should in future be provincial, and adhere to the geographical limits within which differences and rivalries are strongly marked. Let all races, Hindu or Mahomedan of one province be enlisted in one regiment and no others, and having created distinctive regiments, let us keep them so, against the hour of need...... By the system thus indicated two great evils are avoided: firstly, that community of feeling throughout the native army and that mischievous political activity and intrigue which results from association with other races and travel in other Indian provinces." †

* MacMunn and Lovett — *The Armies of India*, pp. 84–85, quoted by Chaudhari.

† As quoted by Chaudhari.

This proposal was supported by many military men before the Peel Commission and was recommended by it as a principle of Indian Army Policy. This principle was known as the principle of Class Composition.

The Special Army Committee of 1879 was concerned with quite a different problem. What the problem was, becomes manifest from the questionnaire issued by the Committee. The questionnaire included the following question :—

> "If the efficient and available reserve of the Indian Army is considered necessary for the safety of the Empire, should it not be recruited and maintained from those parts of the country which give us best soldiers, rather than among the weakest and least warlike races of India, due regard, of course, being had to the necessity of not giving too great strength or prominence to any particular race or religious group and with due regard to the safety of the Empire?"

The principal part of the question is obviously the necessity or otherwise of "not giving too great strength or prominence to any particular race or religious group". On this question official opinion expressed before the Committee was unanimous.

Lt.-General H. J. Warres, Commander-in-Chief of the Bombay Army, stated : —

> "I consider it is not possible to recruit the reserve of the Indian Army altogether from those parts of India which are said to produce best soldiers, without giving undue strength and prominence to the races and religions of these countries."

The Commander-in-Chief, Sir Frederick P. Haines, said :—

> "Distinct in race, language and interests from the more numerous Army of Bengal, it is, in my opinion, eminently politic and wise to maintain these armies (the Madras and Bombay Armies) as a counterpoise to it, and I would in no way diminish their strength in order that a reserve composed of what is called 'the most efficient fighting men whom it is possible to procure' may be established. If by this it is meant to replace Sepoys of Madras and Bombay by a reserve of men passed through the ranks of the Bengal Army and composed of the same classes of which it is formed, I would say that anything more unwise or more impolitic could hardly be conceived."

The Lt.-Governor of the Punjab also shared this view. He too declared that he was "opposed to having one recruiting field for the whole armies" in India. "It will be necessary," he added, "for political reasons, to prevent preponderance of one nationality."

The Special Committee accepted this view and recommended that the composition of the Indian Army should be so regulated that there should be no predominance of any one community or nationality in the Army.

These two principles have been the governing principles of Indian Army policy. Having regard to the principle laid down by the Special Army Committee of 1879, the changes that have taken place in the communal composition of the Indian Army amount to a complete revolution. How this revolution was allowed to take place is beyond comprehension. It is a revolution which has taken place in the teeth of a well-established principle. The principle was really suggested by the fear of the growing predominance of the men of the North-West in the Indian Army and was invoked with the special object of curbing that tendency. The principle was not only enunciated as a rule of guidance but was taken to be rigorously applied. Lord Roberts, who was opposed to this principle because it set a limit upon the recruitment of his pet men of the North-West, had to bow to this principle during his regime as the Commander-in-Chief of India. So well was the principle respected that when in 1903, Lord Kitchener entered upon the project of converting fifteen regiments of Madrasis into Punjab regiments, he immediately set up a counterpoise to the Sikhs and the Punjabi Musalmans by raising the proportion of the Gurkhas and the Pathans. As Sir George Arthur, his biographer, says :—

> "The Government, mindful of the lesson taught by the Mutiny, was alive to the danger of allowing any one element in the Indian Army to preponderate unduly. An increase in the Punjabee infantry had as its necessary sequel a further recruitment of the valuable Gurkha material and the enlistment of more trans-border Pathans in the Frontier Militia."

That a principle, so unanimously upheld and so rigorously applied upto the period of the Great War, should have been thrown to the wind after the Great War, without ceremony and without compunction and in a clandestine manner, is really beyond comprehension. What is the reason which has led the British to allow so great a preponderance of the Muslims in the Indian Army? Two explanations are possible. One is that the Musalmans really proved, in the Great War, that they were better soldiers than the Hindus. The second explanation is that the British have broken the rule and have given the Musalmans such a dominating position in the Army because they wanted to counteract the forces of the Hindu agitation for wresting political power from the hands of the British.

Whatever be the explanation, two glaring facts stand out from the above survey. One is that the Indian Army today is predominantly Muslim in its composition. The other is that the Musalmans who predominate are the Musalmans from the Punjab and the N.-W. F. P. Such a composition of the Indian Army means that the Musalmans of the Punjab and the N.-W. F. P. are made the sole defenders of India from foreign invasion. So patent has this fact become that the Musalmans of the Punjab and the N.-W. F. P. are quite conscious of this proud position which has been assigned to them by the British, for reasons best known to them. For, one often hears them say that they are the 'gate-keepers' of India. The Hindus must consider the problem of the defence of India in the light of this crucial fact.

How far can the Hindus depend upon these 'gate-keepers' to hold the gate and protect the liberty and freedom of India? The answer to this question must depend upon who comes to force the gate open. It is obvious that there are only two foreign countries which are likely to force this gate from the North-West side of India, Russia or Afghanistan, the borders of both of which touch the border of India. Which of them will invade India and when, no one can say definitely. If the invasion came from Russia, it may be hoped that these gate-keepers of India will be staunch and loyal enough to hold the gate and stop the invader. But suppose the Afghans singly or in combination with other Muslim States march on India, will these gate-keepers stop the invaders or will they open the gates and let them in? This is a question which no Hindu can afford to ignore. This is a question on which every Hindu must feel assured, because it is the most crucial question.

It is possible to say that Afghanistan will never think of invading India. But a theory is best tested by examining its capacity to meet the worst case. The loyalty and dependability of this Army of the Punjabi and N.-W.F.P. Muslims can only be tested by considering how it will behave in the event of an invasion by the Afghans. Will they respond to the call of the land of their birth or will they be swayed by the call of their religion, is the question which must be faced if ultimate security is to be obtained. It is not safe to seek to escape from these annoying and discomforting questions by believing that we need not worry about a foreign invasion so long as India is under the protection of the British. Such a complacent attitude is unforgivable to say the least. In the first place, the last war has shown that a situation may arise when Great Britain may not be able to protect India, although, that is the time when India needs her protection most. Secondly, the efficiency of an institution must be tested under natural conditions and not under artificial conditions. The behaviour of the Indian soldier under British control is artificial. His behaviour when he is under Indian control is his natural behaviour. British control does not allow much play to the natural instincts and natural sympathies of the men in the Army. That is why the men in the Army behave so well. But that is an artificial and not a natural condition. That the Indian Army behaves well under British control is no guarantee of its good behaviour under Indian control. A Hindu must be satisfied that it will behave as well when British control is withdrawn.

The question how this army of the Punjabi and the N.-W.F.P. Muslims will behave if Afghanistan invades India, is a very pertinent and crucial question and must be faced, however unpleasant it may be.

Some may say—why assume that the large proportion of Muslims in the Army is a settled fact and that it cannot be unsettled? Those who can unsettle it are welcome to make what efforts they can. But, so far as one can see, it is not going to be unsettled. On the contrary, I should not be surprised if it was entered in the constitution, when revised, as a safeguard for the Muslim Minority. The Musalmans are sure to make this demand and as against the Hindus, the Muslims somehow always succeed. We must, therefore, proceed on the assumption that the composition of the Indian Army will remain what it is at present. The basis remaining the same, the question to be pursued remains what it was: Can the Hindus depend upon such an Army to defend the country against the invasion of Afghanistan? Only the so-called Indian Nationalists will say 'yes' to it. The boldest among the realists must stop to think before he can give an answer to the question. The realist must take note of the fact that the Musalmans look upon the Hindus as Kaffirs, who deserve more to be exterminated than protected. The realist must take note of the fact that while the Musalman accepts the European as his superior, he looks upon the Hindu as his inferior. It is doubtful how far a regiment of Musalmans will accept the authority of their Hindu officers if they be placed under them. The realist must take note that of all the Musalmans, the Musalman of the North-West is the most disaffected Musalman in his relation with the Hindus. The realist must take note that the Punjabi Musalman is fully susceptible to the propaganda in favour of Pan-Islamism. Taking note of all these considerations, there can be very little doubt that he would be a bold Hindu who would say that in any invasion by Muslim countries, the Muslims in the Indian Army would be loyal and that there is no danger of their going over to the invader. Even Theodore Morrison*, writing in 1899, was of the opinion that—

> "The views held by the Mahomedans (certainly the most aggressive and truculent of the peoples of India) are alone sufficient to prevent the establishment of an independent Indian Government. Were the Afghan to descend from the north upon an autonomous India, the Mahomedans, instead of uniting with the Sikhs and the Hindus to repel him, would be drawn by all the ties of kinship and religion to join his flag."

And when it is recalled that in 1919 the Indian Musalmans who were carrying on the Khilafat movement actually went to the length of inviting the Amir of Afghanistan to invade India,

* *Imperial Rule in India*, page 5.

the view expressed by Sir Theodore Morrison acquires added strength and ceases to be a matter of mere speculation.

How this Army composed of the Muslims of the Punjab and N.-W. F. P. will behave in the case of an invasion by Afghanistan is not the only question which the Hindus are called upon to consider. There is another and equally important question on which the Hindus must ponder. That question is: Will the Indian Government be free to use this Army, whatever its loyalties, against the invading Afghans? In this connection, attention must be drawn to the stand taken by the Muslim League. It is to the effect that the Indian Army shall not be used against Muslim powers. There is nothing new in this. This principle was enunciated by the Khilafat Committee long before the League. Apart from this, the question remains how far the Indian Muslims will, in future, make it their article of faith. That the League has not succeeded in this behalf against the British Government does not mean that it will not succeed against an Indian Government. The chances are that it will, because, however unpatriotic the principle may be from the standpoint of the Hindus, it is most agreeable to the Muslim sentiment and the League may find a sanction for it in the general support of the Muslim community in India. If the Muslim League succeeds in enforcing this limitation upon India's right to use her fighting forces, what is going to be the position of the Hindus? This is another question which the Hindus have to consider.

If India remains politically one whole and the two-nation mentality created by Pakistan continues to be fostered, the Hindus will find themselves between the devil and the deep sea, so far as the defence of India is concerned. Having an Army, they will not be free to use it because the League objects. Using it, it will not be possible to depend upon it because its loyalty is doubtful. This is a position which is as pathetic as it is precarious. If the Army continues to be dominated by the Muslims of the Punjab and the N.-W.F.P., the Hindus will have to pay it but will not be able to use it and even if they were free to use it against a Muslim invader, they will find it hazardous to depend upon it. If the League view prevails and India does not remain free to use her Army against Muslim countries, then, even if the Muslims lose their predominance in the Army, India on account of these military limitations, will have to remain on terms of subordinate co-operation with the Muslim countries on her border, as do the Indian States under British paramountcy.

The Hindus have a difficult choice to make: to have a safe Army or a safe border. In this difficulty, what is the wisest course for the Hindus to pursue? Is it in their interest to insist that the Muslim India should remain part of India so that they may have a safe border, or is it in their interest to welcome its separation from India so that they may have a safe Army? The Musalmans of this area are hostile to the Hindus. As to this, there can be no doubt. Which is then better for the Hindus: Should these Musalmans be *without and against or should they be within and against?* If the question is asked to any prudent man, there will be only one answer, namely, that if the Musalmans are to be against the Hindus, it is better that they should be without and against, rather than within and against. Indeed, it is a consummation devoutly to be wished that the Muslims should be without. That is the only way of getting rid of the Muslim preponderance in the Indian Army.

How can it be brought about? Here again, there is only one way to bring it about and that is to support the scheme of Pakistan. Once Pakistan is created, Hindustan, having ample resources in men and money, can have an Army which it can call its own and there will be nobody to dictate as to how it should be used and against whom it should be used. The defence of Hindustan, far from being weakened by the creation of Pakistan, will be infinitely improved by it.

The Hindus do not seem to realize at what disadvantage they are placed from the point of view of their defence, by their exclusion from the Army. Much less do they know that, strange as it may appear, they are in fact purchasing this disadvantage at a very heavy price.

The Pakistan area which is the main recruiting ground of the present Indian Army, contributes very little to the Central Exchequer as will be seen from the following figures:—

Contribution to the Central Exchequer

	Rs.
Punjab	1,18,01,385
North-West Frontier	9,28,294
Sind	5,86,46,915
Baluchistan	Nil
Total ...	7,13,76,594

As against this the provinces of Hindustan contribute as follows:—

	Rs.
Madras	9,53,26,745
Bombay	22,53,44,247
Bengal *	12,00,00,000
U. P.	4,05,53,000
Bihar	1,54,37,742
C. P. & Berar	31,42,682
Assam	1,87,55,967
Orissa	5,67,346
Total ...	51,91,27,729

The Pakistan Provinces, it will be seen, contribute very little. The main contribution comes from the Provinces of Hindustan. In fact, it is the money contributed by the Provinces of Hindustan which enables the Government of India to carry out its activities in the Pakistan Provinces. The Pakistan Provinces are a drain on the Provinces of Hindustan. Not only do they contribute very little to the Central Government but they receive a great deal from the Central Government. The revenue of the Central

* Only ½ revenue is shown because nearly ½ population is Hindu.

Government amounts to Rs. 121 crores. Of this, about Rs. 52 crores are annually spent on the Army. In what area is this amount spent? Who pays the bulk of this amount of Rs. 52 crores? The bulk of this amount of Rs. 52 crores which is spent on the Army is spent over the Muslim Army drawn from the Pakistan area. Now the bulk of this amount of Rs. 52 crores is contributed by the Hindu Provinces and is spent on an Army which for the most part consists of non-Hindus!! How many Hindus are aware of this tragedy? How many know at whose cost this tragedy is being enacted? Today the Hindus are not responsible for it because they cannot prevent it. The question is whether they will allow this tragedy to continue. If they mean to stop it, the surest way of putting an end to it is to allow the scheme of Pakistan to take effect. To oppose it, is to buy a sure weapon of their own destruction. A safe Army is better than a safe border.

CHAPTER VI

PAKISTAN AND COMMUNAL PEACE

Does Pakistan solve the Communal Question is a natural question which every Hindu is sure to ask. A correct answer to this question calls for a close analysis of what is involved in it. One must have a clear idea as to what is exactly meant, when the Hindus and the Muslims speak of the Communal Question. Without it, it will not be possible to say whether Pakistan does or does not solve the Communal Question.

It is not generally known that the Communal Question like the "Forward Policy" for the Frontier has a "greater" and a "lesser intent," and that in its lesser intent it means one thing, and in its greater intent it means quite a different thing.

I

To begin with the Communal Question in its "lesser intent." In its lesser intent, the Communal Question relates to the representation of the Hindus and the Muslims in the Legislatures. Used in this sense, the question involves the settlement of two distinct problems:—

(1) The number of seats to be allotted to the Hindus and the Muslims in the different legislatures, and

(2) The nature of the electorates through which these seats are to be filled in.

The Muslims at the Round Table Conference claimed:—

(1) That their representatives in all the Provincial as well as in the Central Legislatures should be elected by separate electorates;

(2) That they should be allowed to retain the weightage in representation given to Muslim minorities in those Provinces in which they were a minority in the population, and that in addition, they should be given in those Provinces where they were a majority such as the Punjab, Sind, North-West Frontier Province and Bengal, a guaranteed statutory majority of seats.

The Hindus from the beginning objected to both these Muslim demands. They insisted on joint electorates for Hindus and Muslims in all elections to all the Legislatures, Central and Provincial, and on population ratio of representation, for both minorities, Hindus and Muslims, wherever they may be, and raised the strongest objections to a majority of seats being guaranteed to any community by statute.

The Communal Award of His Majesty's Government settled this dispute by the simple, rough and ready method of giving the Muslims all that they wanted, without caring for the Hindu opposition. The Award allowed the Muslims to retain weightage and separate electorates, and in addition, gave them the statutory majority of seats in those provinces where they were a majority in the population.

What is it in the Award that can be said to constitute a problem? Is there any force in the objections of the Hindus to the Communal Award of His Majesty's Government? This question must be considered carefully to find out whether there is substance in the objections of the Hindus to the Award.

Firstly, as to their objection to the weightage to Muslim minorities in the matter of representation. Whatever may be the correct measure of allotting representation to minorities, the Hindus cannot very well object to the weightage given to Muslim minorities, because similar weightage has been given to the Hindus in those Provinces in which they are a minority and where there is sufficient margin for weightage to be allowed. The treatment of the Hindu minorities in Sind and the North-West Frontier Province is a case in point.

Secondly, as to their objection to a statutory majority. That again does not appear to be well founded. A system of guaranteed representation may be wrong and vicious and quite unjustifiable on theoretical and philosophical grounds. But considered in the light of circumstances, such as those obtaining in India, the system of statutory majority appears to be inevitable. Once it is granted that the representation to be given to a minority must not reduce the majority to minority, that very provision creates, as a mere counterpart, a system of statutory majority to the majority community. For, fixing the seats of the minority involves the fixation of the seats of the majority. There is, therefore, no escape from the system of statutory majority, once it is conceded that the minority is not entitled to representation which would convert a majority into a minority. There is, therefore, no great force in the objections of the Hindus to a statutory majority of the Muslims in the Punjab, the N.-W.F. Province, Sind and Bengal. For, even in the Provinces where the Hindus are in a majority and the Muslims are in minority, the Hindus have got a statutory majority over the Muslims. At any rate, there is a parity of position and to that extent there can be said to be no ground for complaint.

This does not mean that because the objections set forth by the Hindus have no substance, there are no real grounds for opposing the Communal Award. There does exist a substantial ground of objection to the Communal Award, although, it does not appear to have been made the basis of attack by the Hindus.

This objection may be formulated in order to bring out its point in the following manner. The Muslim minorities in the Hindu Provinces insisted on separate electorates. The Communal Award gives them the right to determine that issue. This is really what it comes to when one remembers the usual position taken, viz., that the Muslim minorities could not be deprived of their separate electorates without their consent, and the majority community of the Hindus has been made to abide by their determination. The Hindu minorities in Muslim Provinces insisted that there should be joint electorates. Instead of conceding their claim, the Communal Award forced upon them the system of separate electorates to which they objected. If in the Hindu Provinces, the Muslim minorities are allowed the right of self-determination in the matter of electorates, the question arises : Why are not the Hindu minorities in the Muslim Provinces given the right of self-determination in the matter of their electorates? What is the answer to this question? And, if there is no answer, there is undoubtedly a deep-seated inequity in the Communal Award of His Majesty's Government, which calls for redress.

It is no answer that the Hindus also have a statutory majority based on separate electorates* in those Provinces where the Musalmans are in a minority. A little scrutiny will show that there is no parity of position in these two cases. The separate electorates for the Hindu majorities in the Hindu Provinces are not a matter of their choice. It is a consequence resulting from the determination of the Muslim minorities who claimed to have separate electorates for themselves. A minority in one set of circumstances may think that separate electorates would be a better method of self-protection and may have no fear of creating against itself and by its own action a statutory majority based on separate electorates for the opposing community. Another minority or, for the matter of that, the same minority in a different set of circumstances would not like to create by its own action and against itself a statutory majority based upon separate electorates and may, therefore, prefer joint electorates to separate electorates as a better method of self-protection. Obviously the guiding principle, which would influence a minority, would be : Is the majority likely to use its majority in a communal manner and purely for communal purposes? If it felt certain that the majority community is likely to use its communal majority for communal ends, it may well choose joint electorates, because it would be the only method by which it would hope to take away the communal cement of the statutory majority by influencing the elections of the representatives of the majority community in the Legislatures. On the other hand, a majority community may not have the necessary communal cement, which alone would

* It is perhaps not quite correct to speak of a Hindu Electorate. The Electorate is a General Electorate consisting of all those who are not included in any separate electorate. But as the majority in the General Electorate consists of Hindus, it is called a Hindu Electorate.

enable it to use its communal majority for communal ends, in which case a minority, having no fear from the resulting statutory majority and separate electorates for the majority community, may well choose separate electorates for itself. To put it concretely, the Muslim minorities in choosing separate electorates are not afraid of the separate electorates and the statutory majority of the Hindus, because they feel sure that by reason of their deep-seated differences of caste and race the Hindus will never be able to use their majorities against the Muslims. On the other hand, the Hindu minorities in the Muslim Provinces have no doubt that, by reason of their social solidarity, the Muslims will use their statutory majority to set into operation a "Resolute Muslim Government", after the plan proposed by Lord Salisbury for Ireland as a substitute for Home Rule; with this difference, that Salisbury's Resolute Government was to last for twenty years only, while the Muslim Resolute Government was to last as long as the Communal Award stood. The situations, therefore, are not alike. The statutory majority of the Hindus based on separate electorates is the result of the choice made by the Muslim minority. The statutory majority of the Muslims based on separate electorates is something which is not the result of the choice of the Hindu minority. In one case, the Government of the Muslim minority by a Hindu communal majority is the result of the consent of the Muslim minority. In the other case, the Government of the Hindu minority by the Muslim majority is not the result of the consent of the Hindu minority, but is imposed upon it by the might of the British Government.

To sum up this discussion of the Communal Award, it may be said that, as a solution of the Communal Question in its "lesser intent," there is no inequity in the Award on the ground that it gives weightage to the Muslim minorities in the Hindu Provinces. For, it gives weightage also to Hindu minorities in Muslim Provinces. Similarly, it may be said that there is no inequity in the Award, on the ground that it gives a statutory majority to the Muslims in Muslim Provinces in which they are a majority. If there is any, the statutory limitation put upon the Muslim number of seats, also gives to the Hindus in

Hindu Provinces a statutory majority. But the same cannot be said of the Award in the matter of the electorates. The Communal Award is iniquitous inasmuch as it accords unequal treatment to the Hindu and Muslim minorities in the matter of electorates. It grants the Muslim minorities in the Hindu Provinces the right of self-determination in the matter of electorates, but it does not grant the same right to the Hindu minorities in the Muslim Provinces. In the Hindu Provinces, the Muslim minority is allowed to choose the kind of electorates it wants and the Hindu majority is not permitted to have any say in the matter. But in the Muslim Provinces, it is the Muslim majority which is allowed to choose the kind of electorates it prefers and the Hindu minority is not permitted to have any say in the matter. Thus, the Muslims in the Muslim Provinces having been given both statutory majority and separate electorates, the Communal Award must be said to impose upon the Hindu minorities Muslim rule, which they can neither alter nor influence.

This is what constitutes the fundamental wrong in the Communal Award. That this is a grave wrong must be admitted. For, it offends against certain political principles, which have now become axiomatic. First is, not to trust any one with unlimited political power. As has been well said,

> "If in any state there is a body of men who possess unlimited political power, those over whom they rule can never be free. For, the one assured result of historical investigation is the lesson that uncontrolled power is invariably poisonous to those who possess it. They are always tempted to impose their canon of good upon others, and in the end, they assume that the good of the community depends upon the continuance of their power. Liberty always demands a limitation of political authority......"

The second principle is that, as a King has no Divine Right to rule, so also a majority has no Divine Right to rule. Majority Rule is tolerated only because it is for a limited period and subject to the right to have it changed, and secondly because it is a rule of a political majority, i. e., majority which has submitted itself to the suffrage of a minority and not a communal majority. If such is the limited scope of authority permissible to a political majority over a political minority, how can a minority of one community be placed under the perpetual subjection of a majority of another community? To allow a majority of one community to rule a minority of another community without requiring the majority to submit itself to the suffrage of the minority, especially when the minority demands it, is to enact a perversion of democratic principles and to show a callous disregard for the safety and security of the Hindu minorities.

II

To turn to the Communal Question in its "greater intent." What is it, that the Hindus say is a problem? In its greater intent the Communal Question relates to the deliberate creation of Muslim Provinces. At the time of the Lucknow Pact, the Muslims only raised the Communal Question in its lesser intent. At the Round Table Conference, the Muslims put forth, for the first time, the plan covered by the Communal Question in its greater intent. Before the Act of 1935, there were a majority of Provinces in which the Hindus were in a majority and the Muslims in a minority. There were only three Provinces in which the Muslims were in a majority and the Hindus in a minority. They were the Punjab, Bengal and the North-West Frontier Province. Of these, the Muslim majority in the North-West Frontier Province was not effective, because there was no responsible government in that province, the Montagu-Chelmsford Scheme of Political Reforms not being extended to it. So, for all practical purposes, there were only two provinces—the Punjab and Bengal—wherein the Muslims were in majority and the Hindus in minority. The Muslims desired that the number of Muslim Provinces should be increased. With this object in view, they demanded that Sind should be separated from the Bombay Presidency and created into a new self-governing Province, and that the North-West Frontier Province, which was already a separate Province, should be raised to the status of a self-governing Province. Apart from other considerations, from a purely financial point of view, it was not possible to concede this demand. Neither Sind nor the N.-W.F.P. were financially self-supporting. But in order to satisfy the Muslim demand, the British Government went to the length of accepting the responsibility of giving an annual subvention to Sind* and N.-W.F.P. † from the Central Revenues, so as to bring about a budgetary equilibrium in their finances and make them financially self-supporting.

These four Provinces with Muslims in majority and Hindus in minority, now functioning as autonomous and self-governing Provinces, were certainly not created for administrative convenience, nor for purposes of architectural symmetry—the Hindu Provinces poised against the Muslim Provinces. It is also true that the scheme of Muslim Provinces was not a matter of satisfying Muslim pride which demanded Hindu minorities under Muslim majorities to compensate the humiliation of having Muslim minorities under Hindu majorities. What was then, the motive underlying this scheme of Muslim Provinces? The Hindus say that the motive for the Muslim insistence, both on statutory majority and separate electorates, was to enable the Muslims in the Muslim Provinces to mobilize and make effective Muslim power in its exclusive form and to the fullest extent possible. Asked what could be the purpose of having the Muslim political power mobilized in this fashion, the Hindus answer that it was done to place in the hands of the Muslims of the Muslim Provinces an effective weapon to tyrannize their Hindu minorities, in case the Muslim minorities in the Hindu Provinces were tyrannized by their Hindu majorities. The scheme thus became a system of protection, in which blast was to be met by counter-blast, terror by terror and tyranny by tyranny. The plan is, undoubtedly, a dreadful one, involving the maintenance of justice and peace by retaliation, and providing an opportunity for the punishment of an innocent minority, Hindus in Muslim Provinces and Muslims in Hindu Provinces, for the sins of their co-religionists in other Provinces. It is a scheme of communal peace through a system of communal hostages.

That the Muslims were aware from the very start, that the system of communal Provinces was capable of being worked in

* Sind gets an annual subvention of Rs. 1,05,00,000.

† N.-W. F. P. gets an annual subvention of Rs. 1,00,00,000.

this manner, is clear from the speech made by Maulana Abul Kalam Azad as President of the Muslim League Session held in Calcutta in 1927. In that speech the Maulana declared :—

> "That by the Lucknow Pact they had sold away their interests. The Delhi proposals of March last opened the door for the first time to the recognition of the real rights of Mussalmans in India. The separate electorates granted by the Pact of 1916 only ensured Muslim representation, but what was vital for the existence of the community was the recognition of its numerical strength. Delhi opened the way to the creation of such a state of affairs as would guarantee to them in the future of India a proper share. Their existing small majority in Bengal and the Punjab was only a census figure, but the Delhi proposals gave them for the first time five provinces of which no less than three (Sind, the Frontier Province and Baluchistan) contained a real overwhelming Muslim majority. If the Muslims did not recognise this great step they were not fit to live. There would now be nine Hindu provinces against five Muslim provinces, and whatever treatment Hindus accorded in the nine provinces, Muslims would accord the same treatment to Hindus in the five provinces. Was not this a great gain? Was not a new weapon gained for the assertion of Muslim rights?"

That those in charge of these Muslim provinces know the advantage of the scheme, and do not hesitate to put it to the use for which it was intended, is clear from the speeches made not long ago by Mr. Fazl-ul-Huq, as Prime Minister of Bengal.

That this scheme of Communal Provinces, which constitutes the Communal Question in its larger intent, can be used as an engine of communal tyranny, there can be no doubt. The system of hostages, which is the essence of the scheme of communal provinces, supported by separate electorates, is indeed insupportable on any ground. If this is the underlying motive of the demand for the creation of more Muslim provinces, the system resulting from it is undoubtedly a vicious system.

This analysis leaves no doubt that the communal statutory majority based on separate communal electorates and the communal provinces, especially constituted to enable the statutory majority to tyrannize the minority, are the two evils which compose what is called, 'the Communal Problem'.

For the existence of this problem the Hindus hold the Muslims responsible and the Muslims hold the Hindus responsible. The Hindus accuse the Muslims of contumacy. The Muslims accuse Hindus of meanness. Both, however, forget that the communal problem exists not because the Muslims are extravagant and insolent in their demands and the Hindus are mean and grudging in their concessions. It exists and will exist wherever a hostile majority is brought face to face against a hostile minority. Controversies relating to separate *vs.* joint electorates, controversies relating to population ratio *vs.* weightage are all inherent in a situation where a minority is pitted against a majority. The best solution of the communal problem is not to have two communities facing each other, one a majority and the other a minority, welded in the steel-frame of a single government.

How far does Pakistan approximate to the solution of the Communal Question?

The answer to this question is quite obvious. If the scheme of Pakistan is to follow the present boundaries of the Provinces in the North-West and in Bengal, certainly it does not eradicate the evils which lie at the heart of the Communal Question. It retains the very elements which give rise to it, namely, the pitting of a minority against a majority. The rule of the Hindu minorities by the Muslim majorities and the rule of the Muslim minorities by the Hindu majorities are the crying evils of the present situation. This very evil will reproduce itself in Pakistan, if the provinces marked out for it are incorporated into it as they are, i.e., with boundaries drawn as at present. Besides this, the evil which gives rise to the Communal Question in its larger intent, will not only remain as it is but will assume a new malignity. Under the existing system, the power centered in the Communal Provinces to do mischief to their hostages is limited by the power which the Central Government has over the Provincial Governments. At present, the hostages are at least within the pale of a Central Government which is Hindu in its composition and which has power to interfere for their protection. But, when Pakistans become Muslim States with full sovereignty over internal and external affairs, it would be free from the control of the Central Government. The Hindu minorities will have no recourse to an outside authority with overriding powers, to interfere on their behalf and curb this power of mischief, as under the scheme, no such overriding authority is permitted to exist. So, the position of the Hindus in Pakistan may easily become similar to the position of the Armenians under the Turks or of the Jews in Tsarist Russia or in Nazi Germany. Such a scheme would be intolerable and the Hindus may well say that they cannot agree to Pakistan and leave their co-religionist as a helpless prey to the fanaticism of a Muslim National State.

III

This, of course, is a very frank statement of the consequences which will flow from giving effect to the scheme of Pakistan. But care must be taken to locate the source of these consequences. Do they flow from the scheme of Pakistan itself or do they flow from particular boundaries that may be fixed for it. If the evils flow from the scheme itself, i.e., if they are inherent in it, it is unnecessary for any Hindu to waste his time in considering it. He will be justified in summarily dismissing it. On the other hand, if the evils are the result of the boundaries, the question of Pakistan reduces itself to a mere question of changing the boundaries.

A study of the question amply supports the view that the evils of Pakistan are not inherent in it. If any evil results follow from it they will have to be attributed to its boundaries. This becomes clear if one studies the distribution of population. The reason why these evils will be reproduced within Western and Eastern Pakistan is because, with the present boundaries, they do not become single ethnic states. They remain mixed states, composed of a Muslim majority and a Hindu minority as before. The evils are the evils which are inseparable from a mixed state. If Pakistan is made a single unified ethnic state, the evils will automatically vanish. There will be no question of separate electorates within Pakistan, because in such a homogeneous Pakistan, there will be no majorities to rule and no minorities to be protected. Similarly, there will be no majority of one community to hold, in its possession, a minority of an opposing community.

The question, therefore, is one of demarcation of boundaries and reduces itself to this: Is it possible for the boundaries of Pakistan to be so fixed, that instead of producing a mixed state composed of majorities and minorities, with all the evils attendant upon it, Pakistan will be an ethnic state composed of one homogeneous community, namely Muslims? The answer is that in a large part of the area affected by the project of the League, a homogeneous state can be created by shifting merely the boundaries, and in the rest, homogeneity can be produced by shifting only the population.

In this connection, I invite the reader to study carefully the figures given in the Appendices V, X, XI showing the distribution of the population in the areas affected, and also the maps showing how new boundaries can create homogeneous Muslim States. Taking the Punjab, two things will be noted :—

(i) There are certain districts in which the Musalmans predominate. There are certain districts in which the Hindus predominate. There are very few in which the two are, more or less, evenly distributed; and

(ii) The districts in which the Muslims predominate and the districts in which the Hindus predominate are not interspersed. The two sets of districts form two separate areas.

For the formation of the Eastern Pakistan, one has to take into consideration the distribution of population in both the Provinces of Bengal and Assam. A scrutiny of the population figures shows :—

(i) In Bengal, there are some districts in which the Muslims predominate. In others, the Hindus predominate.

(ii) In Assam also, there are some districts in which the Muslims predominate. In others, the Hindus predominate.

(iii) Districts in which the Muslims predominate and those in which the Hindus predominate are not interspersed. They form separate areas.

(iv) The districts of Bengal and Assam in which the Muslims predominate are contiguous.

Given these facts, it is perfectly possible to create homogeneous Muslim States out of the Punjab, Bengal and Assam by drawing their boundaries in such a way that the areas which are predominantly Hindu shall be excluded. That this is possible is shown by the maps given in the appendix.

In the North-West Frontier Province and Sind, the situation is rather hard. How the matter stands in the N.-W. F. P. and Sind may be seen by an examination of the figures given in the appendices VI to IX. As may be seen from the appendices, there are no districts in which the Hindus in the N.-W. F. P. and Sind are concentrated. They are scattered and are to be found in almost every district of the two provinces in small, insignificant numbers. These appendices show quite unmistakably that the Hindus in Sind and the N.-W. F. P. are mostly congregated in urban areas of the districts. In Sind, the Hindus outnumber the Muslims in most of the towns, while the Muslims outnumber the Hindus in villages. In the N.-W. F. P., the Muslims outnumber the Hindus in towns as well as in villages.

The case of the N.-W. F. P. and Sind, therefore, differs totally from the case of the Punjab and Bengal. In the Punjab and Bengal, owing to the natural segregation of the Hindus and Muslims in different areas, it is possible to create a homogeneous State by merely altering their boundaries, involving the shifting of the population in a very small degree. But in the N.-W. F. P. and Sind, owing to the scattered state of the Hindu population, alteration of boundaries cannot suffice for creating a homogeneous State. There is only one remedy and that is to shift the population.

Some scoff at the idea of the shifting and exchange of population. But those who scoff can hardly be aware of the complications, which a minority problem gives rise to and the failures attendant upon almost all the efforts made to protect them. The constitutions of the post-war states, as well as of the older states in Europe which had a minority problem, proceeded on the assumption that constitutional safeguards for minorities should suffice for their protection and so the constitutions of most of the new states with majorities and minorities were studded with long lists of fundamental rights and safeguards to see that they were not violated by the majorities. What was the experience? Experience showed that safeguards did not save the minorities. Experience showed that even a ruthless war on the minorities did not solve the problem. The states then agreed that the best way to solve it was for each to exchange its alien minorities within its border, for its own which was without its border, with a view to bring about homogeneous States. This is what happened in Turkey, Greece and Bulgaria. Those, who scoff at the idea of transfer of population, will do well to study the history of the minority problem, as it arose between Turkey, Greece and Bulgaria. If they do, they will find that these countries found that the only effective way of solving the minorities problem lay in exchange of population. The task undertaken by the three countries was by no means a minor operation. It involved the transfer of some 20 million people from one habitat to another. But undaunted, the three shouldered the task and carried it to a successful end because they felt that the considerations of communal peace must outweigh every other consideration.

That the transfer of minorities is the only lasting remedy for communal peace is beyond doubt. If that is so, there is no reason why the Hindus and the Muslims should keep on trading in safeguards which have proved so unsafe. If small countries, with limited resources like Greece, Turkey and Bulgaria, were capable of such an undertaking, there is no reason to suppose that what they did cannot be accomplished by Indians. After all, the population involved is inconsiderable and because some obstacles require to be removed, it would be the height of folly to give up so sure a way to communal peace.

There is one point of criticism to which no reference has been made so far. As it is likely to be urged, I propose to deal with it here. It is sure to be asked, how will Pakistan affect the position of the Muslims that will be left in Hindustan? The question is natural because the scheme of Pakistan does seem to concern itself with the Muslim majorities who do not need protection and abandons the Muslim minorities who do. But the point is: who can raise it? Surely not the Hindus. Only the

Muslims of Pakistan or the Muslims of Hindustan can raise it. The question was put to Mr. Rehmat Ali, the protagonist of Pakistan and this is the answer given by him:—

> "How will it affect the position of the forty five million Muslims in Hindustan proper?
>
> "The truth is that in this struggle their thought has been more than a wrench to me. They are the flesh of our flesh and the soul of our soul. We can never forget them; nor they, us. Their present position and future security is, and shall ever be, a matter of great importance to us. As things are at present, Pakistan will not adversely affect their position in Hindustan. On the basis of population (one Muslim to four Hindus), they will still be entitled to the same representation in legislative as well as administrative fields which they possess now. As to the future, the only effective guarantee we can offer is that of reciprocity, and, therefore, we solemnly undertake to give all those safeguards to non-Muslim minorities in Pakistan which will be conceded to our Muslim minority in Hindustan.
>
> "But what sustains us most is the fact that they know we are proclaiming Pakistan in the highest interest of the 'Millet'. It is as much theirs as it is ours. While for us it is a national citadel, for them it will ever be a moral anchor. So long as the anchor holds, everything is or can be made safe. But once it gives way, all will be lost."

The answer given by the Muslims of Hindustan is equally clear. They say, "We are not weakened by the separation of Muslims into Pakistan and Hindustan. We are better protected by the existence of separate Islamic States on the Eastern and Western borders of Hindustan than we are by their submersion in Hindustan." Who can say that they are wrong? Has it not been shown that Germany as an outside state was better able to protect the Sudeten Germans in Czechoslovakia than the Sudetens were able to do themselves? *

Be that as it may, the question does not concern the Hindus. The question that concerns the Hindus is: How far does the

* The leaders of the Muslim League seem to have studied deeply Hitler's bullying tactics against Czechoslovakia in the interest of the Sudeten Germans and also learned the lessons which those tactics teach. See their threatening speeches in the Karachi Session of the League held in 1937.

creation of Pakistan remove the communal question from Hindustan? That is a very legitimate question and must be considered. It must be admitted that by the creation of Pakistan, Hindustan is not freed of the communal question. While Pakistan can be made a homogeneous state by redrawing its boundaries, Hindustan must remain a composite state. The Musalmans are scattered all over Hindustan—though they are mostly congregated in towns—and no ingenuity in the matter of redrawing of boundaries can make it homogeneous. The only way to make Hindustan homogeneous is to arrange for exchange of population. Until that is done, it must be admitted that even with the creation of Pakistan, the problem of majority *vs.* minority will remain in Hindustan as before and will continue to produce disharmony in the body politic of Hindustan.

Admitting that Pakistan is not capable of providing a complete solution of the Communal Problem within Hindustan, does it follow that the Hindus on that account should reject Pakistan? Before the Hindus draw any such hasty conclusion, they should consider the following effects of Pakistan.

First, consider the effect of Pakistan on the magnitude of the Communal Problem. That can be best gauged by reference to the Muslim population as it will be grouped within Pakistan and Hindustan.

Muslim Population in Pakistan.		Muslim Population in Hindustan.	
1. Punjab	13,332,460	1. Total Muslim Population in British India (Excluding Burma and Aden).	66,442,766
2. N.-W. F. P.	2,227,303		
3. Sind	2,830,800	2. Muslim Population grouped in Pakistan and Eastern Bengal State.	47,897,301
4. Baluchistan	405,309		
5. Eastern Bengal Muslim State:—		3. Balance of Muslims in British Hindustan.	18,545,465
(i) Eastern Bengal ..	27,497,624		
(ii) Sylhet	1,603,805		
Total ..	47,897,301		

What do these figures indicate? What they indicate is that the Muslims who will be left in British Hindustan will be only 18,545,465 and the rest 47,897,301, forming a vast majority of the total Muslim population, will be out of it and will be the subjects of Pakistan States. This distribution of the Muslim population, in terms of the communal problem, means that while without Pakistan the communal problem in India involves 6½ crores of Muslims, with the creation of Pakistan it will involve only 2 crores of Muslims. Is this to be no consideration for Hindus who want communal peace? To me, it seems that if Pakistan does not solve the communal problem within Hindustan, it substantially reduces its proportion and makes it of minor significance and much easier of peaceful solution.

In the second place, let the Hindus consider the effect of Pakistan on the communal representation in the Central Legislature. The following table gives the distribution of seats in the Central Legislature, as prescribed under the Government of India Act, 1935 and as it would be, if Pakistan came into being.

Name of the Chamber.	Distribution of seats. I.—As at present.			Distribution of seats. II.—After Pakistan.		
	Total seats.	Non-Muslim (Hindu) Territorial seats.	Muslim Territorial Seats.	Total seats.	Non-Muslim (Hindu) Territorial seats.	Muslim Territorial Seats.
Council of State.	150	75	49	126	75	25
Federal Assembly.	250	105	82	211	105	43

To bring out clearly the quantitative change in the communal distribution of seats, which must follow the establishment of

Pakistan, the above figures are reduced to percentages in the table that follows:—

Name of the Chamber.	Distribution of seats. I.—As at present.		Distribution of seats. II.—After Pakistan.	
	Percentage of Muslim seats to total seats.	Percentage of Muslim seats to Hindu seats.	Percentage of Muslim seats to total seats.	Percentage of Muslim seats to Hindu seats.
Council of State ..	33	66	25	33⅓
Federal Assembly..	33	80	21	40

From this table one can see what vast changes must follow the establishment of Pakistan. Under the Government of India Act, the ratio of Muslim seats to the total is 33% in both the Chambers, but to the Hindu seats, the ratio is 66% in the Council of State and 80% in the Assembly—almost a position of equality with the Hindus. After Pakistan, the ratio of Muslim seats to the total seats falls from 33⅓% to 25% in the Council and to 21% in the Assembly, while the ratio to Hindu seats falls from 66% to 33⅓% in the Council and from 80% to 40% in the Assembly. The figures assume that the weightage given to the Muslims will remain the same, even after Hindustan is separated from Pakistan. If the present weightage to Muslims is cancelled or reduced, there would be further improvement in the representation of the Hindus. But assuming that no change in weightage is made, is this a small gain to the Hindus in the matter of representation at the Centre? To me, it appears that it is a great improvement in the position of the Hindus at the Centre, which would never come to them, if they oppose Pakistan.

These are the material advantages of Pakistan. There is another which is psychological. The Muslims, in Southern and Central India, draw their inspiration from the Muslims of the North and the East. If after Pakistan there is communal peace in the North and the East, as there should be, there being no majorities and minorities therein, the Hindus may reasonably expect communal peace in Hindustan. This severance of the bond between the Muslims of the North and the East and the Muslims of Hindustan is another gain to the Hindus of Hindustan.

Taking into consideration these effects of Pakistan, it cannot be disputed that if Pakistan does not wholly solve the communal problem within Hindustan, it frees the Hindus from the turbulence of the Muslims as predominant partners. It is for the Hindus to say whether they will reject such a proposal, simply because it does not offer a complete solution. Some gain is better than much harm.

IV

One last question and this discussion of Pakistan in relation to communal peace may be brought to a close. Will the Hindus and the Muslims of the Punjab and Bengal agree to redraw the boundaries of their provinces to make the scheme of Pakistan as flawless as it can be made?

As for the Muslims, they ought to have no objection to redrawing the boundaries. If they do object, it must be said that they do not understand the nature of their own demand. This is quite possible, since the talk that is going on among Muslim protagonists of Pakistan, is of a very loose character. Some speak of Pakistan as a Muslim National State, others speak of it as a Muslim National Home. Neither care to know whether there is any difference between a National State and a National Home. But there can be no doubt that there is a vital difference between the two. What that difference is was discussed at great length at the time of constituting in Palestine a Jewish National Home. It seems that a clear conception of what this difference is, is necessary, if the likely Muslim opposition to the redrawing of the boundaries is to be overcome.

According to a leading authority :—

> "A National Home connotes a territory in which a people, without receiving the rights of political sovereignty, has

nevertheless a recognised legal position and receives the opportunity of developing its moral, social and intellectual ideals."

The British Government itself, in its statement on Palestine policy issued in 1922, defined its conception of the National Home in the following terms :—

> "When it is asked what is meant by the development of the Jewish national home in Palestine, it may be answered that it is not the imposition of a Jewish nationality upon the inhabitants of Palestine as a whole, but the further development of the existing Jewish Community, with the assistance of Jews in other parts of the world, in order that it may become a centre in which the Jewish people as a whole may take, on grounds of religion and race, an interest and a pride. But in order that this community should have the best prospect of free development and provide a full opportunity for the Jewish people to display its capacities, it is essential that it should know that it is in Palestine as of right and not on sufferance. This is the reason why it is necessary that the existence of a Jewish National Home in Palestine should be internationally guaranteed, and that it should be formally recognized to rest upon ancient historic connection."

From this, it will be clear that there is an essential difference between a National Home and a National State. The difference consists in this : in the case of a National Home, the people who constitute it do not receive the right of political sovereignty over the territory and the right of imposing their nationality on others also living in that territory. All that they get, is a recognized legal position guaranteeing them the right to live as citizens and freedom to maintain their culture. In the case of a National State, people constituting it, receive the rights of political sovereignty with the right of imposing their nationality upon the rest.

This difference is very important and it is in the light of this that one must examine their demand for Pakistan. What do the Muslim want Pakistan for? If they want Pakistan to create a National Home for Muslims, there is no necessity for Pakistan. In the Pakistan Provinces, they already have their National Home with the legal right to live and advance their culture. If they want Pakistan to be a National Muslim State, they are claiming the right of political sovereignty over the territory included in it. This they are entitled to do. But the question is: Should they be allowed to retain, within the boundaries of these Muslim States, Non-Muslim minorities as their subjects, with a right to impose upon them the nationality of these Muslim States? No doubt, such a right is accepted to be an accompaniment of political sovereignty. But it is equally true that in all mixed States, this right has become a source of mischief in modern times. To ignore the possibilities of such mischief in the creation of Pakistan will be to omit to read the bloody pages of recent history on which have been recorded the atrocities, murders, plunders and arsons committed by the Turks, Greeks, Bulgars and the Czechs against their minorities. It is possible to take away from a state this right of imposing its nationality upon its subjects, because it is incidental to political sovereignty. But it is possible not to provide any opportunity for the exercise of such a right. This can be done by allowing the Muslims to have such National Muslim States as are strictly homogeneous, strictly ethnic states. Under no circumstances can they be allowed to carve out mixed states composed of Muslims opposed to Hindus, with the former superior in number to the latter.

This is probably not contemplated by the Muslims who are the authors of Pakistan. It was certainly not contemplated by Sir M. Iqbal, the originator of the scheme. In his Presidential address to the Muslim League in 1930, he expressed his willingness to agree to "the exclusion of Ambala Division and perhaps of some other districts where non-Muslims predominate" on the ground that such exclusion "will make it less extensive and more Muslim in population". On the other hand, it may be that those who are putting forth the Scheme of Pakistan, do contemplate that it will include the Punjab and Bengal with their present boundaries. To them it must become clear, that to insist upon the present boundaries is sure to antagonize even those Hindus who have an open mind on the question. The Hindus can never be expected to consent to the inclusion of the Hindus in a Muslim State deliberately created for the preservation and propagation of Muslim faith and Muslim culture. The Hindus will no doubt oppose. Muslims must not suppose that it will take long to find them out. Muslims, if they insist upon the retention of the present boundaries, will open themselves to the accusation that behind their demand for Pakistan there is something more sinister than a mere desire to create a National Home or a National State. They will be accused of a design to perfect the scheme of Hindu hostages in Muslim hands by increasing the balance of Muslim majorities against Hindu minorities in the Muslim areas.

So much, for considerations which ought to weigh with the Muslims in the matter of changing the provincial boundaries to make Pakistan.

Now, as to the considerations which ought to weigh with the Hindus of the Punjab and Bengal. The Hindus are the more difficult of the two parties to the question. In this connection it is enough to consider the reaction of the high caste Hindus only. For, it is they who guide the Hindu masses and form Hindu opinion. Unfortunately, the high caste Hindus are bad as leaders. They have a trait of character which often leads the Hindus to disaster. This trait is formed by their acquisitive instinct and aversion to share with others the good things of life. They have a monopoly of education and wealth, and with wealth and education they have captured the State. To keep this monopoly to themselves has been the ambition and goal of their life. Charged with this selfish idea of class domination, they take every move to exclude the lower classes of Hindus from wealth, education and power, the surest and the most effective being the preparation of scriptures, inculcating upon the minds of the lower classes of Hindus the teaching that their duty in life is only to serve the higher classes. In keeping this monopoly in their own hands and excluding the lower classes from any share in it, the high caste Hindus have succeeded for a long time and beyond measure. It is only recently that the lower class Hindus rose in revolt against this monopoly by starting the Non-Brahmin Parties in the Madras and the Bombay Presidencies and the C.P. Still the high caste Hindus have successfully maintained their privileged position. This attitude of keeping education, wealth and power as a close preserve for themselves and refusing to share it, which the high caste Hindus have developed in their relation with the lower classes of Hindus, is sought to be extended by them to the

Muslims. They want to exclude the Muslims from place and power, as they have done to the lower class Hindus. This trait of the high caste Hindus is the key to the understanding of their politics.

Two illustrations reveal this trait of theirs. The Hindus in 1929 opposed the separation of Sind from the Bombay Presidency before the Simon Commission, strenuously and vehemently. But in 1915, the Hindus of Sind put forth the opposite plea and wanted Sind to be separated from Bombay. The reason in both the cases was the same. In 1915, there was no representative Government in Sind, which, if there was one would have undoubtedly been a Muslim Government. The Hindus advocated separation because in the absence of a Muslim Government, they could obtain jobs in Government in a greater and greater degree. In 1929, they objected to the separation of Sind because they knew that a separate Sind would be under a Muslim Government, and a Muslim Government was sure to disturb their monopoly and displace them to make room for Muslim candidates. The opposition of the Bengali Hindus to the Partition of Bengal is another illustration of this trait of the high caste Hindus. The Bengali Hindu had the whole of Bengal, Bihar, Orissa, Assam and even U. P. for his pasture. He had captured the civil service in all these Provinces. The partition of Bengal meant a diminution in the area of this pasture. It meant that the Bengali Hindu was to be ousted from Eastern Bengal to make room for the Bengali Musalman who had so far no place in the civil service of Bengal. The opposition to the partition of Bengal on the part of the Bengali Hindus, was due principally to their desire not to allow the Bengal Musalmans to take their place in Eastern Bengal. Little did the Bengali Hindus dream that by opposing partition and at the same time demanding Swaraj they were preparing the way for making the Musalmans the rulers of both Eastern as well as Western Bengal.

These thoughts occur to one's mind because one fears that the high caste Hindus, blinded by their hereditary trait, might oppose Pakistan for no other reason except that it limits the field for their self-seeking careers. Among the many reasons that might come in the way of Pakistan, one need not be surprised, if one of them happens to be the selfishness of the high caste Hindus.

There are two alternatives for the Hindus of the Punjab and Bengal and they may be asked to face them fairly and squarely. The Muslims in the Punjab number 13,332,460 and the Hindus, with Sikhs and the rest, number 11,392,732. The difference is only 1,939,728. This means that the Muslim majority in the Punjab is only a majority of 8 p.c. Given these facts, which is better: To retain the unity of the Punjab and allow the Muslim majority of 54 p.c. to rule the Hindu minority of 46 p.c. or to redraw the boundaries, to allow the Muslims and the Hindus to be under separate national states, and thus rescue the whole body of Hindus from the terrors of the Muslim rule?

The Muslims in Bengal number 27,497,624 and the Hindus number 21,570,407. The difference is only of 5,927,217. This means that the Muslim majority in Bengal is only a majority of 12 p.c. Given these facts, which is better: To oppose the creation of a National Muslim State out of Eastern Bengal and Sylhet by refusing to redraw the boundaries and allow the Muslim majority of only 12 p.c. to rule the Hindu minority of 44 p.c.; or to consent to redraw the boundaries, to have Muslims and Hindus placed under separate National States, and thus rescue the 44 p.c. of the Hindus from the horrors of the Muslim rule?

Let the Hindus of Bengal and the Punjab consider which alternative they should prefer. It seems to me that the moment has come when the high caste Hindus of Bengal and the Punjab should be told that if they propose to resist Pakistan, because it cuts off a field for gainful employment, they are committing the greatest blunder. The time for successfully maintaining in their own hands a monopoly of place and power is gone. They may cheat the lower orders of the Hindus in the name of nationalism, but they cannot cheat the Muslim majorities in the Muslim Provinces and keep their monopoly of place and power. The resolution of the Hindus—if their cry against Pakistan can be regarded as such—to live under a Muslim majority and oppose self-determination may be a very courageous thing. But it will not be a very wise thing if the Hindus believe that they will be able to maintain their place and power by fooling the Musalmans. As Lincoln said, it is not possible to fool all people for all times. If the Hindus choose to live under a Muslim majority the chances are that they may lose all. On the other hand, if the Hindus of Bengal and the Punjab agree to separate, true, they will not get more, but they will certainly not lose all.

PART III

WHAT IF NOT PAKISTAN?

Having stated the Muslim case for Pakistan and the Hindu case against it, it is necessary to turn to the alternatives to Pakistan, if there be any. In forming one's judgment on Pakistan, one must take into account the alternatives to it. Either there is no alternative to Pakistan: or there is an alternative to Pakistan, but it is worse than Pakistan. Thirdly, one must also take into consideration what would be the consequences, if neither Pakistan nor its alternative is found acceptable to the parties concerned. The relevant data, having a bearing on these points, are presented in this part under the following heads :—

1 *Hindu alternative to Pakistan.*

2 *Muslim alternative to Pakistan.*

3 *Lessons from abroad.*

CHAPTER VII

HINDU ALTERNATIVE TO PAKISTAN

I

Thinking of the Hindu alternative to Pakistan, the scheme that at once comes to one's mind is the one put forth by the late Lala Hardyal in 1925. It was published in the form of a statement which appeared in the *Pratap* of Lahore. In this statement, which he called his political testament, Lala Hardyal said :—

> "I declare that the future of the Hindu race, of Hindustan and of the Punjab, rests on these four pillars : (1) Hindu Sangathan, (2) Hindu Raj, (3) Shuddhi of Moslems, and (4) Conquest and Shuddhi of Afghanistan and the Frontiers. So long as the Hindu nation does not accomplish these four things, the safety of our children and great-grand-children will be ever in danger, and the safety of the Hindu race will be impossible. The Hindu race has but one history, and its institutions are homogeneous. But the Musalmans and Christians are far removed from the confines of Hinduism, for their religions are alien and they love Persian, Arab and European institutions. Thus, just as one removes foreign matter from the eye, Shuddhi must be made of these two religions. Afghanistan and the hilly regions of the frontier were formerly part of India, but are at present under the domination of Islam .... Just as there is Hindu religion in Nepal, so there must be Hindu institutions in Afghanistan and the frontier territory; otherwise it is useless to win Swarai. For, mountain tribes are always warlike and hungry. If they become our enemies, the age of Nadirshah and Zamanshah will begin anew. At present English officers are protecting the frontiers; but it cannot always be .... If Hindus want to protect themselves, they must conquer Afghanistan and the frontiers and convert all the mountain tribes."

* See *Times of India* dated 25-7-1925, "Through Indian Eyes".

I do not know how many Hindus would come forward to give their support to this scheme of Lala Hardyal as an alternative to Pakistan.

In the first place, Hindu religion is not a proselytising religion. Maulana Mahomed Ali was quite right when, in the course of his address as President of the Congress, he said:—

> "Now, this has been my complaint for a long time against Hinduism, and on one occasion, lecturing at Allahabad in 1907. I had pointed out the contrast between Musalmans and Hindus, by saying that the worst that can be said of a Muslim was that he had a tasteless mess which he called a dish fit for kings, and wanted all to share it with him, thrusting it down the throats of such as did not relish it and would rather not have it, while his Hindu brother, who prided himself on his cookery, retired into the privacy of his kitchen and greedily devoured all that he had cooked, without permitting even the shadow of his brother to fall on his food, or sparing even a crumb for him. This was said not altogether in levity; and in fact, I once asked Mahatma Gandhi to justify this feature of his faith to me."

What answer the Mahatma gave to his question, Mr. Mahomed Ali did not disclose. The fact is that however much the Hindus may wish, Hindu religion cannot become a missionary religion like Islam or Christianity. It is not that the Hindu religion was never a missionary religion. On the contrary, it was once a missionary religion—indeed could not but have been a missionary religion, otherwise it is difficult to explain how it could have spread over an area so vast as the Indian continent.* But once a missionary religion, Hinduism perforce ceased to be a missionary religion after the time when the Hindu society developed its system of castes. For, caste is incompatible with conversion. To be able to convert a stranger to its religion, it is not enough for a community to offer its creed. It must be in a position to admit the convert to its social life and to absorb and assimilate him among its kindred. It is not possible for the Hindu society to satisfy this prerequisite of effective conversion. There is nothing to prevent a Hindu, with a missionary zeal, to

* On the question whether the Hindu Religion was a missionary Religion and if it was why it ceased to be so, see my essay on *Caste and Conversion* in the Annual Number of the *Telugu Samachar* for 1926.

proceed to convert an alien to the Hindu faith. But before he converts the alien, he is bound to be confronted with the question: What is to be the caste of the convert? According to the Hindus, for a person to belong to a caste he must be born in it. A convert is not born in a caste, therefore he belongs to no caste. This is also an important question. More than political or religious, man is a social animal. He may not have, need not have, religion; he may not have, need not have, politics. He must have society; he cannot do without society. For a Hindu to be without caste is to be without society. Where there is no society for the convert, how can there be any conversion? So long as Hindu society is fragmented in autonomous and autogenic castes, Hindu religion cannot be a missionary religion. The conversion of the Afghans and the frontier tribes to Hinduism is, therefore, an idle dream.

In the second place, Lala Hardyal's scheme must call for financial resources the immensity of which it is hardly possible to compute. Who can furnish the funds necessary for the conversion of the Afghans and the Frontier Tribesmen to Hinduism? The Hindus, having ceased to convert others to their faith for a long time, have also lost the zeal for conversion. Want of zeal is bound to affect the question of finances. Further, Hindu society being moulded in the cast of the *Chaturvarna*, wealth has, from very ancient times, been most unevenly distributed. It is only the Baniya who is the heir to wealth and property among the Hindus. There are, of course, the landlords who are the creation of foreign invaders or native rebels, but they are not as numerous as the Baniya. The Baniya is money-made and his pursuits are solely for private gain. He knows no other use of money except to hold it and to transmit it to his descendants. Spread of religion or acquisition and promotion of culture do not interest him. Even decent living has no place in his budget. This has been his tradition for ages. If money is excepted, he is not much above the brute in the conception and manner of life. Only one new service, on the expenditure side, has found a place in his budget. That service is politics. This happened since the entry of Mr. Gandhi as a political leader. That new service is the support of Gandhian politics. Here again, the reason is not love of politics. The reason is to make private gain out of public affairs. What hope is there that such men will spend money on such a bootless cause as the spread of Hindu religion among the Afghans and Frontier Tribes?

Thirdly, there is the question of facilities for conversion that may be available in Afghanistan. Lala Hardyal evidently thought that it is possible to say in Afghanistan, with the same impunity as in Turkey, that the Koran is wrong or out of date. Only one year before the publication of his political testament by Lala Hardyal i.e. in 1924, one Niamatulla—a follower of Mirza Ghulam Ahamed of Quadiyan—who claimed to be the messiah and Mahdi and a prophet of a sort—was stoned to death* at Kabul by the order of the highest ecclesiastical tribunal of Afghanistan. The crime of this man was, as reported by a Khilafat paper, that he was professing and preaching ideas and beliefs, inconsistent with Islam and Shariat. This man, says the same paper was stoned to death according to the agreeing judgments of the first Sharai (canon) Court, the Central Appellate Court and the Ulema and Divines of the final Appellate Committee of the Ministry of Justice. In the light of these difficulties, the scheme must be said to be wild in its conception and is sure to prove ruinous in its execution. It is adventurous in character and is too fantastic to appeal to any reasonable man except perhaps some fanatical Arya Samajists of the Punjab.

II

The stand taken by the Hindu Mahasabha has been defined by Mr. V. D. Savarkar, the President of the Sabha, in his presidential addresses at the annual sessions of the Sabha. As defined by him, the Hindu Maha Sabha is against Pakistan and proposes to resist it by all means. What these means are we do not know. If they are force, coercion and resistance, they are only negative alternatives and Mr. Savarkar and the Hindu Maha Sabha alone can say how far these means will succeed.

*See Report in *Times of India* 27-11-24, "Through Indian Eyes".

It would, however, not be fair to Mr. Savarkar to say that he has only a negative attitude towards the claim put forth by the Muslims of India. He has put forth his positive proposals in reply to them.

To understand his positive proposals, one must grasp some of his basic conceptions. Mr. Savarkar lays great stress on a proper understanding of the terms, Hinduism, Hindutva and Hindudom. He says :—*

> "In expounding the ideology of the Hindu movement, it is absolutely necessary to have a correct grasp of the meaning attached to these three terms. From the word "Hindu" has been coined the word "Hinduism" in English. It means the schools or system of Religion the Hindus follow. The second word "Hindutva" is far more comprehensive and refers not only to the religious aspects of the Hindu people as the word "Hinduism" does but comprehend even their cultural, linguistic, social and political aspects as well. It is more or less akin to "Hindu Polity" and its nearly exact translation would be "Hinduness". The third word "Hindudom" means the Hindu people spoken of collectively. It is a collective name for the Hindu World, just as Islam denotes the Moslem World."

Mr. Savarkar takes it as a gross misrepresentation to say that the Hindu Maha Sabha is a religious body. In refutation of this misrepresentation, Mr. Savarkar says :—†

> "It has come to my notice that a very large section of the English educated Hindus hold back from joining the Hindu Maha Sabha . . . . . . under the erroneous idea that it is an exclusively Religious organization—something like a Christian Mission. Nothing could be far from truth. The Hindu Maha Sabha is not a Hindu Mission. It leaves Religious questions regarding theism, monotheism, Pantheism or even atheism to be discussed and determined by the different Hindu schools of religious persuasions. It is not a Hindu Dharma Maha Sabha,—but a Hindu-National Maha Sabha. Consequently by its very constitution it is debarred to associate itself exclusively as a partisan with any particular religious school or sect even within the Hindu fold. As a national Hindu body it will of course propagate and defend the National Hindu Church comprising each and all religions of Hindusthani origin against any non-Hindu attack or encroachment. But the sphere of its activity is far more comprehensive

* Speech at the Calcutta Session of the Hindu Maha Sabha held in December 1939, p. 14.

† Ibid., p. 25.

> than that of an exclusively religious body. The Hindu Maha Sabha identifies itself with the National life of Hindudom in all its entirety, in all its social, economical, cultural and above all political aspects and is pledged to protect and promote all that contributes to the freedom, strength and glory of the Hindu Nation; and as an indispensable means to that end to attain Purna Swarajya, absolute political Independence of Hindusthan by all legitimate and proper means."

Mr. Savarkar does not admit that the Hindu Maha Sabha is started to counteract the Muslim League and that as soon as the problems arising out of the Communal Award are solved to the satisfaction of both Hindus and Musalmans, the Hindu Maha Sabha will vanish. Mr. Savarkar insists that the Hindu Maha Sabha must continue to function even after India becomes politically free. He says:—*

> ". . . . Many a superficial critic seems to fancy that the Maha Sabha was only contrived to serve as a make-weight, as a reaction checkmating the Moslem League or the anti-Hindu policy of the present leaders of the Congress and will be out of court or cease automatically to function as soon as it is shorne of this spurious excuse to exist. But if the aims and object of the Maha Sabha mean anything it is clear that it was not the outcome of any frothy effusion, any fussy agitation to remove a grievance here or oppose a seasonal party there. The fact is that every organism whether, individual or social which is living and deserves to survive throws out offensive and defensive organs as soon as it is brought to face adversely changing environments. The Hindu Nation too as soon as it recovered and freed itself from the suffocating grip of the pseudo-Nationalistic ideology of the Congress brand developed a new organ to battle in the struggle for existence under the changed conditions of modern age. This was the Hindu Maha Sabha. It grew up of a fundamental necessity of the National life and not of any ephemeral incident. The constructive side of its aims and objects make it amply clear that its mission is as abiding as the life of the Nation itself. But that apart, even the day to day necessity of adapting its policy to the ever changing political currents makes it incumbent on Hindudom to have an exclusively Hindu organization independent of any moral or intellectual servility or subservience to any non-Hindu or jointly representative institution, to guard Hindu interests and save them from being jeopardised. It is not so only under the present political subjection of Hindustan but it will be all the more necessary to have some such exclusively

* Ibid., pp. 24-27.

Hindu organization, some such Hindu Maha Sabha in substance whether it is identical with this present organization or otherwise to serve as a watchtower at the gates of Hindudom for at least a couple of centuries to come, even after Hindustan is partially or wholly free and a National Parliament controls its political destiny.

"Because, unless something altogether cataclysmic in nature upsets the whole political order of things in the world which practical politics cannot envisage today, all that can be reasonably expected in immediate future is that we Hindus may prevail over England and compel her to recognise India as a self-governing unit with the status contemplated in the Westminster Statute. Now a National Parliament in such a self-governing India can only reflect the electorate as it is, the Hindus and the Moslems as we find them, their relations a bit bettered, perhaps a bit worsened. No realist can be blind to the probability that the extra-territorial designs and the secret urge goading on the Moslem to transform India into a Moslem state may at any time confront the Hindustani state even under self-government either with a Civil War or treacherous overtures to alien invaders by the Moslems. Then again there is every likelihood that there will ever continue at least for a century to come a danger of fanatical riots, the scramble for services, legislative seats, weightages out of proportion to their population on the part of the Moslem minority and consequently a constant danger threatening internal peace. To checkmate this probability which if we are wise we must always keep in view even after Hindustan attains the status of a self-governing country, a powerful and exclusive organization of Hindudom like the Hindu Maha Sabha will always prove a sure and devoted source of strength, a reserve force for the Hindus to fall back upon to voice their grievances more effectively than the joint Parliament can do, to scent danger ahead, to warn the Hindus in time against it and to fight out if need be any treacherous design to which the joint state itself may unwittingly fall a victim.

"The History of Canada, of Palestine, of the movement of the Young Turks will show you that in every state where two or more such conflicting elements as the Hindus and Moslems in India happen to exist as constituents, the wiser of them has to keep its exclusive organization intact, strong and watchful to defeat any attempt at betrayal or capture of the National State by the opposite party; especially so if that party has extra-territorial affinities, religious or cultural, with alien bordering states."

Having stated what is Hindustan, and what is Hindu Maha Sabha, Mr. Savarkar next proceeds to define his conception of Swaraj. According to Mr. Savarkar :—*

> "Swaraj to the Hindus must mean only that in which their "Swatva", their "Hindutva" can assert itself without being overlorded by any non-Hindu people, whether they be Indian Territorials or extra-Territorials—some Englishmen are and may continue to be territorially born Indians. Can, therefore, the overlordship of these Anglo-Indians be a "Swarajya" to the Hindus? Aurangzeb or Tipu were hereditary Indians, nay, were the sons of converted Hindu mothers. Did that mean that the rule of Aurangzeb or Tipu was a "Swarajya" to the Hindus? No! Although they were territorially Indians they proved to be the worst enemies of Hindudom and therefore, a Shivaji, a Gobindsingh, a Pratap or the Peshwas had to fight against the Moslem domination and establish real Hindu Swarajya."

As part of his Swaraj Mr. Savarkar insists upon two things.

Firstly, the retention of the name Hindustan as the proper name for India.†

> "The name "Hindustan" must continue to be the appellation of our country. Such other names as India, Hind etc. being derived from the same original word Sindhu may be used but only to signify the same sense the land of the Hindus, a country which is the abode of the Hindu Nation. Aryavarta, Bharat-Bhumi and such other names are of course the ancient and the most cherished epithets of our Mother Land and will continue to appeal to the cultured elite. In this insistence that the Mother Land of the Hindus must be called but "Hindustan," no encroachment or humiliation is implied in connection with any of our non-Hindu countrymen. Our Parsee and Christian countrymen are already too akin to us culturally and are too patriotic and the Anglo-Indians too sensible to refuse to fall in line with us Hindus on so legitimate a ground. So far as our Moslem countrymen are concerned it is useless to conceal the fact that some of them are already inclined to look upon this molehill also as an insuperable mountain in their way to Hindu-Moslem unity. But they should remember that the Moslems do not dwell only in India nor are the Indian Moslems the only heroic remnants of the Faithful in Islam. China has crores of Moslems, Greece, Palestine and even Hungary and Poland have thousands

* Ibid., p. 18.

† Ibid., pp. 19-20.

of Moslems amongst their nationals. But being there a minority, only a community, their existence in these countries has never been advanced as a ground to change the ancient names of these countries which indicate the abodes of those races whose overwhelming majority owns the land. The country of the Poles continues to be Poland and of the Grecians as Greece. The Moslems there did not or dared not to distort them but are quite content to distinguish themselves as Polish Moslems or Grecian Muslems or Chinese Moslems when occasion arises, so also our Moslem countrymen may distinguish themselves nationally or territorially whenever they want, as "Hindusthanee Moslems" without compromising in the least their separateness as Religious or Cultural entity. Nay, the Moslems have been calling themselves as "Hindusthanis" ever since their advent in India, of their own accord.

"But if inspite of it all some irascible Moslem sections amongst our countrymen object even to this name of our Country, that is no reason why we should play cowards to our own conscience. We Hindus must not betray or break up the continuity of our Nation from the Sindhus in Rigvedic days to the Hindus of our own generation which is implied in "Hindustan," the accepted appellation of our Mother Land. Just as the land of the Germans is Germany, of the English England, of the Turks Turkistan, of the Afghans Afghanistan—even so we must have it indelibly impressed on the map of the earth for all times to come a "Hindustan"—the land of the "Hindus."

The second is the retention of Sanskrit as sacred language, Hindi as national language and Nagari as the script of Hindudom.*

'The Sanskrit shall be our "देवभाषा", (Deva Bhasha)§ our sacred language and the "Sanskrit Nishtha"† Hindi, the Hindi which is derived from Sanskrit and draws its nourishment from the latter, is our "राष्ट्रभाषा," (Rashtra Bhasha)‡ our current national language—besides being the richest and the most cultured of the ancient languages of the world, to us Hindus the Sanskrit is the holiest tongue of tongues. Our scriptures, history, philosophy and culture have their roots so deeply imbedded in the

*. Ibid., pp. 21, 22, 23.

§. Language of Gods.

†. Basically Sanskrit.

‡. National Language.

Sanskrit literature that it forms veritably the brain of our Race. Mother of the majority of our mother tongues, she has suckled the rest of them at her breast. All Hindu languages current today whether derived from Sanskrit or grafted on to it can only grow and flourish on the sap of life they imbibe from Sanskrit. The Sanskrit language therefore must ever be an indispensable constituent of the classical course for Hindu youths.

"In adopting the Hindi as the National tongue of Hindudom no humiliation or any invidious distinction is implied as regards other provincial tongues. We are all as attached to our provincial tongues as to Hindi and they will all grow and flourish in their respective spheres. In fact some of them are today more progressive and richer in literature. But nevertheless, taken all in all the Hindi can serve the purpose of a National Pan-Hindu Language best. It must also be remembered that the Hindi is not made a National Language to order. The fact is that long before either the English or even the Moslems stepped in India the Hindi in its general form had already come to occupy the position of a National tongue throughout Hindustan. The Hindu pilgrim, the tradesman, the tourist, the soldier, the Pandit travelled up and down from Bengal to Sind and Kashmere to Rameshwar by making himself understood from locality to locality through Hindi. Just as the Sanskrit was the National language of the Hindu intellectual world even so Hindi has been for at least a thousand years in the past the National Indian Tongue of the Hindu community.........

"By Hindi we of course mean the pure "Sanskrit Nistha" Hindi, as we find it for example in the "Satyartha Prakash" written by Maharsi Dayananda Saraswati. How simple and untainted with a single unnecessary foreign word is that Hindi and how expressive withal! It may be mentioned in passing that Swami Dayanandaji was about the first Hindu leader who gave conscious and definite expression to the view that Hindi should be the Pan-Hindu National language of India. "This Sanskrit Nistha" Hindi has nothing to do with that hybrid, the so-called Hindusthani which is being hatched up by the Wardha scheme. It is nothing short of a linguistic monstrosity and must be ruthlessly suppressed. Not only that but it is our bounden duty to oust out as ruthlessly all unnecessary alien words whether Arabian or English, from every Hindu tongue—whether provincial or dialectical.........

"......Our Sanskrit alphabetical order is phonetically about the most perfect which the world has yet devised and almost all our current Indian scripts already follow it. The Nagari Script too follows this order. Like the Hindi language the Nagari Script too has already been current for centuries all over India amongst the Hindu literary circles for some two thousand years at any rate in the past and was even popularly nick-named as the "Shastri Lipi" the script of our Hindu Scriptures......It is a matter of common knowledge that if Bengali or Gujarathi is printed in Nagari it is more or less understood by readers in several other provinces. To have only one common language throughout Hindustan at a stroke is impracticable and unwise. But to have the Nagari script as the only common script throughout Hindudom is much more feasible. Nevertheless, it should be borne in mind that the different Hindu scripts current in our different provinces have a future of their own and may flourish side by side with the Nagari. All that is immediately indispensable in the common interest of Hindudom as a whole is that the Nagari Script must be made a compulsory subject along with the Hindi language in every school in the case of Hindu students."

What is to be the position of the Non-Hindu minorities under the Swaraj as contemplated by Mr. Savarkar? On this question, this is what Mr. Savarkar has to say :—*

"When once the Hindu Maha Sabha not only accepts but maintains the principles of "one man one vote" and the public services to go by merit alone added to the fundamental rights and obligations to be shared by all citizens alike irrespective of any distinction of Race or Religion......any further mention of minority rights is on the principle not only unnecessary but self-contradictory. Because it again introduces a consciousness of majority and minority on Communal basis. But as practical politics requires it and as the Hindu Sanghatanists want to relieve our non-Hindu country-men of even a ghost of suspicion, we are prepared to emphasise that the legitimate rights of minorities with regard to their Religion, Culture, and Language will be expressly guaranteed: on one condition only that the equal rights of the majority also must not in any case be encroached upon or abrogated. Every minority may have separate schools to train up their children in their own tongue, their own religious or cultural institutions and can receive Government help also for these,—but always in proportion to the taxes they pay into the common exchequer. The same principle must of course hold good in case of the majority too.

"Over and above this, in case the constitution is not based on joint electorates and on the unalloyed National principle of one man one vote, but is based on the communal basis then those minorities who wish to have separate electorate or reserve seats

*Ibid., p. 4.

will be allowed to have them,—but always in proportion to their population and provided that it does not deprive the majority also of an equal right in proportion to its population too."

That being the position assigned to the minorities, Mr. Savarkar concludes* that under his scheme of Swaraj:—

> "......The Moslem minority in India will have the right to be treated as equal citizens, enjoying equal protection and civic rights in proportion to their population. The Hindu majority will not encroach on the legitimate rights of any non-Hindu minority. But in no case can the Hindu majority resign its right which as a majority it is entitled to exercise under any democratic and legitimate constitution. The Moslem minority in particular has not obliged the Hindus by remaining in minority and therefore, they must remain satisfied with the status they occupy and with the legitimate share of civic and political rights that is their proportionate due. It would be simply preposterous to endow the Moslem minority with the right of exercising a practical veto on the legitimate rights and privileges of the majority and call it a "Swarajya". The Hindus do not want a change of masters, are not going to struggle and fight and die only to replace an Edward by an Aurangazeb simply because the latter happens to be born within Indian borders, but they want henceforth to be masters themselves in their own house, in their own Land."

And it is because he wants his Swaraj to bear the stamp of being a Hindu Raj that Mr. Savarkar wants that India should have the appellation of Hindustan.

This structure has been reared by Mr. Savarkar on two propositions which he regards as fundamental.

The first is that the Hindu are a nation by themselves. He enunciates this proposition with great elaboration and vehemence. Says† Mr. Savarkar:—

> "In my Presidential speech at Nagpur I had, for the first time in the history of our recent politics pointed out in bold relief that the whole Congress ideology was vitiated *ab initio* by its unwitted assumption that the territorial unity, a common habitat, was the only factor that constituted and ought to and must constitute

*Ibid., p. 16.

† Ibid., pp. 14-17.

a Nation. This conception of a Territorial Nationality has since then received a rude shock in Europe itself from which it was imported wholesale to India and the present War has justified my assertion by exploding the myth altogether. All Nations carved out to order on the Territorial design without any other common bond to mould each of them into a national being have gone to rack and ruin, tumbled down like a house of cards. Poland and Czechoslovakia will ever serve as a stern warning against any such efforts to frame hetorogeneous peoples into such hotch-potch Nation, based only on the shifting sands of the conception of Territorial Nationality, not cemented by any cultural, racial or historical affinities and consequently having no common will to incorporate themselves into a Nation. These treaty-Nations broke up at the first opportunity they got: The German part of them went over to Germany, the Russian to Russia, Czechs to Czechs, and Poles to Poles. The cultural, linguistic, historical and such other organic affinities proved stronger than the Territorial one. Only those Nations have persisted in maintaining their National unity and identity during the last three to four centuries in Europe which had developed racial, linguistic cultural and such other organic affinities in addition to their Territorial unity or even at times in spite of it and consequently willed to be homogeneous National units—such as England, France, Germany, Italy, Portugal, etc.

"Judged by any and all of these tests which go severally and collectively to form such a homogeneous and organic Nation, in India we Hindus are marked out as an abiding Nation by ourselves. Not only do we own a common Fatherland, a Territorial unity, but what is scarcely found anywhere else in the world, we have a common Holy Land which is identified with our common Fatherland. This Bharat Bhumi, this Hindustan, India is both our पितृभू and पुण्यभू. Our patriotism therefore is doubly sure. Then, we have common affinities, cultural, religious, historical, linguistic, and racial which through the process of countless centuries of association and assimilation moulded us into a homogeneous and organic nation and above all induced a will to lead a corporate and common national life. The Hindus are no treaty Nation—but an organic National Being.

"One more pertinent point must be met as it often misleads our Congressite Hindu brethren in particular. The homogeneity that wields a people into a National Being does not only imply the total absence of all internal differences, religious, racial or linguistic, of sects and sections amongst themselves. It only means that they differ more from other people as a national unit than they differ amongst themselves. Even the most unitarian nations of today—say the British or the French—cannot be free from any religious, linguistic, cultural, racial or other differences, sects or sections or even some antipathies existing amongst themselves. National homogeneity connotes oneness of a people ,in relation to the contrast they present to any other people as a whole.

"We Hindus, in spite of thousand and one differences within our fold, are bound by such religious, cultural, historical, racial, linguistic and other affinities in common as to stand out as a definitely homogeneous people as soon as we are placed in contrast with any other non-Hindu people—say the English or Japanese or even the Indian Moslems. That is the reason why today we the Hindus from Cashmere to Madras and Sindh to Assam will have to be a Nation by ourselves"....

The second proposition on which Mr. Savarkar has built up his scheme relates to the definition of the term Hindu. According to Mr. Savarkar a Hindu is a person :—

"... who regards and owns this Bharat Bhumi, this land from the Indus to the Seas, as his Fatherland as well as his Holy Land;—i.e., the land of the origin of his religion, the cradle of his faith.

The followers therefore of Vaidicism, Sanatanism, Jainism, Buddhism, Lingaitism, Sikhism, the Arya Samaj, the Brahmosamaj, the Devasamaj, the Prathana Samaj and such other religions of Indian origin are Hindus and constitute Hindudom, i.e., Hindu people as a whole.

Consequently the so-called aboriginal or hill-tribes also are Hindus: because India is their Fatherland as well as their Holy Land, whatever form of religion or worship they follow. The definition rendered in Sanskrit stands thus:—

॥ आसिंधु सिंध पर्यंता यस्य भारत भूमिका ॥

॥ पितृभू : पुण्यभूश्चैव स वै हिंदुरितिस्मृतः ॥ १ ॥

This definition, therefore, should be recognized by the Government and made the test of 'Hindutva' in enumerating the population of Hindus in the Government census to come."

This definition of the term Hindu has been framed with great care and caution. It is designed to serve two purposes which Mr. Savarkar has in view. First, to exclude from it Muslims, Christians, Parsis and Jews by prescribing the recognition of India as a Holy Land as a qualification for being a Hindu. Secondly, to include Buddhists, Jains, Sikhs, etc., by not insisting upon belief in the sanctity of the Vedas as an element in the qualifications.

Such is the scheme of Mr. Savarkar and the Hindu Maha Sabha. As must have been noticed, the scheme has some disturbing features.

One is the categorical assertion that the Hindus are a nation by themselves. This, of course, means that the Muslims are a separate nation by themselves. That this is his view, Mr. Savarkar does not leave to be inferred. He insists upon it in no uncertain terms and with the most absolute emphasis he is capable of. Speaking at the Hindu Maha Sabha Session held at Ahmedabad in 1937, Mr. Savarkar said:—

> "Several infantile politicians commit the serious mistake in supposing that India is already welded into a harmonious nation, or that it could be welded thus for the mere wish to do so. These our well-meaning but unthinking friends take their dreams for realities. That is why they are impatient of communal tangles and attribute them to communal organizations. But the solid fact is that the so-called communal questions are but a legacy handed down to us by centuries of a cultural, religious and national antagonism between the Hindus and the Muslims. When the time is ripe you can solve them; but you cannot suppress them by merely refusing recognition of them. It is safer to diagnose and treat deep-seated disease than to ignore it. Let us bravely face unpleasant facts as they are. India cannot be assumed today to be a unitarian and homogeneous nation, but on the contrary these are two nations in the main, the Hindus and the Muslims in India."

Strange as it may appear, Mr. Savarkar and Mr. Jinnah instead of being opposed to each other on the one nation *versus* two nations issue are in complete agreement about it. Both agree, not only agree but insist that there are two nations in India—one the Muslim nation and the other the Hindu nation. They differ only as regards the terms and conditions on which the two nations should live. Mr. Jinnah says India should be cut up into two, Pakistan and Hindustan, the Muslim nation to occupy Pakistan and the Hindu nation to occupy Hindustan. Mr. Savarkar on the other hand insists that, although there are two nations in India, India shall not be divided into two parts, one for Muslims and the other for the Hindus; that the two nations shall dwell in one country and shall live under the mantle of one single constitution; that the constitution shall be such that the Hindu nation will be enabled to occupy a predominant position that is due to it and the Muslim nation made to live in the position of subordinate co-operation with the Hindu nation. In the struggle for political power between the two nations the rule of the game, which Mr. Savarkar prescribes, is to be one man one vote, be the man Hindu or Muslim. In his scheme a Muslim is to have no advantage which a Hindu does not have. Minority is to be no justification for privilege and majority is to be no ground for penalty. The State will guarantee the Muslims any defined measure of political power in the form of Muslim religion and Muslim culture. But the State will not guarantee secured seats in the Legislature or in the Administration and, if such guarantee is insisted upon by the Muslims,* such guaranteed quota is not to exceed their proportion to the general population. Thus by confiscating its weightages, Mr. Savarkar would even strip the Muslim nation of all the political privileges it has secured so far.

This alternative of Mr. Savarkar to Pakistan has about it a frankness, boldness and definiteness which distinguishes it from the irritating vagueness and indefiniteness which characterizes the Congress declarations about minority rights. Mr. Savarkar's scheme has at least the merit of telling the Muslims, thus far, and no further. The Muslims know where they are with regard to the Hindu Maha Sabha. On the other hand, with the Congress the Musalmans find themselves nowhere because the Congress has been treating the Muslims and the minority question as a game in diplomacy, if not in duplicity.

At the same time, it must be said that Mr. Savarkar's attitude is illogical, if not queer. Mr. Savarkar admits that the Muslims are a separate nation. He concedes that they have a right to cultural autonomy. He allows them to have a national flag. Yet he opposes the demand of the Muslim nation for a separate national home. If he claims a national home for the Hindu nation, how can he refuse the claim of the Muslim nation for a national home?

*It should be noted that Mr. Savarkar is not opposed to separate electorates for the Muslims. It is not clear whether he is in favour of separate electorates for Muslims even where they are in a majority.

It would not have been a matter of much concern if inconsistency was the only fault of Mr. Savarkar. But Mr. Savarkar in advocating his scheme is really creating a most dangerous situation for the safety and security of India. History records two ways as being open to a major nation to deal with a minor nation when they are citizens of the same country and are subject to the same constitution. One way is to destroy the nationality of the minor nation and to assimilate and absorb it into the major nation, so as to make one nation out of two. This is done by denying to the minor nation any right to language, religion or culture and by seeking to enforce upon it the language, religion and culture of the major nation. The other way is to divide the country and to allow the minor nation a separate, autonomous and sovereign existence, independent of the major nation. Both these ways were tried in Austria and Turkey, the second after the failure of the first.

Mr. Savarkar adopts neither of these two ways. He does not propose to suppress the Muslim nation. On the contrary he is nursing and feeding it by allowing it to retain its religion, language and culture, elements which go to sustain the soul of a nation. At the same time he does not consent to divide the country so as to allow the two nations to become separate, autonomous states, each sovereign in its own territory. He wants the Hindus and the Muslims to live as two separate nations in one country, each maintaining its own religion, language and culture. One can understand and even appreciate the wisdom of the theory of suppression of the minor nation by the major nation because the ultimate aim is to bring into being one nation. But one cannot follow what advantage a theory has which says that there must ever be two nations but that there shall be no divorce between them. One can justify this attitude only if the two nations were to live as partners in friendly intercourse with mutual respect and accord. But that is not to be, because Mr. Savarkar will not allow the Muslim nation to be co-equal in authority with the Hindu nation. He wants the Hindu nation to be the dominant nation and the Muslim nation to be the servient nation. Why Mr. Savarkar, after sowing this seed of enmity between the Hindu nation and the Muslim nation should want that they should live under one constitution and occupy one country, is difficult to explain.

One cannot give Mr. Savarkar credit for having found a new formula. What is difficult to understand is that he should believe that his formula is the right formula. Mr. Savarkar has taken old Austria and old Turkey as his model and pattern for his scheme of Swaraj. He sees that in Austria and Turkey there lived one major nation *juxta posed* to other minor nations bound by one constitution with the major nation dominating the minor nations and argues that if this was possible in Austria and Turkey, why should it not be possible for the Hindus to do the same in India.

That Mr. Savarkar should have taken old Austria and old Turkey as his model to build upon is really very strange. Mr. Savarkar does not seem to be aware of the fact that old Austria and old Turkey are no more. Much less does he seem to know the forces which have blown up old Austria and old Turkey to bits. If Mr. Savarkar instead of studying the past — of which he is very fond—were to devote more attention to the present, he would have learnt that old Austria and old Turkey came to ruination for insisting upon maintaining the very scheme of things which Mr. Savarkar has been advising his "Hindudom" to adopt, namely, to establish a Swaraj in which there will be two nations under the mantle of one single constitution in which the major nation will be allowed to hold the minor nation in subordination to itself.

The history of the disruption of Austria, Czechoslovakia, and Turkey is of the utmost importance to India and the members of the Hindu Maha Sabha will do well to peruse the same. I need say nothing here about it because I have drawn attention to lessons from their fateful history in another chapter. Suffice it to say that the scheme of Swaraj formulated by Mr. Savarkar will give the Hindus an empire over the Muslims and thereby satisfy their vanity and their pride in being an imperial race. But it can never ensure a stable and peaceful future for the Hindus, for the simple reason that the Muslims will never yield willing obedience to so dreadful an alternative.

III

Mr. Savarkar is quite unconcerned about the Muslim re-action to his scheme. He formulates his scheme and throws it in the face of the Muslims with the covering letter 'take it or leave it'. He is not perturbed by the Muslim refusal to join in the struggle for Swaraj. He is quite conscious of the strength of the Hindus and the Hindu Maha Sabha and proposes to carry on the struggle in the confident hope that, alone and unaided, the Hindus will be able to wrest Swaraj from the British. Mr. Savarkar is quite prepared to say to the Musalmans:—

> "If you come, with you, if you don't, without you; and if you oppose, in spite of you—the Hindus will continue to fight for their national freedom as best as they can."

Not so Mr. Gandhi. At the very commencement of his career as a political leader of India when Mr. Gandhi startled the people of India by his promise to win Swaraj within six months, Mr. Gandhi said that he could perform the miracle only if certain conditions were fulfilled. One of these conditions was the achievement of Hindu-Muslim unity. Mr. Gandhi is never tired of saying that there is no Swaraj without Hindu-Muslim unity. Mr. Gandhi did not merely make this slogan the currency of Indian politics but he has strenuously worked to bring it about. Mr. Gandhi, it may be said, began his career as a political leader of India with the manifesto dated 2nd March 1919 declaring his intention to launch Satyagraha against the Rowlatt Act and asking those who desired to join him to sign the satyagraha pledge. That campaign of Satyagraha was a short-lived campaign and was suspended by Mr. Gandhi on 18th April 1919. As a part of his programme Mr. Gandhi had fixed* the 6th March 1919 to be observed all over India as a day of protest against the Rowlatt Act. Mass meetings were to be held on that day and Mr. Gandhi had prescribed that the masses attending the meetings should take a vow in the following terms :—

> "With God as witness, we Hindus, and Mahomedans declare that we shall behave towards one another as children of the same parents, that we shall have no differences, that the sorrows of

* See his Manifesto dated 23rd March 1919.

each shall be the sorrows of the other and that each shall help the other in removing them. We shall respect each other's religion and religious feelings and shall not stand in the way of our respective religious practices. We shall always refrain from violence to each other in the name of religion."

There was nothing in the campaign of Satyagraha against the Rowlatt Act which could have led to any clash between the Hindus and the Muslims. Yet Mr. Gandhi asked his followers to take the vow. This shows how insistent he was from the very beginning upon Hindu-Muslim unity.

The Mahomedans started the Khilafat movement in 1919. The objective of the movement was two-fold; to preserve the Khilafat and to maintain the integrity of the Turkish Empire. Both these objectives were unsupportable. The Khilafat could not be saved simply because the Turks, in whose interest this agitation was carried on, did not want the Sultan. They wanted a republic and it was quite unjustifiable to compel the Turks to keep Turkey a monarchy when they wanted to convert it into a republic. It was not open to insist upon the integrity of the Turkish Empire because it meant the perpetual subjection of the different nationalities to the Turkish rule and particularly of the Arabs, especially when it was agreed on all hands that the doctrine of self-determination should be made the basis of the peace settlement.

The movement was started by the Mahomedans. It was taken up by Mr. Gandhi with a tenacity and faith which must have surprised many Mahomedans themselves. There were many people who doubted the ethical basis of the Khilafat movement and tried to dissuade Mr. Gandhi from taking any part in a movement the ethical basis of which was so questionable. But Mr. Gandhi had so completely persuaded himself of the justice of the Khilafat agitation that he refused to yield to their advice. Time and again he argued that the cause was just and it was his duty to join it. The position taken up by him may be summed up in his own words.*

"(1) In my opinion, the Turkish claim is not only not immoral and unjust, but it is highly equitable, if only because Turkey wants to retain what is her own. And the Mahomedan

* *Young India*, 2nd June 1920.

manifesto has definitely declared that whatever guarantees may be necessary to be taken for the protection of the non-Muslim and non-Turkish races, should be taken so as to give the Christians theirs and the Arabs their self-government under the Turkish suzerainty;

(2) I do not believe the Turk to be weak, incapable or cruel. He is certainly disorganised and probably without good generalship. The argument of weakness, incapacity and cruelty one often hears quoted in connection with those from whom power is sought to be taken away. About the alleged massacres a proper commission has been asked for, but never granted. And in any case security can be taken against oppression;

(3) I have already stated that, if I were not interested in the Indian Mahomedans, I would not interest myself in the welfare of the Turks any more than I am in that of the Austrians or the Poles. But I am bound as an Indian to share the sufferings and trials of fellow-Indians. If I deem the Mahomedan to be my brother, it is my duty to help him in his hour of peril to the best of my ability, if his cause commends itself to me as just;

(4) The fourth refers to the extent Hindus should join hands with the Mahomedans. It is, therefore, a matter of feeling and opinion. It is expedient to suffer for my Mahomedan brother to the utmost in a just cause and I should, therefore, travel with him along the whole road so long as the means employed by him are as honourable as his end. I cannot regulate the Mahomedan feeling. I must accept his statement that the Khilafat is with him a religious question in the sense that it binds him to reach the goal even at the cost of his own life."

Mr. Gandhi not only agreed with the Muslims in the Khilafat cause but acted as their guide and their friend. The part played by Mr. Gandhi in the Khilafat agitation and the connection between the Khilafat agitation and the Non-co-operation Movement has become obscure by the reason of the fact that most people believed that it was the Congress which initiated the Non-co-operation Movement and it was done as a means for winning Swaraj. That such a view should prevail is quite understandable because most people content themselves with noting the connection between the Non-co-operation Movement and the special session of the Congress held at Calcutta on 7th and 8th September 1920. But anyone, who cares to go behind September 1920 and examines the situation as it then stood, will find that this view is not true. The truth is that the non-co-operation has its origin in the Khilafat agitation and not in the Congress movement for Swaraj: that it was started by the Khilafatists to help Turkey and adopted by the Congress only to help the Khilafatists: that Swaraj was not its primary object, but its primary object was Khilafat and that Swaraj was added as a secondary object to induce the Hindus to join it will be evident from the following facts.

The Khilafat movement may be said to have begun on 27th October 1919 when the day was observed as the Khilafat Day all over India. On 23rd November 1919 the first Khilafat Conference met at Delhi. It was at this session that the Muslims considered the feasibility of non-co-operation as a means of compelling the British Government to redress the Khilafat wrong. On 10th March 1920 the Khilafat Conference met at Calcutta and decided upon non-co-operation as the best weapon to further the object of their agitation.

On 9th June 1920 the Khilafat Conference met at Allahabad and unanimously reaffirmed their resolve to resort to non-co-operation and appointed an Executive Committee to enforce and lay down a detailed programme. On 22nd June 1920 the Muslims sent a message to the Viceroy stating that they would start non-co-operation if the Turkish grievances were not redressed before 1st August 1920. On 30th June 1920 the Khilafat Committee meeting held at Allahabad resolved to start non-co-operation, after a month's notice to the Viceroy. Notice was given on 1st July 1920 and the non-co-operation commenced on 1st August 1920. This short résumé shows that the non-co-operation was started by the Khilafat Committee and all that the Congress special session at Calcutta did was to adopt what the Khilafat Conference had already done and that too not in the interest of Swaraj but in the interest of helping the Musalmans in furthering the cause of Khilafat. This is clear from the perusal of the Congress Resolution* passed at the special session held at Calcutta.

* "In view of the fact that on the Khilafat question both the Indian and Imperial Governments have signally failed in their duty towards the Muslims of India and the Prime Minister has deliberately broken his pledged word given to them, and that it is the duty of every non-Muslim Indian in every legitimate manner to assist his Muslim brother in his attempt to remove the religious calamity that has overtaken him;

Although the Non-co-operation Movement was launched by the Khilafat Committee and merely adopted by the Congress primarily to help the Khilafat cause, the person who suggested it to the Khilafat Committee and who identified himself with the Committee and took the responsibility of giving effect to it and who brought about its adoption by the Congress was Mr. Gandhi.

At the first Khilafat Conference held at Delhi on 23rd November 1919 Mr. Gandhi was present. Not only was Mr. Gandhi present but also it was he who advised the Muslims to adopt non-co-operation as a method for forcing the British to yield to their demands regarding the Khilafat. The joining of Mr. Gandhi in the Khilafat movement is full of significance. The Muslims were anxious to secure the support of the Hindus in the cause of Khilafat. At the Conference held on 23rd November 1919 the Muslims had invited the Hindus. Again on 3rd June 1920 a joint meeting of the Hindus and the Khilafatist Muslims was held at Allahabad. This meeting was

" And in view of the fact that, in the matter of the events of the April of 1919, both the said Governments have grossly neglected or failed to protect the innocent people of the Punjab and punish officers guilty of unsoldierly and barbarous behaviour towards them, and have exonerated Sir Michael O'Dwyer who proved himself directly responsible for most of the official crimes and callous to the sufferings of the people placed under his administration, and that the debate in the House of Lords betrayed a woeful lack of sympathy with the people of India, and systematic terrorism and frightfulness adopted in the Punjab, and that the latest Viceregal pronouncement is proof of entire absence of repentance in the matters of the Khilafat and the Punjab.

"This Congress is of opinion that there can be no contentment in India without redress of the two aforementioned wrongs, and that the only effectual means to vindicate national honour and to prevent a repetition of similar wrongs in future is the establishment of Swarajya.

"This Congress is further of opinion that there is no course left open for the people of India but to approve of and adopt the policy of progressive non-violent non-co-operation inaugurated by Mahatma Gandhi, until the said wrongs are righted and Swarajya is established."

Mrs. Annie Besant says: "It will be remembered that Mr. Gandhi, in March 1920, had forbidden the mixing up of non-co-operation in defence of the Khilafat with other questions; but it was found that the Khilafat was not sufficiently attractive to Hindus", so at the meeting of the All-India Congress Committee held at Benares on May 30 and 31, the Punjab atrocities and the deficiencies of the Reforms Act were added to the list of provocative causes.—*The Future of Indian Politics*, p. 250.

attended among others by Sapru, Motilal Nehru and Annie Besant. But the Hindus were hesitant in joining the Muslims. Mr. Gandhi was the only Hindu who joined the Muslims. Not only did he show courage to join them, but also he kept step with them, nay, led them. On 9th June 1920 when the Khilafat Conference met at Allahabad and formed an Executive Committee to prepare a detailed programme of non-co-operation and give effect to it, Mr. Gandhi was the only Hindu on that Executive Committee. On 22nd June 1920 the Muslims sent a message to the Viceroy that they would start non-co-operation if the Turkish grievances were not redressed before 1st August 1920. On the same day Mr. Gandhi also sent a letter to the Viceroy explaining the justice of the Khilafat cause, the reasons why he has taken up the cause and the necessity of satisfying the hands of the Khilafatists. For instance the notice given to the Viceroy on 1st July 1920 that non-co-operation will be started on 1st August was given by Mr. Gandhi and not by the Khilafatists. Again when non-co-operation was started by the Khilafatist on 31st August 1920 Mr. Gandhi was the first to give a concrete shape to it by returning his medal. After inaugurating the Non-co-operation Movement as an active member of the Khilafat Committee Mr. Gandhi next directed his energy to the cause of persuading the Congress to adopt non-co-operation and strengthen the Khilafat movement. With that object in view Mr. Gandhi toured the country between 1st August and 1st September 1920 in the company of the Ali Brothers who were the founders of the Khilafat movement impressing upon the people the necessity of non-co-operation. People could notice the disharmony in the tune of Mr. Gandhi and the Ali Brothers. As the *Modern Review* pointed out "Reading between the lines of their speeches, it is not difficult to see that with one of them the sad plight of the Khilafat in distant Turkey is the central fact, while with the other attainment of Swaraj here in India is the object in view." This dichotomy* of interest

* Mr. Gandhi repudiated the suggestion of the *Modern Review* and regarded it as "cruelest cut". Dealing with the criticism of the *Modern Review* in his Article in *Young India* for 20th October 1921 Mr. Gandhi said "I claim that with us both the Khilafat is the central fact, with Maulana Mahomed Ali because it is his religion, with me because, in laying down my life for the Khilafat, I ensure safety of the cow, that is my religion, from the Musalman knife."

did not augur well for the success of the ultimate purpose. Nonetheless Mr. Gandhi succeeded in carrying the Congress with him in support of the Khilafat cause.*

For a long time the Hindus had been engaged in wooing the Muslims to their side. The Congress was very anxious to bridge the gulf between itself and the Muslim League. The ways and means adopted in 1916 for bringing about this consummation and which resulted in the Lucknow Pact signed between the Congress and the Muslim League have been graphically told by Swami Shradhanand in his impressions of the Congress Session held in that year at Lucknow. Says the Swami †:—

> "On sitting on the dais (Lucknow Congress platform) the first thing that I noticed was that the number of Moslem delegates was proportionately fourfold of what it was at Lahore in 1893. The majority of Moslem delegates had donned gold, silver and silk embroidered chogas (flowing robes) over their ordinary coarse suits of wearing apparel. It was rumoured that these 'chogas' had been put by Hindu moneyed men for Congress Tamasha. Of some 433 Moslem delegates only some 30 had come from outside, the rest belonging to Lucknow City. And of these majority was admitted free to delegate seats, board and lodging. Sir Syed Ahmad's anti-Congress League had tried in a public meeting to dissuade Moslems from joining the Congress as delegates. As a countermove the Congress people lighted the whole Congress camp some four nights before the session began and advertised that that night would be free. The result was that all the "Chandul Khanas" of Lucknow were emptied and a huge audience of some thirty thousand Hindus and Moslems was addressed from half a dozen platforms. It was then that the Moslem delegates were elected or selected. All this was admitted by the Lucknow Congress organisers to me in private.
>
> "A show was being made of the Moslem delegates. Moslem delegate gets up to second a resolution in Urdu. He begins: Hozarat, I am a Mahomedan delegate. Some Hindu delegate gets up and calls for three cheers for Mahomedan delegates and the response is so enthusiastic as to be beyond description."

* The Resolution of non-co-operation was carried by 1886 votes against 884. The late Mr. Tairsee once told me that a large majority of the delegates were no others than the taxi drivers of Calcutta who were paid to vote for the non-co-operation resolution

† *Liberator*, 22nd April 1926.

In taking up the cause of Khilafat Mr. Gandhi achieved a double purpose. He carried the Congress plan of winning over the Muslims to its culmination. Secondly he made the Congress a power in the country, which it would not have been, if the Muslims had not joined it. The cause of the Khilafat appealed to the Musalmans far more than political safeguards, with the result that the Musalmans who were outside it trooped into the Congress. The Hindus welcomed them. For, they saw in this a common front against the British, which was their main aim. The credit for this must of course go to Mr. Gandhi. For there can be no doubt that this was an act of great daring.

When the Musalmans in 1919 approached the Hindus for participation in the Non-co-operation Movement which the Muslims desired to start for helping Turkey and the Khilafat, the Hindus were found to be divided in three camps. One was a camp of those who were opposed to non-co-operation in principle. A second camp consisted of those Hindus who were prepared to join the Muslims in their campaign of non-co-operation provided the Musalmans agreed to give up Cow Slaughter. A third group consisted of the Hindus who feared that the Mahomedans might extend their non-co-operation to inviting the Afghans to invade India, in which case the movement instead of resulting in Swaraj might result in the subjection of India to Muslim Raj.

Mr. Gandhi did not care for those Hindus who were opposed to joining the Muslims in the Non-co-operation Movement. But with regard to the others he told them that their attitude was unfortunate. To those Hindus who wanted to give their support on the condition that the Muslims give up cow killing, Mr. Gandhi said * :—

> "I submit that the Hindus may not open the Goraksha (cow protection) question here. The test of friendship is assistance in adversity, and that too, unconditional assistance. Co-operation that needs consideration is a commercial contract and not friendship. Conditional co-operation is like adulterated cement which does not bind. It is the duty of the Hindus, if they see the justice of the Mahomedan cause, to render co-operation. If the Mahomedans feel themselves bound in honour to spare the

* *Young India*, 10th December 1919.

Hindus' feelings and to stop cow killing, they may do so, no matter whether the Hindus co-operate with them or not. Though therefore, I yield to no Hindu in my worship of the cow, I do not want to make the stopping of cow killing a condition precedent to co-operation. Unconditional co-operation means the protection of the cow."

To those Hindus who feared to join the Non-co-operation Movement for the reasons that Muslims may invite the Afghans to invade India, Mr. Gandhi said* :—

"It is easy enough to understand and justify the Hindu caution. It is difficult to resist the Mahomedan position. In my opinion, the best way to prevent India from becoming the battle ground between the forces of Islam and those of the English is for Hindus to make non-co-operation a complete and immediate success, and I have little doubt that, if the Mahomedans remain true to their declared intention and are able to exercise self-restraint and make sacrifices, the Hindus will 'play the game' and join them in the campaign of non-co-operation. I feel equally certain that Hindus will not assist Mahomedans in promoting or bringing about an armed conflict between the British Government and their allies, and Afghanistan. British forces are too well organised to admit of any successful invasion of the Indian frontier. The only way, therefore, the Mahomedans can carry on an effective struggle on behalf of the honour of Islam is to take up non-co-operation in real earnest. It will not only be completely effective if it is adopted by the people on an extensive scale, but it will also provide full scope for individual conscience. If I cannot bear an injustice done by an individual or a corporation, and I am directly or indirectly instrumental in upholding that individual or corporation, I must answer for it before my Maker; but I have done all that is humanly possible for me to do consistently with the moral code that refuses to injure even the wrong-doers, if I cease to support the injustice in the manner described above. In applying, therefore, such a great force, there should be no haste, there should be no temper shown. Non-co-operation must be and remain absolutely a voluntary effort. The whole thing, then, depends upon Mahomedans themselves. If they will but help themselves, Hindu help will come and the Government, great and mighty though it is, will have to bend before this irresistible force. No Government can possibly withstand the bloodless opposition of a whole nation."

Unfortunately, the hope of Mr. Gandhi that 'no Government can possibly withstand the bloodless opposition of a whole

* *Young India*, 9th June 1920.

nation' did not come true. Within a year of the starting of the Non-co-operation Movement, Mr. Gandhi had to admit that the Musalmans had grown impatient and that:—

> "In their impatient anger, the Musalmans ask for more energetic and more prompt action by the Congress and Khilafat organisations. To the Musalmans, Swaraj means, as it must mean, India's ability to deal effectively with the Khilafat question. The Musalmans, therefore, decline to wait if the attainment of Swaraj means indefinite delay or a programme that may require the Musalmans of India to become impotent witnesses of the extinction of Turkey in European waters.
>
> "It is impossible not to sympathise with this attitude. I would gladly recommend immediate action if I could think of any effective course. I would gladly ask for postponement of Swaraj activity if thereby we could advance the interest of the Khilafat. I could gladly take up measures outside non-co-operation, if I could think of any, in order to assuage the pain caused to the millions of the Musalmans.
>
> "But, in my humble opinion, attainment of Swaraj is the quickest method of righting the Khilafat wrong. Hence it is, that for me the solution of the Khilafat question is attainment of Swaraj and *vice versa*. The only way to help the afflicted Turks is for India to generate sufficient power to be able to assert herself. If she cannot develop that power in time, there is no way out for India and she must resign herself to the inevitable. What can a paralytic do to stretch forth a helping hand to a neighbour but to try to cure himself of his paralysis? Mere ignorant, thoughtless and angry outburst of violence may give vent to pent-up rage but can bring no relief to Turkey."

The Musalmans were not in a mood to listen to the advice of Mr. Gandhi. They refused to worship the principle of non-violence. They were not prepared to wait for Swaraj. They were in a hurry to find the most expeditious means of helping Turkey and saving the Khilafat. And the Muslims in their impatience did exactly what the Hindus feared they would do, namely, invite the Afghans to invade India. How far the Khilafatists had proceeded in their negotiations with the Amir of Afghanistan it is not possible to know. But that such a project was entertained by them is beyond question. It needs no saying that the project of an invasion of India was the most dangerous project and every sane Indian would dissociate himself from so mad a project. What part Mr. Gandhi played in this project it is not possible to discover. Certainly he did not dissociate himself from it. On the contrary his misguided zeal for Swaraj and his obsession on Hindu-Moslem unity as the only means of achieving it, led him to support the project. Not only did he advise* the Amir not to enter into any treaty with the British Government but declared—

> "I would, in a sense, certainly assist the Amir of Afghanistan if he waged war against the British Government. That is to say, I would openly tell my countrymen that it would be a crime to help a government which had lost the confidence of the nation to remain in power".

Can any sane man go so far, for the sake of Hindu-Moslem unity? But Mr. Gandhi was so attached to Hindu-Moslem unity that he did not stop to enquire what he was really doing in this mad endeavour. So anxious was Mr. Gandhi in laying the foundation of Hindu-Moslem unity well and truly, that he did not forget to advise his followers regarding the national crisis. In an Article in *Young India* of 8th September 1920 Mr. Gandhi said:—

> "During the Madras tour, at Bezwada I had occasion to remark upon the national crisis and suggested that it would be better to have cries about ideals than men. I asked the audience to replace Mahatma Gandhi-ki-jai and Mahomed Ali Shoukat Ali-ki-jai by Hindu-Musalman-ki-jai. Brother Shoukat Ali, who followed, positively laid down the law. In spite of the Hindu-Muslim unity, he had observed that, if Hindus shouted Bande Mataram, the Muslims rang out with Allaho Akbar and *vice versa*. This, he rightly said jarred on the ear and still showed that the people did not act with one mind. There should be therefore only three cries recognised. Allaho Akbar to be joyously sung out by Hindus and Muslims, showing that God alone was great and no other. The second should be Bande Mataram (Hail Motherland) or Bharat Mata-ki-jai (Victory to Mother Hind). The third should be Hindu-Musalman-ki-jai without which there was no victory for India, and no true demonstration of the greatness of God. I do wish that the newspapers and public men would take up the Maulana's suggestion and lead the people only to use the three cries. They are full of meaning. The first is a prayer and confession of our littleness and therefore a sign of humility. It is a cry in which all Hindus and Muslims should join in reverence and prayfulness. Hindus may not fight shy of Arabic words, when their meaning

* *Young India* dated 4th May 1921.

is not only totally inoffensive but even ennobling. God is no respector of any particular tongue. Bande Mataram, apart from its wonderful associations, expresses the one national wish—the rise of India to her full height. And I should prefer Bande Mataram to Bharat Mata-ki-jai, as it would be a graceful recognition of the intellectual and emotional superiority of Bengal. Since India can be nothing without the union of the Hindu and the Muslim heart, Hindu-Musalman-ki-jai is a cry which we may never forget.

"There should be no discordance in these cries. Immediately some one has taken up any of the three cries, the rest should take it up and not attempt to yell out their favourite. Those, who do not wish to join, may refrain, but they should consider it a breach of etiquette to interpolate their own when a cry has already been raised. It would be better too, always to follow out the three cries in the order given above."

These are not the only things Mr. Gandhi has done to build up Hindu-Moslem unity. He has never called the Muslims to account even when they have been guilty of gross crimes against Hindus.

It is a notorious fact that many prominent Hindus who had offended the religious susceptibilities of the Muslims either by their writings or by their part in the Shudhi movement have been murdered by some fanatic Musalmans. First to suffer was Swami Shradhanand, who was shot by Abdul Rashid on 23 December 1926 when he was lying in his sick bed. This was followed by the murder of Lala Nanakchand, a prominent Arya Samajist of Delhi. Rajpal, the author of the *Rangila Rasool*, was stabbed by Ilamdin on 6th April 1929 while he was sitting in his shop. Nathuramal Sharma was murdered by Abdul Qayum in September 1934. It was an act of great daring. For Sharma was stabbed to death in the Court of the Judicial Commissioner of Sind where he was seated awaiting the hearing of his appeal against his conviction under Section 195, I. P. C. for the publication of a pamphlet on the history of Islam. Khanna, the Secretary of the Hindu Sabha, was severely assaulted in 1938 by the Mahomedans after the Session of the Hindu Maha Sabha held in Ahmedabad and very narrowly escaped death.

This is, of course, a very short list and could be easily expanded. But whether the number of prominent Hindus killed by fanatic Muslims is large or small matters little. What matters is the attitude of those who count towards these murderers. The murderers paid the penalty of law where law is enforced. The leading Moslems, however, never condemned these criminals. On the contrary, they were hailed as religious martyrs and agitation was carried on for clemency being shown to them. As an illustration of this attitude, one may refer to Mr. Barkat Alli, a barrister of Lahore, who argued the appeal of Abdul Qayum. He went to the length of saying that Qayum was not guilty of murder of Nathuramal because his act was justifiable by the law of the Koran. This attitude of the Moslems is quite understandable. What is not understandable is the attitude of Mr. Gandhi.

Mr. Gandhi has been very punctilious in the matter of condemning any and every act of violence and has forced the Congress, much against its will to condemn it. But Mr. Gandhi has never protested against such murders. Not only have the Musalmans not condemned* these outrages but even Mr. Gandhi has never called upon the leading Muslims to condemn them. He has kept silent over them. Such an attitude can be explained only on the ground that Mr. Gandhi was anxious to preserve Hindu-Moslem unity and did not mind the murders of a few Hindus, if it could be achieved by sacrificing their lives.

This attitude to excuse the Muslims any wrong, lest it should injure the cause of unity, is well illustrated by what Mr. Gandhi had to say in the matter of the Mopla riots.

The blood-curdling atrocities committed by the Moplas in Malabar against the Hindus were indescribable. All over Southern India, a wave of horrified feeling had spread among the Hindus of every shade of opinion, which was intensified when certain Khilafat leaders were so misguided as to pass resolutions of "congratulations to the Moplas on the brave fight

*It is reported that for earning merit for the soul of Abdul Rashid, the murderer of Swami Shradhanand, in the next world the students and professors of the famous theological college at Deoband finished five complete recitations of the Koran and had planned to finish daily a lakh and a quarter recitations of Koranic verses. Their prayer was "God Almighty may give the marhoom (i.e. Rashid) a place in the 'a' ala-e-illeeyeen (the summit of the seventh heaven)"—*Times of India*, 30-11-27 Through Indian Eyes columns.

they were conducting for the sake of religion". Any person could have said that this was too heavy a price for Hindu-Moslem unity. But Mr. Gandhi was so much obsessed by the necessity of establishing Hindu-Moslem unity that he was prepared to make light of the doings of the Moplas and the Khilafatists who were congratulating them. He spoke of the Moplas as the "brave God-fearing Moplas who were fighting for what they consider as religion and in a manner which they consider as religious". Speaking of the Muslim silence over the Mopla atrocities Mr. Gandhi told the Hindus :—

> "The Hindus must have the courage and the faith to feel that they can protect their religion in spite of such fanatical eruptions. A verbal disapproval by the Mussalmans of Mopla madness is no test of Mussalman friendship. The Mussalmans must naturally feel the shame and humiliation of the Mopla conduct about forcible conversions and looting, and they must work away so silently and effectively that such a thing might become impossible even on the part of the most fanatical among them. My belief is that the Hindus as a body have received the Mopla madness with equanimity and that the cultured Mussalmans are sincerely sorry of the Mopla's perversion of the teaching of the Prophet."

The Resolution* passed by the Working Committee of the Congress on the Mopla atrocities shows how careful the Congress was not to hurt the feelings of the Musalmans.

> "The Working Committee places on record its sense of deep regret over the deeds of violence done by Moplas in certain areas of Malabar, these deeds being evidence of the fact that there are still people in India who have not understood the message of the Congress and the Central Khilafat Committee, and calls upon every Congress and Khilafat worker to spread the said message of non-violence even under the gravest provocation throughout the length and breadth of India.
>
> "Whilst, however, condemning violence on the part of the Moplas, the Working Committee desires it to be known that the evidence in its possession shows that provocation beyond endurance was given to the Moplas and that the reports published by

*The resolution says that there were only three cases of forcible conversion ! ! In reply to a question in the Central Legislature (Debates 16th January 1922) Sir William Vincent replied "The Madras Government reportthat the number of forcible conversions probably runs to thousands but that for obvious reasons it will never be possible to obtain anything like anaccurate estimate".

and on behalf of the Government have given a one-sided and highly exaggerated account of the wrongs done by the Moplas and an understatement of the needless destruction of life resorted to by the Government in the name of peace and order.

"The Working Committee regrets to find that there have been instances of so-called forcible conversion by some fanatics among the Moplas, but warns the public against believing in the Government and inspired versions. The Report before the Committee says:

"'The families, which have been reported to have been forcibly converted into Mahomedanism, lived in the neighbourhood of Manjeri. It is clear that conversions were forced upon Hindus by a fanatic gang which was always opposed to the Khilafat and Non-co-operation Movement and there were only three cases so far as our information goes.'"

The following instances of Muslim intransigence, over which Mr. Gandhi kept mum are recorded by Swami Shradhanand in his weekly journal called the *Liberator*. Writing in the issue of 30th September 1926 the Swamiji says:—

"As regards the removal of untouchability it has been authoritatively ruled several times that it is the duty of Hindus to expiate for their past sins and non-Hindus should have nothing to do with it. But the Mahomedan and the Christian Congressmen have openly revolted against the dictum of Gandhi at Vaikom and other places. Even such an unbiased leader as Mr. Yakub Hassan, presiding over a meeting called to present an address to me at Madras, openly enjoined upon Musalmans the duty of converting all the untouchables in India to Islam."

But Mr. Gandhi said nothing by way of remonstrance either to the Muslims or to the Christians.

In his issue of July 1926 the Swami writes:—

"There was another prominent fact to which I drew the attention of Mahatma Gandhi. Both of us went together one night to the Khilafat Conference at Nagpur. The Ayats (verses) of the Quoran recited by the Maulanas on that occasion, contained frequent references to Jihad and against, killing of the Kaffirs. But when I drew his attention to this phase of the Khilafat movement, Mahatmaji smiled and said, 'They are alluding to the British Bureaucracy.' In reply I said that it was all subversive of the idea of non-violence and when the reversion of feeling came the Mahomedan Maulanas would not refrain from using these verses against the Hindus."

The Swami's third instance relates to the Mopla riots. Writing in the *Liberator* of 26th August 1926 the Swami says:—

> "The first warning was sounded when the question of condemning the Moplas for their atrocities on Hindus came up in the Subjects Committee. The original resolution condemned the Moplas wholesale for the killing of Hindus and burning of Hindu homes and the forcible conversion to Islam. The Hindu members themselves proposed amendments till it was reduced to condemning only certain individuals who had been guilty of the above crimes. But some of the Moslem leaders could not bear this even. Maulana Fakir and other Maulanas, of course, opposed the resolution and there was no wonder. But I was surprised, an out-and-out Nationalist like Maulana Hasrat Mohani opposed the resolution on the ground that the Mopla country no longer remained Dar-ul-Aman but became Dar-ul-Harab and as they suspected the Hindus of collusion with the British enemies of the Moplas. Therefore, the Moplas were right in presenting the Quoran or sword to the Hindus. And if the Hindus became Mussalmans to save themselves from death, it was a voluntary change of faith and not forcible conversion—Well, even the harmless resolution condemning some of the Moplas was not unanimously passed but had to be accepted by a majority of votes only. There were other indications also, showing that the Mussalmans considered the Congress to be existing on their sufferance and if there was the least attempt to ignore their idiosyncrasies the superficial unity would be scrapped asunder."

The last one refers to the burning of the foreign cloth started by Mr. Gandhi. Writing in the *Liberator* of 13th August 1926 the Swamiji says:—

> "While people came to the conclusion, that the burning of foreign cloth was a religious duty of Indians and Messrs. Das, Nehru and other topmost leaders made bon-fire of cloth worth thousands, the Khilafat Musalmans got permission from Mahatmaji to *send all foreign cloth for the use* of the Turkish brethren. This again was a great shock to me. While Mahatmaji stood adamant and did not have the least regard for Hindu feelings when a question of principle was involved, for the Moslem dereliction of duty, there was always a soft corner in his heart."

In the history of his efforts to bring about Hindu-Moslem unity mention must be made of two incidents. One is the Fast, which Mr. Gandhi underwent in the year 1924. It was a fast of 21 days. Before undertaking the fast Mr. Gandhi explained the reasons for it in a statement from which the following extracts are taken:—

"The fact that Hindus and Musalmans, who were only two years ago apparently working together as friends, are now fighting like cats and dogs in some places, shows conclusively that the non-co-operation they offered was not non-violent. I saw the symptoms in Bombay, Chauri Chaura and in a host of minor cases. I did penance then. It had its effects *protanto*. But this Hindu-Muslim tension was unthinkable. It became unbearable on hearing of the Kohat tragedy. On the eve of my departure from Sabarmati for Delhi, Sarojini Devi wrote to me that speeches and homilies on peace would not do. I must find out an effective remedy. She was right in saddling the responsibility on me. Had I not been instrumental in bringing into being the vast energy of the people? I must find the remedy if the energy proved self-destructive.

* * *

"I was violently shaken by Amethi, Sambhal and Gulbarga. I had read the reports about Amethi and Sambhal prepared by Hindu and Musalman friends. I had learnt the joint finding of Hindu and Musalman friends who went to Gulbarga. I was writing in deep pain and yet I had no remedy. The news of Kohat set the smouldering mass aflame. Something had got to be done. I passed two nights in restlessness and pain. On Wednesday I knew the remedy. I must do penance.

"It is a warning to the Hindus and Musalmans who have professed to love me. If they have loved me truly and if I have been deserving of their love, they will do penance with me for the grave sin of denying God in their hearts.

"The penance of Hindus and Mussalmans is not fasting but retracing their steps. It is true penance for a Mussalman to harbour no ill-will for his Hindu brother and an equally true penance for a Hindu to harbour none for his Mussalman brother.

"I did not consult friends—not even Hakim Saheb who was closeted with me for a long time on Wednesday—not Maulana Mahomed Ali under whose roof I am enjoying the privilege of hospitality.

"But was it right for me to go through the fast under a Mussalman roof? (Gandhi was at the time the guest of Mr. Mahomed Ali at Delhi). Yes, it was. The fast is not born out of ill-will against a single soul. My being under a Mussalman roof ensures it against any such interpretation. It is in the fitness of things that this fast should be taken up and completed in a Mussalman house.

"And who is Mahomed Ali? Only two days before the fast we had a discussion about a private matter in which I told him what was mine was his and what was his was mine. Let me gratefully tell the public that I have never received warmer or better treatment than under Mahomed Ali's roof. Every want of mine is anticipated. The dominant thought of every one of his household is to make me and mine happy and comfortable. Doctors Ansari and Abdur Rehman have constituted themselves my medical advisers. They examine me daily. I have had many a happy occasion in my life. This is no less happy than the previous ones. Bread is not everything. I am experiencing here the richest love. It is more than bread for me.

"It has been whispered that by going so much with Mussalman friends, I make myself unfit to know the Hindu mind. The Hindu mind is myself. Surely I do not live amidst Hindus to know the Hindu mind when every fibre of my being is Hindu. My Hinduism must be a very poor thing if it cannot flourish under influnces the most adverse. I know instinctively what is necessary for Hinduism. But I must labour to discover the Mussalman mind. The closer I come to the best of Mussalmans, the juster I am likely to be in my estimate of the Mussalmans and their doings. I am striving to become the best cement between the two communities. My longing is to be able to cement the two with my blood, if necessary. But, before I can do so, I must prove to the Mussalmans that I love them as well as I love the Hindus. My religion teaches me to love all equally. May God help me to do so! My fast among other things is meant to qualify me for achieving that equal and selfless love."

The fast produced Unity Conferences. But the Unity Conferences produced nothing except pious resolutions which were broken as soon as they were announced.

This short historical sketch of the part Mr. Gandhi played in bringing about Hindu-Moslem unity may be concluded by a reference to the attitude of Mr. Gandhi in the negotiations about the Communal Settlement. He offered the Muslims a blank cheque. The blank cheque only served to exasperate the Muslims as they interpreted it as an act of evasion. He opposed the separate electorates at the Round Table Conference. When they were given to the Muslims by the Communal Award, Mr. Gandhi and the Congress did not approve of them. But when it came to voting upon it, they took the strange attitude of neither approving it nor opposing it.

Such is the history of Mr. Gandhi's efforts to bring about Hindu-Moslem unity. What fruits did these efforts bear? To be able to answer this question it is necessary to examine the relationship between the two communities during 1920-40, the years during which Mr. Gandhi laboured so hard to bring about Hindu-Moslem unity. The relationship is well described in the Annual Reports on the affairs of India submitted year by year to Parliament by the Government of India under the old Government of India Act. It is on these reports* that I have drawn for the facts recorded below.

Beginning with the year 1920 there occurred in that year in Malabar what is known as the Mopla Rebellion. It was the result of the agitation carried out by two Muslim organizations, the Khuddam-i-Kaba (servants of the Mecca Shrine) and the Central Khilafat Committee. Agitators actually preached the doctrine that India under the British Government was Dar-ul-Harab and that the Muslims must fight against it and if they could not, they must carry out the alternative principle of *Hijrat*. The Moplas were suddenly carried off their feet by this agitation. The outbreak was essentially a rebellion against the British Government. The aim was to establish the kingdom of Islam by overthrowing the British Government. Knives, swords and spears were secretly manufactured, bands of desperadoes collected for an attack on British authority. On 20th August a severe encounter took place between the Moplas and the British forces at Pirunangdi. Roads were blocked, telegraph lines cut, and the railway destroyed in a number of places. As soon as the administration had been paralysed, the Moplas declared that Swaraj had been established. A certain Ali Musaliar was proclaimed Raja, Khilafat flags were flown, and Ernad and Walluranad were declared Khilafat Kingdoms. As a rebellion against the British Government it was quite understandable. But what baffled most was the treatment accorded by the Moplas to the Hindus of Malabar. The Hindus were visited by a dire fate at the hands of the Moplas. Massacres, forcible conversions, desecration of temples, foul outrages upon women, such as ripping open pregnant women, pillage, arson and destruction—in short, all the accompaniments of brutal and unrestrained barbarism, were perpetrated freely by the Moplas upon the Hindus until

* The series is known as "India in 1920" & so on.

such time as troops could be hurried to the task of restoring order through a difficult and extensive tract of the country. This was not a Hindu-Moslem riot. This was just a Bartholomew. The number of Hindus who were killed, wounded or converted, is not known. But the number must have been enormous.

In the year 1921-22 communal jealousies did not subside. The Muharram Celebrations had been attended by serious riots both in Bengal and in the Punjab. In the latter province in particular, communal feeling at Multan reached very serious heights, and although the casualty list was comparatively small, a great deal of damage to property was done.

Though the year 1922-23 was a peaceful year the relations between the two communities were strained throughout 1923-24. But in no locality did this tension produce such tragic consequences as in the city of Kohat. The immediate cause of the trouble was the publication and circulation of a pamphlet containing a virulently anti-Islamic poem. Terrible riots broke out on the 9th and 10th of September 1924, the total casualties being about 155 killed and wounded. House property to the estimated value of Rs. 9 lakhs was destroyed, and a large quantity of goods were looted. As a result of this reign of terror the whole Hindu population evacuated the city of Kohat. After protracted negotiations an agreement of reconciliation was concluded between the two communities, Government giving an assurance that, subject to certain reservations, the prosecution pending against persons concerned in rioting should be dropped. With the object of enabling the sufferers to restart their businesses and rebuild their houses, Government sanctioned advances, free of interest in certain instances, amounting to Rs. 5 lakhs. But even after the settlement had been reached and evacuees had returned to Kohat there was no peace and throughout 1924-25 the tension between the Hindu and Musalman masses in various parts of the country increased to a lamentable extent. In the summer months, there was a distressing number of riots. In July, severe fighting broke out between Hindus and Musalmans in Delhi, which was accompanied by serious casualties. In the same month, there was a bad outbreak at Nagpur. August was even worse. There were riots at Lahore, at Lucknow, at Moradabad, at Bhagalpur and Nagpur in British India; while a severe affray took place at

Gulbarga in the Nizam's Dominions. September-October saw severe fighting at Lucknow, Shahajahanpur, Kankinarah and at Allahabad. The most terrible outbreak of the year being the one that took place at Kohat which was accompanied by murder, arson and loot.

In 1925-26 the antagonism between the Hindus and the Muslims became widespread. Very significant features of the Hindu-Muslim rioting, which took place during this year were its wide distribution and its occurrence, in some cases, in small villages. Calcutta, the United Provinces, the Central Provinces and the Bombay Presidency were all scenes of riots, some of which led to regrettable losses of life. Certain minor and local Hindu festivals which occurred at the end of August, gave rise to communal trouble in Calcutta, in Berar, in Gujarat in the Bombay Presidency, and in the United Provinces. In some of these places there were actual clashes between the two communities, but elsewhere, notably at Kankinarah—one of the most thickly populated jute mill centres of Calcutta—serious rioting was prevented by the activity of the police. In Gujarat, Hindu-Muslim feeling was running high in these days and was marked by at least one case of temple desecration. The important Hindu festival of Ramlila, at the end of September, gave rise to acute anxiety in many places, and at Aligarh, an important place in the United Provinces, its celebration was marked by one of the worst riots of the year. The riot assumed such dangerous proportions that the police were compelled to fire in order to restore order, and five persons were killed, either by the police or by rioters. At Lucknow, the same festival gave rise at one time to a threatening situation, but the local authorities prevented actual rioting. October saw another serious riot at Sholapur in the Bombay Presidency. There, the local Hindus were taking a car with Hindu idols through the city, and when they came near a mosque, a dispute arose between them and certain Muslims, which developed into a riot.

A deplorable rioting started in Calcutta in the beginning of April as an affray outside a mosque between Muslims and some Arya Samajists and continued to spread until 5th April, though there was only one occasion on which the police or military were faced by a crowd which showed determined resistance, namely, on the evening of the 5th April, when fire had to be opened. There was also a great deal of incendiarism and in the first three days of this incendiarism, the Fire Brigade had to deal with 110 fires. An unprecedented feature of the riots was the attacks on temples by Muslims and on mosques by Hindus which naturally led to intense bitterness. There were 44 deaths and 584 persons were injured. There was a certain amount of looting and business was suspended, with great economic loss to Calcutta. Shops began to reopen soon after the 5th, but the period of tension was prolonged by the approach of a Hindu festival on the 13th of April, and of the Id on the 14th. The Sikhs were to have taken out a procession on the 13th, but Government were unable to give them the necessary license. The apprehensions with regard to the 13th and 14th of April, fortunately, did not materialise and outward peace prevailed until the 22nd April when it was abruptly broken as a result of a petty quarrel in a street, which restarted the rioting. Fighting between the mobs of the two communities, generally on a small scale, accompanied by isolated assaults and murders continued for six days. During this period there were no attacks on the temples or mosques and there was little arson or looting. But there were more numerous occasions, on which the hostile mobs did not immediately disperse on the appearance of the police and on 12 occasions it was necessary to open fire. The total number of casualties during this second phase of the rioting was 66 deaths and 391 injured. The dislocation of business was much more serious during the first riots and the closing of Marwari business houses was not without an effect on European business firms. Panic caused many of the markets to be wholly or partially closed and for two days the meat supply was practically stopped. So great was the panic that the removal of refuse in the disturbed area was stopped. Arrangements were, however, made to protect supplies, and the difficulty with the Municipal scavengers was overcome, as soon as the Municipality had applied to the police for protection. There was slight extension of the area of rioting, but no disturbances occurred in the mill area around Calcutta. Systematic raiding of the portions of the disturbed area, the arrest of hooligans, the seizure of weapons and the re-inforcement of the police by the posting of British soldiers to act as special police officers had the desired effect, and the last three days of April, in spite of the continuance of isolated assaults and murders, witnessed a steady improvement in the situation. Isolated murders were largely attributable to hooligans of both communities and their persistence during the first as well as the second outbreak induced a general belief that these hooligans were hired assassins. Another equally persistent feature of the riots, namely, the distribution of inflammatory printed leaflets by both sides, together with the employment of hired roughs, strengthened the belief that money had been spent to keep the riots going.

The year 1926-27 was one continuous period of communal riots. Since April 1926, every month witnessed affrays more or less serious between partizans of the two communities and only two months passed without actual rioting in the legal sense of the word. The examination of the circumstances of these numerous riots and affrays shows that they originated either in utterly petty and trivial disputes between individuals, as, for example, between a Hindu shopkeeper and a Mahomedan customer, or else, the immediate cause of trouble was the celebration of some religious festival or the playing of music by Hindu processionists in the neighbourhood of Mahomedan places of worship. One or two of the riots, indeed, were due to nothing more than strained nerves and general excitement. Of these, the most striking example occurred in Delhi on 24th June, when the bolting of a pony in a crowded street gave the impression that a riot had started, upon which both sides immediately attacked each other with brickbats and staves.

Including the two outbursts of rioting in Calcutta during April and May 1926, 40 riots took place during the twelve months ending with April 1st 1927, resulting in the death of 197 and in injuries, more or less severe, to 1,598 persons. These disorders were wide-spread, but Bengal, the Punjab, and the United Provinces were the parts of India most seriously affected. Bengal suffered most from rioting, but on many occasions during the year, tension between Hindus and Mahomedans was high in the Bombay Presidency and also in Sind.

Calcutta remained uneasy throughout the whole of the summer. On 1st June a petty dispute developed into a riot in which forty persons were hurt. After this, there was a lull in overt violence until July 15th on which day fell an important Hindu religious festival. During its celebration the passage of a procession, with bands playing in the neighbourhood of certain mosques, resulted in a conflict, in which 14 persons were killed and 116 injured. The next day saw the beginning of the important Mahomedan festival of Muharram. Rioting broke out on that day and, after a lull, was renewed on the 19th, 20th, 21st and 22nd. Isolated assaults and cases of stabbing occurred on the 23rd, 24th and 25th. The total ascertained casualties during this period of rioting were 28 deaths and 226 injured. There were further riots in Calcutta on the 15th September and 16th October and on the latter day there was also rioting in the adjoining city of Howrah, during which one or two persons were killed and over 30 injured. The April and May riots had been greatly aggravated by incendiarism, but, happily, this feature was almost entirely absent from the later disorders and during the July riots, for example, the Fire Brigade was called upon to deal with only four incendiary fires.

Coming to the year 1927-28 the following facts stare us in the face. Between the beginning of April and the end of September 1927, no fewer than 25 riots were reported. Of these 10 occurred in the United Provinces, six in the Bombay Presidency, 2 each in the Punjab, the Central Provinces, Bengal, and Bihar and Orissa, and one in Delhi. The majority of these riots occurred during the celebration of a religious festival by one or other of the two communities, whilst some arose out of the playing of music by Hindus in the neighbourhood of mosques or out of the slaughter of cows by the Muslims. The total casualties resulting from the above disorders were approximately 103 persons killed and 1,084 wounded.

By far the most serious riot reported during the year was that which took place in Lahore between the 4th and 7th of May 1927. Tension between the two communities had been acute for some time before the outbreak, and the trouble when it came was precipitated by a chance collision between a Mahomedan and two Sikhs. The disorder spread with lightning speed and the heavy casualty list—27 killed 272 injured—was largely swollen by unorganised attacks on individuals. Police and troops were rushed to the scene of rioting quickly and it was impossible for clashes on a big scale to take place between hostile groups. Casual assassinations and assaults were however, reported, for two or three days longer before the streets and lanes of Lahore became safe for the solitary passerby.

After the Lahore riot in May, there was a lull for two months in inter-communal rioting, if we except a minor incident, which happened about the middle of June in Bihar and Orissa; but July witnessed no fewer than eight riots of which the most serious occurred in Multan in the Punjab, on the occasion of the annual Muharram celebrations. Thirteen killed and twenty-four wounded was the toll taken by this riot. But August was to see worse rioting still. In that month, nine riots occurred, two of them resulting in heavy loss of life. In a riot in Bettiah, a town in Bihar and Orissa, arising out of a dispute over a religious procession, eleven persons were killed and over a hundred injured, whilst the passage of a procession in front of a mosque in Bareilly in the United Provinces was the occasion of rioting in which fourteen persons were killed and 165 were injured. Fortunately, this proved to be the turning point in inter-communal trouble during the year, and September witnessed only 4 riots. One of these, however, the riot in Nagpur in the Central Provinces on September 4th, was second only to the Lahore riot in seriousness and in the damage which it caused. The spark, which started the fire, was the trouble in connection with a Muslim procession, but the materials for the combustion had been collected for some time. Nineteen persons were killed and 123 injured were admitted to hospitals as a result of this riot, during the course of which many members of the Muslim community abandoned their homes in Nagpur.

A feature of Hindu-Muslim relations during the year which was hardly less serious than the riots was the number of murderous outrages committed by members of one community against persons belonging to the other. Some of the most serious of these outrages were perpetrated in connection with the agitation relating to *Rangila Rasul* and *Risala Vartman*, two publications containing most scurrilous attack on the Prophet Muhammed and as a result of them, a number of innocent persons lost their lives, sometimes in circumstances of great barbarity. In Lahore a series of outrages against individuals led to a state of great excitement and insecurity during the summer of 1927.

The excitement over the *Rangila Rasul** case had by now travelled far from its original centre and by July had begun to produce unpleasant repercussions on and across the North-West Frontier. The first signs of trouble in this region became apparent early in June, and by the latter part of July the excitement had reached its height. On the British side of the border, firm and tactful handling of the situation by the local authorities averted, what would have been a serious breach of the peace. Economic boycott of Hindus was freely advocated in the British Frontier Districts, especially in Peshawar, but this movement met with little success, and although the Hindus were maltreated in one or two villages, the arrest of the culprits, together with appropriate action under the Criminal Law, quickly restored order. Across the border however, the indignation, aroused by these attacks on the Prophet, gave rise to more serious consequences. The Frontier tribesmen are acutely sensitive to the appeal of religion and when a well-known Mullah started to preach against the Hindus among the Afridis and Shinwaris in the neighbourhood of the Khyber Pass, his words fell on fruitful ground. He called upon the Afridis and Shinwaris to expel all the Hindus living in their midst unless they declared in writing that they dissociated themselves from the doings of their co-religionists down country. The first to expel their Hindu neighbours were two clans of the Khyber Afridis, namely the Kuikhel and Zakkakhel, on the 22nd of July. From these, the excitement spread among their Shinwari neighbours, who gave their Hindu neighbours notice to quit a few days later. However, after the departure of some of the Hindus, the Shinwaris agreed to allow the remainder

* *Rangila Rasul* was written in reply to *Sitaka Chinala*—a pamphlet written by a Muslim alleging that Sita, wife of Rama, the hero of Ramayana, was a prostitute.

to stay on. Some of the Hindus on leaving the Khyber were roughly handled. In two cases, stones were thrown, though happily without any damage resulting. In a third case, a Hindu was wounded and a large amount of property carried off, but this was recovered by Afridi Khassadars in full, and the culprits were fined for the offence. Thereafter, arrangements were made for the picketing of the road for the passage of any Hindus evacuating tribal territory. Under pressure from the Political Agent an Afridi *jirga* decided towards the end of July to suspend the Hindu boycott pending a decision in the Risala Vartman case. In the following week, however, several Hindu families, who had been living at Landi Kotal at the head of the Khyber Pass moved to Peshawar refusing to accept the assurances of the tribal chiefs but leaving one person from each family behind to watch over their interests. All told, between four hundred and four hundred and fifty Hindus, men, women and children, had come into Peshawar by the middle of August, when the trouble was definitely on the wane. Some of the Hindus were definitely expelled, some were induced to leave their homes by threats, some left from fear, some no doubt from sympathy with their neighbours. This expulsion and voluntary exodus from tribal territory were without parallel. Hindus had lived there for more generations than most of them could record as valued and respected, and, indeed, as essential members of the tribal system, for whose protection the tribesmen had been jealous, and whose blood feuds they commonly made their own. In all, about 450 Hindus left the Khyber during the excitement; of these, about 330 had returned to their homes in tribal territory by the close of the year 1927. Most of the remainder had decided to settle, at any rate for the present, amid the more secure conditions of British India.

The year 1928-29 was comparatively more peaceful than the year 1927-28. His Excellency Lord Irwin, by his speeches to the Central Legislature and outside, had given a strong impetus to the attempts to find some basis for agreement between the two communities, on those questions of political importance, which were responsible for the strained relations between them. Fortunately the issues arising out of the inquiry by the Simon Commission which was appointed in 1929, absorbed a large part of the energy and attention of the different communities, with the result that less importance came to be attached to local causes of conflict, and more importance to the broad question of constitutional policy. Moreover, the legislation passed during the autumn session of the Indian Legislature in 1927 penalising the instigation of inter-communal hostility by the press, had some effect in improving the inter-communal position. But the year was not altogether free from communal disturbances. The number of riots during the twelve months ending with March 31st, 1929, was 22. Though the number of riots was comparatively small, the casualties,—swelled heavily by the Bombay riots,—were very serious, no fewer than 204 persons having been killed and nearly a thousand injured. Of these, the fortnight's rioting in Bombay accounts for 149 killed and 739 injured. Seven of these 22 riots, or roughly one-third of them, occurred on the day of the celebration of the annual Muslim festival of Bakr-i-Id at the end of May. The celebration of this festival is always a dangerous time in Hindu-Muslim relations. The Muslims regard it as a day of animal sacrifice, and as the animal chosen is almost always a cow the slightest tension between the two communities is apt to produce an explosion. Of the Bakr-i-Id riots only two were serious and both of them took place in the Punjab. The first took place in a village in the Ambala District in which ten people were killed and nine injured. The other riot which took place in Softa village in the Gurgaon District in the Southern Punjab, attained considerable notoriety because of its sensational features. The village of Softa is about 27 miles south of Delhi and is inhabited by Muslims. This village is surrounded by villages occupied by Hindu cultivators who, on hearing that the Muslims of Softa intended to sacrifice a cow on the 'Id Day', objected to the sacrifice of the particular cow selected on the ground that it had been accustomed to graze in fields belonging to the Hindu cultivators. The dispute over the matter assumed a threatening aspect and the Superintendent of Police of the district accordingly went with a small force of police, about 25 men in all, to try to keep peace. He took charge of the disputed cow and locked it up, but his presence did not deter the Hindu cultivators of a few neighbouring villages from collecting about a thousand people armed with pitchforks, spears and staves, and going to Softa. The Superintendent of Police and an Indian Revenue official, who were present in the village, assured the crowd that the cow, in connection with which the dispute had arisen would not be sacrificed, but this did not satisfy the mob which threatened to burn the whole village if any cow was sacrificed, and also demanded that the cow should be handed over to them. The Superintendent of Police refused to agree to this demand, whereupon the crowd became violent and began to throw stones at the police and to try to get round the latter into the village. The Superintendent of Police warned the crowd to disperse, but to no effect. He, therefore, fired one shot from his revolver as a further warning. Notwithstanding the crowd still continued to advance and the Superintendent had to order his party of police to fire. Only one volley was fired at first, but as this did not cause the retreat of the mob, two more volleys had to be fired before the crowd slowly dispersed, driving off some cattle belonging to the village.

While the police were engaged in this affair a few Hindu cultivators got into Softa at another place and tried to set fire to the village. These were, however, driven away by the police after they had inflicted injuries on three or four men. In all 14 persons were killed and 33 were injured. The Punjab Government deputed a judicial officer to enquire into this affair. His report, which was published on 6th July, justified the action of the police in firing on the mob and recorded the opinion that there was no reason to suppose that the firing was excessive or was continued after the mob had desisted from its unlawful aggression. Had the police not opened fire, the report proceeds, their own lives would have been in immediate danger, as also the lives of the people of Softa. Lastly, in the opinion of the officer writing the report, had Softa village been sacked, there would certainly have broken up, within 24 hours, a terrible communal conflagration in the whole of the surrounding country-side.

The riots of Kharagpur, an important railway centre not far from Calcutta, also resulted in serious loss of life. Two riots took place at Kharagpur, the first on the occasion of the Muharram celebration at the end of June and the second on the 1st

September 1928, when the killing of a cow served as a cause. In the first riot 15 were killed and 21 injured, while in the second riot, the casualties were 9 killed and 35 wounded. But none of these riots is to be compared with those that raged in Bombay from the beginning to the middle of February, when, as we have seen, 149 persons were killed and well over 700 injured.

During the year 1929-30 communal riots, which had been so conspicuous and deplorable a feature of public life during the preceding years, were very much less frequent. Only 12 were of sufficient importance to be reported to Government of India, and of these only the disturbances in the City of Bombay were really serious. Starting on the 23rd of April they continued sporadically until the middle of May, and were responsible for 35 deaths and about 200 other casualties. An event which caused considerable tension in April was the murder at Lahore of Rajpal, whose pamphlet *Rangila Rasul*, containing a scurrilous attack on the Prophet of Islam, was responsible for much of the communal trouble in previous years, and also for a variety of legal and political complications. Fortunately, both communities showed commendable restraint at the time of the murder, and again on the occasion of the execution and funeral of the convicted man; and although feelings ran high no serious trouble occurred.

The year 1930-31 saw the eruption of the Civil Disobedience Movement. It gave rise to riots and disturbances all over the country. They were mostly of a political character and the parties involved in them were the police and the Congress volunteers. But, as it always happens in India, the political disturbances took a communal twist. This was due to the fact that the Muslims refused to submit to the coercive methods used by Congress volunteers to compel them to join in Civil Disobedience. The result was that although the year began with political riots it ended in numerous and quite serious communal riots. The worst of these communal riots took place in and around Sukkur in Sind between the 4th and 11th of August and affected over a hundred villages. The outbreak in the Kishoreganj sub-division of Mymensingh District (Bengal) on the 12th/15th of July was also on a large scale. In addition, there were communal disturbances on the 3rd of August in Ballia (United Provinces); on the 6th of September in Nagpur, and on the 6th/7th September in Bombay; and a Hindu-Christian riot broke out near Tiruchendur (Madras) on the 31st of October. On the 12th of February, in Amritsar, an attempt was made to murder a Hindu cloth merchant who had defied the picketers, and a similar outrage which was perpetrated the day before in Benares had very serious consequences. On this occasion, the victim was a Muslim trader, and the attack proved fatal; as a result, since Hindu-Muslim relations throughout most of Northern India were by this time very strained, a serious communal riot broke out and continued for five days, causing great destruction of property and numerous casualties. Among the other communal clashes during this period were the riots at Nilphamari (Bengal) on the 25th of January and at Rawalpindi on the 31st. Throughout Northern India communal relations had markedly deteriorated during the first two months of 1931, and already, in February, there had been serious communal rioting in Benares. This state of affairs was due chiefly to the increasing exasperation created among Muslims by the paralysis of trade and the general atmosphere of unrest and confusion that resulted from Congress activities. The increased importance which the Congress seemed to be acquiring as a result of the negotiations with the Government aroused in the Muslims serious apprehensions and had the effect of worsening the tension between the two communities. During March, this tension, in the United Provinces at any rate, became greatly increased. Between the 14th and 16th there was serious rioting in the Mirzapur District, and on the 17th, trouble broke out in Agra and continued till the 20th. There was also a communal riot in Dhanbad (Bengal) on the 28th, and in Amritsar District on the 30th; and in many other parts of the country, the relations between members of the two communities had become extremely strained.

In Assam, the communal riot which occurred at Digboi in Lakhimpur District, resulted in the deaths of one Hindu and three Muslims. In Bengal, a communal riot took place in the Asansol division during the Muharram festival. In Bihar and Orissa there was a certain amount of communal tension during the year, particularly in Saran. Altogether there were 16 cases of communal rioting and unlawful assembly. During the Bakr-i-Id festival a clash occurred in the Bhabua sub-division of Shahabad. Some 300 Hindus collected in the mistaken belief that a cow had been sacrificed. The local officers had succeeded in pacifying them when a mob of about 200 Muhammadans armed with lathis, spears and swords, attacked the Hindus, one of whom subsequently died. The prompt action of the police and the appointment of a conciliation committee prevented the spread of the trouble. The Muharram festival was marked by two small riots in Monghyr, the Hindus being the aggressors on one occasion and the Muslims on the other. In the Madras Presidency there were also several riots of a communal nature during the year and the relations between the communities were in places distinctly strained. The most serious disturbance of the year occurred at Vellore on the 8th of June, as a result of the passage of a Muslim procession with Tazias near a Hindu temple; so violent was the conflict between members of the two communities that the police were compelled to open fire in order to restore order; and sporadic fighting continued in the town during the next two or three days. In Salem town, owing to Hindu-Muslim tension a dispute arose on the 13th of July, as to who had been the victor at a largely attended Hindu-Muslim wrestling match at Shevapet. Another riot occurred in October at Kitchipalaiyam near Salem town; the trouble arose from a few Muslims disturbing a street game played by some young Hindus. Hindu-Muslim disturbances also arose in Polikal village, Kurnool District, on the 15th of March, owing to a dispute about the route of a Hindu procession, but the rioters were easily dispersed by a small force of police. In the Punjab there were 907 cases of rioting during the year as compared with 813 in 1929. Many of them were of a communal character, and the tension between the two principal communities remained acute in many parts of the Province. In the United Provinces, although communal tension during 1930 was not nearly so acute as during the first 3 months of 1931, and was for a while overshadowed by the excitement engendered by the Civil Disobedience Movement, indications of it were fairly numerous, and the causes of disagreement remained as potent as ever. In Dehra Dun and Bulandshahr there were communal riots of the usual type, and a very serious riot occurred in Ballia city as a result of a dispute concerning the route taken by a Hindu procession, which necessitated firing by the police. Riots also occurred in Muttra, Azamgarh, Mainpuri and several other places.

Passing on to the events of the year 1931-32, the progress of constitutional discussions at the R.T.C. had a definite reaction in that it bred a certain nervousness among the Muslim and other minority communities as to their position under a constitution functioning on the majority principle. The first session of the Round Table Conference afforded the first "close-up" of the constitutional future. Until then the ideal of Dominion Status had progressed little beyond a vague and general conception, but the declaration of the Princes at the opening of the Conference had brought responsibility at the Centre, in the form of a federal government, within definite view. The Muslims, therefore, felt that it was high time for them to take stock of their position. This uneasiness was intensified by the Irwin-Gandhi settlement, which accorded what appeared to be a privileged position to the Congress, and Congress elation and pose of victory over the Government did not tend to ease Muslim misgivings. Within three weeks of the "pact" occurred the savage communal riots at Cawnpore, which significantly enough began with the attempts of Congress adherents to force Mahomedan shopkeepers to observe a *hartal* in memory of Bhagat Singh who was executed on 23rd March. On the 24th March began the plunder of Hindu shops. On the 25th there was a blaze. Shops and temples were set fire to and burnt to cinders. Disorder, arson, loot, murder, spread like wild fire. Five hundred families abandoned their houses and took shelter in villages. Dr. Ramchandra was one of the worst sufferers. All members of his family, including his wife and aged parents, were killed and their bodies thrown into gutters. In the same slaughter Mr. Ganesh Shanker Vidyarthi lost his life. The Cawnpore Riots Inquiry Committee in its report states that the riot was of unprecedented violence and peculiar atrocity, which spread with unexpected rapidity through the whole city and even beyond it. Murders, arson and looting were wide-spread for three days, before the rioting was definitely brought under control. Afterwards it subsided gradually. The loss of life and property was great. The number of verified deaths was 300, but the death roll is known to have been larger and was probably between four and five hundred. A large number of temples and mosques were desecrated or burnt or destroyed and a very large number of houses were burnt and pillaged.

This communal riot, which need never have occurred but for the provocative conduct of the adherents of the Congress, was the worst which India has experienced for many years. The trouble, moreover, spread from the city to the neighbouring villages, where there were sporadic communal disturbances for several days afterwards.

The year 1932-33 was relatively free from communal agitations and disturbances. This welcome improvement was doubtless in some measure due to the suppression of lawlessness generally and the removal of uncertainty in regard to the position of the Muslims under the new constitution.

But in 1933-34 throughout the country communal tension had been increasing and disorders which occurred not only on the occasion of such festivals as Holi, Id and Muharram, but also many resulting from ordinary incidents of every-day life indicated, that there had been a deterioration in communal relations since the year began. Communal riots during Holi occurred at Benares and Cawnpore in the United Provinces, at Lahore in the Punjab, and at Peshawar. Bakr-i-Id was marked by serious rioting at Ajodhya, in the United Provinces over cow sacrifice, also at Bhagalpore in Bihar and Orissa and at Cannanore in Madras. A serious riot in the Ghazipur District of the United Provinces also resulted in several deaths. During April and May there were Hindu-Muslim riots at several places in Bihar and Orissa, in Bengal, in Sind and Delhi, some of them provoked by very trifling incidents, as for instance, the unintentional spitting by a Muslim shopkeeper of Delhi upon a Hindu passer-by. The increase in communal disputes in British India was also reflected in some of the States where similar incidents occurred.

The position with regard to communal unrest during the months from June to October was indicative of the normal, deep-seated antagonism between the two major communities. June and July months, in which no Hindu or Muhammadan festival of importance took place, were comparatively free from riots, though the situation in certain areas of Bihar necessitated the quartering of additional police. A long-drawn-out dispute started in Agra. The Muslims of this city objected to the noise of religious ceremonies in certain Hindu private houses which they said disturbed worshippers at prayers in a neighbouring mosque. Before the dispute was settled, riots occurred on the 20th July and again on the 2nd September, in the course of which 4 persons were killed and over 80 injured. In Madras a riot, on the 3rd September resulting in one death and injuries to 13 persons, was occasioned by a book published by Hindus containing alleged reflections on the Prophet. During the same month minor riots occurred in several places in the Punjab and the United Provinces.

In 1934-35 serious trouble arose in Lahore on the 29th June as a result of a dispute between Muslims and Sikhs about a mosque situated within the precincts of a Sikh temple known as the Shahidganj Gurudwara. Trouble had been brewing for some time. Ill-feeling became intensified when the Sikhs started to demolish the mosque despite Muslim protests. The building had been in possession of the Sikhs for 170 years and has been the subject of prolonged litigation, which has confirmed the Sikh right of possession.

On the night of the 29th June a crowd of 3 or 4 thousand Muslims assembled in front of the Gurudwara. A struggle between this crowd and the Sikhs inside the Gurudwara was only averted by the prompt action of the local authorities. They subsequently obtained an undertaking from the Sikhs to refrain from further demolition. But during the following week, while strenuous efforts were being made to persuade the leaders to reach an amicable settlement, the Sikhs under pressure of extremist influence again set about demolishing the mosque. This placed the authorities in a most difficult position. The Sikhs were acting within their legal rights. Moreover the only effective method of stopping demolition would have been to resort to firing. As the building was full of Sikhs and was within the precincts of a Sikh place of worship, this would not only have caused much bloodshed but, for religious reasons, would have had serious reactions on the Sikh population throughout the Province. On the other hand, inaction by Government was bound to cause great indignation among the Muslims, for religious reasons: and it was expected that this would show itself in sporadic attacks on the Sikhs and perhaps on the forces of Government.

It was hoped that discussions between leaders of the two communities would effect some rapprochement, but mischief-makers inflamed the minds of their co-religionists. Despite the arrest of the chief offenders, the excitement increased. The Government's gesture in offering to restore to the Muslims another mosque which they had purchased years ago proved unavailing. The situation took a further turn for the worse on the 19th July and during the following two days the situation was acutely dangerous. The Central Police station was practically besieged by huge crowds, which assumed a most menacing attitude. Repeated attempts to disperse them without the use of firearms failed and the troops had to fire twice on the 20th July and eight times on the 21st. In all 23 rounds were fired and 12 persons killed. Casualties, mostly of a minor nature, were numerous amongst the military and police.

As a result of the firing, the crowds dispersed and did not re-assemble. Extra police were brought in from other Provinces and the military garrisons were strengthened. Administrative control was re-established rapidly, but the religious leaders continued to fan the embers of the agitation. Civil litigation was renewed and certain Muslim organisations framed some extravagant demands.

The situation in Lahore continued to cause anxiety up to the close of the year. On the 6th November, a Sikh was mortally wounded by a Muslim. Three days later a huge Sikh-Hindu procession was taken out. The organisers appeared anxious to avoid conflict but nonetheless one serious clash occurred. This was followed by further rioting on the next day. But for the good work of the police and the troops, in breaking up the fights quickly, the casualties might have been very large.

On the 19th March 1935 a serious incident occurred in Karachi after the execution of Abdul Quayum, the Muslim who had murdered Nathuramal, a Hindu, already referred to as the writer of a scurrilous pamphlet about the Prophet. Abdul Quayum's body was taken by the District Magistrate, accompanied by a police party, to be handed over to the deceased's family for burial outside the city. A huge crowd, estimated to be about 25,000 strong, collected at the place of burial. Though the relatives of Abdul Quayum wished to complete the burial at the cemetery, the most violent members of the mob determined to take the body in procession through the city. The local authorities decided to prevent the mob entering, since this would have led to communal rioting. All attempts of the police to stop the procession failed, so a platoon of the Royal Sussex Regiment was brought in to keep peace. It was forced to open fire at short range to stop the advance of the frenzied mob and to prevent itself from being overwhelmed. Forty-seven rounds were fired by which 47 people were killed and 134 injured. The arrival of reinforcements prevented further attempts to advance. The wounded were taken to the Civil Hospital and the body of Abdul Quayum was then interred without further trouble.

On the 25th August 1935 there was a communal riot at Secunderabad.

In the year 1936 there were four communal riots. On the 14th April there occurred a most terrible riot at Firozabad in the Agra District. A Muslim procession was proceeding along the main bazar and it is alleged that bricks were thrown from the roofs of Hindu houses. This enraged the Muslims in the procession who set fire to the house of a Hindu, Dr. Jivaram, and the adjacent temple of Radha Krishna. The inmates of Dr. Jivaram's house in addition to 11 Hindus including 3 children were burnt to death. A second Hindu-Muslim riot broke out in Poona in the Bombay Presidency on 24th April 1936. On the 27th April there occurred a Hindu-Muslim riot in Jamalpur in the Monghyr District. The fourth Hindu-

Muslim riot of the year took place in Bombay on the 15th October 1936.

The year 1937 was full of communal disturbances. On the 27th March 1937 there was a Hindu-Muslim riot at Panipat over the Holi procession and 14 persons were killed. On the 1st May 1937 there occurred a communal riot in Madras in which 50 persons were injured. The month of May was full of communal riots which took place mostly in the C. P. and the Punjab. One that took place in Shikarpur in Sind caused great panic. On 18th June there was a Sikh-Muslim riot in Amritsar. It assumed such proportions that British troops had to be called out to maintain order.

The year 1938 was marked by two communal riots—one in Allahabad on 26th March and another in Bombay in April.

There were 6 Hindu-Muslim riots in 1939. On the 21st January there was a riot at Asansol in which one was killed and 18 injured. It was followed by a riot in Cawnpore on the 11th February in which 42 were killed, 200 injured and 800 arrested. On the 4th March there was a riot at Benares followed by a riot at Cassipore near Calcutta on the 5th of March. On 19th June there was again a riot at Cawnpore over the Rathajatra procession.

A serious riot occurred on 20th November 1939 in Sukkur in Sind. The riot was the culmination of the agitation by the Muslims to take possession, even by force, of a building called Manzilgah which was in the possession of Government as Government property and to the transfer of which the Hindus had raised objections. Mr. E. Weston—now a judge of the Bombay High Court—who was appointed to investigate into the disturbances gives* the following figures of the murdered and the wounded :—

* Report of the Court of Inquiry appointed under Section 3 of the Sind Public Inquiries Act to inquire into the riots which occurred at Sukkur in 1939. p. 65. The total of 142 Hindus under 'murdered' seems to be a mistake. It ought to be 72.

Taluka.	Murders committed.		Persons injured.		Persons subsequently died from injuries.	
	Hindus.	Mdns.	Hindus.	Mdns.	Hindus.	Mdns.
Sukkur Town ..	20	12	11	11	1	...
Sukkur Taluka ..	2	2	23	...	5	...
Shikarpur Taluka ..	5	..	11	...	2	...
Garhi Yasin Taluka ..	24	..	4	...	...	...
Rohri Taluka ..	10	..	3	...	...	...
Pano Akil Taluka ..	6	..	1	...	...	...
Ghorki Taluka ..	1	..	1	...	...	...
Mirpur Mathelo Taluka ..	..	..	1	...	...	...
Ubauro Taluka ..	4	..	3	1	1	...
	142	14	58	12	9	...

Of the many gruesome incidents recorded by him the following may be quoted :—

> "The most terrible of all the disturbances occurred on the night of the 20th at Gosarji village which is eight miles from Sukkur and sixteen from Shikarpur. According to an early statement sent by the District Magistrate to Government, admittedly incomplete, 27 Hindus were murdered there that night. According to the witnesses examined the number was 37.
>
> "Pamanmal a contractor of Gosarji states that at the time of satyagraha the leading Hindus of Gosarji came in deputation to the leading zemindar of the locality Khan Sahib Amirbux who was then at Sukkur. He reassured them and said he was responsible for their safety. On the 20th Khan Sahib Amirbux was at Gosarji, and that morning Mukhi Mahrumal was murdered there. The Hindus went to Khan Sahib Amirbux for protection and were again reassured, but that night wholesale murder and looting took place. Of the 37 murdered, seven were women. Pamanmal states that the following morning he went to the Sub-Inspector of Bagerji, which is one mile from Gosarji, but he was abused and driven from the thana. He then went to Shikarpur and complained to the panchayet, but did not com-

plain to any officer there. I may mention that the Sub-Inspector of Bagerji was afterwards prosecuted under section 211, Indian Penal Code, and has been convicted for failure to make arrests in connection with murders at Gosarji.

"As Khan Sahib Amirbux, the zemindar, who was said to have given assurance of protection to the Hindus of Bagerji, was reported to be attending the Court, he was called and examined as a Court witness. He states that he lives half a mile from Gosarji village. The Sub-Inspector of Bagerji came to Gosarji on the 20th after the murder of Mehrumal, and he acted as a mashir. He says that the Hindus did not ask for help and there was no apprehension of trouble. On the night of the 20th he was not well, and he heard nothing of the murders. He admits that he had heard of the Manzilgah evacuation. Later in his evidence he admits that he told the villagers of Gosarji to be on the alert as there was trouble in Sukkur, and he says he had called the panchayet on the evening of the 19th. He went to Gosarji at sunrise on the 21st after the murders. He admits that he is regarded as the protector of Gosarji."

Mr. Weston adds* :—

"I find it impossible to believe the evidence of this witness. I have no doubt that he was fully aware that there was trouble in Gosarji on the night of 20th and preferred to remain in his house."

Who can deny that this record of rioting presents a picture which is grim in its results and sombre in its tone? But being chronological in order, the record might fail to give an idea of the havoc these riots have caused in any given Province and the paralysis it has brought about in its social and economic life. To give an idea of the paralysis caused by the recurrence of riots in a Province I have recast the record of riots for the Province of Bombay. When recast the general picture appears as follows:

Leaving aside the Presidency and confining oneself to the City of Bombay, there can be no doubt that the record of the city is the blackest. The first Hindu-Muslim riot took place in 1893. This was followed by a long period of communal peace which lasted upto 1929. But the years that have followed have an appalling story to tell. From February 1929 to April 1938—a period of nine years—there were no less than 10 communal riots. In 1929 there were two communal riots. In the first, 149 were

* Ibid., pp. 66-67.

killed and 739 were injured and it lasted for 36 days. In the second riot 35 were killed, 109 were injured and it continued for 22 days. In 1930 there were two riots. Details as to loss of life and its duration are not available. In 1932 there ware again two riots. The first was a small one. In the second 217 were killed, 2,713 were injured and it went on for 49 days. In 1933 there was one riot, details about which are not available. In 1936 there was one riot in which 94 were killed, 632 were injured and it continued to rage for 65 days. In the riot of 1937, 11 were killed, 85 were injured and it occupied 21 days. The riot of 1938 lasted for 2½ hours only but within that time 12 were killed and a little over 100 were injured. Taking the total period of 9 years and 2 months from February 1929 to April 1938 the Hindus and Muslims of the City of Bombay alone were engaged in a sanguinary warfare for 210 days during which period 550 were killed and 4,500 were wounded. This does not of course take into consideration the loss of property which took place through arson and loot.

V

Such is the record of Hindu-Muslim relationship from 1920 to 1940. Placed side by side with the frantic efforts made by Mr. Gandhi to bring about Hindu-Muslim unity, the record makes most painful and heart-rending reading. It would not be much exaggeration to say that it is a record of twenty years of civil war between the Hindus and the Muslims in India, interrupted by brief intervals of armed peace.

In this civil war men were, of course, the principal victims. But women did not altogether escape molestation. It is perhaps not sufficiently known how much women have suffered in communal hostilities. Data relating to the whole of India are not available. But some data relating to Bengal exist.

On the 6th September 1932 questions were asked in the old Bengal Legislative Council regarding the abduction of women in the Province of Bengal. In reply, the Government of the day stated that between 1922 to 1927, the total number of women abducted was 568. Of these, 101 were unmarried and 467 were married. Asked to state the community to which the abducted women belonged, it was disclosed that out of 101 unmarried women 64 were Hindus, 29 Muslims, 4 Christians and 4 non-descript: and that out of 467 married women 331 were Hindus, 122 Muslims, 2 Christians and 12 non-descript. These figures relate to cases which were reported or if reported were not detected. Usually, about 10 p.c. of the cases are reported or detected and 90 p.c. go undetected. Applying this proportion to the facts disclosed by the Bengal Government, it may be said that about 35,000 women were abducted in Bengal during the short period of five years between 1922-27.

The attitude towards women-folk is a good index of the friendly or unfriendly attitude between the two communities. As such, the case which happened on 27th June 1936 in the village of Govindpur in Bengal makes very instructive reading. The following account of it is taken from the opening speech* of the Crown counsel when the trial of 40 Mahomedan accused began on the 10th August 1936. According to the prosecution:—

> "There lived in Govindpur a Hindu by name Radha Vallabh. He had a son Harendra. There lived also in Govindpur a Muslim woman whose occupation was to sell milk. The local Musalmans of the village suspected that Harendra had illicit relationship with this Muslim milk woman. They resented that a Muslim woman should be in the keeping of a Hindu and they decided to wreak their vengeance on the family of Radha Vallabh for this insult. A meeting of the Musalmans of Govindpur was convened and Harendra was summoned to attend this meeting. Soon after Harendra went to the meeting, cries of Harendra were heard. It was found that Harendra was assaulted and was lying senseless in the field where the meeting was held. The Musalmans of Govindpur were not satisfied with this assault. They informed Radha Vallabh that unless he, his wife and his children embraced Islam the Musalmans did not feel satisfied for the wrong his son had done to them. Radha Vallabh was planning to send away to another place his wife and children. The Musalmans came to know of this plan. Next day when Kusum, the wife of Radha Vallabh, was sweeping the courtyard of her house, some Mahomedans came, held down Radha Vallabh and some spirited away Kusum. After having taken her to some distance two Mahomedans by name Laker and

*This is an English version of the report which appeared in the *Savadhan*, a Marathi weekly of Nagpur, in its issue of 25th August 1936.

Mahazar raped her and removed her ornaments. After some time, she came to her senses and ran towards her home. Her assailants again pursued her. She succeeded in reaching her home and locking herself in. Her Muslim assailants broke open the door, caught hold of her and again carried her away on the road. It was suggested by her assailants that she should be again raped on the street. But with the help of another woman by name Rajani, Kusum escaped and took shelter in the house of Rajani. While she was in the house of Rajani the Musalmans of Govindpur paraded her husband Radha Vallabh in the streets in complete disgrace. Next day the Musalmans kept watch on the roads to and from Govindpur to the Police station to prevent Radha Vallabh and Kusum from giving information of the outrage to the Police."

These acts of barbarism against women, committed without remorse, without shame and without condemnation by their fellow brethren show the depth of the antagonism which divided the two communities. The tempers on each side were the tempers of two warring nations. There was carnage, pillage, sacrilege and outrage of every species, perpetrated by Hindus, against Musalmans and by Musalmans against Hindus—more perhaps by Musalmans against Hindus than by Hindus against Musalmans. Cases of arson have occurred in which Musalmans have set fire to the houses of Hindus, in which whole families of Hindus, men, women and children were roasted alive and consumed in the fire, to the great satisfaction of the Muslim spectators. What is astonishing is that these cold and deliberate acts of rank cruelty were not regarded as atrocities to be condemned but were treated as legitimate acts of warfare for which no apology was necessary. Enraged by these hostilities, the editor of the *Hindustan*—a Congress paper—writing in 1926 used the following language to express the painful truth of the utter failure of Mr. Gandhi's efforts to bring about Hindu-Muslim unity. In words of utter despair the editor said*:—

"There is an immense distance between the India of to-day and India a nation, between an uncouth reality which expresses itself in murder and arson and that fond fiction which is in the imagination of patriotic if self-deceiving men. To talk about Hindu-Muslim unity from a thousand platforms or to give it blazoning headlines is to perpetrate an illusion whose cloudy structure dissolves itself at the exchange of brick-bats and the

* Quoted in "Through Indian Eyes" columns of the *Times of India* dated 16-8-26.

> desecration of tombs and temples. To sing a few pious hymns of peace and goodwill *a la Naidu*..........will not benefit the country. The President of the Congress has been improvising on the theme of Hindu-Muslim unity, so dear to her heart, with brilliant variations, which does credit to her genius but leaves the problem untouched. The millions in India can only respond when the unity song is not only on the tongues of the leaders but in the hearts of the millions of their countrymen."

Nothing I could say can so well show the futility of any hope of Hindu-Muslim unity. Hindu-Muslim unity up to now was at least in sight although it was like a mirage. Today it is out of sight and also out of mind. Even Mr. Gandhi has given up what, he perhaps now realizes, is an impossible task.

But there are others who notwithstanding the history of the past twenty years, believe in the possibility of Hindu-Muslim unity. This belief of theirs seems to rest on two grounds. Firstly, they believe in the efficacy of a Central Government to mould diverse set of people into one nation. Secondly, they feel that the satisfaction of Muslim demands will be a sure means of achieving Hindu-Muslim unity.

It is true that Government is a unifying force and that there are many instances where diverse people have become unified into one homogeneous people by reason of their being subjected to a single Government. But the Hindus, who are depending upon Government as a unifying force seem to forget that there are obvious limits to Government acting as a unifying force. The limits to Government working as a unifying force are set by the possibilities of fusion among the people. In a country where race, language and religion do not stand in the way of fusion, Government is most effective as a unifying force. On the other hand, in a country where race, language and religion put an effective bar against fusion, Government can have no effect as a unifying force. If the diverse people in France, England, Italy and Germany became unified nations by reason of a common Government, it was because neither race, language nor religion obstructed the unifying process of Government. On the other hand, if the people in Austria, Hungary, Czechoslovakia and Turkey failed to be unified, although under a common Government, it was because race, language and religion were strong enough to counter and nullify the unifying power of Government. No one can deny that race, language and religion have been too dominant in India to permit the people of India to be welded into a nation by the unifying force of a common Government. It is an illusion to say that the Central Government in India has moulded the Indian people into a nation. What the Central Government has done, is to tie them together by one law and to house them together in one place, as the owner of unruly animals does, by tying them with one rope and keeping them in one stable. All that the Central Government has done is to produce a kind of peace among Indians. It has not made them one nation.

It cannot be said that time has been too short for unification to take place. If one hundred and fifty years of life under a Central Government does not suffice, eternity will not suffice. For this failure the genius of the Indians alone is responsible. There is among Indians no passion for unity, no desire for fusion. There is no desire to have a common dress. There is no desire to have a common language. There is no will to give up what is local and particular for something which is common and national. A Gujarati takes pride in being a Gujarati, a Maharashtrian in being a Maharashtrian, a Punjabi in being a Punjabi, a Madrasi in being a Madrasi and a Bengali in being a Bengali. Such is the mentality of Hindus, who accuse the Musalman of want of national feeling when he says "I am a Musalman first and Indian afterwards." Can any one suggest that there exists anywhere in India even among the Hindus an instinct or a passion that would put any semblance of emotion behind their declaration "*Civis Indianus sum*", or the smallest consciousness of a moral and social unity, which desires to give expression by sacrificing whatever is particular and local in favour of what is common and unifying? There is no such consciousness and no such desire. Without such consciousness and without such desire, to depend upon Government to bring about unification is to deceive oneself.

Regarding the second, it was no doubt the opinion of the Simon Commission :—

> "That the communal riots were a manifestation of the anxieties and ambitions aroused in both the communities by the

prospect of India's political future. So long as authority was firmly established in British hands and self-government was not thought of, Hindu-Muslim rivalry was confined within a narrower field. This was not merely because the presence of a neutral bureaucracy discouraged strife. A further reason was that there was little for members of one community to fear from the predominance of the other. The comparative absence of communal strife in the Indian States today may be similarly explained. Many, who are well acquainted with conditions in British India a generation ago, would testify that at that epoch so much good feeling had been engendered between the two sides that communal tension as a threat to civil peace was at a minimum. But the coming of the Reforms and the anticipation of what may follow them have given new point to Hindu-Muslim competition. The one community naturally lays claim to the rights of a majority and relies upon its qualifications of better education and greater wealth; the other is all the more determined on those accounts to secure effective protection for its members, and does not forget that it represents the previous conquerors of the country. It wishes to be assured of adequate representation and of a full share of official posts."

Assuming that to be a true diagnosis, assuming that Muslim demands are reasonable, assuming that the Hindus were prepared to grant them—and these are all very big assumptions—it is a question whether a true union between Hindus and Muslims can take place through political unity, resulting from the satisfaction of Muslim political demands. Some people seem to think that it is enough if there is a political unity between Hindus and Muslims. I think this is the greatest delusion. Those who take this view seem to be thinking only of how to bring the Muslims to join the Hindus in their demands on the British for Dominion Status or Independence as the mood of the moment be. This, to say the least, is a very shortsighted view. How to make the Muslims join the Hindus in the latter's demands on the British is comparatively a very small question. In what spirit will they work the constitution? Will they work it only as aliens bound by an unwanted tie or will they work it as true kindreds, is the more important question. For working it as true kindreds, what is wanted is not merely political unity but a true union of heart and soul, in other words, social unity. Political unity is worth nothing, if it is not the expression of real union. It is as precarious as the unity between persons, who without being friends become allies of each other.

How very precarious it always is, is best illustrated by what has happened between Germany and Russia. Personally, I do not think that a permanent union can be made to depend upon the satisfaction of mere material interests. Pacts may produce unity. But that unity can never ripen into union. A pact as a basis for a union is worse than useless. As its very nature indicates, a pact is separative in character. A pact cannot produce the desire to accommodate, it cannot instil the spirit of sacrifice, nor can it bind the parties to the main objective. Instead of accommodating each other, parties to a pact strive to get, as much as possible, out of each other. Instead of sacrificing for the common cause, parties to the pact are constantly occupied in seeing that the sacrifice made by one is not used for the good of the other. Instead of fighting for the main objective, parties to the pact are for ever engaged in seeing that in the struggle for reaching the goal the balance of power between the parties is not disturbed. Renan spoke the most profound truth when he said:—

> "Community of interests is assuredly a powerful bond between men. But nevertheless can interests suffice to make a nation? I do not believe it. Community of interests makes commercial treaties. There is a sentimental side to nationality; it is at once body and soul; a Zollverein is not a fatherland."

Equally striking is the view of James Bryce, another well-known student of history. According to Bryce,

> "The permanence of an institution depends not merely on the material interests that support it, but on its conformity to the deep-rooted sentiment of the men for whom it has been made. When it draws to itself and provides a fitting expression for that sentiment, the sentiment becomes thereby not only more vocal but actually stronger, and in its turn imparts a fuller vitality to the institution."

These observations of Bryce were made in connection with the foundation of the German Empire by Bismarck who, according to Bryce, succeeded in creating a durable empire because it was based on a sentiment and that this sentiment was fostered—

> ". . . . most of all by what we call the instinct or passion for nationality, the desire of a people already conscious of a moral and social unity, to see such unity expressed and realized under

a single government, which shall give it a place and name among civilized states."

What is it that produces this moral and social unity which gives permanence and what is it that drives people to see such unity expressed and realized under a single government, which shall give it a place and a name among civilized states?

No one is more competent to answer this question than James Bryce. It was just such a question he had to consider in discussing the vitality of the Holy Roman Empire as contrasted with the Roman Empire. If any Empire can be said to have succeeded in bringing about political unity among its diverse subjects it was the Roman Empire. Paraphrasing for the sake of brevity the language of Bryce:—The gradual extension of Roman citizenship through the founding of colonies, first throughout Italy and then in the provinces, the working of the equalized and equalizing Roman Law, the even pressure of the government on all subjects, the movements of population, caused by commerce and the slave traffic, were steadily assimilating the various peoples. Emperors, who were for the most part natives of the provinces, cared little to cherish Italy or even after the days of the Antonines, to conciliate Rome. It was their policy to keep open for every subject a career by whose freedom they had themselves risen to greatness. Annihilating distinctions of legal status among freemen, it completed the work, which trade and literature and toleration to all beliefs but one were already performing. No quarrel of race or religions disturbed that calm, for all national distinctions were becoming merged in the idea of a common Empire.

This unity produced by the Roman Empire was only a political unity. How long did this political unity last? In the words of Bryce:—

> "Scarcely had these slowly working influences brought about this unity, when other influences began to threaten it. New foes assailed the frontiers; while the loosening of the structure within was shewn by the long struggles for power which followed the death or deposition of each successive emperor. In the period of anarchy after the fall of Valerian, generals were raised by their armies in every part of the Empire, and ruled great provinces as monarchs apart, owning no allegiance to the possessor of the capital. The breaking-up of the western half of the

Empire into separate kingdoms might have been anticipated by two hundred years, had the barbarian tribes on the borders been bolder, or had there not arisen in Diocletian a prince active and skilful enough to bind up the fragments before they had lost all cohesion, meeting altered conditions by new remedies. The policy he adopted of dividing and localizing authority recognized the fact that the weakened heart could no longer make its pulsations felt to the body's extremities. He parcelled out the supreme power among four monarchs, ruling as joint emperors in four capitals, and then sought to give it a factitious strength by surrounding it with an oriental pomp which his earlier predecessors would have scorned............ The prerogative of Rome was menaced by the rivalry of Nicomedia, and the nearer greatness of Milan."

It is, therefore, evident that political unity was not enough to give permanence and stability to the Roman Empire and as Bryce points out that "the breaking-up of the western half (of the Roman Empire) into separate kingdoms might have been anticipated by two hundred years, had the barbarian tribes on the border been bolder, or had there not arisen in Diocletian a prince, active and skilful enough to bind up the fragments before they had lost all cohesion, meeting altered conditions by new remedies." But the fact is that the Roman Empire which was tottering and breaking into bits and whose political unity was not enough to bind it together did last for several hundred years as one cohesive unit after it became the Holy Roman Empire. As Prof. Marvin points out* :—

> "The unity of the Roman Empire was mainly political and military. It lasted for between four and five hundred years. The unity which supervened in the Catholic Church was religious and moral and endured for a thousand years."

The question is what made the Holy Roman Empire more stable than the Roman Empire could ever hope to be? According to Bryce it was a common religion in the shape of Christianity and a common religious organization in the shape of the Christian Church which supplied the cement to the Holy Roman Empire and which was wanting in the Roman Empire. It was this cement which gave to the people of the Empire a moral and social unity and made them see such unity expressed and realized under a single government.

* *The Unity of Western Civilization* (4th Ed.), p. 27.

Speaking of the unifying effect of Christianity as a common religion Bryce says :—

> "It is on religion that the inmost and deepest life of a nation rests. Because Divinity was divided, humanity had been divided, likewise; the doctrine of the unity of God now enforced the unity of man, who had been created in His image. The first lesson of Christianity was love, a love that was to join in one body those whom suspicion and prejudice and pride of race had hitherto kept apart. There was thus formed by the new religion a community of the faithful, a Holy Empire, designed to gather all men into its bosom, and standing opposed to the manifold polytheisms of the older world, exactly as the universal sway of the Caesars was contrasted with the innumerable kingdoms and city republics that had gone before it......"*

If what Bryce has said regarding the instability of the Roman Empire and the comparatively greater stability of its successor, the Holy Roman Empire, has any lesson for India and if the reasoning of Bryce that the Roman Empire was unstable because it had nothing more than political unity to rely on, and that the Holy Roman Empire was more stable, because it rested on the secure foundation of moral and social unity, produced by the possession of a common faith, is valid reasoning and embodies human experience, then it is obvious that there can be no possibility of a union between Hindus and Muslims. The cementing force of a common religion is wanting. From a spiritual point of view, Hindus and Musalmans are not merely two classes or two sects such as Protestants and Catholics or Shaivas and Vaishnavas. They are two distinct species. In this view, neither the Hindu nor the Muslim can be expected to recognize that humanity is an essential quality present in them both, and that they are not many but one and that the differences

* The Christian Church did not play a passive part in the process of unification of the Holy Roman Empire. It took a very active part in bringing it about. "Seeing one institution after another falling to pieces around her, seeing how countries and cities were being severed from each other by the eruption of strange tribes and the increasing difficulty of communication the Christian Church," says Bryce, "strove to save religious fellowship by strengthening the ecclesiastical organization, by drawing tighter every bond of outward union. Necessities of faith were still more powerful. Truth, it was said, is one, and as it must bind into one body all who hold it, so it is only by continuing in that body that they can preserve it. There is one Flock and one Shepherd."

between them are no more than accidents. For them Divinity is divided and with the division of Divinity their humanity is divided and with the division of humanity they must remain divided. There is nothing to bring them in one bosom.

Without social union, political unity is difficult to be achieved. If achieved, it would be as precarious as a summer sapling, liable to be uprooted by the gust of a hostile wind. With mere political unity, India may be a State. But to be a State is not to be a nation and a State, which is not a nation, has small prospects of survival in the struggle for existence. This is especially true where nationalism—the most dynamic force of modern times—is seeking everywhere to free itself by the destruction and disruption of all mixed states. The danger to a mixed and composite state therefore, lies not so much in external aggression as in the internal resurgence of nationalities which are fragmented, entrapped, suppressed and held against their will. Those who oppose Pakistan should not only bear this danger in mind but should also realize that this attempt on the part of suppressed nationalities to disrupt a mixed state and to found a separate home for themselves, instead of being condemned, finds ethical justification from the principle of self-determination.

CHAPTER VIII

MUSLIM ALTERNATIVE TO PAKISTAN

I

The Hindus say they have an alternative to Pakistan. Have the Muslims also an alternative to Pakistan? The Hindus say yes, the Muslims say no. The Hindus believe that the Muslim proposal for Pakistan is only a bargaining manœuvre put forth with the object of making additions to the communal gains already secured under the Communal Award. The Muslims repudiate the suggestion. They say there is no equivalent to Pakistan and, therefore, they will have Pakistan and nothing but Pakistan. It does seem that the Musalmans are devoted to Pakistan and are determined to have nothing else and that the Hindus in hoping for an alternative are merely indulging in wishful thinking. But assuming that the Hindus are shrewd enough in divining what the Muslim game is, will the Hindus be ready to welcome the Muslim alternative to Pakistan? The answer to the question must, of course, depend upon what the Muslim alternative is.

What is the Muslim alternative to Pakistan? No one knows. The Muslims, if they have any, have not disclosed it and perhaps will not disclose it till the day when the rival parties meet to revise and settle the terms on which the Hindus and the Muslims are to associate with each other in the future. To be forewarned is to be forearmed. It is, therefore, necessary for the Hindus to have some idea of the possible Muslim alternative to enable them to meet the shock of it; for the alternative cannot be better than the Communal Award and is sure to be many degrees worse.

In the absence of the exact alternative proposal one can only make a guess. Now one man's guess is as good as that of another, and the party concerned has to choose on which of these he will rely. Among the likely guesses, my guess is that the Muslims will put forth as their alternative some such proposal as the following :—

" That the future constitution of India shall provide:

(i) That the Muslims shall have 50% representation in the Legislature, Central as well as Provincial, through separate electorates.

(ii) That 50% of the Executive in the Centre as well as in the Provinces shall consist of Muslims.

(iii) That in the Civil Service 50% of the posts shall be assigned to the Muslims.

(iv) That in the Fighting Forces the Muslim proportion shall be one half, both in the ranks and in the higher grades.

(v) That Muslims shall have 50% representation in all public bodies, such as councils and commissions, created for public purposes.

(vi) That Muslims shall have 50% representation in all international organizations in which India will participate.

(vii) That if the Prime Minister be a Hindu, the Deputy Prime Minister shall be a Muslim.

(viii) That if the Commander-in-Chief be a Hindu, the Deputy Commander-in-Chief shall be a Muslim.

(ix) That no changes in the Provincial boundaries shall be made except with the consent of 66% of the Muslim members of the Legislature.

(x) That no action or treaty against a Muslim country shall be valid unless the consent of 66% of the Muslim members of the Legislature is obtained.

(xi) That no law affecting the culture or religion or religious usage of Muslims shall be made except with the consent of 66% of the Muslim members of the Legislature.

(xii) That the national language for India shall be Urdu.

(xiii) That no law prohibiting or restricting the slaughter of cows or the propagation of and conversion to Islam shall be valid unless it is passed with the consent of 66% of the Muslim members of the Legislature.

(xiv) That no change in the constitution shall be valid unless the majority required for effecting such changes also includes a 66% majority of the Muslim members of the Legislature."

This guess of mine is not the result of imagination let loose. It is not the result of a desire to frighten the Hindus into an unwilling and hasty acceptance of Pakistan. If I may say so, it is really an intelligent anticipation based upon available data coming from Muslim quarters.

An indication of what the Muslim alternative is likely to be, is obtainable from the nature of the Constitutional Reforms which are contemplated for the Dominions of His Exalted Highness the Nizam of Hyderabad.

The Hyderabad scheme of Reforms is a novel scheme. It rejects the scheme of communal representation obtaining in British India. In its place is substituted what is called Functional Representation, *i.e.* representation by classes and by professions. The composition of the Legislature which is to consist of 70 members is to be as follows:—

Elected

Agriculture		12
Patidars	8	
Tenants	4	
Women		1
Graduates		1
University		1
Jagirdars		2
Maashdars		1
Legal		2
Medical		2
Western	1	
Oriental	1	
Teaching		1
Commerce		1
Industries		2
Banking		2
Indigenous	1	
Co-operative and Joint Stock	1	
Organized Labour		1
Harijan		1
District Municipalities		1
City Municipality		1
Rural Boards		1
Total		33

Nominated

Illakas		8
Sarf-i-Khas	2	
Paigahs	3	
Peshkari	1	
Salar Jung	1	
Samasthans	1	
Officials		18
Rural Arts and Crafts		1
Backward Classes		1
Minor Unrepresented Classes.		3
Others		6
Total		37

Whether the scheme of functional representation will promote better harmony between the various classes and sections than communal representation does is more than doubtful. In addition to perpetuating existing social and religious divisions, it may quite easily intensify class struggle by emphasizing class consciousness. The scheme appears innocuous but its real character will come out when every class will demand representation in proportion to its numbers. Be that as it may, functional representation is not the most significant feature of the Hyderabad scheme of Reforms. The most significant feature of the scheme is the proposed division of seats between Hindus and Musalmans in the new Hyderabad Legislature. Under the scheme as approved by H. E. H. the Nizam, communal representation is not altogether banished. It is retained along with functional representation. It is to operate through joint electorates. But there is to be equal representation for "the two majority communities" on every* elective body including the legislature and no candidate can succeed unless he secures 40 per cent. of the votes polled by members of his community. This principle of equal representation to Hindus and Muslims irrespective of their numbers† is not only to apply to every elective body but it is to apply to both elected as well as nominated members of the body.

In justification of this theory of equal representation it is stated that:—

"The importance of the Muslim community in the state, by virtue of its historical position and its status in the body politic, is so obvious that it cannot be reduced to the status of a minority in the Assembly."

Quite recently there have appeared in the press‡ the proposals formulated by one Mr. Mir Akbar Ali Khan calling himself

* Besides the Central Legislature there are to be constituted under the scheme of Reforms other popular bodies such as *Panchayats*, Rural Boards, Municipalities and Town Committees.

† The distribution of population of Hyderabad State (excluding Berar) is according to the census of 1931 as follows:—

Hindus	Untouchables	Muslims	Christians	Others	Total
96,99,615	24,73,230	15,34,666	1,51,382	5,77,255	1,44,36,148

‡ See *Bombay Sentinel*, June 22nd, 1940. Mr. Mir Akbar Ali Khan says that he discussed his proposals with Mr. Srinivas Iyengar, ex-President of the Congress, and the proposals published by him are really proposals as approved by Mr. Iyengar.

the leader of the Nationalist Party as a means of settling the Hindu-Muslim problem in British India. They are as follows :—

> (1) The future constitution of India must rest upon the broad foundation of adequate military defence of the country and upon making the people reasonably military minded. The Hindus must have the same military mindednes as the Muslims.
>
> (2) The present moment offers a supreme opportunity for the two communities to ask for the defence of India being made over to them. The Indian Army must consist of an equal number of Hindus and Muslims and no regiment should be on a communal, as distinguished from regional basis.
>
> (3) The Governments in the Provinces and at the Centre should be wholly National Governments composed of men who are reasonably military minded. Hindu and Muslim Ministers should be equal in number in the Central as well as all Provincial cabinets; other important minorities might wherever necessary be given special representation. This scheme will function most satisfactorily with joint electorates, but in the present temper of the country separate electorates might be continued. The Hindu Ministers must be elected by the Hindu members of the legislature and the Muslim Ministers by the Muslim members.
>
> (4) The Cabinet is to be removable only on an express vote of no-confidence, against the Cabinet as a whole, passed by a majority of 2/3rds of the whole house which majority must be of Hindus and Muslims taken separately.
>
> (5) The religion, language, script and personal law of each community should be safeguarded by a paramount constitutional check enabling the majority of members, representing that community in the legislature to place a veto on any legislative or other measure affecting it. A similar veto must be provided against any measure designed or calculated to affect adversely the economic well-being of any community.
>
> (6) An adequate communal representation in the services must be agreed to as a practical measure of justice in administration and in the distribution patronage.

If the proposals put forth by a Muslim leader of the Nationalist Party in Hyderabad State is an indication of the direction in which the mind of the Muslims in British India is running, then, the guess I have made as to what is likely to be the alternative to Pakistan derives additional support.

II

It is true that in the month of April 1940 a Conference of Muslims was held in Delhi under the grandiloquent name of "The Azad Muslim Conference." The Muslims who met in the Azad Conference were those who were opposed to the Muslim League as well as to the Nationalist Muslims. They were opposed to the Muslim League firstly, because of their hostility to Pakistan and secondly because they did not want to depend upon the British Government for the protection of their rights.* They were also opposed to the Natonalist Musalmans (i. e. Congressites out and out) because they were accused of indifference to the cultural and religious rights of the Muslims.†

With all this the Azad Muslim Conference was hailed by the Hindus as a Conference of friends. But the resolutions passed by the Conference leave very little to choose between it and the League. Among the resolutions passed by the Azad Muslim Conference the following three bear directly upon the issue in question.

The first of these runs as follows :—

> "This conference, representative of Indian Muslims who desire to secure the fullest freedom of the country, consisting of delegates and representatives of every province, after having given its fullest and most careful consideration to all the vital questions affecting the interest of the Muslim community and the country as a whole declares the following :—
>
> "India will have geographical and political boundaries of an individual whole and as such is the common homeland of all the citizens irrespective of race or religion who are joint owners of its resources. All nooks and corners of the country are hearths and homes of Muslims who cherish the historic eminence of their religion and culture which are dearer to them than their lives.

* Mufti Kifayat Ullah, a prominent member of the conference, in the course of his speech is reported to have said: "They had to demonstrate that they were not behind any other community in the fight for freedom. He wished to declare in clear terms that they did not rely on the British Government for the protection of their rights. They would themselves chalk out the safeguards necessary for the protection of their religious rights and would fight out any party, however powerful, that would refuse to accept those safeguards, as they would fight the Government for freedom" (Prolonged cheers). *Hindustan Times*, April 30, 1940.

† See the speeches of Maulana Hafizul Rehman and Dr. K. M. Ashraf in the same issue of the *Hindustan Times*.

From the national point of view every Muslim is an Indian. The common rights of all residents of the country and their responsibilities, in every walk of life and in every sphere of human activity are the same. The Indian Muslim by virtue of these rights and responsibilities, is unquestionably an Indian national and in every part of the country is entitled to equal privileges with that of every Indian national in every sphere of governmental, economic and other national activities and in public services. For that very reason Muslims own equal responsibilities with other Indians for striving and making sacrifices to achieve the country's independence. This is a self-evident proposition, the truth of which no right thinking Muslim will question. This Conference declares unequivocally and with all emphasis at its command that the goal of Indian Muslims is complete independence along with protection of their religion and communal rights, and that they are anxious to attain this goal as early as possible. Inspired by this aim they have in the past made great sacrifices and are ever ready to make greater sacrifices.

"The Conference unreservedly and strongly repudiates the baseless charge levelled against Indian Muslims by the agents of British Imperialism and others that they are an obstacle in the path of Indian freedom and emphatically declares that the Muslims are fully alive to their responsibilities and consider it inconsistent with their traditions and derogatory to their honour to lag behind others in the struggle for independence."

By this Resolution they repudiated the scheme of Pakistan. Their second Resolution was in the following terms:—

"This is the considered view of this Conference that only that constitution for the future Government of India would be acceptable to the people of India which is framed by the Indians themselves elected by means of adult franchise. The constitution should fully safeguard all the legitimate interests of the Muslims in accordance with the recommendations of the Muslim members of the Constituent Assembly. The representatives of other communities or of an outside power would have no right to interfere in the determination of these safeguards."

By this Resolution the Conference asserted that the safeguards for the Muslims must be determined by the Muslims alone.

Their third Resolution was as under:—

"Whereas in the future constitution of India it would be essential, in order to ensure stability of government and preservation of security, that every citizen and community should feel satisfied, this Conference considers it necessary that a scheme of safeguards as regards vital matters mentioned below should be prepared to the satisfaction of the Muslims.

"This Conference appoints a board consisting of 27 persons. This board, after the fullest investigation, consultation and consideration, shall make its recommendations for submission to the next session of this Conference, so that the Conference may utilise the recommendations as a means of securing a permanent national settlement of the communal question. This recommendation should be submitted within two months. The matters referred to the board are the following:—

"1. The protection of Muslim culture, personal law and religious rights.

"2. Political rights of Muslims and their protection.

"3. The formation of future constitution of India to be non-unitary and federal, with absolutely essential and unavoidable powers for the Federal Government.

"4. The provision of safeguards for the economic, social and cultural rights of Muslims and for their share in public services.

"The board will be empowered to fill up any vacancy in a suitable manner. The board will have the right to co-opt other members. It will be empowered also to consult other Muslim bodies and if it considers necessary, any responsible organisation in the country. The 27 members of the board will be nominated by the president.

"The quorum for the meeting will be nine.

"Since the safeguards of the communal rights of different communities will be determined in the constituent assembly referred to in the resolution which this Conference has passed, this Conference considers it necessary to declare that Muslim members of this constituent assembly will be elected by Muslims themselves."

We must await the report* of this board to know what safeguards the Azad Muslim Conference will devise for the safety and protection of Muslims. But there appears no reason to hope that they will not be in favour of what I have guessed to be the likely alternative for Pakistan. It cannot be overlooked that the Azad Muslim Conference was a body of Muslims who were not only opposed to the Muslim League but were equally opposed to the Nationalist Muslims. There is, therefore, no ground to trust that they will be more merciful to the Hindus than the League has been or will be.

* This report has not appeared even now.

Supposing my guess turns out to be correct, it would be interesting to know what the Hindus will have to say in reply. Should they prefer such an alternative to Pakistan? Or should they rather prefer Pakistan to such an alternative? Those are questions which I must leave the Hindus and their leaders to answer. All I would like to say in this connection is that the Hindus before determining their attitude towards this question should note certain important considerations. In particular they should note that there is a difference between *Macht Politic* * and *Gravamin Politic* †; that there is a difference between *Communitas Communitatum* and a nation of nations; that there is a difference between safeguards to allay apprehensions of the weak and contrivances to satisfy the ambition for power of the strong: that there is a difference between providing safeguards and handing over the country. Further, they should also note that what may with safety be conceded to *Gravamin Politic* may not be conceded to *Macht Politic*. What may be conceded with safety to a community may not be conceded to a nation and what may be conceded with safety to the weak to be used by it as a weapon of defence may not be conceded to the strong who may use it as a weapon of attack.

These are important considerations and, if the Hindus overlook them, they will do so at their peril. For the Muslim alternative is really a frightful and dangerous alternative.

* *Macht Politic* means Power Politics.

† *Gravamin Politic* means in which the main strategy is to gain power by manufacturing grievances

CHAPTER IX

LESSONS FROM ABROAD

Hindus who will not yield to the demand of the Muslims for the division of India into Pakistan and Hindustan and would insist upon maintaining the geographical unity of India without counting the cost, will do well to study the fate that has befallen other countries which, like India, harboured many nations and sought to harmonise them.

It is not necessary to review the history of all such countries. It is enough to recount here the story of two, Turkey and Czechoslovakia.

I

To begin with Turkey. The emergence of the Turks in history was due to the fact that they were driven away by the Mongols from their home in Central Asia, somewhere between 1230-40 A. D., which led them to settle in north-west Anatolia. Their career as the builders of the Turkish Empire began in 1326 with the conquest of Brusa. In 1360-61, they conquered Thrace from the Aegean to the Black Sea; in 1361-62, the Byzantine Government of Constantinople accepted their supremacy. In 1369 Bulgaria followed suit. In 1371-72 Macedonia was conquered. In 1373 Constantinople definitely accepted Ottoman sovereignty. In 1389 Servia was conquered, in 1430 Salonica, in 1453 Constantinople, in 1461 Trebizond, in 1465 Quraman, and in 1475 Kaffa and Tana were annexed. After a short lull, they conquered Mosul in 1514, Syria, Egypt, the Hiaz and the Yaman in 1516-17 and Belgrade in 1521. This was followed in 1526 by victory over the Hungarians at Mohacz. In 1554 took place the first conquest of Baghdad and in 1639 the second conquest of Baghdad. Twice they laid siege to Vienna, first in 1529 and again in 1683 with a view to extend their conquest beyond. But on both occasions they were repulsed with the result that their expansion in Europe was completely checked forever. Still the countries they conquered between 1326 and 1683 formed a vast empire. A few of these territories the Turks had lost to their enemies thereafter, but taking the extent of the Turkish Empire as it stood in 1789 on the eve of the French Revolution, it comprised (1) the Balkans, south of the Danube, (2) Asia Minor, the Levant and the neighbouring islands (i.e., Cyprus), (3) Syria and Palestine, (4) Egypt, and (5) North Africa from Egypt to Morocco.

The tale of the disruption of the Turkish Empire is easily told. The first to break away *de facto*, if not *de jure*, was Egypt in 1769. The next were the Christians in the Balkans. Bessarabia was taken by Russia in 1812 after a war with Turkey. In 1812 Serbia rebelled with the aid of Russia and the Turks were obliged to place Serbia under a separate government. In 1829 similar concessions were granted to two other Danubian provinces, Moldavia and Wallachia. As a result of the Greek war of independence which lasted between 1822-29, Greece was completely freed from the Turkish rule and the Greek independence was recognised by the Powers in 1832. Between 1875-77 there was turmoil amongst the Balkans. There was a revolt in Bosnia and Herzegovina and the Bulgarians resorted to atrocities against the Turks, to which the Turks replied with atrocities in equal measure. As a result, Serbia and Montenegro declared war on Turkey and so did Russia. By the Treaty of Berlin, Bulgaria was given self-government under Turkey and Eastern Rumania was to be ruled by Turkey under a Christian Governor. Russia gained Kars and Batoum. Dobrudja was given to Rumania. Bosnia and Herzegovina were assigned to Austria for administration and England occupied Cyprus. In 1881 Greece gained Thessaly and France occupied Tunis. In 1885 Bulgaria and Eastern Rumania were united into one state.

The story of the growth and decline of the Turkish Empire upto 1906 has been very graphically described by Mr. Lane Poole in the following words* :—

> "In its old extent, when the Porte ruled not merely the narrow territory now called Turkey in Europe, but Greece, Bulgaria and Eastern Rumania, Rumania, Serbia, Bosnia and Herzegovina, with the Crimea and a portion of Southern Russia,

* *Turkey*, pp. 363-64.

Egypt, Syria, Tripoli, Tunis, Algiers and numerous islands in the Mediterranean, not counting the vast but mainly desert tract of Arabia, the total population (at the present time) would be over fifty millions, or nearly twice that of Europe without Russia. One by one her provinces have been taken away. Algiers and Tunis have been incorporated with France, and thus 175,000 square miles and five millions of inhabitants have transferred their allegiance. Egypt is practically independent, and this means a loss of 500,000 miles and over six millions of inhabitants. Asiatic Turkey alone has suffered comparatively little diminution. This forms the bulk of her present dominions, and comprises about 680,000 square miles, and over sixteen millions of population. In Europe her losses have been almost as severe as in Africa where Tripoli alone remains to her. Serbia and Bosnia are administered by Austria and thereby nearly 40,000 miles and three and a half millions of peoples have become Austrian subjects. Wallachia and Moldavia are united in the independent kingdom of Rumania, diminishing the extent of Turkey by 46,000 miles and over five millions of inhabitants. Bulgaria is a dependent state over which the Porte has no real control and Eastern Rumania has lately *de facto* become part of Bulgaria and the two contain nearly 40,000 square miles, and three millions of inhabitants. The kingdom of Greece with its 25,000 miles and two million population has long been separated from its parent. In Europe where the Turkish territory once extended to 230,000 miles, with a population of nearly 20 millions, it now reaches only the total of 66 thousand miles and a population of four and a half millions, it has lost nearly three-fourths of its land, and about the same proportion of its people."

Such was the condition of Turkey in 1907. What has befallen her since then is unfortunately the worst part of her story. In 1908 taking advantage of the revolution brought about by the Young Turks, Austria annexed Bosnia and Herzegovina and Bulgaria declared her independence. In 1911 Italy took possession of Tripoli and in 1912 France occupied Morocco. Encouraged by the successful attack of Italy in 1912, Bulgaria, Greece, Serbia and Montenegro formed themselves into a Balkan League and declared war on Turkey. In this war, known as the first Balkan War, Turkey was completely defeated. By the Treaty of London (1913) the Turkish territory in Europe was reduced to a narrow strip round Constantinople. But the treaty could not take effect because the victors could not agree on the distribution of the spoils of victory. In 1913 Bulgaria declared war on the rest of the Balkan League and Rumania declared war on Bulgaria in the hope of extending her territory. Turkey also did the same. By the Treaty of Bukharest (1913), which ended the second Balkan War, Turkey recovered Adrianople and got Thrace from Bulgaria. Serbia obtained Northern Macedonia and Greece obtained Southern Macedonia (including Salonika), while Montenegro enlarged her territory at the expense of Turkey. By 1914 when the Great European War came on, the Balkans had won their independence from Turkey and the area in Europe that remained under the Turkish Empire was indeed a very small area round about Constantinople and her possessions in Asia. So far as the African continent is concerned, the Sultan's power over Egypt and the rest of North Africa was only nominal; for the European Powers had established real control therein. In the Great War of 1914 the overthrow of Turkey was complete. All the provinces from the Mediterranean to the Persian Gulf were overrun, and the great cities of Baghdad, Jerusalem, Damascus and Alleppo were captured. In Europe the allied troops occupied Constantinople. The Treaty of Sèvres, which brought the war with Turkey to a close, sought to deprive her of all her outlying provinces and even of the fertile plains of Asia Minor. Greek claim for territory was generously allowed at the expense of Turkey in Macedonia, Thrace and Asia Minor and Italy was to receive Adalia and a large tract in the south. Turkey was to be deprived of all her Arab provinces in Asia, Iraq, Syria, Palestine, Hedjaz and Nejd. There was left to Turkey only the capital, Constantinople, and separated from this city, by a "neutral zone of the straits," part of the barren plateau of Anatolia. The treaty though accepted by the Sultan was fiercely attacked by the Nationalist Party under Kemal Pasha. When the Greeks advanced to occupy their new territory, they were attacked and decisively beaten. At the end of the war with Greece, which went on from 1920 to 1922, the Turks had reoccupied Smyrna. As the allies were not prepared to send armies to help the Greeks, they were forced to come to terms with the Nationalist Turks. At the conference at Mudiania the Greeks agreed to revise the terms of the Treaty of Sèvres, which was done by the Treaty of Lausanne in 1923 which granted the demands of Turkey except in Western Thrace. The rest of the Treaty of Sèvres was accepted by the

Turks which meant the loss of her Arab provinces in Asia. Before the War of 1914, Turkey had lost all her provinces in Europe. After the War, she lost her provinces in Asia. As a result of the dismemberment of the old Turkish Empire, what now remains of it is the small state called the Republic of Turkey with an area which is a minute fraction of the old Empire.*

II

Take the case of Czechoslovakia. It is the creation of the Treaty of Trianon which followed the European War of 1914. None of the peace treaties was more drastic in its terms than the Treaty of Trianon. Says Prof. Macartney, "By it Hungary was not so much mutilated as dismembered. Even if we exclude Croatia, Slavonia, which had stood only in a federal relationship to the other lands of the Holy Crown—although one of eight hundred years' standing—Hungary proper was reduced to less than one-third (32.6 per cent.) of her prewar area, and a little over two-fifths (41.6 per cent.) of her population. Territories and peoples formerly Hungarian were distributed among no less than seven states." Of these states, there was one which did not exist before. It was a new creation. That was the state of Czechoslovakia.

The area of the Republic of Czechoslovakia was 54,244 square miles and the population was about 13,613,172. It included the territories formerly known as Bohemia, Moravia, Slovakia and Ruthenia. It was a composite state which included in its bosom three principal nationalities, (i) Czechs occupying Bohemia and Moravia, (ii) Slovaks, occupying Slovakia and (iii) Ruthenians in occupation of Ruthenia.

Czechoslovakia proved to be a very short-lived state. It lived exactly for two decades. On the 15th March 1939 it perished or rather was destroyed as an independent state. It became a protectorate of Germany. The circumstances attending its expiry were of a very bewildering nature. Her death was brought about by the very Powers which had given it birth. By signing the Munich Pact on 30th September 1938—of which the protectorate was an inevitable consequence, Great Britain,

* The area of Turkey is 294,492 square miles exclusive of 3,708 square miles of lakes and swamps. The area of Turkey in Europe is only 9,257 square miles.

France and Italy assisted Germany, their former enemy of the Great War, to conquer Czechoslovakia, their former ally. All the work of the Czechs of the past century to gain freedom was wiped off. They were once more to be the slaves of their former German overlords.

III

What are the reasons for the disruption of Turkey?

Lord Eversley in his *Turkish Empire** has attempted to give reasons for the decay of Turkey, some internal, some external. Among the internal causes there were two. First the degeneracy of the Ottoman dynasty. The supreme power fell into the hands either of the Vaziers of the Sultans or more often in the hands of women of the harem of the Sultan. The harem was always in antagonism to the official administration of the Porte, which ostensibly carried on the administration of the state under the direction of the Sultan. The officials of every degree from the highest to the lowest were interested in the sale of all offices, civil and military, to the highest bidders. For securing their object, they found it expedient to bribe the inmates of the harem and thereby win the assent of the Sultans. The harem thus became the centre from which corruption spread throughout the Turkish Empire and which was one of the main causes of its decay. The second main cause of the decadence of the Turkish Empire was the deterioration of its armies due to two causes. During the last 300 years the army had lost the élan and the daring by which the Ottomans won their many victories in the early period of their career. The loss of this élan and daring by the Turkish army was due to the composition of the army, recruitment to which was restricted to Turks and Arabs, and also to the diminution of opportunities of plunder and the hope of acquiring lands for distribution among the soldiers as an incentive to victory and valour in the latter period when the Empire was on the defensive and when it was no longer a question of making fresh conquests, but of retaining what had already been won.

Among the external causes of the disruption of Turkey, the chief one is said to be the rapacity of the European nations. But

* See abridgment by Sheikh Abdur Rashid.

this view omits to take note of the true cause. The true and the principal cause of the disruption of Turkey was the growth of the spirit of nationalism among its subject peoples. The Greek revolt, the revolts of the Serbs, Bulgarians and other Balkans against the Turkish authority were no doubt represented as a conflict between Christianity and Islam. That is one way of looking at it, but only a superficial way. These revolts were simply the manifestations of the spirit of nationalism by which they were generated. These revolts no doubt had for their immediate causes Turkish misrule, Christian antipathy to Islam and the machinations of European nations. But this does not explain the real force which motivated them. The real motive force was the spirit of nationalism and their revolts were only a manifestation of this inner urge brought on by it. That it was nationalism which had brought about the disruption of Turkey is proved by the revolt of the Arabs in the last war and their will to be independent. Here there was no conflict between Islam and Christianity, nor was the relationship between the two that of the oppressor and the oppressed. Yet, the Arab claimed to be freed from the Turkish Empire. Why? Because he was moved by Arab nationalism and preferred to be an Arab nationalist to being a Turkish subject.

What is the cause of the destruction of Czechoslovakia?

The general impression is that it was the result of German aggression. To some extent that is true. But it is not the whole truth. If Germany was the only enemy of Czechoslovakia, all that she would have lost was the fringe of her borderland which was inhabited by the Sudeten Germans. German aggression need have cost her nothing more. Really speaking the destruction of Czechoslovakia was brought about by an enemy within her own borders. That enemy was the intransigent nationalism of the Slovaks who were out to break up the unity of the state and secure the independence of Slovakia.

The union of the Slovaks with the Czechs, as units of a single state, was based upon certain assumptions. First, the two were believed to be so closely akin as to be one people, and that the Slovaks were only a branch of Czechoslovaks. Second, the two spoke a single 'Czechoslovak' language. Third, there was no separate Slovak national consciousness. Nobody examined these assumptions at the time, because the Slovaks themselves desired this union, expressing their wish in 1918 by formal declaration of their representatives at the Peace Conference. This was a superficial and hasty view of the matter. As Prof. Macartney* points out

> "....'the central political fact which emerges from the consideration of this history (of the relations between the Czechs and Slovaks) for the purposes of the present age is the final crystallization of a Slovak national consciousness.....' The genuine and uncompromising believers in a single indivisible Czechoslovak language and people were certainly never so large, at least in Slovakia, as they were made to appear. Today they have dwindled to a mere handful, under the influence of actual experience of the considerable differences which exist between the Czechs and the Slovaks. At present Slovak is in practice recognized by the Czechs themselves as the official language of Slovakia. The political and national resistance has been no less tenacious, and to-day the name of 'Czechoslovakia' is practically confined to official documents and to literature issued for the benefit of foreigners. During many weeks in the country I only remember hearing one person use the term for herself; this was a half-German, half-Hungarian girl, who used it in a purely political sense, meaning that she thought irridentism futile. No Czech and no Slovak feels or calls himself, when speaking naturally, anything but a Czech or a Slovak as the case may be."

This national consciousness of the Slovaks, which was always alive, began to burst forth on seeing that the Sudeten Germans had made certain demands on Czechoslovakia for autonomy. The Germans sought to achieve their objective by the application of gangster morality to international politics, saying "Give us what we ask or we shall burst up your shop." The Slovaks followed suit by making their demands for autonomy but with a different face. They did not resort to gangster methods but modulated their demands to autonomy only. They had eschewed all idea of independence, and, in the proclamation issued on October 8 by Dr. Tiso, the leading man in the autonomist movement in Slovakia, it was said "We shall proceed in the spirit of our motto, for God and the Nation, in a Christian and national spirit." Believing in their *bona fides* and desiring to give no room to the *Gravamin Politic* of which the Slovaks were making full use to disturb the friendly relations between the

* C. A. Macartney—*Hungary and Her Successors* (Oxford), 1937, p. 136.

Czechs and the Slovaks, the National Assembly in Prague passed an Act in November 1938—immediately after the Munich Pact —called the "Constitutional Act on the Autonomy of Slovakia." Its provisions were of a far-reaching character. There was to be a separate parliament for Slovakia and this parliament was to decide the constitution of Slovakia within the framework of the legal system of the Czechoslovak Republic. An alteration in the territory of Slovakia was to be with the consent of the two-third majority in the Slovak parliament. The consent of the Slovak parliament was made necessary for international treaties which exclusively concerned Slovakia. Officials of the central state administration in Slovakia were to be primarily Slovaks. Proportional representation of Slovakia was guaranteed in all central institutions, councils, commissions and other organizations. Similarly, Slovakia was to be proportionally represented on all international organizations in which the Czechoslovak Republic was called upon to participate. Slovak soldiers, in peace time, were to be stationed in Slovakia as far as possible. As far as legislative authority was concerned all subjects which were strictly of common concern were assigned to the parliament of Czechoslovakia. By way of guaranteeing these rights to the Slovaks, the Constitution Act provided that the decision of the National Assembly to make constitutional changes shall be valid only if the majority constitutionally required for such changes includes also a proportionate majority of the members of the National Assembly elected in Slovakia. Similarly, the election of the President of the Republic required the consent not merely of the constitutionally determined majority of the members of the parliament, but also of a proportionate majority of the Slovak members. Further to emphasize that the central government must enjoy the confidence of the Slovaks it was provided by the constitution that one-third of the Slovak members of parliament may propose a motion of 'No Confidence'.

These constitutional changes introduced, much against the will of the Czechs, a hyphen between the Czechs and the Slovaks which did not exist before. But it was done in the hope that, once the relatively minor quarrels between the two were got out of the way, the very nationalism of the Slovaks was more likely to bring them closer to the Czechs than otherwise. With the constitutional changes guaranteeing an independent status to Slovakia and the fact that the status so guaranteed could not be changed without the consent of the Slovaks themselves, there was no question of the Slovaks ever losing their national identity through submergence by the Czechs. The autonomy introduced by the hyphen separated the cultural waters and saved the Slovaks from losing their colour.

The first Slovak parliament elected under the new constitution was opened on January 18, 1939, and Dr. Martin Sokol, the President of the parliament, declared "The period of the Slovak's struggle for freedom is ended. Now begins the period of national rebirth". Other speeches made on the occasion indicated that now that Slovakia had its autonomy the Slovaks would never feel animosity towards the Czechs again and that both would loyally abide by the Czecho-Slovak State.

Not even a month elapsed since the inauguration of the Slovak parliament before the Slovak politicians began their battle against the hyphen and for complete separation. They made excited speeches in which they attacked the Czechs, talked about Czech oppression and demanded a completely independent Slovakia. By the beginning of March, the various forms of separatism in Slovakia were seriously threatening the integrity of the Czecho-Slovak State. On March 9 it was learnt that Tiso, the Slovak Premier, had decided to proclaim the independence of Slovakia. On the 10th in anticipation of such an act troops were moved in Slovakia and Tiso, the Prime Minister, was dismissed along with other Slovak ministers by the President of the Republic, Dr. Hacha. On the next day Tiso, supposed to be under police supervision, telephoned to Berlin and asked for help. On Monday Tiso and Hitler met and had an hour and a half's talk in Berlin. Immediately after the talk with Hitler, Tiso got on the phone to Prague and passed on the German orders. They were :—

(i) All Czech troops to be withdrawn from Slovakia ;

(ii) Slovakia to be an independent state under German protection ;

(iii) The Slovak parliament to be summoned by President Hacha to hear the proclamation of independence.

There was nothing that President Hacha and the Prague Government could do except say 'yes,' for they knew very well that dozens of divisions of German troops were massed round the defenceless frontiers of Czechoslovakia ready to march in at any moment if the demands made by Germany in the interest of and at the instance of Slovakia were refused. Thus ended the new state of Czechoslovakia.

IV

What is the lesson to be drawn from the story of these two countries?

There is some difference as to how the matters should be put. Mr. Sydney Brooks would say that the cause of these wars of disruption is nationalism, which according to him is the enemy of the universal peace. Mr. Norman Angell, on the other hand, would say it is not nationalism but the threat to nationalism which is the cause. To Mr. Robertson nationalism is an irrational instinct, if not a positive hallucination, and the sooner humanity got rid of it the better for all.

In whatever way the matter is put and howsoever ardently one may wish for the elimination of nationalism, the lesson to be drawn is quite clear: that nationalism is a fact which can neither be eluded nor denied. Whether one calls it an irrational instinct or positive hallucination, the fact remains that it is a potent force which has a dynamic power to disrupt empires. Whether nationalism is the cause or the threat to nationalism is the cause, is a difference of emphasis only. The real thing is to recognize, as does Mr. Toynbee, that "nationalism is strong enough to produce war in spite of us. It has terribly proved itself to be no outworn creed, but a vital force to be reckoned with." As was pointed out by him, "the right reading of nationality has become an affair of life and death." It was not only so for Europe. It was so for Turkey. It was so for Czechoslovakia. And what was a question of life and death to them could not but be one of life and death to India. Prof. Toynbee pleaded ,as was done before him by Guizot, for the recognition of nationality as the necessary foundation of European peace. Could India ignore to recognize this plea? If she does, she will be acting at her peril. That nationalism is a disruptive force is not the only lesson to be learnt from the history of these two countries. Their experience embodies much else of equal if not of greater significance. What that is, will be evident if certain facts are recalled to memory.

The Turks were by no means as illiberal as they are painted. They allowed their minorities a large measure of autonomy. The Turks had gone far towards solving the problem of how people of different communities with different social heritages are to live together in harmony when they are geographically intermingled. The Ottoman Empire had accorded, as a matter of course, to the non-Muslim and non-Turkish communities within its frontiers a degree of territorial as well as cultural autonomy which had never been dreamt of in the political philosophy of the West. Ought not the Christian subjects to have been satisfied with this? Say what one may, the nationalism of Christian minorities was not satisfied with this local autonomy. It fought for complete freedom and in that fight Turkey was slit open.

The Turks were bound to the Arabs by the tie of religion. The religious tie of Islam is the strongest known to humanity. No social confederacy can claim to rival the Islamic brotherhood in point of solidarity. Add to this the fact that while the Turk treated his Christian subjects as his inferior, he acknowledged the Arab as his equal. All non-Muslims were excluded from the Ottoman army. But the Arab soldiers and officers served side by side with Turks and Kurds. The Arab officer class, educated in Turkish schools, served in military and civil capacities on the same terms as the Turks. There was no derogating distinction between the Turk and the Arab, and there was nothing to prevent the Arab from rising to the highest rank in the Ottoman services. Not only politically but even socially the Arab was treated as his equal by the Turk and Arabs married Turkish wives and Turks married Arab wives. Ought not the Arabs to have been satisfied with this Islamic brotherhood of Arabs and Turks based on fraternity, liberty and equality? Say what one may, the Arabs were not satisfied. Arab nationalism broke the bonds of Islam and fought against his fellow Muslim, the Turk, for its independence. It won, but Turkey was completely dismantled.

As to Czechoslovakia, she began with the recognition that both the Czechs and the Slovaks were one people. Within a few years, the Slovaks claimed to be a separate nation. They would not even admit that they were a branch of the same stock as the Czechs. Their nationalism compelled the Czechs to recognize the fact that they were a distinct people. The Czechs sought to pacify the nationalism of the Slovaks by drawing a hyphen as a mark indicating distinctness. In place of Czechoslovakia they agreed to have Czecho-Slovakia. But even with the hyphen the Slovak nationalism remained discontented. The act of autonomy was both a hyphen separating them from the Czechs as well as a link joining them with the Czechs. The hyphen as making separation was welcome to the Slovaks but as making a link with the Czechs was very irksome to them. The Slovaks accepted the autonomy with its hyphen with great relief and promised to be content and loyal to the state. But evidently this was only a matter of strategy. They did not accept it as an ultimate end. They accepted it because they thought that they could use it as a vantage ground for destroying the hyphen which was their main aim and convert autonomy into independence. The nationalism of the Slovaks was not content with a hyphen. It wanted a bar in place of the hyphen. Immediately the hyphen was introduced, they began their battle to replace the hyphen between the Czechs and the Slovaks by a bar. They did not care what means they should employ. Their nationalism was so wrong-headed and so intense that when they failed they did not hesitate to call the aid of the Germans.

Thus a deeper study of the disruption of Turkey and Czechoslovakia shows that neither local autonomy nor the bond of religion is sufficient to withstand the force of nationalism, once it is set on the go.

This is a lesson which the Hindus will do well to grasp. They should ask themselves: if the Greek, Balkan and Arab nationalism has blown up the Turkish State and if Slovak nationalism has caused the dismantling of Czechoslovakia, what is there to prevent Muslim nationalism from disrupting the Indian State? If experience of other countries teaches that this is the inevitable consequence of pent-up nationalism, why not profit by their experience and avoid the catastrophe by agreeing to divide India into Pakistan and Hindustan? Let the Hindus take the warning that if they refuse to divide India into two before they launch on their career as a free people, they will be sailing in those shoal waters in which Turkey, Czechoslovakia and many others have foundered. If they wish to avoid shipwreck in mid-ocean, they must lighten the draught by throwing overboard all superfluous cargo. They will ease the course of their voyage considerably if they—to use the language of Prof. Toynbee—reconcile themselves to making jetsam of less cherished and more combustible cargo.

V

Will the Hindus really lose if they agree to divide India into two, Pakistan and Hindustan?

With regard to Czechoslovakia it is instructive to note the real feelings of its government on the loss of their territory caused by the Munich Pact. They were well expressed by the Prime Minister of Czechoslovakia in his message to the people of Czechoslovakia. In it he said*:—

> "Citizens and soldiers.... I am living through the hardest hour of my life; I am carrying out the most painful task, in comparison with which death would be easy. But precisely because I have fought and because I know under what conditions a war is won, I must tell you frankly ... that the forces opposed to us at this moment compel us to recognize their superior strength and to act accordingly....
>
> "In Munich four European Great Powers met and decided to demand of us the acceptance of new frontiers, according to which the German areas of our State would be taken away. We had the choice between desperate and hopeless defence, which would have meant the sacrifice not only of the adult generation but also of women and children, and the acceptance of conditions which in their ruthlessness, and because they were imposed by pressure without war, have no parallel in history. We desired to make a contribution to peace; we would gladly have made it. But not by any means in the way it has been forced upon us.
>
> "But we were abandoned, and were alone.... Deeply moved, all your leaders considered, together with the army and the President of the Republic, all the possibilities which remained.

* Alexander Henderson—*Eyewitness in Czechoslovakia* (Harrap, 1939), pp. 229-30.

> *They recognized that in choosing between narrower frontiers and the death of the nation it was their sacred duty to save the life of our people, so that we may not emerge weakened from these terrible times, and so that we may remain certain that our nation will gather itself together again, as it has done so often in the past. Let us all see that our State re-establishes itself soundly within its new frontiers, and that its population is assured of a new life of peace and fruitful labour.* With your help we shall succeed. We rely upon you, and you have confidence in us."

It is evident that the Czechs refused to be led by the force of historic sentiment. They were ready to have narrower frontiers and a smaller Czechoslovakia to the ultimate destruction of their people.

With regard to Turkey the prevalent view was the one that was expressed in 1853 by the Czar Nicholas I, during a conversation with British Ambassador in St. Petersburg in which he said "We have on our hand a sick man—a very sick man .... He may suddenly die upon our hands." From that day the imminent decease of Turkey, the sick man of Europe, was awaited by all his neighbours. The shedding of the territories was considered as the convulsions of a dying man who is alleged to have breathed his last by affixing his signature to the Treaty of Sèvres.

Is this really a correct view to take of Turkey in the process of dissolution? It is instructive to note the comments of Arnold Toynbee on this view. Referring to the Czar's description of Turkey as the sick man who may suddenly die, he says*:—

> "In this second and more sensational part of his diagnosis Czar Nicholas went astray because he did not understand the nature of the symptoms. If a person totally ignorant of natural history stumbled upon a snake in course of shedding its skin, he would pronounce dogmatically that the creature could not possibly recover. He could point out that when a man (or other mammal) has the misfortune to lose his skin, he is never known to survive. Yet while it is perfectly true that the leopard cannot change his spots nor the Ethiopian his skin, a wider study would have informed our amateur naturalist that a snake can do both and does both habitually. Doubtless, even for the snake, the process is awkward and uncomfortable. He becomes temporarily torpid, and in this condition he is dangerously at the mercy of his enemies. Yet, if he escapes the kites and crows

* Arnold Toynbee—*Turkey*, p. 141.

> until his metamorphosis is complete, he not only recovers his health but renews his youth with the replacement of his mortal coils. This is the recent experience of the Turk, and 'moulting snake' is better simile than sick man for a description of his distemper."

In this view, the loss of her possessions by Turkey is the removal of an anomalous excrescence and the gain of a new skin. Turkey is certainly homogeneous and has no fear of any disruption from within.

The Muslim areas are an anomalous excrescence on Hindustan and Hindustan is an anomalous excrescence on them. Tied together they will make India the sick man of Asia. Welded together they will make India a heterogeneous unit. If Pakistan has the demerit of cutting away parts of India, it has also the merit of introducing harmony in place of conflict.

Severed into two, each becomes a more homogeneous unit. The homogeneity of the two areas is obvious enough. Each has a cultural unity. Each has a religious unity. Pakistan has a linguistic unity. If there is no such unity in Hindustan, it is possible to have it without any controversy as to whether the common language should be Hindustani, Hindi or Urdu. Separated, each can become a strong and well-knit state. India needs a strong Central Government. But it cannot have it so long as Pakistan remains a part of India. Compare the structure of the Federal Government as embodied in the Government of India Act, 1935, and it will be found, that the Central Government as constituted under it is an effete ramshackle thing with very little life in it.* As has already been pointed out, this weakening of the Central Government is brought about by the desire to placate the Muslim Provinces who wish to be independent of the authority of the Central Government on the ground that the Central Government is bound to be predominantly Hindu in character and composition. When Pakistan comes into being these considerations can have no force. Hindustan can then have a strong Central Government and a homogeneous population, which are necessary elements for the stability of the state and neither of which will be secured unless there is severance of Pakistan from Hindustan.

* For further light on this topic, see my tract on *Federation vs. Freedom*.

PART IV

PAKISTAN AND THE MALAISE

The Hindu-Muslim problem has two aspects to it. In its first aspect, the problem that presents itself is the problem of two separate communities facing each other and seeking adjustment of their respective rights and privileges. In its other aspect, the problem is the problem of the reflex influences which this separation and conflict produces upon each of them. In the course of the foregoing discussion we have looked at the project of Pakistan in relation to the first of the aspects of the Hindu-Muslim problem. We have not examined the project of Pakistan in relation to the second aspect of that problem. Yet, such an examination is necessary because that aspect of the Hindu-Muslim problem is not unimportant. It is a very superficial if not an incomplete view to stop with the problem of the adjustment of their claims. It cannot be overlooked that their lot is cast together: as such they have to participate in a course of common activity whether they like it or not. And if in this common activity they face each other as two combatants do, then their actions and reactions are worth study, for they affect both and produce a state of affairs from which, if it is a deceased state, the question of escape must be faced. A study of the situation shows that the actions and reactions have produced a malaise which exhibits itself in three ways: (1) *Social Stagnation,* (2) *Communal Aggression, and* (3) *National Frustration of Political Destiny. This malaise is a grave one. Will Pakistan be a remedy for the malaise? or, will it aggravate the malaise? The following chapters are devoted to the consideration of these questions.*

CHAPTER X

SOCIAL STAGNATION

I

The social evils which characterize the Hindu Society, have been well known. The publication of *Mother India* by Miss Mayo gave these evils the widest publicity. But while *Mother India* served the purpose of exposing the evils and calling their authors at the bar of the world to answer for their sins, it created the unfortunate impression throughout the world that while the Hindus were grovelling in the mud of these social evils and were conservative, the Muslims in India were free from them, and as compared to the Hindus, were a progressive people. That, such an impression should prevail, is surprising to those who know the Muslim Society in India at close quarters.

One may well ask if there is any social evil which is found among the Hindus and is not found among the Muslims?

Take child-marriage. The Secretary of the Anti-Child-marriage Committee, constituted by the All-India Women's Conference, published a bulletin which gives the extent of the evil of child-marriage in the different communities in the country. The figures which were taken from the Census Report of 1931 are as follows:—

TABLE

Married Females aged 0-15 per 1000 Females of that age.

		Hindus.	Muslims.	Jains.	Sikhs.	Christians.
1881	..	208	153	189	170	33
1891	..	193	141	172	143	37
1901	..	186	131	164	101	38
1911	..	184	123	130	88	39
1921	..	170	111	117	72	32
1931	..	199	186	125	80	43

Can the position among the Musalmans so far as child-marriage goes, be considered better than the position among the Hindus?

Take the position of women. It is insisted by Muslims that the legal rights given to Muslim women, ensure them a greater measure of independence than that allowed to other Eastern women, for example, Hindu women, and are in excess of the rights given to women in some Western countries. Reliance is placed on some of the provisions of the Muslim Law.

Firstly, it is said the Muslim Law does not fix any age for marriage, and recognizes the right of a girl to marry any time. Further, except where the marriage is celebrated by the father or the grandfather, a Muslim girl, if given in marriage in childhood, has the power to repudiate her marriage on attaining puberty.

Secondly, it is held out that marriage among the Musalmans is a contract. Being a contract, the husband has a right to divorce his wife and the Muslim Law has provided ample safeguards for the wife which, if availed of, would place the Muslim wife on the same footing as the husband in the matter of divorce. For, it is claimed that the wife under the Muslim Law can, at the time of the marriage, or even thereafter in some cases, enter into a contract by which she may under certain circumstances obtain a divorce.

Thirdly, the Mahomedan Law requires that a wife can claim from her husband, by way of consideration for the surrender of her person, a sum of money or other property—known as her "dower". The dower may be fixed even after marriage and if no amount is fixed, the wife is entitled to proper dower. The amount of dower is usually split into two parts, one is called "prompt" which is payable on demand, and the other "deferred" which is payable on dissolution of marriage by death or divorce. Her claim for dower will be treated as a debt against the husband's estate. She has complete dominion over her dower which is intended to give her economic independence. She can remit it or she can appropriate the income of it as she pleases.

Granting all these provisions of law in her favour, the Muslim woman is the most helpless person in the world. To quote an Egyption Muslim leader :—

> "Islam has set its seal of inferiority upon her, and given the sanction of religion to social customs which have deprived her

of the full opportunity for self-expression and development of personality."

No Muslim girl has the courage to repudiate her marriage, although it may be open to her on the ground that she was a child and that it was brought about by persons other than her parents. No Muslim wife will think it proper to have a clause entered into her marriage contract reserving her the right to divorce. In that event, her fate is "once married, always married." She cannot escape the marriage tie, however irksome it may be. While she cannot repudiate the marriage, the husband can always do it without having to show any cause. Utter the word "*Tallak*" and observe continence for three weeks and the woman is cast away. The only restraint on his caprice is the obligation to pay dower. If the dower has already been remitted, his right to divorce is a matter of his sweet will.

This latitude in the matter of divorce destroys that sense of security which is so fundamental for a full, free and happy life for a woman. This insecurity of life, to which a Muslim woman is exposed, is greatly augmented by the right of polygamy and concubinage, which the Muslim Law gives to the husband.

Mahomedan Law allows a Muslim to marry four wives at a time. It is not unoften said that this is an improvement over the Hindu Law which places no restriction on the number of wives a Hindu can have at any given time. But it is forgotten that in addition to the four legal wives, the Muslim Law permits a Mahomedan to cohabit with his female slaves. In the case of female slaves nothing is said as to the number. They are allowed to him without any restriction whatever and without any obligation to marry them.

No words can adequately express the great and many evils of polygamy and concubinage and especially as a source of misery to a Muslim woman. It is true that because polygamy and concubinage are sanctioned, one must not suppose they are indulged in by the generality of Muslims; still the fact remains that they are privileges which are easy for a Muslim to abuse to the misery and unhappiness of his wife. Mr. John J. Pool, no enemy of Islam, observes*:—

* *Studies in Mahomedanism*, pp. 34-35.

"This latitude in the matter of divorce is very greatly taken advantage of by some Mohamedans. Stobart, commenting on this subject in his book, *Islam, and its Founder*, says: 'Some Mohamedans make a habit of continually changing their wives. We read of young men who have had twenty and thirty wives, a new one every three months; and thus it comes about that women are liable to be indefinitely transferred from one man to another, obliged to accept a husband and a home whenever they can find one, or in case of destitution, to which divorce may have driven them, to resort to other more degrading means of living.' Thus while keeping the strict letter of the law, and possessing only one or certainly not more than four wives, unscrupulous characters may yet by divorce obtain in a lifetime as many wives as they please.

"In another way also a Mohamedan may really have more than four wives, and yet keep within the law. This is by means of living with concubines, which the Koran expressly permits. In that *sura* which allows four wives, the words are added, 'of the slaves which ye shall have acquired.' Then in the 70th *sura*, it is revealed that it is no sin to live with slaves. The very words are: 'The slaves which their right hands possess, as to them they shall be blameless.' At the present day, as in days past, in multitudes of Mohamedan homes, slaves are found; as Muir says, in his *Life of Mahomet* 'so long as this unlimited permission of living with their female slaves continues, it cannot be expected that there will be any hearty attempt to put a stop to slavery in Mohamedan countries.' Thus the Koran, in this matter of slavery, is the enemy of the mankind. And women, as usual, are the greater sufferers."

Take the caste system. Islam speaks of brotherhood. Everybody infers that Islam must be free from slavery and caste. Regarding slavery nothing needs to be said. It stands abolished now by law. But while it existed much of its support was derived from Islam and Islamic countries.* While the prescriptions by the Prophet regarding the just and humane treatment of slaves contained in the Koran are praiseworthy, there is nothing whatever in Islam that lends support to the abolition of this curse. As Sir W. Muir has well said†:—

"... rather, while lightening, he rivetted the fetter.... There is no obligation on a Muslim to release his slaves...."

But if slavery has gone, caste among Musalmans has remained. As an illustration one may take the conditions prevalent

* Ibid., Chapter XXXIX.

† *The Koran, its Composition and Teaching*, p. 58.

among the Bengal Muslims. The Superintendent of the Census for 1901 for the Province of Bengal records the following interesting facts regarding the Muslims of Bengal :—

> "The conventional division of the Mahomedans into four tribes—Sheikh, Saiad, Moghul and Pathan—has very little application to this Province (Bengal). The Mahomedans themselves recognize two main social divisions, (1) Ashraf or Sharaf and (2) Ajlaf. Ashraf means 'noble' and includes all undoubted descendants of foreigners and converts from high caste Hindus. All other Mahomedans including the occupational groups and all converts of lower ranks, are known by the contemptuous terms, 'Ajlaf', 'wretches' or 'mean people': they are also called Kamina or Itar, 'base' or Rasil, a corruption of Rizal, 'worthless'. In some places a third class, called Arzal or 'lowest of all,' is added. With them no other Mahomedan would associate, and they are forbidden to enter the mosque or to use the public burial ground.
>
> "Within these groups there are castes with social precedence of exactly the same nature as one finds among the Hindus.
>
> I. *Ashraf* or better class Mahomedans.
>
> (1) Saiads.
> (2) Sheikhs.
> (3) Pathans.
> (4) Moghul.
> (5) Mallik.
> (6) Mirza.
>
> II. *Ajlaf* or lower class Mahomedans.
>
> (1) Cultivating Sheikhs, and others who were originally Hindus but who do not belong to any functional group, and have not gained admittance to the Ashraf Community, e.g. Pirali and Thakrai.
> (2) Darzi, Jolaha, Fakir, and Rangrez.
> (3) Barhi, Bhathiara, Chik, Churihar, Dai, Dhawa, Dhunia, Gaddi, Kalal, Kasai, Kula Kunjara, Laheri, Mahifarosh, Mallah, Naliya, Nikari.
> (4) Abdal, Bako, Bediya, Bhat, Chamba, Dafali, Dhobi, Hajjam, Mucho, Nagarchi, Nat, Panwaria, Madaria, Tuntia.
>
> III. *Arzal* or degraded class.
>
> Bhanar, Halalkhor, Hijra, Kasbi, Lalbegi, Maugta, Mehtar."

The Census Superintendent mentions another feature of the Muslim social system, namely, the prevalence of the "panchayet system." He states :—

"The authority of the panchayat extends to social as well as trade matters and . . . marriage with people of other communities is one of the offences of which the governing body takes cognizance. The result is that these groups are often as strictly endogamous as Hindu castes. The prohibition on inter-marriage extends to higher as well as to lower castes, and a Dhuma, for example, may marry no one but a Dhuma. If this rule is transgressed, the offender is at once hauled up before the panchayat and ejected ignominiously from his community. A member of one such group cannot ordinarily gain admission to another, and he retains the designation of the community in which he was born even if he abandons its distinctive occupation and takes to other means of livelihood . . . thousands of Jolahas are butchers, yet they are still known as Jolahas."

Similar facts from other Provinces of India could be gathered from their respective Census Reports and those who are curious may refer to them. But the facts for Bengal are enough to show that the Mahomedans observe not only caste but also untouchability.

There can thus be no manner of doubt that the Muslim Society in India is afflicted by the same social evils as afflict the Hindu Society. Indeed, the Muslims have all the social evils of the Hindus and something more. That something more is the compulsory system of *purdah* for Muslim women.

As a consequence of the *purdah* system a segregation of the Muslim women is brought about. The ladies are not expected to visit the outer rooms, verandahs or gardens, their quarters are in the back-yard. All of them, young and old, are confined in the same room. No male servant can work in their presence. A woman is allowed to see only her sons, brothers, father, uncles and husband, or any other near relation who may be admitted to a position of trust. She cannot go even to the mosque to pray and must wear *burka* (veil) whenever she has to go out. These *burka* women walking in the streets is one of the most hideous sights one can witness in India. Such seclusion cannot but have its deteriorating effects upon the physical constitution of Muslim women. They are usually victims to anæmia, tuberculosis and pyorrhœa. Their bodies are deformed, with their backs bent, bones protruded, hands and feet crooked. Ribs, joints and nearly all their bones ache. Heart palpitation is very often present in them. The result of this pelvic deformity is untimely death at the time of delivery. *Purdah* deprives Muslim women of mental and moral nourishment. Being deprived of healthy social life, the process of moral degeneration must and does set in. Being completely secluded from the outer world, they engage their minds in petty family quarrels with the result that they become narrow and restricted in their outlook.

They lag behind their sisters from other communities, cannot take part in any outdoor activity and are weighed down by a slavish mentality and an inferiority complex. They have no desire for knowledge, because they are taught not to be interested in anything outside the four walls of the house. *Purdah* women in particular become helpless, timid, and unfit for any fight in life. Considering the large number of *purdah* women among Muslims in India, one can easily understand the vastness and seriousness of the problem of *purdah.**

The physical and intellectual effects of *purdah* are nothing as compared with its effects on morals. The origin of *purdah* lies of course in the deep-rooted suspicion of sexual appetites in both sexes and the purpose is to check them by segregating the sexes. But far from achieving the purpose, *purdah* has adversely affected the morals of Muslim men. Owing to *purdah* a Muslim has no contact with any woman outside those who belong to his own household. Even with them his contact extends only to occasional conversation. For a male there is no company of and no commingling with the females except those who are children or aged. This isolation of the males from females is sure to produce bad effects on the morals of men. It requires no psychoanalyst to say that a social system which cuts off all contact between the two sexes produces an unhealthy tendency towards sexual excesses and unnatural and other morbid habits and ways.

The evil consequences of *purdah* are not confined to the Muslim community only. It is responsible for the social segregation of Hindus from Muslims which is the bane of public life in India. This argument may appear far fetched and one is inclined to attribute this segregation to the unsociability of the Hindus rather than to *purdah* among the Muslims. But the

* For the position of Muslim women, see *Our Cause*, edited by Shyam Kumar Nehru.

Hindus are right when they say that it is not possible to establish social contact between Hindus and Muslims because such contact can only mean contact between women from one side and men from the other.*

Not that *purdah* and the evils consequent thereon are not to be found among certain sections of the Hindus in certain parts of the country. But the point of distinction is that among the Muslims, *purdah* has a religious sanctity which it has not with the Hindus. *Purdah* has deeper roots among the Muslims than it has among the Hindus and can only be removed by facing the inevitable conflict between religious injunctions and social needs. The problem of *purdah* is a real problem with the Muslims—apart from its origin—which it is not with the Hindus. Of any attempt by the Muslims to do away with it, there is no evidence.

There is thus a stagnation not only in the social life but also in the political life of the Muslim community of India. The Muslims have no interest in politics as such. Their predominant interest is religion. This can be easily seen by the terms and conditions that a Muslim constituency makes for its support to a candidate fighting for a seat. The Muslim constituency does not care to examine the programme of the candidate. All that the constituency wants from the candidate is that he should agree to replace the old lamps of the masjid by supplying new ones at his cost, to provide a new carpet for the masjid because the old one is torn, or to repair the masjid because it has become dilapidated. In some places a Muslim constituency is quite satisfied if the candidate agrees to give a sumptuous feast and in other places if he agrees to buy votes for so much a piece. With the Muslims, election is a mere matter of money and is very seldom a matter of social programme of general improvement. Muslim politics takes no note of purely secular categories of life, namely, the differences between rich and poor, capital and labour, landlord and tenant, priest and layman, reason and

*It is interesting to note the argument which the Europeans who are accused by Indians for not admitting them to their clubs use to defend themselves. They say, "We bring our women to the clubs. If you agree to bring your women to the club, you can be admitted. We can't expose our women to your company if you deny us the company of your women. Be ready to go fifty-fifty, then ask for entry in our clubs."

superstition. Muslim politics is essentially clerical and recognizes only one difference, namely, that existing between Hindus and Muslims. None of the secular categories of life have any place in the politics of the Muslim community and if they do find a place—and they must because they are irrepressible—they are subordinated to one and the only governing principle of the Muslim political universe, namely, religion.

II

The existence of these evils among the Muslims is distressing enough. But far more distressing is the fact that there is no organized movement of social reform among the Musalmans of India on a scale sufficient to bring about their eradication. The Hindus have their social evils. But there is this relieving feature about them—namely, that some of them are conscious of their existence and a few of them are actively agitating for their removal. The Muslims, on the other hand, do not realize that they are evils and consequently do not agitate for their removal. Indeed, they oppose any change in their existing practices. It is noteworthy that the Muslims opposed the Child-Marriage Bill brought in the Central Assembly in 1930, whereby the age for marriage of a girl was raised to 14 and of a boy to 18 on the ground that it was opposed to the Muslim canon law. Not only did they oppose the bill at every stage but that when it became law they started a campaign of Civil Disobedience against that Act. Fortunately the Civil Disobedience campaign of the Muslims against the Act did not swell and was submerged in the Congress Civil Disobedience campaign which synchronized with it. But the campaign only proves how strongly the Muslims are opposed to social reform.

The question may be asked why are the Muslims opposed to social reform?

The usual answer given is that the Muslims all over the world are an unprogressive people. This view no doubt accords with the facts of history. After the first spurts of their activity—the scale of which was undoubtedly stupendous leading to the foundations of vast empires—the Muslims suddenly fell into a strange condition of torpor, from which they never seem to have become awake. The cause assigned for this torpor by those, who have made a study of their condition, is said to be the fundamental assumption made by all Muslims that Islam is a world religion, suitable for all peoples, for all times and for all conditions. It has been contended that :—

> "The Musalman, remaining faithful to his religion, has not progressed; he has remained stationary in a world of swiftly moving modern forces. It is, indeed, one of the salient features of Islam that it immobilizes in their native barbarism, the races whom it enslaves. It is fixed in a crystallization, inert and impenetrable. It is unchangeable; and political, social or economic changes have no repercussion upon it.
>
> "Having been taught that outside Islam there can be no safety; outside its law no truth and outside its spiritual message there is no happiness, the Muslim has become incapable of conceiving any other condition than his own, any other mode of thought than the Islamic thought. He firmly believes that he has arrived at an unequalled pitch of perfection; that he is the sole possessor of true faith, of the true doctrine, the true wisdom; that he alone is in possession of the truth—no relative truth subject to revision, but absolute truth.
>
> "The religious law of the Muslims has had the effect of imparting to the very diverse individuals of whom the world is composed, a unity of thought, of feeling, of ideas, of judgment."

It is urged that this uniformity is deadening and is not merely imparted to the Muslims, but is imposed upon them by a spirit of intolerance which is unknown anywhere outside the Muslim world for its severity and its violence and which is directed towards the suppression of all rational thinking which is in conflict with the teachings of Islam. As Renan observes*:—

> "Islam is a close union of the spiritual and the temporal; it is the reign of a dogma, it is the heaviest chain that humanity has ever borne.... Islam has its beauties as a religion;....But to the human reason Islamism has only been injurious. The minds that it has shut from the light were, no doubt, already closed in their own internal limits; but it has persecuted free thought, I shall not say more violently than other religions, but more effectually. It has made of the countries that it has conquered a closed field to the rational culture of the mind. What is, in fact essentially distinctive of the Musalman is his hatred of science, his persuasion that research is useless, frivolous, almost impious—the natural sciences, because they are attempts at

* *Nationality and other Essays.*

> rivalry with God; the historical sciences, because they apply to times anterior to Islam, they may revive ancient heresies . . . ."

Renan concludes by saying :—

> "Islam, in treating science as an enemy, is only consistent, but it is a dangerous thing to be consistent. To its own misfortune Islam has been successful. By slaying science it has slain itself; and is condemned in the world to a complete inferiority."

This answer though obvious, cannot be the true answer. If it were the true answer, how are we to account for the stir and ferment that is going on in all Muslim countries outside India, where the spirit of inquiry, the spirit of change and the desire to reform are noticeable in every walk of life. Indeed, the social reforms which have taken place in Turkey have been of the most revolutionary character. If Islam has not come in the way of the Muslims of these countries, why should it come in the way of the Muslims of India? There must be some special reason for the social and political stagnation of the Muslim community in India.

What can that special reason be? It seems to me that the reason for the absence of the spirit of change in the Indian Musalman is to be sought in the peculiar position he occupies in India. He is placed in a social environment which is predominantly Hindu. That Hindu environment is always silently but surely encroaching upon him. He feels that it is de-musalmanazing him. As a protection against this gradual weaning away he is led to insist on preserving everything that is Islamic without caring to examine whether it is helpful or harmful to his society. Secondly, the Muslims in India are placed in a political environment which is also predominantly Hindu. He feels that he will be suppressed and that political suppression will make the Muslims a depressed class. It is this consciousness that he has to save himself from being submerged by the Hindus socially and politically, which to my mind is the primary cause why the Indian Muslims as compared with their fellows outside are backward in the matter of social reform. Their energies are directed to maintaining a constant struggle against the Hindus for seats and posts in which there is no time, no thought and no room for questions relating to social reform. And if there is any, it is all overweighed and suppressed by the desire, generated by pressure of communal tension, to close the ranks and offer a united front to the menace of the Hindus and Hinduism by maintaining their socio-religious unity at any cost.

The same is the explanation of the political stagnation in the Muslim community of India. Muslim politicians do not recognize secular categories of life as the basis of their politics because to them it means the weakening of the community in its fight against the Hindus. The poor Muslims will not join the poor Hindus to get justice from the rich. Muslim tenants will not join Hindu tenants to prevent the tyranny of the landlord. Muslim labourers will not join Hindu labourers in the fight of labour against capital. Why? The answer is simple. The poor Muslim sees that if he joins in the fight of the poor against the rich, he may be fighting against a rich Muslim. The Muslim tenant feels that if he joins in the campaign against the landlord, he may have to fight against a Muslim landlord. A Muslim labourer feels that if he joins in the onslaught of labour against capital, he will be injuring a Muslim mill-owner. He is conscious that any injury to a rich Muslim, to a Muslim landlord or to a Muslim mill-owner, is a disservice to the Muslim community, for it is thereby weakened in its struggle against the Hindu community.

How Muslim politics has become perverted is shown by the attitude of the Muslim leaders to the political reforms in the Indian States. The Muslims and their leaders carried on a great agitation for the introduction of representative government in the Hindu State of Kashmir. The same Muslims and their leaders are deadly opposed to the introduction of representative governments in other Muslim States. The reason for this strange attitude is quite simple. In all matters, the determining question with the Muslims is how it will affect the Muslims *vis-à-vis* the Hindus. If representative government can help the Muslims, they will demand it, and fight for it. In the State of Kashmir the ruler is a Hindu, but the majority of the subjects are Muslims. The Muslims fought for representative government in Kashmir, because representative government in Kashmir meant the transfer of power from a Hindu king to the Muslim masses. In other Muslim States, the ruler is a Muslim but the majority of his subjects are Hindus. In such States representative government means the transfer of power from a Muslim ruler to the Hindu masses, and that is why the Muslims support the introduction of representative government in one case and oppose it in the other. The dominating consideration with the Muslims is not democracy. The dominating consideration is how democracy with majority rule will affect the Muslims in their struggle against the Hindus. Will it strengthen them or will it weaken them? If democracy weakens them, they will not have democracy. They will prefer the rotten state to continue in the Muslim States rather than weaken the Muslim ruler in his hold upon his Hindu subjects.

The political and social stagnation in the Muslim community can be explained by one and only one reason. The Muslims think that the Hindus and Muslims must perpetually struggle; the Hindus to establish their dominance over the Muslims and the Muslims to establish their historical position as the ruling community—that in this struggle the strong will win, and to ensure strength they must suppress or put in cold storage everything which causes dissension in their ranks.

If the Muslims in other countries have undertaken the task of reforming their society and the Muslims of India have refused to do so, it is because the former are free from communal and political clashes with rival communities, while the latter are not.

III

It is not that this blind spirit of conservatism which does not recognize the need of repair to the social structure has taken hold of the Muslims only. It has taken hold of the Hindus also. The Hindus at one time did recognize that without social efficiency no permanent progress in other fields of activity was possible, that, owing to the mischief wrought by evil customs Hindu Society was not in a state of efficiency and that ceaseless efforts must be made to eradicate these evils. It was due to the recognition of this fact that the birth of the National Congress was accompanied by the foundation of the Social Conference. While the Congress was concerned with defining the weak points in the political organisation of the country, the Social Conference was engaged in removing the weak points in the social organisation of the Hindu Society. For some time, the Congress and the Conference worked as two wings of one common body and held their annual sessions in the same pandal. But soon the two wings developed into two parties, a Political Reform Party and a Social Reform Party, between whom raged fierce controversy. The Political Reform Party supported the National Congress and the Social Reform Party supported the Social Conference. The two bodies became two hostile camps. The point at issue was whether social reform should precede political reform. For a decade the forces were evenly balanced and the battle was fought without victory to either side. It was, however, evident that the fortunes of the Social Conference were ebbing fast. The gentlemen who presided over the sessions of the Social Conference lamented that the majority of the educated Hindus were for political advancement and indifferent to social reform and that while the number of those who attended the Congress was very large and the number who did not attend but who sympathized with it even larger, the number of those who attended the Social Conference was very much smaller. This indifference, this thinning of its ranks was soon followed by active hostility from the politicians, like the late Mr. Tilak. In course of time, the party in favour of political reform won and the Social Conference vanished and was forgotten.* With it also vanished from the Hindu Society the urge for social reform. Under the leadership of Mr. Gandhi, the Hindu Society, if it did not become a political mad-house, certainly became mad after politics. Non-co-operation, Civil Disobedience, and the cry for Swaraj took the place which social reform once had in the minds of the Hindus. In the din and dust of political agitation, the Hindus do not even know that there are any evils to be remedied. Those who are conscious of it, do not believe that social reform is as important as political reform, and when forced to admit its importance argue that there can be no social reform unless political power is first achieved. They are so eager to possess political power that they are impatient even of propaganda in favour of social reform, as it means so much time and energy deducted from political propaganda. A correspondent of Mr. Gandhi put the point of view of the Nationalists

* For a more detailed statement, see my tract on *Annihilation of Caste.*

very appropriately, if bluntly, when he wrote* to Mr. Gandhi, saying :—

> "Don't you think that it is impossible to achieve any great reform without winning political power? The present economic structure has got to be tackled? No reconstruction is possible without political reconstruction and I am afraid all this talk of polished and unpolished rice, balanced diet and so on and so forth is mere moonshine."

The Social Reform Party, led by Ranade, died leaving the field to the Congress. There has grown up among the Hindus another party which is also a rival to the Congress. It is the Hindu Maha Sabha. One would expect from its name that it was a body for bringing about the reform of Hindu Society. But it is not. Its rivalry with the Congress has nothing to do with the issue of social reform *vs.* political reform. Its quarrel with the Congress has its origin in the pro-Muslim policy of the Congress. It is organized for the protection of Hindu rights against Muslim encroachment. Its plan is to organize the Hindus for offering a united front to the Muslims. As a body organized to protect Hindu rights it is all the time engaged in keeping an eye on political movements, on seats and posts. It cannot spare any thought for social reform. As a body keen on bringing about a united front of all Hindus, it cannot afford to create dissensions among its elements which would be the case if it undertook to bring about social reforms. For the sake of the consolidation of the Hindu rank and file, the Hindu Maha Sabha is ready to suffer all social evils to remain as they are. For the sake of consolidation of the Hindus, it is prepared to welcome the Federation as devised by the Act of 1935 in spite of its many iniquities and defects. For the same purpose, the Hindu Maha Sabha favours the retention of the Indian States, with their administration as it is. 'Hands off the Hindu States' has been the battle-cry of its President. This attitude is stranger than that of the Muslims. Representative government in Hindu States cannot do harm to the Hindus. Why then should the President of the Hindu Maha Sabha oppose it? Probably because it helps the Muslims, whom he cannot tolerate.

* *Harijan* — 11th January 1936.

IV

To what length this concern for the conservation of their forces can lead the Hindus and the Musalmans cannot be better illustrated than by the debates on the Dissolution of Muslim Marriage Act VIII of 1939 in the Central Assembly. Before 1939, the law was that apostasy of a male or a female married under the Muslim law *ipso facto* dissolved the marriage with the result that if a married Muslim woman changed her religion, she was free to marry a person professing her new religion. This was the rule of law enforced by the courts, throughout India at any rate, for the last 60 years.*

This law was annulled by Act VIII of 1939, section 4 of which reads as follows :—

> "The renunciation of Islam by a married Muslim woman or her conversion to a faith other than Islam shall not by itself operate to dissolve her marriage:
>
> Provided that after such renunciation or conversion the woman shall be entitled to obtain a decree for the dissolution of marriage on any of the grounds mentioned in section 2 :
>
> Provided further that the provisions of this section shall not apply to a woman converted to Islam from some other faith who re-embraces her former faith."

According to this Act, the marriage of a married Muslim woman is not dissolved by reason of her conversion to another religion. All that she gets is a right of divorce. It is very intriguing to find that section 2 does not refer to conversion or apostasy as a ground for divorce. The effect of the law is that a married Muslim woman has no liberty of conscience and is tied for ever to her husband whose religious faith may be quite abhorrent to her.

The grounds urged in support of this change are well worth attention. The mover of the Bill, Quazi Kazmi, M.L.A., adopted a very ingenious line of argument in support of the change. In his speech† on the motion to refer the Bill he said :—

> "Apostasy was considered by Islam, as by any other religion, as a great crime, almost amounting to a crime against the State.

* The earliest reported decision was that given by the High Court of the North-West Province in 1870 in the case of *Zabaroast Khan vs. His wife*.

† *Legislative Assembly Debates*, 1938, Vol. V, pp. 1098-101.

It is not novel for the religion of Islam to have that provision. If we look up the older Acts of any nation, we will find that similar provision also exists in other Codes as well. For the male a severer punishment was awarded, that of death, and for females, only the punishment of imprisonment was awarded. This main provision was that because it was a sin, it was a crime, it was to be punished, and the woman was to be deprived of her status as wife. It was not only this status that she lost, but she lost all her status in society; she was deprived of her property and civil rights as well. But we find that as early as 1850 an Act was passed here, called the Caste Disabilities Removal Act of 1850, Act XXI of 1850.....

"....by this Act, the forfeiture of civil rights that could be imposed on a woman on her apostasy has been taken away. She can no longer be subjected to any forfeiture of property or her right of inheritance or anything of the kind. The only question is that the Legislature has come to her help, it has given her a certain amount of liberty of thought, some kind of liberty of religion to adopt any faith she likes, and has removed the forfeiture clause from which she could suffer, and which was a restraint upon her changing the faith. The question is how far we are entitled after that to continue placing the restriction on her status as a wife. Her status as a wife is of some importance in society. She belongs to some family, she has got children, she has got other connections too. If she has got a liberal mind, she may not like to continue the same old religion. If she changes her religion, why should we, according to our modern ideas, inflict upon her a further penalty that she will cease to be the wife of her husband. I submit, in these days when we are advocating freedom of thought and freedom of religion, when we are advocating inter-marriages between different communities, it would be inconsistent for us to support a provision that a mere change of faith or change of religion would entail forfeiture of her rights as the wife of her husband. So, from a modern point of view, I have got no hesitation in saying that we cannot, in any way, support the contrary proposition that apostasy must be allowed to finish her relationship with her husband. But that is only one part of the argument.

"Section 32 of the Parsi Marriage and Divorce Act, 1936, is to the effect that a married woman may sue for divorce on the grounds 'that the defendant has ceased to be a Parsi....'

"There are two things apparent from this. The first is, that it is a ground for dissolution, not from any religious idea or religious sentiment, because, if two years have passed after the conversion and if plaintiff does not object, then either the male or female has no right to sue for dissolution of marriage. The second thing is, that it is the plaintiff who has got the complaint that the other party has changed the religion, who has got the right of getting the marriage dissolved.........In addition to this Act, as regards other communities we can have an idea of the effect of conversion on marriage tie from the Native Converts' Marriage Dissolution Act, Act XXI of 1886........It applies to all the communities of India, and this legislation recognises the fact that mere conversion of an Indian to Christianity would not dissolve the marriage but he will have the right of going to a law court and saying that the other party, who is not converted, must perform the marital duties in respect of him........then they are given a year's time and the judge directs that they shall have an interview with each other in the presence of certain other persons to induce them to resume their conjugal relationship, and if they do not agree, then on the ground of desertion the marriage is dissolved. The marriage is dissolved no doubt, but not on the ground of change of faith.........So, every community in India has got this accepted principle that conversion to another religion cannot amount to a dissolution of marriage."

Syed Gulam Bikh Nairang, another Muslim member of the Assembly and a protagonist of the Bill, was brutally frank. In support of the principle of the Bill he said*:—

"For a very long time the courts in British India have held without reservation and qualification that under all circumstances apostasy automatically and immediately puts an end to the married state without any judicial proceedings, any decree of court, or any other ceremony. That has been the position which was taken up by the Courts. Now, there are three distinct views of *Hanafi jurists* on the point. One view which is attributed to the Bokhara jurists was adopted and even that not in its entirety but in what I may call a mutilated and maimed condition. What that Bokhara view is has been already stated by Mr. Kazmi and some other speakers. The Bokhara jurists say that marriage is dissolved by apostasy. In fact, I should be more accurate in saying—I have got authority for that—that it is, according to the Bokhara view, not dissolved but suspended. The marriage is suspended but the wife is then kept in custody or confinement till she repents and embraces Islam again, and then she is induced to marry the husband, whose marriage was only suspended and not put an end to or cancelled. The second view is that on apostasy a married Muslim woman ceases to be the wife of her husband but becomes his bond woman. One view, which is a sort of corollary to this view, is that she is not necessarily the bond woman of her ex-husband but she becomes the bond woman of the entire Muslim community and anybody can employ her as a bond woman. The third view, that of the Ulema of

* *Legislative Assembly Debates*, 1938, Vol. V, pp. 1953-55.

Samarkand and Balkh, is that the marriage tie is not affected by such apostasy and that the woman still continues to be the wife of the husband. These are the three views. A portion of the first view, the Bokhara view, was taken hold of by the Courts and rulings after rulings were based on that portion.

"This House is well aware that it is not only in this solitary instance that judicial error is sought to be corrected by legislation, but in many other cases, too, there have been judicial errors or conflicts of judicial opinion or uncertainties and vagueness of law. Errors of judicial view are being constantly corrected by legislation. In this particular matter there has been an error after error and a tragedy of errors. To show me those rulings is begging the question. Surely, it should be realized that it is no answer to my Bill that because the High Courts have decided against me, I have no business to come to this House and ask it to legislate this way or that way."

Having regard to the profundity of the change, the arguments urged in support of it were indeed very insubstantial. Mr. Kazmi failed to realize that if there was a difference between the divorce law relating to Parsis, Christians and Muslims, once it is established that the conversion is genuine, the Muslim law was in advance of the Parsi and the Christian law and instead of making the Muslim law retrograde, the proper thing ought to have been to make the Parsi and the Christian law progress. Mr. Nairang did not stop to inquire that, if there were different schools of thought among the Muslim jurists, whether it was not more in consonance with justice to adopt the more enlightened view which recognized the freedom of the Muslim woman and not to replace it by the barbaric one which made her a bondswoman.

Be that as it may, the legal arguments had nothing to do with the real motive underlying the change. The real motive was to put a stop to the illicit conversion of women to alien faiths, followed by immediate and hurried marriages with some one professing the faith she happened to have joined, with a view to locking her in the new community and preventing her from going back to the community to which she originally belonged. The conversion of Muslim women to Hinduism and of Hindu women to Islam looked at from a social and political point of view cannot but be fraught with tremendous consequences. It means a disturbance in the numerical balance between the two communities. As the disturbance was being brought about by the abduction of women, it could not be overlooked. For woman is at once the seed-bed of and the hot-house for nationalism in a degree that man can never be.* These conversions of women and their subsequent marriages were therefore regarded, and rightly, as a series of depredations practised by Hindus against Muslims and by Muslims against Hindus with a view to bringing about a change in their relative numerical strength. This abominable practice of woman-lifting had become as common as cattle-lifting and, with its obvious danger to communal balance, efforts had to be made to stop it. That this was the real reason behind this legislation can be seen from the two provisions to section 4 of the Act. In proviso 1 the Hindus concede to the Musalmans that if they convert a woman who was originally a Muslim she will remain bound to her former Muslim husband notwithstanding her conversion. By proviso 2 the Muslims concede to the Hindus that if they convert a Hindu married woman and she is married to a Musalman, her marriage will be deemed to be dissolved if she renounces Islam and she will be free to return to her Hindu fold. Thus what underlies the change in law is the desire to keep the numerical balance and it is for this purpose that the rights of women were sacrificed.

There are two other features of this malaise which have not been sufficiently noted.

One such feature is the jealousy with which one of them looks upon any reform by the other in its social system. If the effect of such reform is to give it increase of strength for resistance, it at once creates hostility.

Swami Shradanand relates a very curious incident which well illustrates this attitude. Writing in the *Liberator* † his recollections, he refers to this incident. He says:—

> "Mr. Ranade was there .... to guide the Social Conference to which the title of 'National' was for the first and last time given. It was from the beginning a Hindu Conference in all walks of life. The only Mahomedan delegate who joined the National Social Conference was a Mufti Saheb of Barreily. Well! The conference began when the resolution in favour of

* The part played by woman in sustaining nationalism has not been sufficiently noticed. See the observations of Renan on this point in his *Essay on Nationality*.

† 26th April 1926.

remarriage of child-widows was moved by a Hindu delegate and by me. Sanatanist Pandits opposed it. Then the Mufti asked permission to speak. The late Baijnath told Mufti Saheb that as the resolution concerned the Hindus only, he need not speak. At this the Mufti flared up.

"There was no loophole left for the President and Mufti Saheb was allowed to have his say. Mufti Saheb's argument was that as Hindu Shastras did not allow remarriage, it was a sin to press for it. Again, when the resolution about the reconversion of those who had become Christians and Musalmans came up, Mufti Saheb urged that when a man abandoned the Hindu religion he ought not to be allowed to come back."

Another illustration would be the attitude of the Muslims towards the problem of the Untouchables. The Muslims have always been looking at the Depressed Classes with a sense of longing and much of the jealousy between Hindus and Muslims arises out of the fear of the latter that the former might become stronger by assimilating the Depressed Classes. In 1909 the Muslims took the bold step of suggesting that the Depressed Classes should not be enrolled in the census as Hindus. In 1923 Mr. Mahomed Ali in his address as the President of the Congress went much beyond the position taken by the Muslims in 1909. He said :—

"The quarrels about ALAMS and PIPAL trees and musical processions are truly childish; but there is one question which can easily furnish a ground for complaint of unfriendly action if communal activities are not amicably adjusted. It is the question of the conversion of the Suppressed Classes, if Hindu society does not speedily absorb them. The Christian missionary is already busy and no one quarrels with him. But the moment some Muslim Missionary Society is organized for the same purpose there is every likelihood of an outcry in the Hindu press. It has been suggested to me by an influential and wealthy gentleman who is able to organize a Missionary Society on a large scale for the conversion of the Suppressed Classes, that it should be possible to reach a settlement with leading Hindu gentlemen and divide the country into separate areas where Hindu and Muslim missionaries could respectively work, each community preparing for each year, or longer unit of time if necessary, an estimate of the numbers it is prepared to absorb or convert. These estimates would, of course, be based on the number of workers and funds each had to spare, and tested by the actual figures of the previous period. In this way each community would be free to do the work of absorption and conversion, or rather, of reform without chances of collision with one another. I cannot

> say in what light my Hindu brethren will take it and I place this suggestion tentatively in all frankness and sincerity before them. All that I say for myself is that I have seen the condition of the 'Kali Praja' in the Baroda State and of the Gonds in the Central Provinces and I frankly confess it is a reproach to us all. If the Hindus will not absorb them into their own society, others will and must, and then the orthodox Hindu too will cease to treat them as untouchables. Conversion seems to transmute them by a strong alchemy. But does this not place a premium upon conversion?"

The other feature is the "preparations" which the Muslims and Hindus are making against each other without abatement. It is like a race in armaments between two hostile nations. If the Hindus have the Benares University, the Musalmans must have the Aligarh University. If the Hindus start Shudhi movement, the Muslims must launch the Tablig movement. If the Hindus start Sangathan, the Muslims must meet it by Tanjim. If the Hindus have the R. S. S. S.,* the Muslims must reply by organizing the Khaksars.† This race in social armament and equipment is run with the determination and apprehension characteristic of nations which are on the war path. The Muslims fear that the Hindus are subjugating them. The Hindus feel that the Muslims are engaged in reconquering them. Both appear to be preparing for war and each is watching the "preparations" of the other.

Such a state of things cannot but be ominous. It is a vicious circle. If the Hindus make themselves stronger, the Musalmans feel menaced. The Muslims endeavour to increase their forces to meet the menace and the Hindus then do the same to equalize the position. As the preparations proceed, so does the suspicion, the secrecy, and the plotting. The possibilities of peaceful adjustment are poisoned at the source and precisely because everyone is fearing and preparing for it that "war" between the two tends to become inevitable. But in the situation in which they find themselves, for the Hindus and the Muslims not to attend to anything, except to prepare themselves to meet the challenge of each other, is quite natural. It is a struggle for

---

* Short for the Rashtriya Swayam Sevaka Sangh which is a Hindu volunteer corps.

† Khaksar is a Muslim volunteer corps.

existence and the issue, that counts, is survival and not the quality or the plane of survival.

Two things must be said to have emerged from this discussion. One is that the Hindus and the Muslims regard each other as a menace. The second is that to meet this menace, both have suspended the cause of removing the social evils with which they are infested. Is this a desirable state of things? If it is not how then can it be ended?

No one can say that to have the problems of social reform put aside is a desirable state of things. Wherever there are social evils, the health of the body politic requires that they shall be removed before they become the symbols of suffering and injustice. For it is the social and economic evils which everywhere are the parent of revolution or decay. Whether social reform should precede political reform or political reform should precede social reform may be a matter of controversy. But there can be no two opinions on the question that the sole object of political power is the use to which it can be put in the cause of social and economic reform. The whole struggle for political power would be a barren and bootless effort if it was not justified by the feeling that, because of the want of political power, urgent and crying social evils are eating into the vitals of society and are destroying it. But suppose the Hindus and the Muslims somehow come into possession of political power, what hope is there that they will use it for purposes of social reform? There is hardly any hope in that behalf. So long as the Hindus and the Muslims regard each other as a menace, their attention will be engrossed in preparations for meeting the menace. The exigencies of a common front by Musalmans against Hindus and by Hindus against Musalmans generate—and is bound to generate—a conspiracy of silence over social evils. Neither the Muslims nor the Hindus will attend to them even though the evils may be running sores and requiring immediate attention, for the simple reason that they regard every measure of social reform as bound to create dissension and division and thereby weaken the ranks when they ought to be closed to meet the menace of the other community. It is obvious that so long as one community looks upon the other as a menace there will be no social progress and the spirit of conservatism will continue to dominate the thoughts and actions of both.

How long will this menace last? It is sure to last as long as the Hindus and Muslims are required to live as members of one country under the mantle of a single constitution. For, it is the fear of the single constitution with the possibility of the shifting of the balance—for nothing can keep the balance at the point originally fixed by the constitution—which makes the Hindus a menace to the Muslims and the Muslims a menace to the Hindus. If this is so, Pakistan is the obvious remedy. It certainly removes the chief condition which makes for the menace. Pakistan liberates both the Hindus and the Muslims from the fear of enslavement of and encroachment against each other. It removes, by providing a separate constitution for each, Pakistan and Hindustan, the very basis which leads to this perpetual struggle for keeping a balance of power in the day-to-day life and frees them to take in hand those vital matters of urgent social importance which they are now forced to put aside in cold storage, and improve the lives of their people, which after all is the main object of this fight for Swaraj.

Without some such arrangement, the Hindus and the Muslims will act and react as though they were two nations, one fearing to be conquered by the other. Preparations for aggression will always have precedence over social reform, so that the social stagnation which has set in must continue. This is quite natural and no one need be surprised at it. For, as Bernard Shaw pointed out:—

> "A conquered nation is like a man with cancer; he can think of nothing else.... A healthy nation is as unconscious of its nationality as a healthy man of his bones. But if you break a nation's nationality, it will think of nothing else but getting it set again. It will listen to no reformer, to no philosopher, to no preacher until the demand of the nationalist is granted. It will attend to no business, however vital, except the business of unification and liberation."

Unless there is unification of the Muslims who wish to separate from the Hindus and unless there is liberation of each from the fear of domination by the other, there can be no doubt that this malaise of social stagnation will not be set right.

CHAPTER XI

COMMUNAL AGGRESSION

Even a superficial observer cannot fail to notice that a spirit of aggression underlies the Hindu attitude towards the Muslim and the Muslim attitude towards the Hindu. The Hindu's spirit of aggression is a new phase which he has just begun to cultivate. The Muslim's spirit of aggression is his native endowment and is ancient as compared with that of the Hindu. It is not that the Hindu, if given time, will not pick up and overtake the Muslim. But as matters stand to-day, the Muslim in this exhibition of the spirit of aggression leaves the Hindu far behind.

Enough has been said about the social aggression of the Muslims in the chapter dealing with communal riots. It is necessary to speak briefly of the political aggression of the Muslims. For this political aggression has created a malaise which cannot be overlooked.

Three things are noticeable about this political aggression of the Muslims.

First is the ever-growing catalogue of the Muslim's political demands. Their origin goes back to the year 1892.

In 1885 the Indian National Congress was founded. It began with a demand for good government as distinguished from self-government. In response to this demand the British Government felt the necessity of altering the nature of the Legislative Councils, Provincial and Central, established under the Act of 1861. In that nascent stage of Congress agitation, the British Government did not feel called upon to make them fully popular. It thought it enough to give them a popular colouring. Accordingly the British Parliament passed in 1892 what is called the Indian Councils Act. This Act is memorable for two things. It was in this Act of 1892 that the British Government for the first time accepted the semblance of the principle of popular representation as the basis for the constitution of the Legislatures in India. It was not a principle of election. It was a principle of nomination, only it was qualified by the requirement that before nomination a person must be selected by important public bodies such as municipalities, district boards, universities and the associations of merchants, etc. Secondly, it was in the legislatures that were constituted under this Act that the principle of separate representation for Musalmans was for the first time introduced in the political constitution of India.

The introduction of this principle is shrouded in mystery. It is a mystery because it was introduced so silently and so stealthily. The principle of separate representation does not find a place in the Act. The Act says nothing about it. It was in the directions—but not in the Act—issued to those charged with the duty of framing regulations as to the classes and interests to whom representation was to be given that the Muslims were named as a class to be provided for.

It is a mystery as to who was responsible for its introduction. This scheme of separate representation was not the result of any demand put forth by any organized Muslim association. In whom did it then originate? It is suggested* that it originated with the Viceroy, Lord Dufferin, who, as far back as the year 1888, when dealing with the question of representation in the Legislative Councils, emphasized the necessity that in India representation will have to be, not in the way representation is secured in England, but representation by interests. Curiosity leads to a further question, namely, what could have led Lord Dufferin to propose such a plan? It is suggested† that the idea was to wean‡ away the Musalmans from the Congress which had already been started three years before. Be that as it may, it is certain that it is by this Act that separate representation for Muslims became, for the first time, a feature of the Indian Constitution. It should, however, be noted that neither the Act

* See the speech of Sir Mahomad Shafi in the Minorities Sub-Committee of the first R.T.C. (Indian Edition), p. 57.

† See the speech of Raja Narendranath, Ibid., p. 65.

‡ The Musalmans had already been told by Sir Sayad Ahmad not to join the Congress in the two speeches, one delivered at Lucknow on 28th December 1887, and the other at Meerut on 16th March 1888. Mr. Mahomed Ali in his presidential address speaks of them as historic speeches.

nor the Regulations conferred any right of selection upon the Muslim community, nor did the Act give the Muslim community a right to claim a fixed number of seats. All that it did was to give the Muslims the right to separate representation.

Though, to start with, the suggestion of separate representation came from the British, the Muslims did not fail to appreciate the social value of separate political rights with the result that when in 1909 the Muslims came to know that the next step in the reform of the Legislative Councils was contemplated, they waited of their own accord in deputation* upon the Viceroy, Lord Minto, and placed before him the following demands:—

(i) Communal representation in accordance with their numerical strength, social position and local influence, on district and municipal boards.

(ii) An assurance of Muhammadan representation on the governing bodies of Universities.

(iii) Communal representation on provincial councils, election being by special electoral colleges composed of Muhammadan landlords, lawyers, merchants, and representatives of other important interests, University graduates of a certain standing and members of district and municipal boards.

(iv) The number of Muhammadan representatives in the Imperial Legislative Council should not depend on their numerical strength, and Muhammadans should never be in an ineffective minority. They should be elected as far as possible (as opposed to being nominated), election being by special Muhammadan colleges composed of landowners, lawyers, merchants, members of provincial councils, Fellows of Universities, etc.

These demands were granted and given effect to in the Act of 1909. Under this Act the Muhammadans were given (1) the right to elect their representatives, (2) the right to elect their representatives by separate electorates, (3) the right to vote in the general electorates as well, and (4) the right to weightage in representation. The following table shows the proportion of representation secured to the Muslims in the Legislatures by the Act of 1909 and the Regulations made thereunder:—

* Mr. Mahomed Ali in his speech as the President of the Congress said that this deputation was a "command performance".

Composition of Legislative Councils under the Act of 1909 showing Communal Proportion between Hindus and Muslims

Province.	Maximum number of Additional Members prescribed by the Act of 1909.	Maximum number of Additional Members allowed by Regulations: columns 5 and 12.	Ex-officio Members.	Strength of the Councils under the Regulations.									Total strength columns 4, 5, 12.
				Elected Members.			Nominated Members.						
							Officials.						
				Total.	Non-Muslims.	Muslims.	Law Officers.	Others*	Non-Officials.	Experts.	Total.		
1	2	3	4	5	6	7	8	9	10	11	12		13
India	60	60	8	27	22	5	...	28	5	...	33		68
Madras	50	45	4	21	19	2	1	16	5	2	24		49
Bombay	50	45	4	21	17	4	1	14	7	2	24		49
Bengal	50	50	4	28	23	5	...	16	4	2	22		54
Bihar	50	41	4	21	17	4	...	15	4	1	20		45
U. P.	50	49	1	21	17	4	...	20	6	2	28		50
Punjab	30	26	1	8	8	none.	...	10	6	2	18		27
Burma	30	17	1	1	1	none.	...	6	8	2	16		18
Assam	30	25	1	11	9	2	...	9	4	1	14		25

* The numbers in column 9 represent the maximum of Official Members permitted under the Regulations.

The provisions were applied to all Provinces except the Punjab and the C. P. It was not applied to the Punjab because such special protection was considered unnecessary for the Musalmans of the Punjab and it was not applied to the C. P. because it had no Legislative Council at the time.*

In October 1916, 19 members of the Imperial Legislative Council presented the Viceroy (Lord Chelmsford) a memorandum demanding a reform of the Constitution. Immediately the Muslims came forward with a number of demands on behalf of the Muslim community. These were :—

(i) The extension of the principle of separate representation to the Punjab and the C. P.

(ii) Fixing the numerical strength of the Muslim representatives in the Provincial and Imperial Legislative Councils.

(iii) Safeguards against legislation affecting Muslims, their religion and religious usages.

The negotiations following upon these demands resulted in agreement between the Hindus and the Muslims which is known as the Lucknow Pact. It may be said to contain two clauses. One related to legislation, under which it was agreed that :—

> "No Bill, nor any clause thereof, nor a resolution introduced by a non-official affecting one or other community (which question is to be determined by the members of that community in the Legislative Council concerned) shall be proceeded with, if three-fourths of the members of that community in the particular Council, Imperial and Provincial, oppose the Bill or any clause thereof or the resolution."

The other clause related to the proportion of Muslim representation. With regard to the Imperial Legislative Council the Pact provided :—

> "That one-third of the Indian elected members should be Muhammadans, elected by separate electorates in the several Provinces, in the proportion, as nearly as might be, in which they were represented on the provincial legislative councils by separate Muhammadan electorates."

* The C. P. Legislative Council was established in 1914.

In the matter of Muslim representation in the Provincial Legislative Councils it was agreed that the proportion of Muslim representation should be as follows*:—

	Percentage of elected Indian Members to the Provincial Legislature
Punjab	50
United Provinces	30
Bengal	40
Bihar and Orissa	25
Central Provinces	15
Madras	15
Bombay	33

While allowing this proportion of seats to the Muslims, the right to second vote in the general electorates which they had under the arrangement of 1909 was taken away.

The Lucknow Pact was adversely criticized by the Montagu-Chelmsford Report. But being an agreement between the parties Government did not like to reject it and to substitute in its place its own decision. Both clauses of the agreement were accepted by Government and embodied in the Government of India Act of 1919. The clause relating to legislation was given effect to but in a different form. Instead of leaving it to the members of the Legislature to oppose it, it was provided† that legislation affecting the religion or religious rites and usages of any class of British subjects in India shall not be introduced at any meeting of either Chamber of the Indian Legislature without the previous sanction of the Governor-General.

The clause relating to representation was accepted by the Government, though in the opinion of the Government the Punjab and Bengal Muslims were not fairly treated.

The effect of these concessions can be seen by reference to the composition of the Legislatures constituted under the Government of India Act, 1919, which was as follows:—

* For some reason the Pact did not settle the proportion of Muslim representation in Assam.

† Government of India Act, 1919, section 67 (2) (*b*).

Composition of the Legislatures

—	Statutory Minimum.	Elected Members.			Nominated Members.		Actual Total.
		Total	Muslims	Non-Muslims	Officials	Non-Officials	
1	2	3	4	5	6	7	8
Legislative Assembly ...	145	104	52	52	26	15	145
Council of State	60	33	11	22	17	10	60
Madras Provincial Council	118	98	13	85	11	23	132
Bombay Provincial Council	111	86	27	59	19	9	114
Bengal Provincial Council	125	114	39	75	16	10	140
U. P. Provincial Council ...	118	110	29	71	17	6	123
Punjab Provincial Council	83	71	32	39	15	8	. 94
Bihar Provincial Council ...	98	76	18	58	15	12	103
C. P. Provincial Council ...	70	55	7	48	10	8	73
Assam Provincial Council	53	39	12	27	7	7	53

The extent of representation secured by the Muslims by the Lucknow Pact can be seen from the following table*:—

Legislative Body.	Percentage of Muslims to total population of the electoral area (1921 Census).	Percentage of Muslim Members to total No. of Members.	Percentage of elected Muslim Members to total No. of elected Indian Members.	Percentage of Muslim Members to total Members in seats filled by election from Indian general (communal) constituencies.	Lucknow Pact Percentage
.	1	2	3	4	5
Punjab	55·2	40	48·5	50	50
United Provinces	14·3	25	30	32·5	30
Bengal	54·6	30	40·5	46	40
Bihar and Orissa	10·9	18·5	25	27	25
Central Provinces ...	4·4	9·5	13	14·5	15
Madras	6·7	10·5	14	16·5	15
Bombay	19·8	25·5	35	37	33·3
Assam	32·2	30	35·5	37·5	No provision.
Legislative Assembly ...	24·0	26	34	38	33·3

*Statutory Commission, 1929, Report, Vol. I, p. 189.

† Column 3 includes Indians elected by special constituencies, e.g. Commerce, whose communal proportions may of course vary slightly from time to time. Similarly column 2, including also officials and nominated non-officials, will show slightly different results at different periods.

This table does not show quite clearly the weightage obtained by the Muslims under the Lucknow Pact. It was worked out by the Government of India in their despatch* on the Report of Franchise Committee of which Lord Southborough was the Chairman. The following table is taken from that despatch which shows that the Muslims got a weightage under the Lucknow Pact far in excess of what Government gave them in 1909.

....	Muslim percentage of Population. 1	Percentage of Muslim seats Proposed. 2	Percentage (2) of (1). 3
Bengal	52·6	40	76
Bihar and Orissa	10·5	25	238
Bombay	20·4	33·3	163
Central Provinces	4·3	15	349
Madras	6·5	15	231
Punjab	54·8	50	91
United Provinces	14·0	30	214

In 1927 the British Government announced the appointment of the Simon Commission to examine the working of the Indian Constitution and to suggest further reforms. Immediately the Muslims came forward with further political demands. These demands were put forth from various Muslim platforms such as the Muslim League, All-India Muslim Conference, All-Parties Muslim Conference, Jamiat-ul-Ulema and the Khilafat Conference. The demands were substantially the same. It would suffice to state those that were formulated by Mr. Jinnah† on behalf of the Muslim League.

* Fifth despatch on Indian Constitutional Reforms (Franchises), dated 23rd April 1919, para 21.

† The demands are known as Mr. Jinnah's 14 points. As a matter of fact they are 15 in number and were formulated at a meeting of Muslim leaders of all shades of opinion held at Delhi in March 1927 and were known as the Delhi Proposals. For Mr. Jinnah's explanation of the origin of his 14 points, see *All-India Register*, 1929, Vol. I, p. 367.

They were in the following terms:—

1. The form of the future Constitution should be federal with residuary powers vested in the provinces.

2. A uniform measure of autonomy should be granted to all provinces.

3. All legislatures in the country and other elected bodies should be reconstituted on the definite principle of adequate and effective representation of minorities in every province without reducing the majority of any province to a minority or even equality.

4. In the Central Legislature Muslim representation should not be less than one-third.

5. The representation of communal groups should continue to be by means of separate electorates as at present, provided that it should be open to any community at any time to abandon its separate electorate in favour of joint electorates.

6. Any territorial redistribution that might at any time be necessary should not in any way affect the Muslim majority in the Punjab, Bengal and North-West Province.

7. Full religious liberty, that is, liberty of belief, worship, observances, propaganda, association and education should be guaranteed to all communities.

8. No bill or resolution, or any part thereof, should be passed in any legislature or any other elected body if three-fourths of the members of any community in that particular body oppose such bill or resolution or part thereof on the ground that it would be injurious to the interests of that community or, in the alternative, such other method as may be devised or as may be found feasible and practicable to deal with such cases.

9. Sind should be separated from the Bombay Presidency.

10. Reforms should be introduced in the North-West Frontier Province and Baluchistan on the same footing as in other provinces.

11. Provision should be made in the Constitution giving the Muslims an adequate share along with other Indians in all the Services of the State and in self-governing bodies, having due regard to the requirements of efficiency.

12. The constitution should embody adequate safeguards for the protection of Muslim religion, culture and personal law, and the promotion of Muslim education, language, religion, personal laws, Muslim charitable institutions, and for their due share in grants-in-aid given by the State and by self-governing bodies.

13. No Cabinet, either Central or Provincial, should be formed without there being a proportion of Muslim Ministers of at least one-third.

14. No change to be made in the Constitution by the Central Legislature except with the concurrence of the States constituting the Indian Federation.

15. That in the present circumstances the representation of Musalmans in the different legislatures of the country and of the other elected bodies through separate electorates is inevitable, and, further, Government being pledged not to deprive the Musalmans of this right, it cannot be taken away without their consent, and so long as the Musalmans are not satisfied that their rights and interests are safeguarded in the manner specified above (or herein) they would in no way consent to the establishment of joint electorates with or without conditions.

Note:—The question of excess representation of Musalmans over and above their population in the provinces where they are in minority to be considered hereafter.

This is a consolidated statement of Muslim demands. In it there are some which are old, and some which are new. The old ones are included because the aim is to retain the advantages accruing therefrom. The new ones are added in order to remove the weaknesses in the Muslim position. The new ones are five in number: (1) Representation in proportion to population to Muslim majorities in the Punjab and Bengal, (2) One-third representation to Muslims in the cabinets both Central and Provincial, (3) Adequate representation of Muslims in the Services, (4) Separation of Sind from the Bombay Presidency and the raising of N.-W.F.P. and Baluchistan to the status of self-governing provinces, and (5) Vesting of residuary powers in the provinces instead of in the Central Government.

These new demands are self-explanatory except perhaps 1, 4 and 5. The object of demands 1 and 4 was to place, in four provinces, the Muslim community in a statutory majority where it had only communal majority, as a force counteracting the six provinces in which the Hindu community happened to be in a majority. This was insisted upon as a guarantee of good treatment by both the communities of its minorities. The object of demand No. 5 was to guarantee Muslim rule in Sind, N.-W.F.P., the Punjab and Bengal. But a Muslim majority rule in these Muslim Provinces, it was feared, would not be effective if they remained under the control of the Central Government which could not but be in the hand of the Hindus. To free the Muslim Provinces from the control of the Hindu Government at the Centre was the object for which demand No. 5 was put forth.

These demands were opposed by the Hindus. There may not be much in this. But what is significant is that they were also rejected by the Simon Commission. The Simon Commission, which was by no means unfriendly to the Muslims, gave some very cogent reasons for rejecting the Muslim demands. It said* :—

> "This claim goes to the length of seeking to preserve the full security for representation now provided for Muslims in these six provinces and at the same time to enlarge in Bengal and the Punjab the present proportion of seats secured to the community by separate electorates to figures proportionate to their ratio of population. This would give Muhammadans a fixed and unalterable majority of the general constituency seats in both provinces. We cannot go so far. The continuance of the present scale of weightage in the six provinces could not — in the absence of a new general agreement between the communities — equitably be combined with so great a departure from the existing allocation in Bengal and the Punjab.
>
> "It would be unfair that Muhammadans should retain the very considerable weightage they enjoy in the six provinces, and that there should at the same time be imposed, in face of Hindu and Sikh opposition, a definite Muslim majority in the Punjab and Bengal unalterable by any appeal to the electorate..... ..."

Notwithstanding the opposition of the Hindus and the Sikhs and the rejection by the Simon Commission, the British Government when called upon to act as an arbiter granted the Muslims all their demands old and new.

By a Notification† in the *Gazette of India* dated 25th January 1932 the Government of India, in exercise of the powers conferred by sub-section (2) of section 52 A of the Government of India Act, 1916, declared that the N.-W. F. Province shall be treated as a

* Report, Vol. II, p. 71.

† Notification No. F. 173/31- R in the *Gazette of India Extraordinary*, dated 25th January 1932.

Governor's Province.* By an Order in Council, issued under the provisions contained in sub-section (1) of section 289 of the Government of India Act of 1935, Sind was separated from Bombay as from 1st April 1936 and declared to be a Governor's Province to be known as the province of Sind. By the Resolution issued by the Secretary of State for India and published on 7th July 1934 the Muslim share in the public services was fixed at 25 per cent. of all appointments Imperial and Provincial. With regard to residuary powers, it is true that the Muslim demand that they should be vested in the Provinces was not accepted. But in another sense the Muslim demand in this respect may be deemed to have been granted. The essence of the Muslim demand was that the residuary powers should not be vested in the Centre, which, put in different language, meant that they should not be in the hands of the Hindus. This is precisely what is done by section 104 of the Government of India Act, 1935, which vests the residuary powers in the Governor-General to be exercised in his discretion. The demand for 33⅓ per cent. representation in the Cabinets, Central and Provincial, was not given effect to by a legal provision in the Act. The right of Muslims to representation in the Cabinets was however accepted by the British Government and provision for giving effect to it was made in the Instruments of Instructions issued to the Governors and Governor-General. As to the remaining demand which related to a statutory majority in the Punjab and Bengal, the demand was given effect to by the Communal Award. True, a statutory majority in the whole House has not been given to the Muslims and could not be given having regard to the necessity for providing representation to other interests. But a statutory majority as against Hindus has been given to the Muslims of the Punjab and Bengal without touching the weightages obtained by the Muslim minorities under the Lucknow Pact.

* The Simon Commission had rejected the claim saying: "We entirely share the view of the Bray Committee that provision ought now to be made for the constitutional advance of the N.-W.F.P................But we also agree that the situation of the Province and its intimate relation with the problem of Indian defence are such that special arrangements are required. It is not possible, therefore, to apply to it automatically proposals which may be suited for provincial areas in other parts of India." They justified it by saying: "The inherent right of a man to smoke a cigarette must necessarily be curtailed if he lives in a powder magazine."—Report, Vol. II, paras 120-121.

These political grants to the Muslim community by the British Government lacked security and it was feared by the Muslims that pressure might be brought upon them or upon His Majesty's Government by the Hindus to alter the terms of the grants to the prejudice of the Muslims. This fear was due to two reasons. One was the success of Mr. Gandhi in getting that part of the Award which related to the Depressed Classes revised by means of the pressure of a fast unto death.* Some people encouraged by this success actually agitated for revision of that part of the Award which related to the Muslims and some Muslims were even found to be in favour of entering into such negotiations.† This alarmed the Muslim community. The other reason for the fear of a revision of the terms of the grants arose out of certain amendments in the clauses in the Government of India Bill which were made in the House of Commons permitting such revision under certain conditions. To remove these fears and to give complete security to the Muslims against hasty and hurried revision of the grants, His Majesty's Government authorized the Government of India to issue the following communique‡ :—

> "It has come to the notice of His Majesty's Government that the impression is prevalent that what is now Clause 304 of the Government of India Bill (numbered 285 in the Bill as first introduced and 299 in the Bill as amended by the Commons in Committee) has been amended during the passage of the Bill through the Commons in such a way as to give His Majesty's Government unfettered power to alter at any time they may think fit the constitutional provisions based upon what is commonly known as Government's Communal Award.
>
> "His Majesty's Government think it desirable to give the following brief explanation both of what they consider is the practical effect of Clause 304 in relation to any change in the Communal Award and of their own policy in relation to any such change.
>
> "Under this Clause there is conferred on the Governments and Legislatures in India, after the expiry of ten years, the right of initiating a proposal to modify the provisions and regulating

* This resulted in the Poona Pact which was signed on 24th September 1932.

† For the efforts to get the Muslim part of the Award revised, see *All-India Register*, 1932, Vol. II, pp. 281-315.

‡ The communique is dated Simla July 2, 1935.

various matters relating to the constitution of the Legislature, including such questions as were covered by the Communal Award.

"The Clause also imposes on the Secretary of State the duty of laying before Parliament from the Governor-General or the Governor as the case may be his opinion as to the proposed amendment and in particular as to the effect which it would have on the interests of any minority and of informing Parliament of any action which he proposed to take.

"Any change in the constitutional provisions resulting from this procedure can be effected by an Order in Council, but this is subject to the proviso that the draft of the proposed Order has been affirmatively approved by both Houses of Parliament by a resolution. The condition is secured by Clause 305 of the Bill.

"Before the expiry of ten years there is no similar constitutional initiative residing in the Governments and the Legislatures of India. Power is, however, conferred by the Clause to make such a change by an Order in Council (always with the approval of both Houses of Parliament) even before the end of ten years, but within the first ten years (and indeed subsequently, if the initiative has not come from the Legislatures of India) it is incumbent upon the Secretary of State to consult the Governments and the Legislatures of India who will be affected (unless the change is of a minor character) before any Order in Council is laid before Parliament for its approval.

"The necessity for the powers referred to in the preceding paragraph is due to such reasons as the following :—

"(a) It is impossible to foresee when the necessity may arise for amending minor details connected with the franchise and the constitution of legislatures, and for such amendment it will be clearly disadvantageous to have no method available short of a fresh amending Act of Parliament, nor is it practicable statutorily to separate such details from the more important matter such as the terms of the Communal Award;

"(b) It might also become desirable, in the event of a unanimous agreement between the communities in India, to make a modification in the provisions based on the Communal Award ; and for such an agreed change it would also be disadvantageous to have no other method available than an amending Act of Parliament.

"Within the range of the Communal Award His Majesty's Government would not propose, in the exercise of any power conferred by this Clause, to recommend to Parliament any change unless such changes had been agreed to between the communities concerned.

"In conclusion, His Majesty's Government would again emphasise the fact that none of the powers in Clause 304 can, in view of the provisions in Clause 305, be exercised unless both Houses of Parliament agreed by an affirmative resolution."

After taking into account what the Muslims demanded at the R.T.C. and what was conceded to them, any one could have thought that the limit of Muslim demands was reached and that the 1932 settlement was a final settlement. But, it appears that even with this the Musalmans are not satisfied. A further list of new demands for safeguarding the Muslim position seems to be ready. In the controversy that went on between Mr. Jinnah and the Congress in the year 1938, Mr. Jinnah was asked to disclose his demands which he refused to do. But these demands have come to the surface in the correspondence that passed between Pandit Nehru and Mr. Jinnah in the course of the controversy and they have been tabulated by Pandit Nehru in one of his letters to Mr. Jinnah. His tabulation gives the following items as being matters of disputes and requiring settlement*:—

(1) The fourteen points formulated by the Muslim League in 1929.

(2) The Congress should withdraw all opposition to the Communal Award and should not describe it as a negation of nationalism.

(3) The share of the Muslims in the state services should be definitely fixed in the constitution by statutory enactment.

(4) Muslim personal law and culture should be guaranteed by statute.

(5) The Congress should take in hand the agitation in connection with the Sahidganj Mosque and should use its moral pressure to enable the Muslims to gain possession of the Mosque.

(6) The Muslims' right to call Azan and perform their religious ceremonies should not be fettered in any way.

(7) Muslims should have freedom to perform cow-slaughter.

* *Indian Annual Register*, 1938, Vol. I, p. 369.

(8) Muslim majorities in the Provinces, where such majorities exist at present, must not be affected by any territorial re-distribution or adjustments.

(9) The 'Bande Mataram' song should be given up.

(10) Muslims want Urdu to be the national language of India and they desire to have statutory guarantees that the use of Urdu shall not be curtailed or damaged.

(11) Muslim representation in the local bodies should be governed by the principles underlying the Communal Award, that is, separate electorates and population strength.

(12) The tricolour flag should be changed or alternately the flag of the Muslim League should be given equal importance.

(13) Recognition of the Muslim League as the one authoritative and representative organization of Indian Muslims.

(14) Coalition Ministries should be formed.

With this new list, there is no knowing where the Muslims are going to stop in their demands. Within one year, that is, between 1938 and 1939, one more demand and that too of a substantial character, namely 50 per cent. share in everything, has been added to it. In this catalogue of new demands there are some which on the face of them are extravagant and impossible, if not irresponsible. As an instance, one may refer to the demand for fifty-fifty and the demand for the recognition of Urdu as the national language of India. In 1929, the Muslims insisted that in allotting seats in Legislatures, a majority shall not be reduced to a minority or equality.* This principle, enunciated by themselves, it is now demanded, shall be abandoned and a majority shall be reduced to equality. The Muslims in 1929 admitted that the other minorities required protection and that they must have it in the same manner as the Muslims. The only distinction made between the Muslims and other minorities was as to the extent of the protection. The Muslims claimed a higher degree of protection than was conceded to the other minorities on the ground of their political importance.

* See point No. 3 in Mr. Jinnah's 14 points.

The necessity and adequacy of protection for the other minorities the Muslims never denied. But with this new demand of 50 per cent. the Muslims are not only seeking to reduce the Hindu majority to a minority but they are also cutting into the political rights of the other minorities. The Muslims are now speaking the language of Hitler and claiming a place in the sun as Hitler has been doing for Germany. For their demand for 50 per cent. is nothing but a counterpart of the German claims for *Deutschland Uber Alles* and *Lebensraum* for themselves, irrespective of what happens to other minorities.

Their claim for the recognition of Urdu as the national language of India is equally extravagant. Urdu is not only not spoken all over India but is not even the language of all the Musalmans of India. Of the 68 millions of Muslims* only 28 millions speak Urdu. The proposal of making Urdu the national language means that the language of 28 millions of Muslims is to be imposed particularly upon 40 millions of Musalmans or generally upon 322 millions of Indians.

It will thus be seen that every time a proposal for the reform of the constitution comes forth, the Muslims are there, ready with some new political demand or demands. The only check upon such indefinite expansion of Muslim demands is the power of the British Government, which must be the final arbiter in any dispute between the Hindus and the Muslims. Who can confidently say that the decision of the British will not be in favour of the Muslims if the dispute relating to these new demands was referred to them for arbitration? The more the Muslims demand the more accommodating the British seem to become. At any rate, past experience shows that the British have been inclined to give the Muslims more than what the Muslims had themselves asked. Two such instances can be cited.

One of these relates to the Lucknow Pact. The question was whether the British Government should accept the Pact. The authors of the Montagu-Chelmsford Report were disinclined to accept it for reasons which were very weighty. Speak-

* These figures relate to the Census of 1921.

ing of the weightages granted to the Muslims by the Lucknow Pact, the authors of the Joint Report observed* :—

> "Now a privileged position of this kind is open to the objection, that if any other community hereafter makes good a claim to separate representation, it can be satisfied only by deducting the non-Muslim seats, or by a rateable deduction from both Muslim and non-Muslim; and Hindu and Muslim opinion are not likely to agree which process should be adopted. While, therefore, for reasons that we explain subsequently we assent to the maintenance of separate representation for Muhammadans, we are bound to reserve our approval of the particular proposals set before us, until we have ascertained what the effect upon other interests will be, and have made fair provision for them."

Notwithstanding this grave flaw in the Lucknow Pact, the Government of India, in its despatch referred to above, recommended that the terms of the Pact should be improved in so far as it related to the Muslims of Bengal. Its reasons make a strange reading. It argued that:—

> "The Muhammadan representation which they [the authors of the Pact] propose for Bengal is manifestly insufficient.† It is questionable whether the claims of the Muhammadan population of Eastern Bengal were adequately pressed when the Congress-League compact was in the making. They are conspicuously a backward and impoverished community. The repartition of the presidency in 1912 came as a severe disappointment to them, and we should be very loath to fail in seeing that their interests are now generously secured. In order to give the Bengal Muslims a representation proportionate to their numbers, and no more, we should allot them 44 instead of 34 seats [due to them under the Pact]."

This enthusiasm for the Bengal Muslims shown by the Government of India was not shared by the British Government. It felt that as the number of seats given to the Bengal Muslims was the result of an agreement, any interference to improve the bargain when there was no dispute about the genuineness of the agreement, could not but create the impression that the British Government was in some special sense and for some special reason the friend of the Muslims. In suggesting this

* Montagu-Chelmsford Report, 1918, para 163.

† The Government of India felt that injustice was done to the Punjab as well. But as there was no such special reason as there was in the case of Bengal, namely, the unsettling of the partition, they did not propose any augmentation in its representation as settled by the Pact.

augmentation in the seats, the Government of India forgot to take note of the reason why the Muslims of the Punjab and Bengal were not given by the Pact seats in proportion to their population. The Lucknow Pact was based upon the principle, now thrown to the winds, that a community as such was not entitled to political protection. A community was entitled to protection when it was in a minority. That was the principle underlying the Lucknow Pact. The Muslim community in the Punjab and Bengal was not in a minority and, therefore, was not entitled to the same protection which it got in other Provinces where it was in a minority. Notwithstanding their being in a majority, the Muslims of the Punjab and Bengal felt the necessity of separate electorates. According to the principle underlying the Pact they could qualify themselves for this only by becoming a minority which they did by agreeing to a minority of seats. This is the reason why the Muslims of Bengal and the Punjab did not get the majority of seats they were entitled to on the population basis.*

The proposal of the Government of India to give to the Bengal Muslims more than what they had asked for did not go through. But the fact that they wanted to do so remains as evidence of their inclinations.

The second occasion when the British Government as an arbiter gave the Muslims more than they asked for was when the Communal Decision was given in 1932. Sir Muhammad Shafi made two different proposals in the Minorities Sub-Committee of the R. T. C. In his speech on 6th January 1931, Sir

* There is no doubt that this was well understood by the Muslims who were parties to the Pact. This is what Mr. Jinnah said as a witness appearing before the Joint Select Committee appointed by Parliament on the Government of India Bill, 1919, in reply to question No. 3808: "The position of Bengal was this: In Bengal the Muslims are in a majority, and the argument was advanced that any section or any community which is in the majority cannot claim a separate electorate: separate electorate is to protect the minority. But the counter-argument was perfectly true that numerically we are in a majority but as voters we are in the minority in Bengal, because of poverty and backwardness and so on. It was said: Very well, then fix 40 per cent., because if you are really put to test you will not get 40 per cent. because you will not be qualified as voters. Then we had the advantage in other Provinces."

Muhammad Shafi put forth the following proposal as a basis for communal settlement* :—

> "We are prepared to accept joint electorates on the conditions named by me: Firstly, that the rights at present enjoyed by the Musalmans in the minority Provinces should be continued to them; that in the Punjab and in Bengal they should have two joint electorates and representation on a population basis; that there should be the principle of reservation of seats coupled with Maulana Mahomed Ali's condition."†

In his speech on 14th January 1931 before the same Committee he made a different offer. He said‡ :—

> "To-day I am authorized to make this offer: that in the Punjab the Musalmans should have through communal electorates 49 per cent. of the entire number of seats in the whole House, and should have liberty to contest the special constituencies which it is proposed to create in that Province: so far as Bengal is concerned that Musalmans should have through communal electorates 46 per cent. representation in the whole House, and should have the liberty to contest the special constituencies which it is proposed to create in that Province; in so far as the minority Provinces are concerned, the Musalmans should continue to enjoy the weightage which they have at present through separate electorates, similar weightage to be given to our Hindu brethren in Sind, and to our Hindu and Sikh brethren in the North-West Frontier Province. If at any time hereafter two-thirds of the representatives of any community in any Provincial Legislative Council or in the Central Legislative Council desire to give up communal electorates and to accept joint electorates then thereafter the system of joint electorates should come into being."

The difference between the two proposals is clear. "Joint electorates, if accompanied by statutory majority. If statutory majority was refused, then a minority of seats with separate electorates." The British Government took statutory majority from the first demand and separate electorates from the second demand and gave the Muslims both when they had not asked for both.

* Report of the Minorities Sub-Committee of the first R. T. C. (Indian Edition), p. 96.

† Mr. Mahomed Ali's formula was for Joint Electorates and Reserved Seats with this proviso that no candidate shall be declared elected unless he had secured at least 40 per cent. of the votes of his own community and at least 5 or 10 per cent. of the votes of the other community.

‡ Ibid., p. 123.

The second thing that is noticeable among the Muslims is the spirit of exploiting the weaknesses of the Hindus. If the Hindus object to anything, the Muslim policy seems to be to insist upon it and give it up only when the Hindus show themselves ready to offer a price for it by giving the Muslims some other concessions. As an illustration of this, one can refer to the question of separate and joint electorates. The Hindus have been to my mind utterly foolish in fighting over joint electorates especially in Provinces in which the Muslims are in a minority. Joint electorates can never suffice for a basis for nationalism. Nationalism is not a matter of political nexus or cash nexus, for the simple reason that union cannot be the result of calculation of mere externals. Where two communities live a life which is exclusive and self-inclosed for five years, they will not be one, because, they are made to come together on one day in five years for the purposes of voting in an election. Joint electorates may produce the enslavement of the minor community by the major community: but by themselves they cannot produce nationalism. Be that as it may, because the Hindus have been insisting upon joint electorates the Muslims have been insisting upon separate electorates. That this insistence is a matter of bargain only can be seen from Mr. Jinnah's 14 points* and the resolution† passed in the Calcutta session of the All-India Muslim League held on 30th December 1927. Therein it was stipulated that only when the Hindus agreed to the separation of Sind and to the raising of the N.-W. F. P. to the status of a self-governing Province the Musalmans would consent to give up separate electorates.‡ The Musalmans evidently did not regard separate electorates as vital. They regarded them as a good *quid pro quo* for obtaining their other claims.

Another illustration of this spirit of exploitation is furnished by the Muslim insistence upon cow-slaughter and the stoppage of music before mosques. Islamic law does not insist upon the slaughter of the cow for sacrificial purposes and no Musalman,

*See point No. 15 in Mr. Jinnah's points.

†For the resolution and the speech of Mr. Barkat Ali thereon, see the *Indian Quarterly Register*, 1927, Vol. II, pp. 447-48.

‡The unfortunate thing for the Hindus is that they did not get joint electorates although the Musalmans got the concessions.

when he goes to Haj, sacrifices the cow in Mecca or Medina. But in India they will not be content with the sacrifice of any other animal. Music may be played before a mosque in all Muslim countries without any objection. Even in Afghanistan, which is not a secularized country, no objection is taken to music before a mosque. But in India the Musalmans must insist upon its stoppage for no other reason except that the Hindus claim a right to it.

The third thing that is noticeable is the adoption by the Muslims of the gangster's method in politics. The riots are a sufficient indication that gangsterism has become a settled part of their strategy in politics. They seem to be consciously and deliberately imitating the Sudeten Germans in the means employed by them against the Czechs.* So long as the Muslims were the aggressors, the Hindus were passive, and in the conflict they suffered more than the Muslims did. But this is no longer true. The Hindus have learned to retaliate and no longer feel any compunction in knifing a Musalman. This spirit of retaliation bids fair to produce the ugly spectacle of gangsterism against gangsterism.

How to meet this problem must exercise the minds of all concerned. There are the simple-minded Hindu Maha Sabha patriots who believe that the Hindus have only to make up their minds to wipe the Musalmans and they will be brought to their senses. On the other hand, there are the Congress Hindu Nationalists whose policy is to tolerate and appease the Musalmans by political and other concessions, because they believe that they cannot reach their cherished goal of independence unless the Musalmans back their demand. The Hindu Maha Sabha plan is no way to unity. On the contrary, it is a sure block to progress. The slogan of the Hindu Maha Sabha President—Hindustan for Hindus—is not merely arrogant but is arrant nonsense. The question, however, is: is the Congress way the right way? It seems to me that the Congress has failed to realize two things. The first thing which the Congress has failed to realize is that there is a difference between appeasement

*In the Karachi session of the All-India Muslim League both Mr. Jinnah and Sir Abdullah Haroon compared the Muslims of India to the "Sudeten" of the Muslim world and capable of doing what the Sudeten Germans did to Czechoslovakia.

and settlement, and that the difference is an essential one. Appeasement means buying off the aggressor by conniving at his acts of murder, rape, arson and loot against innocent persons who happen for the moment to be the victims of his displeasure. On the other hand, settlement means laying down the bounds which neither party to it can transgress. Appeasement sets no limits to the demands and aspirations of the aggressor. Settlement does. The second thing the Congress has failed to realize is that the policy of concession has increased Muslim aggressiveness, and what is worse, Muslims interpret these concessions as a sign of defeatism on the part of the Hindus and the absence of the will to resist. This policy of appeasement will involve the Hindus in the same fearful situation in which the Allies found themselves as a result of the policy of appeasement which they adopted towards Hitler. This is another malaise, no less acute than the malaise of social stagnation. Appeasement will surely aggravate it. The only remedy for it is a settlement. If Pakistan is a settlement, it is a proposition worth consideration. As a settlement it will do away with this constant need of appeasement and ought to be welcomed by all those who prefer the peace and tranquillity of a settlement to the insecurity due to the growing political appetite shown by the Muslims in their dealings with the Hindus.

CHAPTER XII

NATIONAL FRUSTRATION

I

Suppose an Indian was asked, what is the highest destiny you wish for your country, what would be his answer? The question is important, and the answer cannot but be instructive.

There can be no doubt that other things being equal, a hundred per cent Indian, proud of his country, would say, "An integral and independent India is my ideal of India's destiny." It will be equally true to say that unless this destiny was accepted by both Hindus as well as Muslims, the ideal can only convey a pious wish, and can never take a concrete form. Is it only a pious wish of some or is it a goal to be pursued by all?

So far as profession of political aims goes, all parties seem to be in agreement inasmuch as all of them have declared that the goal of India's political evolution is Independence. The Congress was the first to announce that its aim was to achieve political independence for India. In its Madras session, held in December 1927, the creed of the Congress was defined in a special resolution to the effect that the goal of the Indian people* was complete national independence. The Hindu Maha Sabha until 1932 was content to have Responsible Government as the goal of India's political evolution. It made no change in its political creed till 1937 when in its session held at Ahmedabad it declared that the Hindu Maha Sabha believed in "Poorna Swaraj", i.e., absolute political independence for India. The Muslim League declared its political creed in 1912 to be the establishment of

*The creed of the Congress was not changed at Madras. It was changed at the Lahore session of the Congress by a resolution passed on 31st December 1929. In the Madras session only a resolution in favour of independence was passed. In the Calcutta session of the Congress held in December 1928 both Mr. Gandhi and the President of the Congress declared themselves willing to accept Dominion Status if it was offered by the British Government by midnight of 31st December 1929.

Responsible Government in India. In 1937 it made a similar advance by changing its creed from Responsible Government to Independence and thereby brought itself in line with the Congress and the Hindu Maha Sabha.

This independence defined by the three political bodies means freedom from British Imperialism. But an agreement on freedom from the yoke of British Imperialism is not enough. There must be an agreement upon maintaining an independent India. For this, there must be an agreement that India shall not only be free and independent of the British but that her freedom and independence shall be maintained as against any other foreign power. Indeed, the obligation to maintain her freedom is more important than merely winning freedom from the British. But on this more important obligation there does not seem to be the same unanimity. At any rate, the attitude of the Muslims on this point has not been very assuring. It is obvious from the numerous utterances of Muslim leaders that they do not accept the obligation to maintain India's freedom. I give below two such utterances.

In a meeting held in Lahore in 1925 Dr. Kitchlew said* :—

> "The Congress was lifeless till the Khilafat Committee put life in it. When the Khilafat Committee joined it, it did in one year what the Hindu Congress had not done in 40 years. The Congress also did the work of uplifting the seven crores of untouchables. This was purely a work for the Hindus, and yet the money of the Congress was spent on it. Mine and my Musalman brethren's money was spent on it like water. But the brave Musalmans did not mind. Then why should the Hindus quarrel with us when we Musalmans take up the Tanzim work and spend on it money that belongs neither to the Hindus nor to the Congress?
>
> "If we remove British rule from this country and establish Swaraj, and if the Afghans or other Muslims invade India, then we Muslims will oppose them and sacrifice all our sons in order to save the country from the invasion. But one thing I shall declare plainly. Listen, my dear Hindu brothers, listen very attentively! If you put obstacles in the path of our Tanzim movement, and do not give us our rights, we shall make common cause with Afghanistan or some other Musalman power and establish our rule in this country."

* "Through Indian Eyes." *Times of India* dated 14-3-25.

Maulana Azad Sobhani in his speech* made on the 27th January 1939 at Sylhet expressed sentiments which are worthy of attention. In reply to the question of a Maulana, Maulana Azad Sobhani said:—

"If there is any eminent leader in India who is in favour of driving out the English from this country, then I am that leader. In spite of this I want that there should be no fight with the English on behalf of the Muslim League. Our big fight is with the 22 crores of our Hindu enemies, who constitute the majority. Only 4½ crores of Englishmen have practically swallowed the whole world by becoming powerful. And if these 22 crores of Hindus who are equally advanced in learning, intelligence and wealth as in numbers, if they become powerful, then these Hindus will swallow Muslim India and gradually even Egypt, Turkey, Kabul, Mecca, Medina and other Muslim principalities, like Yajuj-Majuj (it is so mentioned in the Koran that before the destruction of the world, they will appear on the earth and will devour whatever they will find).

"The English are gradually becoming weak.... they will go away from India in the near future. So if we do not fight the greatest enemies of Islam, the Hindus, from now on and make them weak, then they will not only establish *Ramrajya* in India but also gradually spread all over the world. It depends on the 9 crores of Indian Muslims either to strengthen or to weaken them (the Hindus). So it is the essential duty of every devout Muslim to fight on by joining the Muslim League so that the Hindus may not be established here and a Muslim rule may be established in India as soon as the English depart.

"Though the English are the enemies of the Muslims, yet for the present our fight is not with the English. At first we have to come to some understanding with the Hindus through the Muslim League. Then we shall be easily able to drive out the English and establish Muslim rule in India.

"Be careful! Don't fall into the trap of Congress Maulvis; because the Muslim world is never safe in the hands of 22 crores of Hindu enemies."

According to the summary of the speech given by the correspondent of the *Anand Bazar Patrika* Maulana Azad Sobhani then narrated various imaginary incidents of oppressions on Muslims in Congress provinces.

"He said that when the Congress accepted ministry after the introduction of Provincial Autonomy, he felt that Muslim

* The Bengali version of the speech appeared in the *Anand Bazar Patrika*. The English version of it given here is a translation made for me by the Editor of the *Hindustan Standard*.

interests were not safe in the hands of the Hindu-dominated Congress; but the Hindu leaders felt indifferently and so he left the Congress and joined the League. What he had feared has been put in reality by the Congress ministers. This forestalling of the future is called politics. He was, therefore, a great politician. He was again thinking that before India became independent some sort of understanding had to be arrived at with the Hindus either by force or in a friendly way. Otherwise, the Hindus, who had been the slaves of the Muslims for 700 years, would enslave the Muslims."

The Hindus are aware of what is passing in the mind of the Muslims and dread the possibility of Muslims using independence to enslave them. As a result Hindus are lukewarm towards making independence as the goal of India's political evolution. These are not the fears of those who are not qualified to judge. On the contrary, the Hindus who have expressed their apprehensions as to the wisdom of heading for independence are those who are eminently qualified by their contact with Muslim leaders to express an opinion.

Mrs. Annie Besant says* :—

"Another serious question arises with regard to the Muhammadans of India. If the relation between Muslims and Hindus were as it was in the Lucknow days, this question would not be so urgent, though it would even then have almost certainly arisen, sooner or later, in an Independent India. But since the Khilafat agitation, things have changed and it has been one of the many injuries inflicted on India by the encouragement of the Khilafat crusade, that the inner Muslim feeling of hatred against 'unbelievers' has sprung up, naked and unashamed, as in years gone by. We have seen revived, as guide in practical politics, the old Muslim religion of the sword, we have seen the dragging out of centuries of forgetfulness, the old exclusiveness, claiming the Jazirut-Arab, the island of Arabia, as a holy land which may not be trodden by the polluting foot of a non-Muslim, we have heard Muslim leaders declare that if the Afghans invaded India, they would join their fellow believers, and would slay the Hindus who defended their motherland against the foe: we have been forced to see that the primary allegiance of Musalmans is to Islamic countries, not to our motherland; we have learned that their dearest hope is to establish the 'Kingdom of God', not God as Father of the world, loving all his creatures, but as a God seen through Musalman spectacles resembling in his command through one of the prophets, as to the treatment of unbeliever—the Mosaic *JEHOVA* of the early Hebrews, when

* *The Future of Indian Politics*, pp. 301-305.

they were fighting as did the early Muslims, for freedom to follow the religion given to them by their prophet. The world has gone beyond such so-called theocracies, in which God's commands are given through a man. The claim now put forward by Musalman leaders that they must obey the laws of their particular prophet above the laws of the State in which they live, is subversive of civic order and the stability of the State; it makes them bad citizens for their centre of allegiance is outside the nation and they cannot, while they hold the views proclaimed by Maulanas Mahomed Ali and Shaukat Ali, to name the most prominent of these Muslim leaders, be trusted by their fellow citizens. If India were independent the Muslim part of the population — for the ignorant masses would follow those who appealed to them in the name of their prophet — would become an immediate peril to India's freedom. Allying themselves with Afghanistan, Baluchistan, Persia, Iraq, Arabia, Turkey and Egypt and with such of the tribes of Central Asia who are Musalmans, they would rise to place India under the Rule of Islam — those in 'British India' being helped by the Muslims in Indian States — and would establish Musalman rule. We had thought that Indian Musalmans were loyal to their motherland, and indeed, we still hope that some of the educated class might strive to prevent such a Musalman rising; but they are too few for effective resistance and would be murdered as apostates. Malabar has taught us what Islamic rule still means, and we do not want to see another specimen of the 'Khilafat Raj' in India. How much sympathy with the Moplas is felt by Muslims outside Malabar has been proved by the defence raised for them by their fellow believers, and by Mr. Gandhi himself, who stated that they had acted as they believed that religion taught them to act. I fear that that is true; but there is no place in a civilised land for people who believe that their religion teaches them to murder, rob, rape, burn, or drive away out of the country those who refuse to apostatise from their ancestral faiths, except in its schools, under surveillance, or in its gaols. The Thugs believed that their particular form of God commanded them to strangle people — especially travellers with money. Such 'Laws of God' cannot be allowed to override the laws of a civilised country, and people living in the twentieth century must either educate people who hold these Middle Age views, or else exile them. Their place is in countries sharing their opinions, where they can still use such arguments against any who differ from them — as indeed, Persia and with the Parsis long ago, and the Bahaists in our own time. In fact, Muslim sects are not safe in a country ruled by orthodox Muslims. British rule in India has protected the freedom of all sects: Shiahs, Sunnis, Sufis, Bahaists live in safety under her sceptre, although it cannot protect any of them from social ostracism, where it is in a minority. Musalmans are more free under British rule, than in countries where there are Muslim rulers. In thinking of an Independent India, the menace of Muhammadan rule has to be considered."

Similar fear was expressed by Lala Lajpatrai in a letter* to Mr. C. R. Das :—

"There is one point more which has been troubling me very much of late and one which I want you to think carefully and that is the question of Hindu-Mohamedan unity. I have devoted most of my time during the last six months to the study of Muslim history and Muslim Law and I am inclined to think, it is neither possible nor practicable. Assuming and admitting the sincerity of the Mohamedan leaders in the Non-co-operation movement, I think their religion provides an effective bar to anything of the kind. You remember the conversation, I reported to you in Calcutta, which I had with Hakim Ajmalkhan and Dr. Kitchlew. There is no finer Mohamedan in Hindustan than Hakimsaheb but can any other Muslim leader override the Quran? I can only hope that my reading of Islamic Law is incorrect, and nothing would relieve me more than to be convinced that it is so. But if it is right then it comes to this that although we can unite against the British we cannot do so to rule Hindustan on British lines, we cannot do so to rule Hindustan on democratic lines. What is then the remedy? I am not afraid of seven crores in Hindustan but I think the seven crores of Hindustan plus the armed hosts of Afghanistan, Central Asia, Arabia, Mesopotamia and Turkey will be irresistible. I do honestly and sincerely believe in the necessity or desirability of Hindu-Muslim unity. I am also fully prepared to trust the Muslim leaders, but what about the injunctions of the Quran and Hadis? The leaders cannot override them. Are we then doomed? I hope not. I hope your learned mind and wise head will find some way out of this difficulty."

In 1924 the editor of a Bengalee paper had an interview with the poet Dr. Rabindra Nath Tagore. The report of this interview states† :—

"....another very important factor which, according to the poet, was making it almost impossible for the Hindu-Mohamedan unity to become an accomplished fact was that the Mohamedans could not confine their patriotism to any one country.... The poet said that he had very frankly asked many Mohamedans whether, in the event of any Mohamedan power invading India, they would stand side by side with their Hindu neighbours to defend their common land. He could not be

* Quoted in *Life of Savarkar* by Indra Prakash.

† Quoted in "Through Indian Eyes" in the *Times of India* dated 18-4-24.

satisfied with the reply he got from them. He said that he could definitely state that even such men as Mr. Mahomed Ali had declared that under no circumstances was it permissible for any Mohamedan, whatever his country might be, to stand against any other Mohamedan."

II

If independence is impossible, then the destiny acceptable to a hundred per cent. Indian as the next best would be for India to have the status of a Dominion within the British Empire. Who would be content with such a destiny? I feel certain that left to themselves the Musalmans will not be content with Dominion Status while the Hindus most certainly will. Such a statement is sure to jar on the ears of Indians and Englishmen. The Congress being loud and vociferous in its insistence of independence, the impression prevails that the Hindus are for independence and the Muslims are for Dominion Status. Those who were present at the R. T. C., could not have failed to realize how strong a hold this impression had taken of the English mind and how the claims and interests of the Hindus suffered an injury because of the twin cries raised by the Congress, namely, independence and repudiation of debts. Listening to these cries, Englishmen felt that the Hindus were the enemies of the British and the Muslims, who did not ask either for independence or repudiation, were their friends. This impression, however true it may be in the light of the avowed plans of the Congress, is a false impression created by false propaganda. For, there can be no doubt that the Hindus are at heart for Dominion Status and that the Muslims are at heart for Independence. If proof is wanted there is an abundance of it.

The question of independence was first raised in 1921. In that year the Indian National Congress, the All-India Khilafat Conference and the All-India Muslim League held their annual sessions in the city of Ahmedabad. Each had a resolution in favour of Independence moved in its session. It is interesting to note the fate which the resolution met at the hands of the Congress, the Khilafat Conference and the Muslim League.

The President of the Congress was Hakim Ajmal Khan who acted for Mr. C. R. Das, who though duly elected could not preside owing to his arrest by Government before the session commenced. In the session of the Congress, Maulana Hasrat Mohani moved a resolution pressing for a change in the creed of the Congress. The following is the summary of the proceedings* relating to the resolution:—

> "Maulana Hasrat Mohani in proposing his resolution on complete independence made a long and impassioned speech in Urdu. He said, although they had been promised Swaraj last year, the redress of the Khilafat and the Punjab wrongs within a year, they had so far achieved nothing of the sort. Therefore it was no use sticking to the programme. If remaining within the British Empire or the British Commonwealth they could not have freedom, he felt that, if necessary, they should not hesitate to go out of it. In the words of Lok. Tilak 'liberty was their birth-right,' and any Government which denied this elementary right of freedom of speech and freedom of action did not deserve allegiance from the people. Home Rule on Dominion lines or Colonial Self-Government could not be a substitute to them for their inborn liberty. A Government which could clap into jail such distinguished leaders of the people as Mr. Chitta Ranjan Das, Pandit Motilal Nehru, Lala Lajpat Rai and others, had forfeited all claim to respect from the people. And since the end of the year did not bring them Swaraj nothing should prevent them from taking the only course left open to them now, that of winning their freedom free from all foreign control. The resolution reads as follows:—
>
> "'The object of the Indian National Congress is the attainment of Swaraj or complete independence free from all foreign control by the people of India by all legitimate and peaceful means.'"

After several delegates had spoken in favour of it, Mr. Gandhi came forward to oppose the resolution. In opposing the resolution, Mr. Gandhi said:—

> "Friends, I have said only a few words in Hindi in connection with the proposition of Mr. Hasrat Mohani. All I want to say to you in English is that the levity with which that proposition has been taken by some of you has grieved me. It has grieved me because it shows lack of responsibility. As responsible men and women we should go back to the days of Nagpur and Calcutta and we should remember what we did only an hour ago. An hour ago we passed a resolution which actually contemplates a final settlement of the Khilafat and the Punjab wrongs and transference of the power from the hands of the

* See *The Indian Annual Register*, 1922, Appendix, pp. 64-66.

bureaucracy into the hands of the people by certain definite means. Are you going to rub the whole of that position from your mind by raising a false issue and by throwing a bombshell in the midst of the Indian atmosphere? I hope that those of you who have voted for the previous resolution, will think fifty times before taking up this resolution and voting for it. We shall be charged by the thinking portion of the world that we do not know really where we are. Let us understand, too, our limitations. Let Hindus and Musalmans have absolute, indissoluble unity. Who is here who can say today with confidence: 'Yes Hindu-Muslim unity has become an indissoluble factor of Indian Nationalism?' Who is here who can tell me that the Parsis and the Sikhs and the Christians and the Jews and the untouchables about whom you heard this afternoon—who will tell me that those very people will not rise against any such idea? Think therefore fifty times before you take a step which will redound not to your credit, not to your advantage, but which may cause you irreparable injury. Let us first of all gather up our strength; let us first of all sound our own depths. Let us not go into waters whose depths we do not know, and this proposition of Mr. Hasrat Mohani lands you into depths unfathomable. I ask you in all confidence to reject that proposition, if you believe in the proposition that you passed only an hour ago. The proposition now before you rubs off the whole of the effect of the proposition that you passed only a moment ago. Are creeds such simple things like clothes which a man can change at will? For creeds people die, and for creeds people live from age to age. Are you going to change the creed which with all deliberation and after great debate in Nagpur, you accepted? There was no limitation of one year when you accepted that creed. It is an extensive creed; it takes in all, the weakest and the strongest, and you will deny yourselves the privilege of clothing the weakest amongst yourselves with protection if you accept this limited creed of Maulana Hasrat Mohani, which does not admit the weakest of your brethren. I, therefore, ask you in all confidence to reject his proposition."

The resolution when put to vote was declared to be lost.

The session of the All-India Khilafat Conference was presided over also by Hakim Ajmal Khan. A resolution in favour of independence was also moved in the subjects committee of this Conference. What happened to the resolution is clear from the following summary of its proceedings. The report of the proceedings says* :—

"Before the Conference adjourned at eleven in the night till the next day the President, Hakim Ajmalkhan, announced that

* *The Indian Annual Register*, 1922, Appendix, pp. 133-34.

the Subjects Committee of the Conference had, on the motion of Mr. Azad Sobhani, supported by Mr. Hasrat Mohani, by a majority resolved to ask all Mohamedans and other communities to endeavour to destroy British imperialism and secure complete independence.

"This resolution stated that whereas through the persistent policy and attitude of the British Government it cannot be expected that British Imperialism would permit the Jazirat-ul-Arab and the Islamic world to be completely free from the influence and control of non-Muslims, which means that the Khilafat cannot be secured to the extent that the Shariat demands its safety, therefore, in order to secure permanent safety of the Khilafat and the prosperity of India, it is necessary to endeavour to destroy British Imperialism. This Conference holds the view that the only way to make this effort is, for the Muslims, conjointly with other inhabitants of India, to make India completely free, and that this Conference is of opinion that Muslim opinion about Swaraj is the same, that is, complete independence, and it expects that other inhabitants of India would also hold the same point of view.

"On the Conference resuming its sitting on the second day, December 27th, 1921, a split was found to have taken place in the camp over this resolution about independence. When Mr. Hasrat Mohani was going to move his resolution declaring as their goal, independence and the destruction of British Imperialism, objection was taken to its consideration by a member of the Khilafat Subjects Committee on the ground that according to their constitution no motion which contemplated a change in their creed could be taken as adopted, unless it was voted for in the Subjects Committee by a majority of two-third.

"The President, Hakim Ajmalkhan, upheld this objection and ruled the independence motion out of order.

"Mr. Hasrat Mohani strongly protested and pointed out that the President had disallowed a similar objection by the same member in the Subjects Committee, while he had allowed it in the open Conference. He said that the President had manœuvred to rule his motion out of order in order to stand in their way of declaring from that Conference that their Swaraj meant complete independence."

The President of the All-India Muslim League was Maulana Hasrat Mohani. The report of the proceedings of the League bearing on the resolution says* :—

"The Muslim League met at 9 p. m. on 31st December 1921. After it had passed some non-contentious resolutions the

* Ibid., Appendix, p. 78.

President Hasrat Mohani made an announcement amidst applause that he proposed that the decision of the Subjects Committee rejecting his resolution regarding the attainment of independence and destruction of British Imperialism would be held as final and representing the opinion of the majority in the League, but that in view of the great importance of the subject he would allow a discussion on that resolution without taking any vote.

"Mr. Azad Sobhani, who had moved the resolution in the Subjects Committee, also moved it in the League. He said he believed in Hindu-Muslim unity as absolutely essential, in non-violent non-co-operation as the only way to fight their battle and Mr. Gandhi was fully deserving the dictatorship which had been invested on him by the Congress but that he also believed that British Imperialism was the greatest danger to India and the Muslim world and must be destroyed by placing before them an ideal of independence.

"Mr. Azad Sobhani was followed by several speakers who supported him in the same vein.

"The Hon'ble Mr. Raza Ali announced that the reason for the ruling of the President was that the League did not want to take a step which the Congress had not taken. He warned them against saying big things without understanding them and reminded the audience that India was at present not ready for maintaining liberty even if it was attained.

"He asked, who would, for instance, be their Commander-in-Chief if the British left tomorrow. (A voice, 'Enver Pasha'.)

"The speaker emphatically declared that he would not tolerate any foreigner. He wanted an Indian Commander-in-Chief."

The question of Independence was again raised at the Congress session held in March 1923 at Coconada but with no success.

In 1924 Mr. Gandhi presiding over the Congress session held in Belgaum said:—

"In my opinion, if the British Government mean what they say and honestly help us to equality, it would be a greater triumph than a complete severance of the British connection. I would, therefore, strive for Swaraj within the Empire but would not hesitate to sever all connection if it became a necessity through Britain's own fault. I would thus throw the burden of separation on the British people."

In 1925 Mr. C. R. Das again took up the theme. In his address to the Bengal Provincial Conference held in May of that year he, with the deliberate object of giving a deadly blow to the idea of independence, took particular pains to show the inferiority of the idea of Independence as compared with that of Dominion Status :—

"... Independence, to my mind, is a narrower ideal than that of Swaraj. It implies, it is true, the negation of dependence; but by itself it gives us no positive ideal. I do not for a moment suggest that independence is not consistent with Swaraj. But what is necessary is not mere independence but the establishment of Swaraj. India may be independent tomorrow in the sense that the British people may leave us to our destiny but that will not necessarily give us what I understand by Swaraj. As I pointed out in my Presidential address at Gaya, India presents an interesting but a complicated problem of consolidating the many apparently conflicting elements which go to make up the Indian people. This work of consolidation is a long process, may even be a weary process; but without this no Swaraj is possible. . . .

"Independence, in the second place, does not give you that idea of order which is the essence of Swaraj. The work of consolidation which I have mentioned means the establishment of that order. But let it be clearly understood that what is sought to be established must be consistent with the genius, the temperament and the traditions of the Indian people. To my mind, Swaraj implies, firstly, that we must have the freedom of working out the consolidation of the diverse elements of the Indian people; secondly, we must proceed with this work on National lines, not going back two thousand years ago, but going forward in the light and in the spirit of our national genius and temperament. . . .

"Thirdly, in the work before us, we must not be obstructed by any foreign power. What then we have to fix upon in the matter of ideal is what I call Swaraj and not mere independence which may be the negation of Swaraj. When we are asked as to what is our national ideal of freedom, the only answer which is possible to give is Swaraj. I do not like either Home Rule or Self-Government. Possibly they come within what I have described as Swaraj. But my culture somehow or other is antagonistic to the word 'rule' — be it Home Rule or Foreign Rule."

* * * * *

"Then comes the question as to whether this ideal is to be realised within the Empire or outside? The answer which the Congress has always given is 'within the Empire if the Empire will recognise our right' and 'outside the Empire, if it does not.' We must have opportunity to live our life, — opportunity for self-realization, self-development, and self-fulfilment. The question is of living our life. If the Empire furnishes sufficient scope for the growth and development of our national life the

Empire idea is to be preferred. If, on the contrary, the Empire like the Car of Jagannath crushes our life in the sweep of its imperialistic march, there will be justification for the idea of the establishment of Swaraj outside the Empire.

"Indeed, the Empire idea gives us a vivid sense of many advantages. Dominion Status is in no sense servitude. It is essentially an alliance by consent of those who form part of the Empire for material advantages in the real spirit of co-operation. Free alliance necessarily carries with it the right of separation. Before the War it was generally believed that it is only as a great confederation that the Empire or its component parts can live. It is realised that under modern conditions no nation can live in isolation and the Dominion Status, while it affords complete protection to each constituent composing the great Commonwealth of Nations called the British Empire, secures to each the right to realise itself, develop itself and fulfil itself and therefore it expresses and implies all the elements of Swaraj which I have mentioned.

"To me the idea is specially attractive because of its deep spiritual significance. I believe in world peace, in the ultimate federation of the world ; and I think that the great Commonwealth of Nations called the Britsh Empire—a federation of diverse races, each with its distinct life, distinct civilization, its distinct mental outlook—if properly led with statesmen at the helm is bound to make lasting contribution to the great problem that awaits the statesmen, the problem of knitting the world into the greatest federation the mind can conceive—the federation of the human race. But if only properly led with statesmen at the helm ;—for the development of the idea involves apparent sacrifice on the part of the constituent nations and it certainly involves the giving up for good the Empire idea with its ugly attribute of domination. I think it is for the good of India, for the good of the world that India should strive for freedom within the Commonwealth and so serve the cause of humanity."

Mr. Das not only insisted that Dominion Status was better than Independence but went further and got the Conference to pass the following resolution on the goal of India's political evolution :—

"1. This Conference declares that the National ideal of Swaraj involves the right of the Indian Nation to live its own life, to have the opportunity of self-realization, self-development and self-fulfilment and the liberty to work for the consolidation of the diverse elements which go to make up the Indian Nation unimpeded and unobstructed by any outside domination.

"2. That if the British Empire recognises such right and does not obstruct the realisation of Swaraj and is prepared to give such opportunity and undertakes to make the necessary sacrifices to make such rights effective, this Conference calls upon the Indian Nation to realise its Swaraj within the British Commonwealth."

It may be noted that Mr. Gandhi was present throughout the session. But there was no word of dissent coming from him. On the contrary, he approved of the stand taken by Mr. Das.

With these facts, who can doubt that the Hindus are for Dominion Status and the Muslims are for Independence? But if there be any doubt still remaining, the repercussions in Muslim quarters over the Nehru Committee's Report in 1928 must dissolve it completely. The Nehru Committee appointed by the Congress to frame a constitution for India accepted Dominion Status as the basis for India's constitution and rejected independence. It is instructive to note the attitude adopted by the Congress and the Muslim political organizations in the country towards the Nehru Report.

The Congress in its session held at Calcutta in 1928 passed a resolution moved by Mr. Gandhi which was in the following terms :—

> "This Congress, having considered the constitution recommended by the All-Parties Committee Report, welcomes it as a great contribution towards the solution of India's political and communal problems, and congratulates the Committee on the virtual unanimity of its recommendations and, whilst adhering to the resolution relating to complete independence passed at the Madras Congress approves of the constitution drawn up by the Committee as a great step in political advance, especially as it represents the largest measure of agreement attained among the important parties in the country.
>
> "Subject to the exigencies of the political situation this Congress will adopt the constitution in its entirety if it is accepted by the British Parliament on or before December 31, 1929, but in the event of its non-acceptance by that date or its earlier rejection, Congress will organise a non-violent non-co-operation by advising the country to refuse taxation or in such other manner as may be decided upon. Consistently with the above, nothing in this resolution shall interfere with the carrying on, in the name of the Congress, of the propaganda for complete independence."

This shows that Hindu opinion is not in favour of Independence but in favour of Dominion Status. Some will take exception to this statement. It may be asked what about the Congress resolution of 1927? It is true that the Congress in its Madras session held in 1927 did pass the following resolution moved by Pandit Jawaharlal Nehru :—

> "This Congress declares the goal of the Indian people to be complete National Independence."

But there is enough evidence to support the contention that this resolution did not and does not speak the real mind of the Hindus in the Congress.

The resolution came as a surprise. There was no indication of it in the speech of Dr. Ansari* who presided over the 1927 session. The Chairman† of the Reception Committee only referred to it in passing, not as an urgent but a contingent line of action.

There was no forethought about the resolution. It was the result of a coup and the coup was successful because of three factors.

In the first place, there was then a section in the Congress which was opposed to the domination of Pandit Motilal Nehru and Mr. Gandhi, particularly the former. This group was led by Mr. Srinivas Iyengar who was the political rival of Pandit Motilal. They were searching for a plan which would destroy the power and prestige of Pandit Motilal and Mr. Gandhi. They knew that the only way to win people to their side was to take a more extreme position and to show that their rivals were really moderates, and as moderation was deemed by Congressmen to be a sin, they felt that this plan was sure to succeed. They

* This is all that Dr. Ansari said about the subject in his speech:

"Whatever be the final form of the constitution, one thing may be said with some degree of certainty, that it will have to be on federal lines providing for a United States of India with existing Indian States as autonomous units of the Federation taking their proper share in the defence of the country, in the regulation of the nation's foreign affairs and other joint and common interests." —*The Indian Quarterly Register*, 1927, Vol. II, p. 372.

† Mr. Muthuranga Mudaliar said:

"We ought to make it known that if Parliament continues in its present insolent mood, we must definitely start on an intensive propaganda for the severance of India from the Empire. Whenever the time may come for the effective assertion of Indian nationalism, Indian aspiration will then be towards free nationhood, untrammelled even by the nominal suzerainty of the King of England. It behoves English statesmanship to take careful note of this fact. Let them not drive us to despair."—Ibid., p. 356.

made the goal of India the battle-ground, and knowing that Pandit Motilal and Gandhi were for Dominion Status, put forth the goal of Independence. In the second place, there was a section in the Congress which was led by Mr. Vithalbhai Patel. This section was in touch with the Irish Sinn Fein party and was canvassing its help in the cause of India. The Irish Sinn Fein party was not willing to render any help unless the Indians declared that their goal was Independence. This section was anxious to change the goal from Dominion Status to Independence in order to secure Irish help. To these two factors was added a third, namely, the speech made by Lord Birkenhead, the then Secretary of State for India, on the occasion of the appointment of the Simon Commission when he taunted the Indians on their incapacity to produce a constitution. The speech was regarded as a great insult by Indian politicians. It is the combination of these three factors which was responsible for the passing of this resolution. Indeed, the resolution was passed more from the motive* of giving a fitting reply to Lord Birkenhead than from the motive of defining the political goal of the country and if Mr. Gandhi and Pandit Motilal Nehru kept quiet it was largely because the storm created by the intemperate language of Lord Birkenhead against Indians was so great that they thought it wise to bow to it rather than engage upon the task of sweeping it off which they would have otherwise easily done.

That this resolution did not speak the real mind of the Hindus in the Congress is beyond doubt. Otherwise, it is not possible to explain how the Nehru Committee could have flouted the Madras resolution of 1927 by adopting Dominion Status as the basis of the constitutional structure framed by it. Nor is it possible to explain how the Congress adopted Dominion Status in 1928 if it had really accepted† independence in 1927 as the resolution says. The clause in the resolution that the Congress

---

* Mr. Sambamurti in seconding the resolution said:

"The resolution is the only reply to the arrogant challenge thrown by Lord Birkenhead."—*The Indian Quarterly Register*, 1927, Vol. II, p. 381.

† Pandit Jawaharlal Nehru in moving the resolution said:

"It declares that the Congress stands today for complete Independence. Nonetheless it leaves the doors of the Congress open to such persons as may perhaps be satisfied with a lesser goal."—Ibid., p. 381.

would accept Dominion Status if given before 31st December 1929, if not, it would change its faith from Dominion Status to Independence was only a face-saving device and did not connote a real change of mind. For time can never be of the essence in a matter of such deep concern as the political destiny of the country.

That notwithstanding the resolution of 1927, the Congress continued to believe in Dominion Status and did not believe in Independence, is amply borne out by the pronouncements made from time to time by Mr. Gandhi who is the oracle of the Congress. Anyone, who studies Mr. Gandhi's pronouncements on this subject from 1929 onwards, cannot help feeling that Mr. Gandhi has not been happy about the resolution on Independence and that he has ever since felt necessary to wheel the Congress back to Dominion Status. He began with the gentle process of interpreting it away. The goal was first reduced from Independence to substance of Independence. From substance of Independence it was reduced to equal partnership and from equal partnership it was brought back to its original position. The wheel completed the turn when Mr. Gandhi in 1937 gave the following letter to Mr. Pollock for the information of the English people:—

> "Your question is whether I retain the same opinion as I did at the Round Table Conference in 1931. I said then, and repeat now, that, so far as I am concerned, if Dominion Status were offered to India in terms of the Statute of Westminster, i.e., the right to secede at will, I would unhesitatingly accept."*

Turning to the pronouncements of Muslim political organizations on the Nehru Report it is interesting to note the reasons given by them for its rejection. These reasons are wholly unexpected. No doubt some Muslim organizations such as the Muslim League rejected the Report because it recommended the abolition of separate electorates. But that was certainly not the reason why it was condemned by the Khilafat Conference or the Jamiat-ul-Ulema—the two Muslim organizations which went with the

* *Times of India* 1-2-37. In view of this, the declaration made by the National Convention—consisting of the members elected to the new Provincial Legislatures under the new constitution—on the 20th March 1937 held at Delhi in favour of independence has no significance. But from his having launched the Quit India movement it may be said that Mr. Gandhi now believes in Independence.

Congress through the same fiery ordeal of non-co-operation and civil disobedience and whose utterances expressed far more truly the real opinion of Muslim masses on the issues relating to the political affairs of the country than did the utterances of any other Muslim organization.

Maulana Mahomed Ali set out his reasons for the rejection of the Nehru Report in his Presidential address to the All-India Khilafat Conference held in Calcutta in 1928. He said* :—

> "[I] was a member of the Indian National Congress, its Working Committee, the All-India Muslim League and [I] have come to the Khilafat Conference to express (my views) on the important political issues of the time, which should have the serious attention of the whole Muslim community.
>
> * * * * *
>
> "In the All-Parties Convention he had said that India should have complete independence and there was no communalism in it. Yet he was being heckled at every moment and stopped during his speech at every step.
>
> * * * * *
>
> "The Nehru Report had as its preamble admitted the bondage of servitude . . . . Freedom and Dominion Status were widely divergent things . . . .
>
> * * * * *
>
> "I ask, when you boast of your nationalism and condemn communalism, show me a country in the world like your India—your nationalist India.
>
> * * * * *
>
> " You make compromises in your constitution every day with false doctrines, immoral conceptions and wrong ideas but you make no compromise with our communalists—with separate electorates and reserved seats. Twenty-five per cent. is our portion of population and yet you will not give us 33 per cent. in the Assembly. You are a Jew, a Bania. But to the English you give the status of your dominion."

The Conference passed a short resolution in the following pithy terms :—

> " This Conference declares once more that complete independence is our goal."

---

* *The Indian Quarterly Register*, 1928, Vol. II, pp. 402-403.

Maulana Hasrat Mohani, as President of the Jamiat-ul-Ulema Conference held in Allahabad in 1931, gave the same reasons for condemning the Nehru Report in words more measured but not less scathing. Said* the Maulana :—

"My political creed with regard to India is now well known to everybody. I cannot accept anything short of complete independence, and, that too, on the model of the United States of America or the Soviet Russia which is essentially (1) democratic, (2) federal and (3) centrifugal, and in which the rights of Muslim minorities are safeguarded.

"For some time the Jamiat-ul-Ulema of Delhi held fast to the creed of complete independence and it was mostly for this reason that it repudiated the Nehru Report which devised a unitary constitution instead of a federal one. Besides, when, after the Lahore session, the Congress, at the instance of Mahatma Gandhi, declared the burial of the Nehru Report on the banks of the Ravi and the resolution of complete independence was unanimously agreed upon, the Delhi Jamiat ventured to co-operate with the Congress and its programme of civil disobedience simply because it was the duty of every Indian, Hindu or Muslim, to take part in the struggle for independence.

"But unfortunately Gandhiji very soon went back upon his words and (1) while yet in jail he told the British journalist Mr. Slocombe that by complete independence he meant only the substance of independence, (2) besides, when he was released on expressing his inclination for compromise he devised the illusory term of 'Purna Swaraj' in place of complete independence and openly declared that in 'Purna Swaraj' there was no place for severance of the British connection, (3) by making a secret pact with Lord Irwin he definitely adopted the ideal of Dominion Status under the British Crown.

"After this change of front by Gandhiji the Delhi Jamiat ought to have desisted from blindly supporting the Mahatma and like the Nehru Report it should have completely rejected this formula of the Congress Working Committee by which the Nehru Report was sought to be revived at Bombay.

"But we do not know what unintelligible reasons induced the Delhi Jamiat-ul-Ulema to adopt 'Purna Swaraj' as their ideal, in spite of the knowledge that it does not mean complete independence but something even worse than complete independence. And the only explanation for adopting this creed is said to be that, although Gandhiji has accepted Dominion Status, he still insists that Britain should concede the right of secession from the British Empire to the Indians.

* Ibid., 1931, Vol. II, pp. 238-39.

"Although it is quite clear that insistence on this right has no better worth than the previous declaration of complete independence, in other words, just as Gandhiji insisted on complete independence with the sole object of forcing the British Government to accede to the demand of Dominion Status, which was the sole ultimate aim of the Mahatma, in the same way the leaders of the Congress insisted upon the right of secession with the object of extorting the largest measure of political rights from the British people who might not go beyond a certain limit in displeasing them. Otherwise Gandhiji and his followers know it full well that even if this right of secession is given to Indians, it would perhaps be never put into practice.

"If someone considers this contention of mine to be based on suspicion and contends that the Congress will certainly declare for secession from the Empire whenever there is need of it, I will ask him to let me know what will be the form of Indian Government after the British connection is withdrawn. It is clear that no one can conceive of a despotic form and a democratic form, whether it be unitary or federal but centripetal, will be nothing more than Hindu Raj which the Musalmans can in no circumstances accept. Now remains only one form, viz. after complete withdrawal of the British connection India with its autonomous Provinces and States forms into united centrifugal democratic government on the model of the United States Republic or Soviet Russia. But this can never be acceptable to the Mahasabhaite Congress or a lover of Britain like Mahatma Gandhi.

"Thus the Jamiat-ul-Ulema of Delhi after washing its hands of complete independence has stultified itself, but thank God the Ulemas of Cawnpore, Lucknow, Badaun, etc., still hold fast to their pledge and will remain so, God willing. Some weak-kneed persons urge against this highest ideal that, when it is not possible for the present to attain it, there is no use talking about it. We say to them that it is not at all useless but rather absolutely necessary, for if the highest ideal is not always kept before view, it is liable to be forgotten.

"We must, therefore, oppose Dominion Status in all circumstances as this is not the half-way house or part of our ultimate aim, but its very negation and rival. If Gandhiji reaches England and the Round Table Conference is successfully concluded, giving India Dominion Status of any kind, with or without safeguards, the conception of complete independence will completely vanish or at any rate will not be thought of for a very long time to come."

The All-India Khilafat Conference and the Jamiat-ul-Ulema were surely extremist bodies avowedly anti-British. But the All-Parties Muslim Conference was not at all a body of extremists or anti-British Musalmans. Yet the U. P. Branch of it in its session held at Cawnpore on 4th November 1928 passed the following resolution :—

> "In the opinion of the All-Parties U. P. Muslim Conference, Musalmans of India stand for the goal of complete independence, which shall necessarily take the form of a federal republic."

In the opinion of the mover, Islam always taught freedom, and for the matter of that the Muslims of India would fail in their religious duty, if they were against complete independence. Indian Muslims were poor, yet they were, the speaker was sure, devoted to Islam more than any other people on earth.

In this Conference an incident* of some interest occurred in the Subjects Committee when Maulana Azad Sobhani proposed that the Conference should declare itself in favour of complete independence.

Khan Bahadur Masoodul Hassan and some other persons, objected to such declaration, which, in their opinion, would go against the best interests of Musalmans. Upon this, a number of women from their *puraah* gallery sent a written statement to the President saying that if men had not the courage to stand for complete independence, women would come out of *purdah*, and take their place in the struggle for independence.

III

Notwithstanding this difference in their ultimate destiny, an attempt is made to force the Hindus and Muslims to live in one country, as one people, bound by the political ties of a single constitution. Assuming that this is done and that the Muslims are somehow manœuvred into it, what guarantee is there that the constitution will not break down?

The successful working of a Parliamentary Government assumes the existence of certain conditions. It is only when these conditions exist that Parliamentary Government can take roots. One such condition was pointed out by the late Lord

* See *The Indian Quarterly Register*, 1928, Vol. II. pp. 425.

Balfour when in 1925 he had an occasion to discuss the political future of the Arab peoples in conversation with his niece Blanche Dugdale.

In the course of this conversation he said* :—

> "It is partly the fault of the British nation — and of the Americans; we can't exonerate them from blame either — that this idea of 'representative government' has got into the heads of nations who haven't the smallest notion of what its basis must be. It's difficult to explain, and the Anglo-Saxon races are bad at exposition. Moreover we know it so well ourselves that it does not strike us as necessary to explain it. I doubt if you would *find it* written in any book on the British Constitution that the whole essence of British Parliamentary Government lies in the *intention to make the thing work*. We take that for granted. We have spent hundreds of years in elaborating a system that rests on that alone. It is so deep in us that we have lost sight of it. But it is not so obvious to others. These peoples — Indians, Egyptians, and so on — study our learning. They read our history, our philosophy, and politics. They learn about our parliamentary methods of obstruction, but nobody explains to them that when it comes to the point, all our parliamentary parties are determined that the machinery shan't stop. 'The king's government must go on' as the Duke of Wellington said. But their idea is that the function of opposition is to stop the machine. Nothing easier, of course, but hopeless."

Asked why the opposition in England does not go to the length of stopping the machine, he said :—

> "Our whole political machinery presupposes a people... fundamentally at one."

Laski has well summarized these observations of Balfour on the condition necessary for the successful working of Parliamentary Government when he says† :

> "The strength of Parliamentary Government is exactly measured by the unity of political parties upon its fundamental objects."

Having stated the condition necessary for the successful working of the machinery of representative government it will be well to examine whether these conditions are present in India.

How far can we say that there is an intention in the Hindus and the Muslims to make representative government work?

* Dugdale's *Balfour* (Hutchinson), Vol. II, pp. 363-64.
† *Parliamentary Government in England*, p. 37.

To prove the futility and unworkability of representative and responsible government, it is enough even if one of the two parties shows an intention to stop the machinery of government. If such an intention is enough, then it does not matter much whether it is found in the Hindus or in the Muslims. The Muslims being more outspoken than the Hindus, one gets to know their mind more than one gets to know the mind of the Hindus. How the Muslim mind will work and by what factors it is likely to be swayed will be clear if the fundamental tenets of Islam which dominate Muslim politics and the views expressed by prominent Muslims bearing on Muslim attitude towards an Indian Government are taken into consideration. Certain of such religious tenets of Islam and the views of some of the Muslim leaders are given below to enable all those who are capable of looking at things dispassionately, to judge for themselves whether the condition postulated by Balfour can be said to exist in India.

Among the tenets one that calls for notice is the tenet of Islam which says that in a country which is not under Muslim rule wherever there is a conflict between Muslim law and the law of the land, the former must prevail over the latter and a Muslim will be justified in obeying the Muslim law and defying the law of the land.

What the duty of the Musalmans is in such cases was well pointed out by Maulana Mahomed Ali in the course of his statement made in 1921 before the Committing Magistrate of Karachi in answer to the charges for which he was prosecuted by the Government. The prosecution arose out of a resolution passed at the session of the All-India Khilafat Conference held in Karachi on 8th July 1921 at which Mr. Mahomed Ali presided and introduced the resolution in question.

The resolution was as follows :—

> "This meeting clearly proclaims that it is in every way religiously unlawful for a Musalman at the present moment to continue in the British Army, or to enter the Army, or to induce others to join the Army. And it is the duty of all Musalmans in general and of the Ulemas in particular to see that these religious commandments are brought home to every Musalman in the Army."

Along with Maulana Mahomed Ali six other persons* were prosecuted under Section 120-B read with Sec. 131 I. P. C. and under Sec. 505 or 505 read with Sec. 114 and Sec. 505 read with Sec.117 I. P. C. Maulana Mahomed Ali in justification of his plea of not guilty, said† :—

> "After all what is the meaning of this precious prosecution. By whose convictions are we to be guided, we the Musalmans and the Hindus of India? Speaking as a Musalman, if I am supposed to err from the right path, the only way to convince me of my error is to refer me to the Holy Koran or to the authentic traditions of the last Prophet—on whom be peace and God's benediction—or the religious pronouncements of recognized Muslim divines, past and present, which purport to be based on these two original sources of Islamic authority demands from me in the present circumstances, the precise action for which a Government, that does not like to be called satanic, is prosecuting me to-day.
>
> "If that which I neglect, becomes by my neglect a deadly sin, and is yet a crime when I do not neglect it, how am I to consider myself safe in this country?
>
> "I must either be a sinner or a criminal .... Islam recognizes one sovereignty alone, the sovereignty of God, which is supreme and unconditional, indivisible and inalienable .....
>
> "The only allegiance a Musalman, whether civilian or soldier, whether living under a Muslim or under a non-Muslim administration, is commanded by the Koran to acknowledge is his allegiance to God, to his Prophet and to those in authority from among the Musalmans chief among the last mentioned being of course that Prophet's successor or commander of the faithful .... This doctrine of unity is not a mathematical formula elaborated by abstruse thinkers but a work-a-day belief of every Musalman learned or unlettered .... Musalmans have before this also and elsewhere too, lived in peaceful subjection to non-Muslim administrations. But the unalterable rule is and has always been that as Musalmans they can obey only such laws and orders issued by their secular rulers as do not involve disobedience to the commandments of God who in the expressive language of the Holy Koran is 'the all-ruling ruler.' These very clear and rigidly definite limits of obedience are not laid down with regard to the authority of non-

* Strange enough one of them was the Shankaracharya of Sharda Peeth.

† *The Trial of Ali Brothers*, by R. V. Thadani, pp. 69-71.

> Muslim administration only. On the contrary they are of universal application and can neither be enlarged nor reduced in any case."

This must make anyone wishing for a stable government very apprehensive. But this is nothing to the Muslim tenets which prescribe when a country is a motherland to the Muslim and when it is not.

According to Muslim Canon Law the world is divided into two camps, Dar-ul-Islam (abode of Islam) and Dar-ul-Harb (abode of war). A country is Dar-ul-Islam when it is ruled by Muslims. A country is Dar-ul-Harb when Muslims only reside in it but are not rulers of it. That being the Canon Law of the Muslims, India cannot be the common motherland of the Hindus *and* the Musalmans. It can be the land of the Musalmans—but it cannot be the land of the 'Hindus and the Musalmans living as equals.' Further, it can be the land of the Musalmans only when it is governed by the Muslims. The moment the land becomes subject to the authority of a non-Muslim power, it ceases to be the land of the Muslims. Instead of being Dar-ul-Islam it becomes Dar-ul-Harb.

It must not be supposed that this view is only of academic interest. For it is capable of becoming an active force capable of influencing the conduct of the Muslims. It did greatly influence the conduct of the Muslims when the British occupied India. The British occupation raised no qualms in the minds of the Hindus. But so far as the Muslims were concerned, it at once raised the question whether India was any longer a suitable place of residence for Muslims. A discussion was started in the Muslim community, which Dr. Titus says lasted for half a century, as to whether India was Dar-ul-Harb or Dar-ul-Islam. Some of the more zealous elements, under the leadership of Sayyed Ahmad, actually did declare a holy war, preached the necessity of emigration (*Hijrat*) to lands under Muslim rule, and carried their agitation all over India.

It took all the ingenuity of Sir Sayyed Ahmad, the founder of the Aligarh movement, to persuade the Indian Musalmans not to regard India under the British as Dar-ul-Harb merely because it was not under Muslim rule. He urged upon the Muslims to regard it as Dar-ul-Islam, because the Muslims were perfectly free to exercise all the essential rites and ceremonies of their religion. The movement for *Hijrat* for the time being died down. But the doctrine that India was Dar-ul-Harb had not been given up. It was again preached by Muslim patriots during 1920-21, when the Khilafat agitation was going on. The agitation was not without response from the Muslim masses and there was a goodly number of Muslims who not only showed themselves ready to act in accordance with the Muslim Canon Law but actually abandoned their homes in India and crossed over to Afghanistan.

It might also be mentioned that *Hijrat* is not the only way of escape to Muslims who find themselves in a Dar-ul-Harb. There is another injunction of Muslim Canon Law called *Jihad* (crusade) by which it becomes "incumbent on a Muslim ruler to extend the rule of Islam until the whole world shall have been brought under its sway. The world, being divided into two camps, Dar-ul-Islam (abode of Islam), Dar-ul-Harb (abode of war), all countries come under one category or the other. Technically, it is the duty of the Muslim ruler, who is capable of doing so, to transform Dar-ul-Harb into Dar-ul-Islam." And just as there are instances of the Muslims in India resorting to *Hijrat*, there are instances showing that they have not hesitated to proclaim *Jihad*. The curious may examine the history of the Mutiny of 1857 and if he does, he will find that, in part, at any rate, it was really a *Jihad* proclaimed by the Muslims against the British, and that the Mutiny so far as the Muslims were concerned was a recrudescence of revolt which had been fostered by Sayyed Ahmad who preached to the Musalmans for several decades that owing to the occupation of India by the British the country had become a Dar-ul-Harb. The Mutiny was an attempt by the Muslims to re-convert India into a Dar-ul-Islam. A more recent instance was the invasion of India by Afghanistan in 1919. It was engineered by the Musalmans of India who led by the Khilafatists' antipathy to the British Government sought the assistance of Afghanistan to emancipate India.* Whether the invasion would have resulted in the emancipation of India or

* This interesting and awful episode has been examined in some details, giving the part played therein by Mr. Gandhi, in a series of articles in the issues of the *Maratha*, for the year by Mr. Karandikar.

whether it would have resulted in its subjugation, it is not possible to say because the invasion failed to take effect. Apart from this, the fact remains that India, if not exclusively under Muslim rule, is a Dar-ul-Harb and the Musalmans according to the tenets of Islam are justified in proclaiming a *Jihad.*

Not only can they proclaim *Jihad* but they can call the aid of a foreign Muslim power to make *Jihad* a success, or if the foreign Muslim power intends to proclaim a *Jihad*, help that power in making its endeavour a success. This was clearly explained by Mr. Mahomed Ali in his address to the Jury in the Sessions Court. Mr. Mahomed Ali said:—

> "But since the Government is apparently uninformed about the manner in which our Faith colours and is meant to colour all our actions, including those which, for the sake of convenience, are generally characterised as mundane, one thing must be made clear, and it is this: Islam does not permit the believer to pronounce an adverse judgment against another believer without more convincing proof; and we could not, of course, fight against our Muslim brothers without making sure that they were guilty of wanton aggression, and did not take up arms in defence of their faith." (This was in relation to the war that was going on between the British and the Afghans in 1919.) "Now our position is this. Without better proof of the Amir's malice or madness we certainly do not want Indian soldiers, including the Musalmans, and particularly with our own encouragement and assistance, to attack Afghanistan and effectively occupy it first, and then be a prey to more perplexity and perturbation afterwards.
>
> "But if on the contrary His Majesty the Amir has no quarrel with India and her people and if his motive must be attributed, as the Secretary of State has publicly said, to the unrest which exists throughout the Mahomedan world, an unrest with which he openly professed to be in cordial sympathy, that is to say, if impelled by the same religious motive that has forced Muslims to contemplate *Hijrat*, the alternative of the weak, which is all that is within our restricted means, His Majesty has been forced to contemplate *Jihad*, the alternative of those comparatively stronger which he may have found within his means; if he has taken up the challenge of those who believed in force and yet more force, and he intends to try conclusions with those who require Musalmans to wage war against the Khilafat and those engaged in *Jihad*; who are in wrongful occupation of the Jazirut-ul-Arab and the holy places; who aim at the weakening of Islam; discriminate against it; and deny to us full freedom to advocate its cause; then the clear law of Islam requires that in the first place,

in no case whatever should a Musalman render anyone any assistance against him; and in the next place if the *Jihad* approaches my region—every Musalman in that region must join the Mujahidin and assist them to the best of his or her power.

"Such is the clear and undisputed law of Islam; and we had explained this to the Committee investigating our case when it had put to us a question about the religious duty of a Muslim subject of a non-Muslim power when *Jihad* had been declared against it, long before there was any notion of trouble on the Frontiers, and when the late Amir was still alive."

A third tenet which calls for notice as being relevant to the issue is that Islam does not recognize territorial affinities. Its affinities are social and religious and therefore extra-territorial. Here again Maulana Mahomed Ali will be the best witness. When he was committed to the Sessions Court in Karachi Mr. Mahomed Ali addressing the Jury said:—

"One thing has to be made clear as we have since discovered that the doctrine to which we shall now advert is not so generally known in non-Muslim and particularly in official circles as it ought to be. A Musalman's faith does not consist merely in believing in a set of doctrines and living up to that belief himself; he must also exert himself to the fullest extent of his power, of course without resort to any compulsion, to the end that others also conform to the prescribed belief and practices. This is spoken of in the Holy Koran as *Amribilmaroof* and *Nahi anilmunkar*; and certain distinct chapters of the Holy Prophet's traditions relate to this essential doctrine of Islam. A Musalman cannot say: 'I am not my brother's keeper,' for in a sense he is and his own salvation cannot be assured to him unless he exhorts others also to do good and dehorts them against doing evil. If therefore any Musalman is being compelled to wage war against the Mujahid of Islam, he must not only be a conscientious objector himself, but must, if he values his own salvation, persuade his brothers also at whatever risk to himself to take similar objection. Then and not until then, can he hope for salvation. This is our belief as well as the belief of every other Musalman and in our humble way we seek to live up to it; and if we are denied freedom to inculcate this doctrine, we must conclude that the land, where this freedom does not exist, is not safe for Islam."

This is the basis of Pan-Islamism. It is this which leads every Musalman in India to say that he is a Muslim first and Indian afterwards. It is this sentiment which explains why the Indian Muslim has taken so small a part in the advancement of

India but has spent himself to exhaustion* by taking up the cause of Muslim countries and why Muslim countries occupy the first place and India occupies a second place in his thoughts.

His Highness the Aga Khan justifies it by saying† :—

> "This is a right and legitimate Pan-Islamism to which every sincere and believing Mahomedan belongs—that is, the theory of the spiritual brotherhood and unity of the children of the Prophet. It is a deep, perennial element in that Perso-Arabian culture, that great family of civilization to which we gave the name Islamic in the first chapter. It connotes charity and good-will towards fellow-believers everywhere from China to Morocco, from the Volga to Singapore. It means an abiding interest in the literature of Islam, in her beautiful arts, in her lovely architecture, in her entrancing poetry. It also means a true reformation—a return to the early and pure simplicity of the faith, to its preaching by persuasion and argument, to the manifestation of a spiritual power in individual lives, to beneficent activity of mankind. This natural and worthy spiritual movement makes not only the Master and His teaching but also His children of all climes an object of affection to the Turk or the Afghan, to the Indian or the Egyptian. A famine or a desolating fire in the Muslim quarters of Kashgar or Sarajevo would immediately draw the sympathy and material assistance of the Mahomedan of Delhi or Cairo. The real spiritual and cultural unity of Islam must ever grow, for to the follower of the Prophet it is the foundation of the life of the soul."

If this spiritual Pan-Islamism seeks to issue forth in political Pan-Islamism, it cannot be said to be unnatural. It is perhaps that feeling which was in the mind of the Aga Khan when he said‡ :—

> "It is for the Indian patriot to recognise that Persia, Afghanistan and possibly Arabia must sooner or later come within the orbit of some Continental Power—such as Germany, or what may grow out of the break-up of Russia—or must throw in their lot with that of the Indian Empire, with which they have so much more genuine affinity. The world forces that move small States into closer contact with powerful neighbours, though so far most visible in Europe, will inevitably make themselves felt

* Between 1912 when the first Balkan war began and 1922 when Turkey made peace with the European Powers, the Indian Muslims did not bother about Indian politics in the least. They were completely absorbed in the fate of Turkey and Arabia.

† *India in Transition*, p. 157.

‡ Ibid., p. 169.

in Asia. Unless she is willing to accept the prospect of having powerful and possibly inimical neighbours to watch, and the heavy military burdens thereby entailed, India cannot afford to neglect to draw her Mahomedan neighbour States to herself by the ties of mutual interest and goodwill.

"In a word, the path of beneficent and growing union must be based on a federal India, with every member exercising her individual rights, her historic peculiarities and natural interests, yet protected by a common defensive system and customs union from external danger and economic exploitation by stronger forces. Such a federal India would promptly bring Ceylon to the bosom of her natural mother, and the further developments we have indicated would follow. We can build a great South Asiatic Federation by now laying the foundations wide and deep on justice, on liberty, and on recognition for every race, every religion, and every historical entity.

"A sincere policy of assisting both Persia and Afghanistan in the onward march which modern conditions demand, will raise two natural ramparts for India in the north-west that neither German nor Slav, Turk nor Mongol, can ever hope to destroy. They will be drawn of their own accord towards the Power which provides the object lesson of a healthy form of federalism in India, with real autonomy for each province, with the internal freedom of principalities assured, with a revived and liberalised kingdom of Hyderabad, including the Berars, under the Nizam. They would see in India freedom and order, autonomy and yet Imperial union, and would appreciate for themselves the advantages of a confederation assuring the continuance of internal self-government buttressed by goodwill, the immense and unlimited strength of that great Empire on which the sun never sets. The British position in Mesopotamia and Arabia also, whatever its nominal form may be, would be infinitely strengthened by the policy I have advocated."

This South Asiatic Federation was more for the good of the Muslim countries such as Arabia, Mesopotamia and Afghanistan than for the good of India.* This shows how very naturally the thoughts of Indian Musalmans are occupied by considerations of Muslim countries other than those of India.

* What a terrible thing it would have been if this South Asiatic Federation had come into being? Hindus would have been reduced to the position of a distressed minority. The *Indian Annual Register* says: "Supporters of British Imperialism in the Muslim community of India have also been active trying by the organization of an Anglo-Muslim alliance to stabilize the rule of Britain in Southern Asia, from Arabia to the Malaya Archipelago, wherein the Muslims will be junior partners in the firm at present, hoping to rise in time to the senior partnership. It was to some such

Government is based on obedience to authority. But those, who are eager to establish self-government of Hindus and Muslims, do not seem to have stopped to inquire on what such obedience depends and how far such obedience would be forthcoming in the usual course and in moments of crisis. This is a very important question. For, if obedience fails, self-government means working together and not working under. That may be so in an ideal sense. But in the practical and work-a-day world, if the elements brought under one representative government are disproportionate in numbers, the minor section will have to work under the major section and whether it works under the major section or not will depend upon how far it is disposed to obey the authority of the government carried on by the major section. So important is this factor in the success of self-government that Balfour may be said to have spoken only part of the truth when he made its success dependent upon parties being fundamentally at one. He failed to note that willingness to obey the authority of government is a factor equally necessary for the success of any scheme of self-government.

The importance of this second condition, the existence of which is necessary for a successful working of parliamentary government, has been discussed by* James Bryce. While dealing with the basis of political cohesion, Bryce points out that while force may have done much to build up States, force is only one among many factors and not the most important. In creating, moulding, expanding and knitting together political communities what is more important than force is obedience. This willingness to obey and comply with the sanctions of a government depends upon certain psychological attributes of the individual citizens and groups. According to Bryce the attitude which

---

feeling and anticipation that we must trace the scheme adumbrated by His Highness the Aga Khan in his book *India in Transition* published during the war years. The scheme had planned for the setting up of a South Western Asiatic Federation of which India might be a constituent unit. After the war when Mr. Winston Churchill was Secretary of State for the Colonies in the British Cabinet, he found in the archives of the Middle Eastern Department a scheme ready-made of a Middle Eastern Empire" —1938, Vol. II, Section on "India in Home Polity," p. 48.

* *Studies in History and Jurisprudence*, Vol. II, Essay I.

produces obedience are indolence, deference, sympathy, fear and reason. All are not of the same value. Indeed they are relative in their importance as causes producing a disposition to obey. As formulated by Bryce, in the sum total of obedience the percentage due to fear and to reason respectively is much less than that due to indolence and less also than that due to deference or sympathy. According to this view deference and sympathy are, therefore, the two most powerful factors which predispose a people to obey the authority of its government.

Willingness to render obedience to the authority of the government is as essential for the stability of government as the unity of political parties on the fundamentals of the state. It is impossible for any sane person to question the importance of obedience in the maintenance of the state. To believe in civil disobedience is to believe in anarchy.

How far will Muslims obey the authority of a government manned and controlled by the Hindus? The answer to this question need not call for much inquiry. To the Muslims a Hindu is a Kaffir.* A Kaffir is not worthy of respect. He is low-born and without status. That is why a country which is ruled by a Kaffir is Dar-ul-Harb to a Musalman. Given this, no further evidence seems to be necessary to prove that the Muslims will not obey a Hindu government. The basic feelings of deference and sympathy, which predispose persons to obey the authority of government, do not simply exist. But if proof is wanted, there is no dearth of it. It is so abundant that the problem is what to tender and what to omit.

In the midst of the Khilafat agitation when the Hindus were doing so much to help the Musalmans, the Muslims did not forget that as compared with them the Hindus were a low and an inferior race. A Musalman wrote † in the Khilafat paper called *Insaf*:—

> "What is the meaning of Swami and Mahatma? Can Muslims use in speech or writing these words about non-Muslims? He says that Swami means 'Master', and 'Mahatma'

* The Hindus have no right to feel hurt at being called Kaffirs. They call the Muslims *Mlechas*—persons not fit to associate with.

† See "Through Indian Eyes," *Times of India*, dated 11-3-24.

means 'possessed of the highest spiritual powers' and is equivalent to 'Ruh-i-aazam', and the supreme spirit."

He asked the Muslim divines to decide by an authoritative *fatwa* whether it was lawful for Muslims to call non-Muslims by such deferential and reverential titles.

A remarkable incident was reported* in connection with the celebration of Mr. Gandhi's release from gaol in 1924 at the Tibbia College of Yunani medicine run by Hakim Ajmal Khan at Delhi. According to the report, a Hindu student compared Mr. Gandhi to Hazarat Isa (Jesus) and at this sacrilege to the Musalman sentiment all the Musalman students flared up and threatened the Hindu student with violence, and, it is alleged, even the Musalman professors joined with their co-religionists in this demonstration of their outraged feelings.

In 1923 Mr. Mahomed Ali presided over the session of the Indian National Congress. In this address he spoke of Mr. Gandhi in the following terms :—

> "Many have compared the Mahatma's teachings, and latterly his personal sufferings, to those of Jesus (on whom be peace) .... When Jesus contemplated the world at the outset of his ministry he was called upon to make his choice of the weapons of reform...... The idea of being all-powerful by suffering and resignation, and of triumphing over force by purity of heart, is as old as the days of Abel and Cain, the first progeny of man......
>
> "Be that as it may, it was just as peculiar to Mahatma Gandhi also; but it was reserved for a Christian Government to treat as felon the most Christ like man of our time (*Shame, Shame*) and to penalize as a disturber of the public peace the one man engaged in public affairs who comes nearest to the Prince of Peace. The political conditions of India just before the advent of the Mahatma resembled those of Judea on the eve of the advent of Jesus, and the prescription that he offered to those in search of a remedy for the ills of India was the same that Jesus had dispensed before in Judea. Self-purification through suffering; a moral preparation for the responsibilities of government; self-discipline as the condition precedent of Swaraj—this was Mahatma's creed and conviction; and those of us, who have been privileged to have lived in the glorious year that culminated in the Congress session at Ahmedabad, have seen what a remarkable and rapid

* See "Through Indian Eyes," *Times of India*, dated 21-3-24.

change he wrought in the thoughts, feelings and actions of such large masses of mankind."

A year after, Mr. Mahomed Ali speaking at Aligarh and Ajmere said :—

> "However pure Mr. Gandhi's character may be, he must appear to me from the point of view of religion inferior to any Musalman, even though he be without character."

The statement created a great stir. Many did not believe that Mr. Mahomed Ali, who testified to so much veneration for Mr. Gandhi, was capable of entertaining such ungenerous and contemptuous sentiments about him. When Mr. Mahomed Ali was speaking at a meeting held at Aminabad Park in Lucknow, he was asked whether the sentiments attributed to him were true. Mr. Mahomed Ali without any hesitation or compunction replied* :—

> "Yes, according to my religion and creed, I do hold an adulterous and a fallen Musalman to be better than Mr. Gandhi."

It was suggested† at the time that Mr. Mahomed Ali had to recant because the whole of the orthodox Muslim community had taken offence for his having shown such deference to Mr. Gandhi, who was a Kaffir, as to put him on the same pedestal as Jesus. Such praise of a Kaffir, they felt, was forbidden by the Muslim Canon Law.

In a manifesto‡ on Hindu-Muslim relations issued in 1928 Khwaja Hasan Nizami declared :—

> "Musalmans are separate from Hindus; they cannot unite with the Hindus. After bloody wars the Musalmans conquered India, and the English took India from them. The Musalmans are one united nation and they alone will be masters of India. They will never give up their individuality. They have ruled India for hundreds of years, and hence they have a prescriptive right over the country. The Hindus are a minor community in the world. They are never free from internecine quarrels; they believe in Gandhi and worship the cow; they are polluted by taking other people's water. The Hindus do not care for self-government; they have no time to spare for it: let them go on with their internal squabbles. What capacity have they for

* "Through Indian Eyes," *Times of India*, dated 21-3-24.

† Ibid., dated 26-4-24.

‡ Ibid., dated 14-3-28.

ruling over men? The Musalmans did rule, and the Musalmans will rule."

Far from rendering obedience to Hindus, the Muslims seem to be ready to try conclusions with the Hindus again. In 1926 there arose a controversy as to who really won the third battle of Panipat, fought in 1761. It was contended for the Muslims that it was a great victory for them because Ahmad Sha Abdali had 1 lakh of soldiers while the Mahrattas had 4 to 6 lakhs. The Hindus replied that it was a victory to them—a victory to the vanquished—because it stemmed the tide of Muslim invasions. The Muslims were not prepared to admit defeat at the hands of the Hindus and claimed that they will always prove superior to the Hindus. To prove the eternal superiority of Muslims over Hindus it was proposed by one Maulana Akbar Shah Khan of Najibabad in all seriousness, that the Hindus and Muslims should fight, under test conditions, fourth battle on the same fateful plain of Panipat. The Maulana accordingly issued* a challenge to Pandit Madan Mohan Malaviya in the following terms :—

> "If you, Malaviyaji, are making efforts to falsify the result at Panipat, I shall show you an easy and an excellent way (of testing it). Use your well-known influence and induce the British Government to permit the fourth battle of Panipat to be fought out without hindrance from the authorities. I am ready to provide . . . a comparative test of the valour and fighting spirit of the Hindus and the Musalmans. . . . As there are seven crores of Musalmans in India, I shall arrive on a fixed date on the plain of Panipat with 700 Musalmans representing the seven crores of Muslims in India and as there are 22 crores of Hindus I allow you to come with 2,200 Hindus. The proper thing is not to use cannon, machine guns or bombs: only swords and javelins and spears, bows and arrows and daggers should be used. If you cannot accept the post of generalissimo of the Hindu host, you may give it to any descendant of Sadashivrao† or Vishwasrao† so that their scions may have an opportunity to avenge the defeat of their ancestors in 1761. But any way do come as a spectator ; for on seeing the result of this battle you will have to change your views, and I hope there will be then an end of the present discord and fighting in the country. . . . In conclusion I beg to add that among the 700 men that I shall bring

* Quoted in "Through Indian Eyes," *Times of India*, dated 20-6-26.

† They were the Military Commanders on the side of the Hindus in the third battle of Panipat.

there will be no Pathans or Afghans as you are mortally afraid of them. So I shall bring with me only Indian Musalmans of good family who are staunch adherents of Shariat."

IV

Such are the religious beliefs, social attitudes and ultimate destinies of the Hindus and Muslims and their communal and political manifestations. These religious beliefs, social attitudes and views regarding ultimate destinies constitute the motive force which determines the lines of their action, whether they will be co-operative or conflicting. Past experience shows that they are too irreconcilable and too incompatible to permit Hindus and Muslims ever forming one single nation or even two harmonious parts of one whole. These differences have the sure effect not only of keeping them asunder but also of keeping them at war. The differences are permanent and the Hindu-Muslim problem bids fair to be eternal. To attempt to solve it on the footing that Hindus and Muslims are one or if they are not one now they will be one hereafter is bound to be a barren occupation—as barren as it proved to be in the case of Czechoslovakia. On the contrary, time has come when certain facts must be admitted as beyond dispute, however unpleasant such admission may be.

In the first place, it should be admitted that every possible attempt to bring about union between Hindus and Muslims has been made and that all of them have failed.

The history of these attempts may be said to begin with the year 1909. The demands of the Muslim deputation, if they were granted by the British, were assented to by the Hindus, prominent amongst whom was Mr. Gokhale. He has been blamed by many Hindus for giving his consent to the principle of separate electorates. His critics forget that withholding consent would not have been a part of wisdom. For, as has been well said by Mr. Mahomed Ali:—

> "....paradoxical as it may seem, the creation of separate electorates was hastening the advent of Hindu-Muslim unity. For the first time a real franchise, however restricted, was being offered to Indians, and if Hindus and Musalmans remained just as divided as they had hitherto been since the commencement

of the British rule, and often hostile to one another, mixed electorates would have provided the best battle-ground for inter-communal strifes, and would have still further widened the gulf separating the two communities. Each candidate for election would have appealed to his own community for votes and would have based his claims for preference on the intensity of his ill-will towards the rival community, however disguised this may have been under some such formula as 'the defence of his community's interests'. Bad as this would have been, the results of an election in which the two communities were not equally matched would have been even worse, for the community that failed to get its representative elected would have inevitably borne a yet deeper grudge against its successful rival. Divided as the two communities were, there was no change for any political principles coming into prominence during the elections. The creation of separate electorates did a great deal to stop this inter-communal warfare, though I am far from oblivious of the fact that when inter-communal jealousies are acute the men that are more likely to be returned even from communal electorates are just those who are noted for the ill-will towards the rival community."

But the concession in favour of separate electorates made by the Hindus in 1909 did not result in Hindu-Muslim unity. Then came the Lucknow Pact in 1916. Under it the Hindus gave satisfaction to the Muslims on every count. Yet, it did not produce any accord between the two. Six years later, another attempt was made to bring about Hindu-Muslim unity. The All-India Muslim League at its annual session held at Lucknow in March 1923 passed a resolution* urging the establishment of a national pact to ensure unity and harmony among the various communities and sects in India and appointed a committee to collaborate with committees to be appointed by other organizations. The Indian National Congress in its special session held in September 1923 at Delhi under the presidentship of Maulana Abul Kalam Azad passed a resolution reciprocating the sentiments expressed by the League. The Congress resolved to appoint two committees (1) to revise the constitution and (2) to prepare a draft of a national pact. The report† of the committee on the Indian National Pact was signed by Dr. Ansari and Lala Lajpat Rai and was presented at the

* For the full text of the resolution of the League, see *Indian Annual Register*, 1923, Vol. I., pp. 395-96 .

† For the terms of the Bengal Pact, see Ibid., p. 127.

session of the Congress held at Coconada in 1923. Side by side with the making of the terms of the Indian National Pact there was forged the Bengal Pact* by the Bengal Provincial Congress Committee with the Bengal Muslims under the inspiration of Mr. C. R. Das. Both the Indian National Pact and the Bengal Pact came up for discussion† in the Subjects Committee of the Congress. The Bengal Pact was rejected by 678 votes against 458. With regard to the Indian National Pact, the Congress resolved‡ that the Committee do call for further opinions on the draft of the Pact prepared by them and submit their report by 31st March 1924 to the A. I. C. C. for its consideration. The Committee, however, did not proceed any further in the matter. This was because the feeling among the Hindus against the Bengal Pact was so strong that according to Lala Lajpat Rai§ it was not considered opportune to proceed with the Committee's labours. Moreover, Mr. Gandhi was then released from jail and it was thought that he would take up the question. Dr. Ansari, therefore, contented himself with handing over to the A. I. C. C. the material he had collected.

Mr. Gandhi took up the threads as soon as he came out of the gaol. In November 1924 informal discussions were held in Bombay. As a result of these discussions, an All-Parties Conference was constituted and a committee was appointed to deal with the question of bringing about unity. The Conference was truly an All-Parties Conference inasmuch as the representatives were drawn from the Congress, the Hindu Maha Sabha, the Justice Party, Liberal Federation, Indian Christians, Muslim League, etc. On the 23rd January 1925, a meeting of the committee¶ appointed by the All-Parties Conference was held in Delhi at the Western Hotel. Mr. Gandhi presided. On the 24th January the committee appointed a representative sub-committee

* For the report and the draft terms of the Pact, see the *Indian Annual Register*, 1923, Vol. II, supplement, pp. 104-108.

† For the debate on these two Pacts, see Ibid., pp. 121-127.

‡ For the resolution, see Ibid., p. 122.

§ See his statement on the All-Parties Conference held in 1925 in the *Indian Quarterly Register*, 1925, Vol. I, p. 70.

¶ For the proceedings of the committee, see the *Indian Quarterly Register*, 1925, Vol. I, pp. 66-77.

consisting of 40 members (a) to frame such recommendations as would enable all parties to join the Congress, (b) to frame a scheme for the representation of all communities, races and sub-divisions on the legislative and other elective bodies under Swaraj and recommended the best method of securing a just and proper representation of the communities in the services without detriment to efficiency, and (c) to frame a scheme of Swaraj that will meet the present needs of the country. The committee was instructed to report on or before the 15th February. In the interest of expediting the work some members formed themselves into a smaller committee for drawing up a scheme of Swaraj leaving the work of framing the scheme of communal representation to the main committee.

The Swaraj sub-committee under the chairmanship of Mrs. Besant succeeded in framing its report on the constitution and submitted the same to the general committee of the All-Parties Conference. But the sub-committee appointed to frame a scheme of communal representation met at Delhi on the 1st March and adjourned *sine die* without coming to any conclusion. This was due to the fact that Lala Lajpat Rai and other representatives of the Hindus would not attend the meeting of the sub-committee. Mr. Gandhi and Pandit Motilal Nehru issued the following statement*:—

> "Lala Lajpat Rai had asked for a postponement by reason of the inability of Messrs. Jayakar, Srinivas Iyengar and Jai Ram Das to attend. We were unable to postpone the meeting on our own responsibility. We, therefore, informed Lala Lajpat Rai that the question of postponement be placed before the meeting. This was consequently done but apart from the absence of Lala Lajpat Rai and of the gentlemen named by him the attendance was otherwise also too meagre for coming to any decision. In our opinion there was moreover no material for coming to any definite conclusions nor is there likelihood of any being reached in the near future......"

There is no doubt that this statement truly summed up the state of mind of the parties concerned. The late Lala Lajpat Rai, the spokesman of the Hindus on the committee, had already said in an article in the *Leader* of Allahabad that there was no immediate hurry for a fresh pact and that he declined to accept

* For the proceedings of the committee, see the *Indian Quarterly Register*, 1925, Vol. I, p. 77.

the view that a Hindu majority in some provinces and a Muslim majority in others was the only way to Hindu-Muslim unity.

The question of Hindu-Muslim unity was again taken up in 1927. This attempt was made just prior to the Simon Commission inquiry, in the hope that it would be successful as the attempt made prior to the Montagu-Chelmsford inquiry in 1916 and which had fructified in the Lucknow Pact. As a preliminary, a conference of leading Muslims was held in Delhi on the 20th March 1927 at which certain proposals* for safeguarding the interest of the Muslims were considered. These proposals, which were known as the Delhi proposals, were considered by the Congress at its session held in Madras in December 1927. At the same time, the Congress passed a resolution† authorizing its Working Committee to confer with similar committees to be appointed by other organizations to draft a Swaraj constitution for India. The Liberal Federation and the Muslim League passed similar resolutions appointing their representatives to join in the deliberations. Other organizations were also invited by the Congress Working Committee to send their spokesmen. The All-Parties Conference,‡ as the committee came to be called, met on 12th February 1928 and appointed a sub-committee to frame a constitution. The committee prepared a report with a draft of the constitution — which is known as the Nehru Report. The report was placed before the All-Parties Convention which met under the presidentship of Dr. Ansari on 22nd December 1928 at Calcutta just prior to the Congress session. On the 1st January 1929 the Convention adjourned *sine die* without coming to any agreement, on any question, not even on the communal question.

This is rather surprising because the points of difference between the Muslim proposals and the proposals made in the Nehru Committee report were not substantial. This is quite

* These proposals will be found in the *Indian Quarterly Register*, 1927, Vol. I, p. 33. These proposals subsequently became the basis of Mr. Jinnah's 14 points.

† For the resolution of the Congress on these proposals, see Ibid., 1927, Vol. II, pp. 397-98.

‡ For the origin, history and composition of the All-Parties Convention and for the text of the report, Ibid., 1928, Vol. I, pp. 1-142.

obvious from the speech* of Mr. Jinnah in the All-Parties Convention in support of his amendments. Mr. Jinnah wanted four amendments to be made in the report of the Nehru Committee. Speaking on his first amendment relating to the Muslim demand for 33⅓ per cent. representation in the Central Legislature, Mr. Jinnah said:—

> "The Nehru Report has stated that according to the scheme which they propose the Muslims are likely to get one-third in the Central Legislature and perhaps more, and it is argued that the Punjab and Bengal will get much more than their population proportion. What we feel is this. If one-third is going to be obtained by Muslims, then the method which you have adopted is not quite fair to the provinces where the Muslims are in a minority because the Punjab and Bengal will obtain more than their population basis in the Central Legislature. You are going to give to the rich more and keeping the poor according to population. It may be sound reasoning but it is not wisdom. . . .
>
> "Therefore, if the Muslims are, as the Nehru Report suggest, to get one-third, or more, they cannot give the Punjab or Bengal more, but let six or seven extra seats be distributed among provinces which are already in a very small minority, such as, Madras and Bombay, because, remember, if Sind is separated, the Bombay Province will be reduced to something like 8 per cent. There are other provinces where we have small minorities. This is the reason why we say, fix one-third and let it be distributed among Muslims according to our own adjustment."

His second amendment related to the reservation of seats on population basis in the Punjab and in Bengal, i.e. the claim to a statutory majority. On this Mr. Jinnah said:—

> "You remember that originally proposals emanated from certain Muslim leaders in March 1927 known as the 'Delhi Proposals.' They were dealt with by the A. I. C. C. in Bombay and at the Madras Congress and the Muslim League in Calcutta last year substantially endorsed at least this part of the proposal. I am not going into the detailed arguments. It really reduces itself into one proposition, that the voting strength of Mahomedans in the Punjab and Bengal, although they are in a majority, is not in proportion to their population. That was one of the reasons. The Nehru Report has now found a substitute and they say that if adult franchise is established then there is no need for reservation, but in the event of its not being established we want to have no doubt that in that case there should be reservation for Muslims in the Punjab and Bengal, according

* See the *Indian Quarterly Register*, 1928, Vol. I, pp. 123-24.

> to their population, but they shall not be entitled to additional seats."

His third amendment was in regard to residuary powers which the Nehru Committee had vested in the Central Government. In moving his amendment that they should be lodged in the Provincial Governments Mr. Jinnah pleaded:—

> "Gentlemen, this is purely a constitutional question and has nothing to do with the communal aspect. We strongly hold—I know Hindus will say Muslims are carried away by communal consideration—we strongly hold the view that, if you examine this question carefully, we submit that the residuary powers should rest with the provinces."

His fourth amendment was concerned with the separation of Sind. The Nehru Committee had agreed to the separation of Sind but had subjected it to one proviso, namely, that the separation should come "only on the establishment of the system of government outlined in the report." Mr. Jinnah in moving for the deletion of the proviso said:—

> "We feel this difficulty ...... Suppose the Government choose, within the next six months, or a year or two years, to separate Sind before the establishment of a government under this constitution, are the Mahomedans to say, 'we do not want it' ..... So long as this clause stands its meaning is that Mahomedans should oppose its separation until simultaneously a government is established under this constitution. We say delete these words and I am supporting my argument by the fact that you do not make such a remark about the N.-W. F. Province. .... The Committee says it cannot accept it as the resolution records an agreement arrived at by parties who signed at Lucknow. With the utmost deference to the members of the Committee I venture to say that that is not valid ground .... Are we bound, in this Convention, bound because a particular resolution was passed by an agreement between certain persons?"

These amendments show that the gulf between the Hindus and Muslims was not in any way a wide one. Yet there was no desire to bridge the same. It was left to the British Government to do what the Hindus and the Muslims failed to do and it did it by the Communal Award.

The Poona Pact between the Hindus and the Depressed Classes gave another spurt to the efforts to bring about unity.*

* For an account of these efforts, see the *Indian Quarterly Register* 1932, Vol. II, p. 296 *et seq.*

During the months of November and December 1932 Muslims and Hindus did their best to come to some agreement. Muslims met in their All-Parties Conferences, Hindus, Muslims and Sikhs met in Unity Conferences. Proposals and counter-proposals were made but nothing came out of these negotiations to replace the Award by a Pact and they were in the end abandoned after the Committee had held 23 sittings.

Just as attempts were made to bring about unity on political questions, attempts were also made to bring about unity on social and religious questions such as:—

(1) Cow slaughter, (2) music before Mosques and (3) conversions over which differences existed. The first attempt in this direction was made in 1923 when the Indian National Pact was proposed. It failed. Mr. Gandhi was then in gaol. Mr. Gandhi was released from gaol on the 5th February 1924. Stunned by the destruction of his work for Hindu-Muslim unity, Mr. Gandhi decided to go on a twenty-one days' fast, holding himself morally responsible for the murderous riots that had taken place between Hindus and Muslims. Advantage was taken of the fast to gather leading Indians of all communities at a Unity Conference,* which was attended also by the Metropolitan of Calcutta. The Conference held prolonged sittings from September 26th to October 2nd, 1924. The members of the Conference pledged themselves to use their utmost endeavours to enforce the principles of freedom of conscience and religion and condemn any deviation from them even under provocation. A Central National Panchayet was appointed with Mr. Gandhi as the chairman. The Conference laid down certain fundamental rights relating to liberty of holding and expressing religious beliefs and following religious practices, sacredness of places of worship, cow slaughter, and music before mosques, with a statement of the limitations they must be subject to. This Unity Conference did not produce peace between the two communities. It only produced a lull in the rioting which had become the order of the day. Between 1925 and 1926, rioting was renewed with an intensity and malignity unknown before. Shocked by this rioting, Lord Irwin, the then Viceroy of India, in his address to the Central Legislature

* Pattabhi Sitarammaya—*History of the Congress*, p. 532.

on 29th August 1927 made an appeal to the two communities to stop the rioting and establish amity. Lord Irwin's exhortation to establish amity was followed by another Unity Conference which was known as the Simla Unity Conference.* This Unity Conference met on the 30th August 1927 and issued an appeal beseeching both the communities to support the leaders in their efforts to arrive at a satisfactory settlement. The Conference appointed a Unity Committee which sat in Simla from 16th to 22nd September under the chairmanship of Mr. Jinnah. No conclusions were reached on any of the principal points involved in the cow and music questions and others pending before the Committee were not even touched. Some members felt that the Committee might break up. The Hindu members pressed that the Committee should meet again on some future convenient date. The Muslim members of the Committee were first divided in their opinion, but at last agreed to break up the Committee and the President was requested to summon a meeting if he received a requisition within six weeks from eleven specified members. Such a requisition never came and the Committee never met again.

The Simla Conference having failed, Mr. Srinivas Iyengar, the then President of the Congress, called a special conference of Hindus and Muslims which sat in Calcutta on the 27th and 28th October 1927. It came to be known as the Calcutta Unity Conference.† The Conference passed certain resolutions on the three burning questions. But the resolution had no support behind them as neither the Hindu Maha Sabha nor the Muslim League was represented at the Conference.

At one time it was possible to say that Hindu-Muslim unity was an ideal which not only must be realized but could be realized and leaders were blamed for not making sufficient efforts for its realization. Such was the view expressed in 1911 even by Maulana Mahomed Ali who had not then made any particular efforts to achieve Hindu-Muslim unity. Writing in the *Comrade* of 14th January 1911 Mr. Mahomed Ali said‡ :—

* For the proceedings of this Conference, see the *Indian Quarterly Register*, Vol. II, pp. 39-50.

† For the proceedings of the Conference, see Ibid., pp. 50-58.

‡ Quoted in his presidential address at Coconada session of the Congress, 1923.

"We have no faith in the cry that India is united. If India was united where was the need of dragging the venerable President of this year's Congress from a distant home? The bare imagination of a feast will not dull the edge of hunger. We have less faith still in the sanctimoniousness that transmutes in its subtle alchemy a rapacious monopoly into fervent patriotism .... the person we love best, fear the most, and trust the least is the impatient idealist. Goethe said of Byron that he was a prodigious poet, but that when he reflected he was a child. Well, we think no better and no worse of the man who combines great ideals and a greater impatience. So many efforts, well meaning as well as ill-begotten, have failed in bringing unity to this distracted land, that we cannot spare even cheap and scentless flowers of sentiment for the grave of another ill-judged endeavour. We shall not make the mistake of gumming together pieces of broken glass, and then cry over the unsuccessful result, or blame the refractory material. In other words, we shall endeavour to face the situation boldly, and respect facts, howsoever ugly and ill-favoured. It is poor statesmanship to slur over inconvenient realities, and not the least important success in achieving unity is the honest and frank recognition of the deep-seated prejudices that hinder it and the yawning differences that divide."

Looking back on the history of these 30 years, one can well ask whether Hindu-Muslim unity has been realized? Whether efforts have not been made for its realization? And whether any efforts remain to be made? The history of the last 30 years shows that Hindu-Muslim unity has not been realized. On the contrary, there now exists the greatest disunity between them: that efforts — sincere and persistent — have been made to achieve it and that nothing now remains to be done to achieve it except surrender by one party to the other. If anyone, who is not in the habit of cultivating optimism where there is no justification for it, said that the pursuit of Hindu-Muslim unity is like a mirage and that the idea must now be given up, no one can have the courage to call him a pessimist or an impatient idealist. It is for the Hindus to say whether they will engage themselves in this vain pursuit in spite of the tragic end of all their past endeavours or give up the pursuit of unity and try for a settlement on another basis.

In the second place, it must be admitted that the Muslim point of view has undergone a complete revolution. How complete the revolution is can be seen by reference to the past pronouncements of some of those who insist on the two-nation theory and believe that Pakistan is the only solution of the Hindu-Muslim problem. Among these Mr. Jinnah, of course, must be accepted as the foremost. The revolution in his views on the Hindu-Muslim question is striking, if not staggering. To realize the nature, character and vastness of this revolution it is necessary to know his pronouncements in the past relating to the subject so that they may be compared with those he is making now.

A study of his past pronouncements may well begin with the year 1906 when the leaders of the Muslim community waited upon Lord Minto and demanded separate electorates for the Muslim community. It is to be noted that Mr. Jinnah was not a member of the deputation. Whether he was not invited to join the deputation or whether he was invited to join and declined is not known. But the fact remains that he did not lend his support to the Muslim claim to separate representation when it was put forth in 1906.

In 1918 Mr. Jinnah resigned his membership of the Imperial Legislative Council as a protest against the Rowlatt Bill.* In tendering his resignation Mr. Jinnah said :—

> "I feel that under the prevailing conditions, I can be of no use to my people in the Council, nor consistently with one's self-respect is co-operation possible with a Government that shows such utter disregard for the opinion of the representatives of the people at the Council Chamber and the feelings and the sentiments of the people outside."

In 1919 Mr. Jinnah gave evidence before the Joint Select Committee appointed by Parliament on the Government of India Reform Bill, then on the anvil. The following views were expressed by him in answer to questions put by members of the Committee on the Hindu-Muslim question.

EXAMINED BY MAJOR ORMSBY-GORE.

> Q. 3806.—You appear on behalf of the Moslem League—that is, on behalf of the only widely extended Mohammedan organisation in India?—Yes.

* The Bill notwithstanding the protest of the Indian members of the Council was passed into law and became Act XI of 1919 as "The Anarchical and Revolutionary Crimes Act."

Q. 3807.—I was very much struck by the fact that neither in your answers to the questions nor in your opening speech this morning did you make any reference to the special interest of the Mohammedans in India: is that because you did not wish to say anything?—No, but because I take it the Southborough Committee have accepted that, and I left it to the members of the Committee to put any questions they wanted to. I took a very prominent part in the settlement of Lucknow. I was representing the Mussalmans on that occasion.

Q. 3809.—On behalf of the All-India Moslem League, you ask this Committee to reject the proposal of the Government of India?—I am authorised to say that—to ask you to reject the proposal of the Government of India with regard to Bengal [i.e. to give the Bengal Muslims more representation than was given them by the Lucknow Pact].

Q. 3810.—You said you spoke from the point of view of India. You speak really as an Indian Nationalist?—I do.

Q. 3811.—Holding that view, do you contemplate the early disappearance of separate communal representation of the Mohammedan community?—I think so.

Q. 3812.—That is to say, at the earliest possible moment you wish to do away in political life with any distinction between Mohammedans and Hindus?—Yes. Nothing will please me more than when that day comes.

Q. 3813.—You do not think it is true to say that the Mohammedans of India have many special political interests not merely in India but outside India, which they are always particularly anxious to press as a distinct Mohammedan community? —There are two things. In India the Mohammedans have very few things really which you can call matters of special interest for them—I mean secular things.

Q. 3814.—I am only referring to them, of course?—And therefore that is why I really hope and expect that the day is not very far distant when these separate electorates will disappear.

Q. 3815.—It is true, at the same time, that the Mohammedans in India take a special interest in the foreign policy of the Government of India?—They do: a very,—No, because what you propose to do is to frame very keen interest and the large majority of them hold very strong sentiments and very strong views.

Q. 3816.—Is that one of the reasons why you, speaking on behalf of the Mohammedan community, are so anxious to get the Government of India more responsible to an electorate? —No.

Q. 3817.—Do you think it is possible, consistently with remaining in the British Empire, for India to have one foreign policy and for His Majesty, as advised by his Ministers in London, to have another?—Let me make it clear. It is not a question of foreign policy at all. What the Moslems of India feel is that it is a very difficult position for them. Spiritually, the Sultan or the Khalif is their head.

Q. 3818.—Of one community?—Of the Sunni sect, but that is the largest; it is in an overwhelming majority all over India. The Khalif is the only rightful custodian of the Holy Places according to our view, and nobody else has a right. What the Moslems feel very keenly is this, that the Holy Places should not be severed from the Ottoman Empire—that they should remain with the Ottoman Empire under the Sultan.

Q. 3819.—I do not want to get away from the Reform Bill on to foreign policy.—I say it has nothing to do with foreign policy. Your point is whether in India the Moslems will adopt a certain attitude with regard to foreign policy in matters concerning Moslems all over the world.

Q. 3820.—My point is, are they seeking for some control over the Central Government in order to impress their views on foreign policy on the Government of India?—No.

EXAMINED BY MR. BENNETT

Q. 3853.—.................. Would it not be an advantage in the case of an occurrence of that kind [i.e. a 'communal riot] if the maintenance of law and order were left with the executive side of the Government?—I do not think so, if you ask me, but I do not want to go into unpleasant matters, as you say.

Q. 3854.—It is with no desire to bring up old troubles that I ask the question; I would like to forget them?—If you ask me, very often these riots are based on some misunderstanding, and it is because the police have taken one side or the other, and that has enraged one side or the other. I know very well that in the Indian States you hardly ever hear of any Hindu-Mohammedan riots, and I do not mind telling the Committee, without mentioning the name, that I happened to ask one of the ruling Princes, "How do you account for this?" and he told me, "As soon as there is some trouble we have invariably traced it to the police, through the police taking one side or the other, and the only remedy we have found is that as soon as we come to know we move that police officer from that place, and there is an end of it."

Q. 3855.—That is a useful piece of information, but the fact remains that these riots have been inter-racial, Hindu on the one side and Mohammedan on the other. Would it be an advantage at a time like that the Minister, the representative of one community or the other, should be in charge of the maintenance of law and order?—Certainly.

Q. 3856.—It would?—If I thought otherwise I should be casting a reflection on myself. If I was the Minister, I would make bold to say that nothing would weigh with me except justice, and what is right.

Q. 3857.—I can understand that you would do more than justice to the other side; but even then, there is what might be called the subjective side. It is not only that there is impartiality, but there is the view which may be entertained by the public, who may harbour some feeling of suspicion?—With regard to one section or the other, you mean they would feel that an injustice was done to them, or that justice would not be done?

Q. 3858.—Yes: that is quite apart from the objective part of it?—My answer is this: That these difficulties are fast disappearing. Even recently, in the whole district of Thana, Bombay, every officer was an Indian officer from top to bottom, and I do not think there was a single Mohammedan—they were all Hindus—and I never heard any complaint. Recently that has been so. I quite agree with you that ten years ago there was that feeling what you are now suggesting to me, but it is fast disappearing.

EXAMINED BY LORD ISLINGTON

Q. 3892.—............... You said just now about the communal representation, I think in answer to Major Ormsby-Gore, that you hope in a very few years you would be able to extinguish communal representation, which was at present proposed to be established and is established in order that Mahommedans may have their representation with Hindus. You said you desired to see that. How soon do you think that happy state of affairs is likely to be realized?—I can only give you certain facts: I cannot say anything more than that: I can give you this, which will give you some idea: that in 1913, at the All-India Moslem League sessions at Agra, we put this matter to the test whether separate electorates should be insisted upon or not by the Mussalmans, and we got a division, and that division is based upon Provinces; only a certain number of votes represent each Province, and the division came to 40 in favour of doing away with the separate electorate, and 80 odd—I do not remember the exact number—were for keeping the separate electorate. That was in 1913. Since then I have had many opportunities of discussing this matter with various Mussalman leaders; and they are changing their angle of vision with regard to this matter. I cannot give you the period, but I think it cannot last very long. Perhaps the next inquiry may hear something about it.

Q. 3893.—You think at the next inquiry the Mahommedans will ask to be absorbed into the whole?—Yes. I think the next inquiry will probably hear something about it.

Although Mr. Jinnah appeared as a witness on behalf of the Muslim League, he did not allow his membership of the League to come in the way of his loyalty to other political organizations in the country. Besides being a member of the Muslim League, Mr. Jinnah was a member of the Home Rule League and also of the Congress. As he said in his evidence before the Joint Parliamentary Committee, he was a member of all three bodies although he openly disagreed with the Congress, with the Muslim League and that there were some views which the Home Rule League held which he did not share. That he was an independent but a nationalist is shown by his relationship with the Khilafatist Musalmans. In 1920 the Musalmans organized the Khilafat Conference. It became so powerful an organization that the Muslim League went under and lived in a state of suspended animation till 1924. During these years no Muslim leader could speak to the Muslim masses from a Muslim platform unless he was a member of the Khilafat Conference. That was the only platform for Muslims to meet Muslims. Even then Mr. Jinnah refused to join the Khilafat Conference. This was no doubt due to the fact that then he was only a statutory Musalman with none of the religious fire of the orthodox which he now says is burning within him. But the real reason why he did not join the Khilafat was because he was opposed to the Indian Musalmans engaging themselves in extra-territorial affairs relating to Muslims outside India.

After the Congress accepted non-co-operation, civil disobedience and boycott of Councils, Mr. Jinnah left the Congress. He became its critic but never accused it of being a Hindu body. He protested when such a statement was attributed to him by his opponents. There is a letter by Mr. Jinnah to the Editor of the *Times of India* written about the time which puts in a strange contrast the present opinion of Mr. Jinnah about the Congress and his opinion in the past. The letter* reads as follows :—

"To the Editor of "The Times of India"

* Published in the *Times of India* of 3-10-25.

Sir,—I wish again to correct the statement which is attributed to me and to which you have given currency more than once and now again repeated by your correspondent 'Banker' in the second column of your issue of the 1st October that I denounced the Congress as 'a Hindu Institution.' I publicly corrected this misleading report of my speech in your columns soon after it appeared; but it did not find a place in the columns of your paper and so may I now request you to publish this and oblige."

After the Khilafat storm had blown over and the Muslims had shown a desire to return to the internal politics of India, the Muslim League was resuscitated. The session of the League held in Bombay on 30th December 1924 under the presidentship of Mr. Raza Ali was a lively one. Both Mr. Jinnah and Mr. Mahomed Ali took part in it.*

In this session of the League, a resolution was moved which affirmed the desirability of representatives of the various Muslim associations of India representing different shades of political thought meeting in a conference at an early date at Delhi or at some other central place with a view to develop "a united and sound practical activity" to supply the needs of the Muslim community. Mr. Jinnah in explaining the resolution said†:—

> "The object was to organize the Muslim community, not with a view to quarrel with the Hindu community, but with a view to unite and co-operate with it for their motherland. He was sure once they had organized themselves they would join hands with the Hindu Mahasabha and declare to the world that Hindus and Mahomedans are brothers."

The League also passed another resolution in the same session for appointing a committee of 33 prominent Musalmans to formulate the political demands of the Muslim community. The resolution was moved by Mr. Jinnah. In moving the resolution, Mr. Jinnah‡:—

* Mr. Mahomed Ali in his presidential address to the Congress at Coconada humorously said: " Mr. Jinnah would soon come back to us (*cheers*). I may mention that an infidel becomes a Kaffir and a Kaffir becomes an infidel; likewise, when Mr. Jinnah was in the Congress I was not with him in those days, and when I was in the Congress and in the Muslim League he was away from me. I hope some day we would reconcile (*Laughter*)."

† From the report in the *Times of India*, 1st January 1925.

‡ The *Indian Quarterly Register*, 1924, Vol. II, p. 481.

> "Repudiated the charge that he was standing on the platform of the League as a communalist. He assured them that he was, as ever, a nationalist. Personally he had no hesitation. He wanted the best and the fittest men to represent them in the Legislatures of the land (Hear, Hear and Applause). But unfortunately his Muslim compatriots were not prepared to go as far as he. He could not be blind to the situation. The fact was that there was a large number of Muslims who wanted representation separately in Legislatures and in the country's Services. They were talking of communal unity, but where was unity? It had to be achieved by arriving at some suitable settlement. He knew, he said amidst deafening cheers, that his fellow-religionists were ready and prepared to fight for Swaraj, but wanted some safeguards. Whatever his view, and they knew that as a practical politician he had to take stock of the situation, the real block to unity was not the communities themselves, but a few mischief makers on both sides."

And he did not thus hesitate to arraign mischief makers in the sternest possible language that could only emanate from an earnest nationalist. In his capacity as the President of the session of the League held in Lahore on 24th May 1924 he said*:—

> "If we wish to be free people, let us unite, but if we wish to continue slaves of Bureaucracy, let us fight among ourselves and gratify petty vanity over petty matters, Englishmen being our arbiters."

In the two All-Parties Conferences, one held in 1925 and the other in 1928, Mr. Jinnah was prepared to settle the Hindu-Muslim question on the basis of joint electorates. In 1927 he openly said† from the League platform:—

> "I am not wedded to separate electorates, although I must say that the overwhelming majority of the Musalmans firmly and honestly believe that it is the only method by which they can be sure."

In 1928, Mr. Jinnah joined the Congress in the boycott of the Simon Commission. He did so even though the Hindus and Muslims had failed to come to a settlement and he did so at the cost of splitting the League into two.

Even when the ship of the Round Table Conference was about to break on the communal rock, Mr. Jinnah resented being

* See the *Indian Quarterly Review*, 1924, Vol. I, p. 658.

† *The Indian Quarterly Register*, 1927, Vol. I, p. 37.

named as a communalist who was responsible for the result and said that he preferred an agreed solution of the communal problem to the arbitration of the British Government. Addressing* the U. P. Muslim Conference held at Allahabad on 8th August 1931 Mr. Jinnah said:—

> "The first thing that I wish to tell you is that it is now absolutely essential and vital that Muslims should stand united. For Heaven's sake close all your ranks and files and stop this internecine war. I urged this most vehemently and I pleaded to the best of my ability before Dr. Ansari, Mr. T. A. K. Sherwani, Maulana Abul Kalam Azad and Dr. Syed Mahmud. I hope that before I leave the shores of India I shall hear the good news that whatever may be our differences, whatever may be our convictions between ourselves, this is not the moment to quarrel between ourselves.
>
> "Another thing I want to tell you is this. There is a certain section of the press, there is a certain section of the Hindus, who constantly misrepresent me in various ways. I was only reading the speech of Mr. Gandhi this morning and Mr. Gandhi said that he loves Hindus and Muslims alike. I again say standing here on this platform that although I may not put forward that claim but I do put forward this honestly and sincerely that I want fair play between the two communities."
>
> Continuing further Mr. Jinnah said: "As to the most important question, which to my mind is the question of Hindu-Muslim settlement—all I can say to you is that I honestly believe that the Hindus should concede to the Muslims a majority in the Punjab and Bengal and if that is conceded, I think a settlement can be arrived at in a very short time.
>
> "The next question that arises is one of separate *vs.* joint electorates. As most of you know, if a majority is conceded in the Punjab and Bengal, I would personally prefer a settlement on the basis of joint electorate. (Applause.) But I also know that there is a large body of Muslims—and I believe a majority of Muslims—who are holding on to separate electorate. My position is that I would rather have a settlement even on the footing of separate electorate, hoping and trusting that when we work our new constitution and when both Hindus and Muslims get rid of distrust, suspicion and fears and when they get their freedom, we would rise to the occasion and probably separate electorate will go sooner than most of us think.
>
> "Therefore I am for a settlement and peace among the Muslims first; I am for a settlement and peace between the Hindus and Mahommedans. This is not a time for argument,

* *The Indian Annual Register*, 1931, Vol. II, pp. 230-231.

not a time for propaganda work and not a time for embittering feelings between the two communities, because the enemy is at the door of both of us and I say without hesitation that if the Hindu-Muslim question is not settled, I have no doubt that the British will have to arbitrate and that he who arbitrates will keep to himself the substance of power and authority. Therefore, I hope they will not vilify me. After all, Mr. Gandhi himself says that he is willing to give the Muslims whatever they want, and my only sin is that I say to the Hindus give to the Muslims only 14 points, which is much less than the 'blank cheque' which Mr. Gandhi is willing to give. I do not want a blank cheque, why not concede the 14 points? When Pandit Jawaharlal Nehru says: 'Give us a blank cheque' when Mr. Patel says: 'Give us a blank cheque and we will sign it with a Swadeshi pen on a Swadeshi paper' they are not communalists and I am a communalist! I say to Hindus not to misrepresent everybody. I hope and trust that we shall be yet in a position to settle the question which will bring peace and happiness to the millions in our country.

"One thing more I want to tell you and I have done. During the time of the Round Table Conference,—it is now an open book and anybody who cares to read it can learn for himself—I observed the one and the only principle and it was that when I left the shores of Bombay I said to the people that I would hold the interests of India sacred, and believe me—if you care to read the proceedings of the Conference, I am not bragging because I have done my duty—that I have loyally and faithfully fulfilled my promise to the fullest extent and I venture to say that if the Congress or Mr. Gandhi can get anything more than I fought for, I would congratulate them.

"Concluding Mr. Jinnah said that they must come to a settlement, they must become friends eventually and he, therefore, appealed to the Muslims to show moderation, wisdom and conciliation, if possible, in the deliberation that might take place and the resolution that might be passed at the Conference."

As an additional illustration of the transformation in Muslim ideology, I propose to record the opinions once held by Mr. Barkat Ali who is now a follower of Mr. Jinnah and a staunch supporter of Pakistan.

When the Muslim League split into two over the question of co-operation with the Simon Commission, one section led by Sir Mahommad Shafi favouring co-operation and another section led by Mr. Jinnah supporting the Congress plan of boycott, Mr. Barkat Ali belonged to the Jinnah section of the League. The two wings of the League held their annual sessions in 1928 at two different places. The Shafi wing met in Lahore and the Jinnah wing met in Calcutta. Mr. Barkat Ali, who was the Secretary of the Punjab Muslim League, attended the Calcutta session of the Jinnah wing of the League and moved the resolution relating to the communal settlement. The basis of the settlement was joint electorates. In moving the resolution Mr. Barkat Ali said* :—

> "For the first time in the history of the League there was a change in its angle of vision. We are offering by this change a sincere hand of fellowship to those of our Hindu countrymen who have objected to the principle of separate electorates."

In 1928 there was formed a Nationalist Muslim Party under the leadership of Dr. Ansari.† The Nationalist Muslim Party was a step in advance of the Jinnah wing of the Muslim League and was prepared to accept the Nehru Report, as it was, without any amendments—not even those which Mr. Jinnah was insisting upon. Mr. Barkat Ali, who in 1927 was with the Jinnah wing of the League, left the same as not being nationalistic enough and joined the Nationalist Muslim Party of Dr. Ansari. How great a nationalist Mr. Barkat Ali then was can be seen by his trenchant and vehement attack on Sir Muhammad Iqbal for his having put forth in his presidential address to the annual session of the All-India Muslim League held at Allahabad in 1930 a scheme‡ for the division of India which is now taken up by Mr. Jinnah and Mr. Barkat Ali and which goes by the name of Pakistan. In 1931 there was held in Lahore the Punjab Nationalist Muslim Conference and Mr. Barkat Ali was the Chairman of the Reception Committee. The views he then expressed on Pakistan are worth recalling.§ Reiterating and reaffirming the conviction and the political faith of his party, Malik Barkat Ali, Chairman of the Reception Committee of the Conference, said :—

> "We believe, first and foremost in the full freedom and honour of India. India, the country of our birth and the place with which all our most valued and dearly cherished associations are knit, must claim its first place in our affection and in our

* *The Indian Quarterly Register*, 1927, Vol. II, p. 448.

† *The Indian Quarterly Register*, 1929, Vol. II, p. 350.

‡ For his speech see *The Indian Annual Register*, 1930, Vol. II, pp. 334-345.

§ *Indian Annual Register*, 1931, Vol. II, pp. 234-235.

desires. We refuse to be parties to that sinister type of propaganda which would try to appeal to ignorant sentiment by professing to be Muslim first and Indian afterwards. To us a slogan of this kind is not only bare, meaningless cant, but downright mischievous. We cannot conceive of Islam in its best and last interests as in any way inimical to or in conflict with the best and permanent interests of India. India and Islam in India are identical, and whatever is to the detriment of India must, from the nature of it, be detrimental to Islam whether economically, politically, socially or even morally. Those politicians, therefore, are a class of false prophets and at bottom the foes of Islam, who talk of any inherent conflict between Islam and the welfare of India. Further, howsoever much our sympathy with our Muslim brethren outside India, i.e. the Turks and the Egyptians or the Arabs,—and it is a sentiment which is at once noble and healthy,—we can never allow that sympathy to work to the detriment of the essential interests of India. Our sympathy, in fact, with those countries can only be valuable to them, if India as the source, nursery and fountain of that sympathy, is really great. And if ever the time comes, God forbid, when any Muslim Power from across the Frontier chooses to enslave India and snatch away the liberties of its people, no amount of pan-Islamic feeling, whatever it may mean, can stand in the way of Muslim India fighting shoulder to shoulder with non-Muslim India in defence of its liberties.

"Let there be, therefore, no misgivings of any kind in that respect in any non-Muslim quarters. I am conscious that a certain class of narrow-minded Hindu politicians is constantly harping on the bogey of an Islamic danger to India from beyond the N.-W. Frontier passes but I desire to repeat that such statements and such fears are fundamentally wrong and unfounded. Muslim India shall as much defend India's liberties as non-Muslim India, even if the invader happens to be a follower of Islam.

"Next, we not only believe in a free India but we also believe in a united India—not the India of the Muslim, not the India of the Hindu or of the Sikh, not the India of this community or of that community but the India of all. And as this is our abiding faith, we refuse to be parties to any division of the India of the future into a Hindu or a Muslim India. However much the conception of a Hindu and a Muslim India may appeal and send into frenzied ecstasies abnormally orthodox mentalities of their party, we offer our full throated opposition to it, not only because it is singularly unpractical and utterly obnoxious but because it not only sounds the death-knell of all that is noble and lasting in modern political activity in India, but is also contrary to and opposed to India's chief historical tradition.

"India was one in the days of Asoka and Chandragupta and India remained one even when the sceptre and rod of Imperial sway passed from Hindu into Moghul or Muslim hands. And India shall remain one when we shall have attained the object of our desires and reached those uplands of freedom, where all the light illuminating us shall not be reflected glory but shall be light proceeding direct as it were from our very faces.

"The conception of a divided India, which Sir Muhammad Iqbal put forward recently in the course of his presidential utterance from the platform of the League at a time when that body had virtually become extinct and ceased to represent free Islam—I am glad to be able to say that Sir Muhammad Iqbal has since recanted it—must not therefore delude anybody into thinking that it is Islam's conception of the India to be. Even if Dr. Sir Muhammad Iqbal had not recanted it as something which could not be put forward by any sane person, I should have emphatically and unhesitatingly repudiated it as something foreign to the genius and the spirit of the rising generation of Islam, and I really deem it a proud duty to affirm today that not only must there be no division of India into communal provinces but that both Islam and Hinduism must run coterminously with the boundaries of India and must not be cribbed, cabined and confined within any shorter bounds. To the same category as Dr. Iqbal's conception of a Muslim India and a Hindu India, belongs the sinister proposals of some Sikh communalists to partition and divide the Punjab.

"With a creed so expansive, namely a free and united India with its people all enjoying in equal measure and without any kinds of distinctions and disabilities the protection of laws made by the chosen representatives of the people on the widest possible basis of a true democracy, namely, adult franchise, and through the medium of joint electorates—and an administration charged with the duty of an impartial execution of the laws, fully accountable for its actions, not to a distant or remote Parliament of foreigners but to the chosen representatives of the land,—you would not expect me to enter into the details and lay before you, all the colours of my picture. And I should have really liked to conclude my general observations on the aims and objects of the Nationalist Muslim Party here, were it not that the much discussed question of joint or separate electorates, has today assumed proportions where no public man can possibly ignore it.

"Whatever may have been the value or utility of separate electorates at a time when an artificially manipulated high-propertied franchise had the effect of converting a majority of the people in the population of a province into a minority in the electoral roll, and when communal passions and feelings ran particularly high, universal distrust poisoning the whole atmosphere like a general and all-pervading miasma,—we feel that in the circumstances of today and in the India of the future, separate electorates should have no place whatever."

Such were the views which Mr. Jinnah and Mr. Barkat Ali held on nationalism, on separate electorates and on Pakistan. How diametrically opposed are the views now held by them on these very problems?

So far I have laboured to point out two things, the utter failure of the attempts made to bring about Hindu-Muslim unity and the emergence of a new ideology in the minds of the Muslim leaders. There is also a third thing which I must discuss in the present context for reasons arising both from its relevance as well as from its bearing on the point under consideration, namely whether this Muslim ideology has behind it a justification which political philosophers can accept.

Many Hindus seem to hold that Pakistan has no justification. If we confine ourselves to the theory of Pakistan there can be no doubt that this is a greatly mistaken view. The philosophical justification for Pakistan rests upon the distinction between a community and a nation. In the first place, it is recognized comparatively recently. Political philosophers for a long time were concerned, mainly, with the controversy summed up in the two questions, how far should the right of a mere majority to rule the minority be accepted as a rational basis for government and how far the legitimacy of a government be said to depend upon the consent of the governed. Even those who insisted, that the legitimacy of a government depended upon the consent of the governed, remained content with a victory for their proposition and did not care to probe further into the matter. They did not feel the necessity for making any distinctions within the category of the "governed." They evidently thought that it was a matter of no moment whether those who were included in the category of the governed formed a community or a nation. Force of circumstances has, however, compelled political philosophers to accept this distinction. In the second place, it is not a mere distinction without a difference. It is a distinction which is substantial and the difference is consequentially fundamental. That this distinction between a community and a nation is fundamental, is clear from the difference in the political rights which political philosophers are prepared to permit to a community and those they are prepared to allow to a nation, against the Government established by law. To a community they are prepared to allow only the right of insurrection. But to a nation they are willing to concede the right of disruption. The distinction between the two is as obvious as it is fundamental. A right of insurrection is restricted only to insisting on a change in the mode and manner of government. The right of disruption is greater than the right of insurrection and extends to the secession of a group of the members of a State with a secession of the portion of the State's territory in its occupation. One wonders what must be the basis of this difference. Writers on political philosophy, who have discussed this subject, have given their reasons for the justification of a community's right to insurrection* and of a nation's right to demand disruption.† The difference comes to

* Sidgwick justifies it in these words: ".... the evils of insurrection may reasonably be thought to be outweighed by the evils of submission, when the question at issue is of vital importance.... an insurrection may sometimes induce redress of grievances, even when the insurgents are clearly weaker in physical force; since it may bring home to the majority the intensity of the sense of injury aroused by their actions. For similar reasons, again a conflict in prospect may be anticipated by a compromise; in short, the fear of provoking disorder may be a salutary check on the persons constitutionally invested with supreme power under a democratic as under other forms of government.... I conceive, then that a moral right of insurrection must be held to exist in the most popularly governed community."— *Elements of Politics* (1929), pp. 646-47.

† This is what Sidgwick has to say on the right to disruption: "....some of those who hold that a government to be legitimate, must rest on the consent of the governed, appear not to shrink from drawing this inference: they appear to qualify the right of the majority of members of a state to rule by allowing the claim of a minority that suffers from the exercise of this right to secede and form a new state, when it is in a majority in a continuous portion of its old state's territory.... and I conceive that there are cases in which the true interests of the whole may be promoted by disruption. For instance, where two portions of a state's territory are separated by a long interval of sea, or other physical obstacles, from any very active intercommunication, and when, from differences of race or religion, past history, or present social conditions, their respective inhabitants have divergent needs and demands in respect of legislation and other governmental interference, it may easily be inexpedient that they should have a common government for internal affairs; while if, at the same time, their external relations, apart from their union, would be very different, it is quite possible that each part may lose more through the risk of implication in the other's quarrels, than it is likely to gain from the aid of its military force. Under such conditions as these, it is not to be desired that any

this: a community has a right to safeguards, a nation has a right to demand separation. The difference is at once clear and crucial. But they have not given any reasons why the right of one is limited to insurrection and why that of the other extends to disruption. They have not even raised such a question. Nor are the reasons apparent on the face of them. But it is both interesting and instructive to know why this difference is made. To my mind the reason for this difference pertains to questions of ultimate destiny. A state either consists of a series of communities or it consists of a series of nations. In a state, which is composed of a series of communities, one community may be arrayed against another community and the two may be opposed to each other. But in the matter of their ultimate destiny they feel they are one. But in a state, which is composed of a series of nations, when one nation rises against the other, the conflict is one as to differences of ultimate destiny. This is the distinction between communities and nations and it is this distinction which explains the difference in their political rights. There is nothing new or original in this explanation. It is merely another way of stating why the community has one kind of right and the nation another of quite a different kind. A community has a right of insurrection because it is satisfied with it. All that it wants is a change in the mode and form of government. Its quarrel is not over any difference of ultimate destiny. A nation has to be accorded the right of disruption because it will not be satisfied with mere change in the form of government. Its quarrel is over the question of ultimate destiny. If it will not be satisfied unless the unnatural bond that binds them is dissolved, then prudence and even ethics demands that the bond shall be dissolved and they shall be freed each to pursue its own destiny.

V

While it is necessary to admit that the efforts at Hindu-Muslim unity have failed and that the Muslim ideology has

sentiment of historical patriotism, or any pride in the national ownership of an extensive territory, should permanently prevent a peaceful dissolution of the incoherent whole into its natural parts."—*Elements of Politics* (1929), pp. 648-49.

undergone a complete revolution, it is equally necessary to know the precise causes which have produced these effects. The Hindus say that the British policy of divide and rule is the real cause of this failure and of this ideological revolution. There is nothing surprising in this. The Hindus having cultivated the Irish mentality to have no other politics except that of being always against the Government, are ready to blame the Government for everything including bad weather. But time has come to discard the facile explanation so dear to the Hindus. For it fails to take into account two very important circumstances. In the first place, it overlooks the fact that the policy of divide and rule, allowing that the British do resort to it, cannot succeed unless there are elements which make division possible, and further, if the policy succeeds for such a long time, it means that the elements which divide are more or less permanent and irreconcilable and are not transitory or superficial. Secondly, it forgets that Mr. Jinnah, who represents this ideological transformation, can never be suspected of being a tool in the hands of the British even by the worst of his enemies. He may be too self-opinionated, an egotist without the mask and has perhaps a degree of arrogance which is not compensated by any extraordinary intellect or equipment. It may be on that account he is unable to reconcile himself to a second place and work with others in that capacity for a public cause. He may not be overflowing with ideas although he is not, as his critics make him out to be, an empty-headed dandy living upon the ideas of others. It may be that his fame is built up more upon art and less on substance. At the same time, it is doubtful if there is a politician in India to whom the adjective incorruptible can be more fittingly applied. Anyone who knows what his relations with the British Government have been, will admit that he has always been their critic, if indeed, he has not been their adversary. No one can buy him. For it must be said to his credit that he has never been a soldier of fortune. The customary Hindu explanation fails to account for the ideological transformation of Mr. Jinnah.

What is then the real explanation of these tragic phenomena, this failure of the efforts for unity, this transformation in the Muslim ideology?

The real explanation of this failure of Hindu-Muslim unity lies in the failure to realize that what stands between the Hindus and Muslims is not a mere matter of difference, and that this antagonism is not to be attributed to material causes. It is spiritual in its character. It is formed by causes which take their origin in historical, religious, cultural and social antipathy, of which political antipathy is only a reflection. These form one deep river of discontent which, being regularly fed by these sources, keeps on mounting to a head and overflowing its ordinary channels. Any current of water flowing from another source however pure, when it joins it, instead of altering the colour or diluting its strength becomes lost in the main stream. The silt of this antagonism which this current has deposited, has become permanent and deep. So long as this silt keeps on accumulating and so long as this antagonism lasts, it is unnatural to expect this antipathy between Hindus and Muslims to give place to unity.

Like the Christians and Muslims in the Turkish Empire, the Hindus and Muslims of India have met as enemies on many fields, and the result of the struggle has often brought them into the relation of conquerors and conquered. Whichever party has triumphed, a great gulf has remained fixed between the two and their enforced political union either under the Moghuls or the British instead of passing over, as in so many other cases, into organic unity, has only accentuated their mutual antipathy. Neither religion nor social code can bridge this gulf. The two faiths are mutually exclusive and whatever harmonies may be forged in the interest of good social behaviour, at their core and centre they are irreconcilable. There seems to be an inherent antagonism between the two which centuries have not been able to dissolve. Notwithstanding the efforts made to bring the creeds together by reformers like Akbar and Kabir, the ethical realities behind each have still remained, to use a mathematical phrase, which nothing can alter or make integers capable of having a common denominator. A Hindu can go from Hinduism to Christianity without causing any commotion or shock. But he cannot pass from Hinduism to Islam without causing a communal riot, certainly not without causing qualms. That shows the depth of the antagonism which divides the Hindus from the Musalmans.

If Islam and Hinduism keep Muslims and Hindus apart in the matter of their faith, they also prevent their social assimilation. That Hinduism prohibits intermarriage between Hindus and Muslims is quite well known. This narrow-mindedness is not the vice of Hinduism only. Islam is equally narrow in its social code. It also prohibits intermarriage between Muslims and Hindus. With these social laws there can be no social assimilation and consequently no socialization of ways, modes and outlooks, no blunting of the edges and no modulation of age-old angularities.

There are other defects in Hinduism and in Islam which are responsible for keeping the sore between Hindus and Muslims open and running. Hinduism is said to divide people and in contrast Islam is said to bind people together. This is only a half truth. For Islam divides as inexorably as it binds. Islam is a close corporation and the distinction that it makes between Muslims and non-Muslims is a very real, very positive and very alienating distinction. The brotherhood of Islam is not the universal brotherhood of man. It is brotherhood of Muslims for Muslims only. There is a fraternity but its benefit is confined to those within that corporation. For those who are outside the corporation, there is nothing but contempt and enmity. The second defect of Islam is that it is a system of *social* self-government and is incompatible with *local* self-government, because the allegiance of a Muslim does not rest on his domicile in the country which is his but on the faith to which he belongs. To the Muslim *ibi bene ibi patria* is unthinkable. Wherever there is the rule of Islam, there is his own country. In other words, Islam can never allow a true Muslim to adopt India as his motherland and regard a Hindu as his kith and kin. That is probably the reason why Maulana Mahomed Ali, a great Indian but a true Muslim, preferred to be buried in Jerusalem rather than in India.

The real explanation of the ideological transformation of the Muslim leaders is not to be attributed to any dishonest drift in their opinion. It appears to be the dawn of a new vision pointing to a new destiny symbolized by a new name, Pakistan. The Muslims appear to have started a new worship of a new destiny for the first time. This is really not so. The worship is new because the sun of their new destiny which was so far hidden in the clouds has only now made its appearance in full glow. The magnetism of this new destiny cannot but draw the Muslims towards it. The pull is so great that even men like Mr. Jinnah have been violently shaken and have not been able to resist its force. This destiny spreads itself out in a concrete form over the map of India. No one, who just looks at the map, can miss it. It lies there as though it is deliberately planned by Providence as a separate National State for Muslims. Not only is this new destiny capable of being easily worked out and put in concrete shape but it is also catching because it opens up the possibilities of realizing the Muslim idea of linking up all the Muslim kindred in one Islamic State and thus avert the danger of Muslims in different countries adopting the nationality of the country to which they belong and thereby bring about the disintegration of the Islamic brotherhood.* With the separation of Pakistan from Hindustan, Iran, Iraq, Arabia, Turkey and Egypt are forming a federation of Muslim countries constituting one Islamic State extending from Constantinople down to Lahore. A Musalman must be really very stupid if he is not attracted by the glamour of this new destiny and completely transformed in his view of the place of Muslims in the Indian cosmos.

So obvious is the destiny that it is somewhat surprising that the Muslims should have taken so long to own it up. There is evidence that some of them knew this to be the ultimate destiny of the Muslims as early as 1923. In support of this, reference may be made to the evidence of Khan Saheb Sardar M. Gul Khan who appeared as a witness before the North-West Frontier Committee appointed in that year by the Government of India under the chairmanship of Sir Dennis Bray, to report upon the administrative relationship between the Settled Districts of the

* Sir Muhammad Iqbal strongly condemned nationalism in Musalmans of any non-Muslim country including Indian Musalmans in the sense of an attachment to the mother country.

N.-W.F. Province and the Tribal Area and upon the amalgamation of the Settled Districts with the Punjab. The importance of his evidence was not realized by any member of the Committee except Mr. N. M. Samarth who was the one member who drew pointed attention to it in his Minority Report. The following extracts from his report illuminate a dark corner in the history of the evolution of this new destiny.* Says Mr. Samarth :—

"There was not before the Committee another witness who could claim to speak with the authority of personal knowledge and experience of not only the North-West Frontier Province and Independent Territory but Baluchistan, Persia and Afghanistan, which this witness could justly lay claim to. It is noteworthy that he appeared before the Committee as a witness in his capacity as 'President, Islamic Anjuman, Dera Ismail Khan.' This witness (Khan Saheb Sardar Muhammad Gul Khan) was asked by me: 'Now suppose the Civil Government of the Frontier Province is so modelled as to be on the same basis as in Sind, then this Province will be part and parcel of the Punjab as Sind is of the Bombay Presidency. What have you to say to it?' He gave me, in the course of his reply, the following straight answer: 'As far as Islam is concerned and the Mahomedan idea of the League of Nations goes, I am against it.' On this answer, I asked him some further questions to which he gave me frank, outspoken replies without mincing matters. I extract the pertinent portions below:—

'Q.—The idea at the back of your Anjuman is the Pan-Islamic idea which is that Islam is a League of Nations and as such amalgamating this Province with the Punjab will be detrimental, will be prejudicial, to that idea. That is the dominant idea at the back of those who think with you? Is it so?

'A.—It is so, but I have to add something. Their idea is that the Hindu-Muslim unity will never become a fact, it will never become a *fait accompli*, and they think that this Province should remain separate and a link between Islam and Britannic Commonwealth. In fact, when I am asked what my opinion is—I, as a member of the Anjuman, am expressing this opinion—we would very much rather see the separation of the Hindus and Muhammadans, 23 crores of Hindus to the south and 8 crores of Muslims to the north. Give the whole portion from Raskumari† to Agra to Hindus and from Agra to Peshawar to

* Report of the North-West Frontier Inquiry Committee, 1924, pp. 122-23.

† This is as in the original. It is probably a misprint for Kanya Kumari.

Muhammadans, I mean transmigration from one place to the other. This is an idea of exchange. It is not an idea of annihilation. Bolshevism at present does away with the possession of private property. It nationalizes the whole thing and this is an idea which of course appertains to only exchange. This is of course impracticable. But if it were practicable, we would rather want this than the other.

'Q.—That is the dominant idea which compels you not to have amalgamation with the Punjab?

'A. – Exactly.

* * * *

'Q.—When you referred to the Islamic League of Nations, I believe you had the religious side of it more prominently in your mind than the political side?

'A.—Of course, political. Anjuman is a political thing. Initially, of course, anything Muhammadan is religious, but of course Anjuman is a political association.

'Q.— I am not referring to your Anjuman but I am referring to the Musalmans. I want to know what the Musalmans think of this Islamic League of Nations, what have they most prominently in mind, is it the religious side or the political side?

'A.— Islam, as you know, is both religious and political.

'Q.—Therefore politics and religion are intermingled?

'A.—Yes, certainly.'

* * * *

Mr. Samarth used this evidence for the limited purpose of showing that to perpetuate a separate Pathan Province by refusing to amalgamate the N.-W.F.P. with the Punjab was dangerous in vew of the Pathan's affiliations with Afghanistan and with other Muslim countries outside India. But this evidence also shows that the idea underlying the scheme of Pakistan had taken birth sometime before 1923.

In 1924 Mr. Mahomed Ali speaking on the resolution on the extension of the Montagu-Chelmsford Reforms to the N.-W. F. Province, which was moved in the session of the Muslim League held in Bombay in that year is said to have suggested* that the Mahomedans of the Frontier Province should

* For reference see Lala Lajpatrai's Presidential address to the Hindu Maha Sabha session held at Calcutta on 11th April 1925 in the *Indian Quarterly Register*, 1925, Vol. I, p. 379.

have the right of self-determination to choose between an affiliation with India or with Kabul. He also quoted a certain Englishman who had said that if a straight line be drawn from Constantinople to Delhi, it will disclose a Mahomedan corridor right up to Shaharanpur. It is possible that Mr. Mahomed Ali knew the whole scheme of Pakistan which came out in the evidence of the witness referred to by Mr. Samarth and in an unguarded moment gave out what the witness had failed to disclose, namely, the ultimate linking of Pakistan to Afghanistan.

Nothing seems to have been said or done by the Muslims about this scheme between 1924 and 1930. The Muslims appear to have buried it and conducted negotiations with the Hindus for safeguards, as distinguished from partition, on the basis of the traditional one-nation theory. But in 1930 when the Round Table Conference was going on, certain Muslims had formed themselves into a committee with headquarters in London for the purpose of getting the R. T. C. to entertain the project of Pakistan. Leaflets and circulars were issued by the committee and sent round to members of the R. T. C. in support of Pakistan. Even then nobody took any interest in it, and the Muslim members of the R. T. C. did not countenance it in any way.*

It is possible that the Muslims in the beginning, thought that this destiny was just a dream incapable of realization. It is possible that later on when they felt that it could be a reality they did not raise any issue about it because they were not sufficiently well organized to compel the British as well as the Hindus to agree to it. It is difficult to explain why the Muslims did not press for Pakistan at the R. T. C. Perhaps they knew that the scheme would offend† the British and as they had to

* If opposition to one common central government be taken as a principal feature of the scheme of Pakistan, then the only member of the R. T. C. who may be said to have supported it without mentioning it by name was Sir Muhammad Iqbal who expressed the view at the third session of the R. T. C. that there should be no central government for India, that the provinces should be autonomous and independent dominions in direct relationship to the Secretary of State in London.

† It is said that it was privately discussed with the British authorities who were not in favour of it. It is possible that the Muslims did not insist on it for fear of incurring their displeasure.

depend upon the British for a decision on the 14 points of dispute between them and the Hindus, the Musalmans, perfect statesmen as they are and knowing full well that politics, as Bismarck said, was always the game of the possible, preferred to wait and not to show their teeth till they had got a decision from the British in their favour on the 14 points of dispute.

There is another explanation for this delay in putting forth the scheme of Pakistan. It is far more possible that the Muslim leaders did not until very recently know the philosophical justification for Pakistan. After all, Pakistan is no small move on the Indian political chess-board. It is the biggest move ever taken, for it involves the disruption of the state. Any Mahomedan, if he had ventured to come forward to advocate it, was sure to have been asked what moral and philosophical justification he had in support of so violent a project. The reason why they had not so far discovered what the philosophical justification for Pakistan is, is equally understandable. The Muslim leaders were, therefore, speaking of the Musalmans of India as a community or a minority. They never spoke of the Muslims as a nation. The distinction between a community and a nation is rather thin, and even if it is otherwise, it is not so striking in all cases. Every state is more or less a composite state and there is, in most of them, a great diversity of populations, with varying languages, religious codes and social traditions, forming a congeries of loosely associated groups. No state is ever a single society, an inclusive and permeating body of thought and action. Such being the case, a group may mistakenly call itself a community even when it has in it the elements of being a nation. Secondly, as has been pointed out earlier, a people may not be possessed of a national consciousness although there may be present all the elements which go to make a nation.

Again from the point of view of minority rights and safeguards this difference is unimportant. Whether the minority is a community or a nation, it is a minority and the safeguards for the protection of a minor nation cannot be very different from the safeguards necessary for the protection of a minor community. The protection asked for is against the tyranny of the majority, and once the possibility of such a tyranny of the majority over a minority is established, it matters very little whether the minority driven to ask for safeguards is a community or is a nation. Not that there is no distinction between a community and a nation. The difference indeed is very great. It may be summed up by saying that a community, however different from and however opposed to other communities, major or minor, is one with the rest in the matter of the ultimate destiny of all. A nation, on the other hand, is not only different from other components of the state but it believes in and cherishes a different destiny totally antagonistic to the destiny entertained by other component elements in the state. The difference appears to me so profound that speaking for myself I would not hesitate to adopt it as a test to distinguish a community from a nation. A people who, notwithstanding their differences accept a common destiny for themselves as well as for their opponents, are a community. A people who are not only different from the rest but who refuse to accept for themselves the same destiny which others do, are a nation. It is this acceptance or non-acceptance of a common destiny which alone can explain why the Untouchables, the Christians and the Parsis are in relation to the Hindus only communities and why the Muslims are a nation. Thus, from the point of view of harmony in the body politic the difference is of the most vital character as the difference is one of ultimate destiny. The dynamic character of this difference is undeniable. If it persists, it cannot but have the effect of rending the State in fragments. But so far as safeguards are concerned, there cannot be any difference between a nation and a community. A community is entitled to claim the same rights and safeguards as a nation can.

The delay in discovering the philosophical justification for Pakistan is due to the fact that the Muslim leaders had become habituated to speaking of Muslims as a community and as a minority. The use of this terminology took them in a false direction and brought them to a dead end. As they acknowledged themselves to be a minority community, they felt that there was nothing else open to them except to ask for safeguards which they did and with which they concerned themselves for practically half a century. If it had struck them that they need not stop with acknowledging themselves to be a minority, but that they could proceed further to distinguish a minority which is a community from a minority which is a nation, they might have been led on to the way to discover this philosophical justification for Pakistan. In that case, Pakistan would, in all probability, have come much earlier than it has done.

Be that as it may, the fact remains that the Muslims have undergone a complete transformation and that the transformation is brought about not by any criminal inducement but by the discovery of what is their true and ultimate destiny. To some, this suddenness of the transformation may give a shock. But those who have studied the course of Hindu-Muslim politics for the last twenty years, cannot but admit feeling that this transformation, this parting of the two, was on the way. For the course of Hindu-Muslim politics has been marked by a tragic and ominous parallelism. The Hindus and Muslims have trodden parallel paths. No doubt, they went in the same direction. But they never travelled the same road. In 1885, the Hindus started the Congress to vindicate the political rights of Indians as against the British. The Muslims refused to be lured by the Hindus into joining the Congress. Between 1885 and 1906 the Muslims kept out of this stream of Hindu politics. In 1906 they felt the necessity for the Muslim community taking part in political activity. Even then they dug their own separate channel for the flow of Muslim political life. The flow was to be controlled by a separate political organization called the Muslim League. Ever since the formation of the Muslim League the waters of Muslim politics have flown in this separate channel. Except on rare occasions, the Congress and the League have lived apart and have worked apart. Their aims and objects have not always been the same. They have even avoided holding their annual sessions at one and the same place, lest the shadow of one should fall upon the other. It is not that the League and the Congress have not met. The two have met but only for negotiations, a few times with success and most times without success. They met in 1916 at Lucknow and their efforts were crowned with success. In 1925 they met but without success. In 1928 a section of the Muslims were prepared to meet the Congress. Another section refused to meet. It rather preferred to depend upon the British. The point is, they have met but have never merged. Only during the Khilafat agitation did the waters of the two channels leave their appointed course and flow as one stream in one channel. It was believed that nothing would separate the waters which God was pleased to join. But that hope was belied. It was found that there was something in the composition of the two waters which would compel their separation. Within a few years of their confluence and as soon as the substance of the Khilafat cause vanished —the water from the one stream reacted violently to the presence of the other, as one does to a foreign substance entering one's body. Each began to show a tendency to throw out and to separate from the other. The result was that when the waters did separate, they did with such impatient velocity and determined violence—if one can use such language in speaking of water—against each other that thereafter they have been flowing in channels far deeper and far more distant from each other than those existing before. Indeed, the velocity and violence with which the two waters have burst out from the pool in which they had temporarily gathered have altered the direction in which they were flowing. At one time their direction was parallel. Now they are opposite. One is flowing towards the east as before. The other has started to flow in the opposite direction, towards the west. Apart from any possible objection to the particular figure of speech, I am sure, it cannot be said that this is a wrong reading of the history of Hindu-Muslim politics. If one bears this parallelism in mind, he will know that there is nothing sudden about the transformation. For if the transformation is a revolution, the parallelism in Hindu-Muslim politics marks the evolution of that revolution. That Muslim politics should have run a parallel course and should never have merged in the Hindu current of politics is a strange fact of modern Indian history. In so segregating themselves the Muslims were influenced by some mysterious feeling, the source of which they could not define and guided by a hidden hand which they could not see but which was all the same directing them to keep apart from Hindus. This mysterious feeling and this hidden hand was no other than their pre-appointed destiny, symbolized by Pakistan, which, unknown to them, was working within them. Thus viewed, there is nothing new or nothing sudden in the idea of Pakistan. The only thing that has happened is that, what was indistinct appears now in full glow, and what was nameless has taken a name.

VI

Summing up the whole discussion, it appears that an integral India is incompatible with an independent India or even with India as a dominion. On the footing that India is to be one integral whole there is a frustration of all her hopes of freedom writ large on her future. There is frustration, if the national destiny is conceived in terms of independence, because the Hindus will not follow that path. They have reason not to follow it. They fear that that way lies the establishment of the domination of the Muslims over the Hindus. The Hindus see that the Muslim move for independence is not innocent. It is to be used only to bring the Hindus out of the protecting shield of the British Empire in the open and then by alliance with the neighbouring Muslim countries and by their aid subjugate them. For the Muslims independence is not the end. It is only a means to establish Muslim Raj. There is frustration if the national destiny is conceived of in terms of Dominion Status because the Muslims will not agree to abide by it. They fear that under Dominion Status, the Hindus will establish Hindu Raj over them by taking benefit of the principle of one man one vote and one vote one value, and that however much the benefit of the principle is curtailed by weightage to Muslims, the result cannot fail to be a government of the Hindus, by the Hindus and therefore for the Hindus. Complete frustration of her destiny therefore seems to be the fate of India if it is insisted that India shall remain as one integral whole.

It is a question to be considered whether integral India is an ideal worth fighting for. In the first place, even if India remained as one integral whole it will never be an organic whole. India may in name continue to be known as one country, but in reality it will be two separate countries — Pakistan and Hindustan — joined together by a forced and artificial union.

This will be specially so under the stress of the two-nation theory. As it is, the idea of unity has had little hold on the Indian world of fact and reality, little charm for the common Indian, Hindu or Muslim, whose vision is bounded by the valley in which he lives. But it did appeal to the imaginative and unsophisticated minds on both sides. The two-nation theory will not leave room even for the growth of that sentimental desire for unity. The spread of that virus of dualism in the body politic must some day create a mentality which is sure to call for a life and death struggle for the dissolution of this forced union. If by reason of some superior force the dissolution does not take place, one thing is sure to happen to India—namely, that this continued union will go on sapping her vitality, loosening its cohesion, weakening its hold on the love and faith of her people and preventing the use, if not retarding the growth, of its moral and material resources. India will be an anæmic and sickly state, ineffective, a living corpse, dead though not buried.

The second disadvantage of this forced union will be the necessity for finding a basis for Hindu-Muslim settlement. How difficult it is to reach a settlement no one needs to be told. Short of dividing India into Pakistan and Hindustan what more can be offered—without injury to the other interests in the country,—than what has already been conceded with a view to bring about a settlement, it is difficult to conceive. But whatever the difficulties, it cannot be gainsaid that if this forced union continues, there can be no political advance for India unless it is accompanied by communal settlement. Indeed, a communal settlement—rather an international settlement for now and hereafter the Hindus and the Muslims must be treated as two nations—will remain under this scheme of forced union a condition precedent for every inch of political progress.

There will be a third disadvantage of this forced political union. It cannot eliminate the presence of a third party. In the first place the constitution, if one comes in existence, will be a federation of mutually suspicious and unfriendly states. They will of their own accord want the presence of a third party to appeal to in cases of dispute. For their suspicious and unfriendly relationship towards each other will come in the way of the two nations ever reaching satisfaction by the method of negotiation. India will not have in future even that unity of opposition to the British which used to gladden the hearts of so many in the past. For the two nations will be more opposed to each other than before, ever to become united against the British. In the second place, the basis of the constitution will be the settlement between the Hindus and the Muslims, and for the successful working of such a constitution the presence of a third party, and be it noted, with sufficient armed force, will be necessary to see that the settlement is not broken.

All this, of course, means the frustration of the political destiny, which both Hindus and Muslims profess to cherish and the early consummation of which they so devoutly wish. What else, however, can be expected if two warring nations are locked in the bosom of one country and one constitution?

Compare with this dark vista, the vista that opens out if India is divided into Pakistan and Hindustan. The partition opens the way to a fulfilment of the destiny each may fix for itself. Muslims will be free to choose for their Pakistan independence or dominion status, whatever they think good for themselves. Hindus will be free to choose for their Hindustan independence or dominion status, whatever they may think wise for their condition. The Muslims will be freed from the nightmare of Hindu Raj and Hindus will save themselves from the hazard of a Muslim Raj. Thus the path of political progress becomes smooth for both. The fear of the object being frustrated gives place to the hope of fulfilment. Communal settlement must remain a necessary condition precedent, if India, as one integral whole, desires to make any political advance. But Pakistan and Hindustan are free from the rigorous trammels of such a condition precedent and even if a communal settlement with minorities remained to be a condition precedent it will not be difficult to fulfil. The path of each is cleared of this obstacle. There is another advantage of Pakistan which must be mentioned. It is generally admitted that there does exist a kind of antagonism between Hindus and Muslims which if not dissolved will prove ruinous to the peace and progress of India. But, it is not realized that the mischief is caused not so much by the existence of mutual antagonism as by the existence of a common theatre for its display. It is the common theatre which calls this antagonism into action. It cannot but be so. When the two are called to participate in acts of common concern what else can happen except a display of that antagonism which is inherent in them. Now the scheme of Pakistan has this advantage, namely, that it leaves no theatre for the play of that social antagonism which is the cause of disaffection among the Hindus and the Muslims. There is no fear of Hindustan and Pakistan suffering from that disturbance of peace and tranquillity which has torn and shattered India for so many years. Last, but by no means least, is the elimination of the necessity of a third party to maintain peace. Freed from the trammels which one imposes upon the other by reason of this forced union, Pakistan and Hindustan can each grow into a strong stable State with no fear of disruption from within. As two separate entities, they can reach their respective destinies which as parts of one whole they never can.

Those who want an integral India must note what Mr. Mahomed Ali as President of the Congress in 1923 said. Speaking about the unity among Indians, Mr. Mahomed Ali said:—

> "Unless some new force other than the misleading unity of opposition unites this vast continent of India, it will remain a geographical misnomer."

Is there any new force which remains to be harnessed? All other forces having failed, the Congress, after it became the Government of the day, saw a new force in the plan of *mass contact*. It was intended to produce political unity between Hindus and Muslim masses by ignoring or circumventing the leaders of the Muslims. In its essence, it was the plan of the British Conservative Party to buy Labour with "Tory gold." The plan was as mischievous as it was futile. The Congress forgot that there are things so precious that no owner, who knows their value, will part with and any attempt to cheat him to part with them is sure to cause resentment and bitterness. Political power is the most precious thing in the life of a community especially if its position is constantly being challenged and the community is required to maintain it by meeting the challenge. Political power is the only means by which it can sustain its position. To attempt to make it part with it by false propaganda, by misrepresentation or by the lure of office or of gold is equivalent to disarming the community, to silencing its guns and to making it ineffective and servile. It may be a way of producing unity. But the way is despicable for it means suppressing the opposition by a false and unfair method. It cannot produce any unity. It can only create exasperation, bitterness and hostility.* This is precisely what the *mass contact* plan of the Congress did. For there can be no doubt that this mad plan of mass contact has had a great deal to do with the emergence of Pakistan.

It might be said that it was unfortunate that mass contact was conceived and employed as a political lever and that it might have been used as a force for social unity with greater success. But could it have succeeded in breaking the social wall which divides the Hindus and the Muslims? It cannot but be matter of the deepest regret to every Indian that there is no social tie to draw them together. There is no inter-dining and no inter-marriage between the two. Can they be introduced? Their festivals are different. Can the Hindus be induced to adopt them or join in them? Their religious notions are not only divergent but repugnant to each other so that on a religious platform, the entry of the one means the exit of the other. Their cultures are different; their literatures and their histories are

* So sober a person as Sir Abdur Rahim, in his presidential address to the session of the Muslim League held in Aligarh on 30th December 1925, gave expression to this bitterness caused by Hindu tactics wherein he "deplored the attacks on the Muslim community in the form of Shuddhi, Sangathan and Hindu Maha Sabha movements and activities led by politicians like Lala Lajpat Rai and Swami Shradhanand" and said "Some of the Hindu leaders had spoken publicly of driving out Muslims from India as Spaniards expelled Moors from Spain. Musalmans would be too big a mouthful for their Hindu friends to swallow. Thanks to the artificial conditions under which they lived they had to admit that Hindus were in a position of great advantage and even the English had learned to dread their venomous propaganda. Hindus were equally adept in the art of belittling in every way possible the best Musalmans in public positions excepting only those who had subscribed to the Hindu political creed. They had in fact by their provocative and aggressive conduct made it clearer than ever to Muslims that the latter could not entrust their fate to Hindus and must adopt every possible measure of self-defence."—*All-India Register*, 1925, Vol. II, p. 356.

different. They are not only different, but so distasteful to each other, that they are sure to cause aversion and nausea. Can any-one make them drink from the same fount of these perennial sources of life? No common meeting ground exists. None can be cultivated. There is not even sufficient physical contact, let alone their sharing a common cultural and emotional life. They do not live together. Hindus and Muslims live in separate worlds of their own. Hindus live in villages and Muslims in towns in those provinces where the Hindus are in a majority. Muslims live in villages and Hindus in towns in those provinces where the Muslims are in a majority. Wherever they live, they live apart. Every town, every village has its Hindu quarters and Muslim quarters, which are quite separate from each other. There is no common continuous cycle of participation. They meet to trade or they meet to murder. They do not meet to befriend one another. When there is no call to trade or when there is no call to murder, they cease to meet. When there is peace, the Hindu quarters and the Muslim quarters appear like two alien settlements. The moment war is declared, the settle-ments become armed camps. The periods of peace and the periods of war are brief. But the interval is one of continuous tension. What can mass contact do against such barriers? It cannot even get over on the other side of the barrier, much less can it produce organic unity.

PART V

Different people have thought differently of what has been said in the foregoing pages on the question of Pakistan. One set of people have alleged that I have only stated the two sides of the issue and the problems arising out of it but have not expressed my personal views on either of them. This is not correct. Anyone who has read the preceding parts will have to admit that I have expressed my views in quite positive terms, if not on all, certainly on many questions. In particular I may refer to two of the most important ones in the controversy, namely, Are the Muslims a Nation, and Have they a case for Pakistan. There are others whose line of criticism is of a different sort. They do not complain that I have failed to express my personal views. What they complain is that in coming to my conclusions I have relied on propositions as though they were absolute in their application and have admitted no exception. I am told, "Have you not stated your conclusions in too general terms? Is not a general proposition subject to conditions and limitations? Have you not disposed of certain complicated problems in a brief and cavalier fashion? Have you shown how Pakistan can be brought into existence in a just and peaceful manner?" Even this criticism is not altogether correct. It is not right to say that I have omitted to deal with these points. It may be that my treatment of them is brief, and scattered. However, I am prepared to admit that there is much force in this criticism and I am in duty bound to make good the default. This part is therefore intended and is devoted to the consideration of the following subjects :—

1. *What are the limiting considerations which affect the Muslim case for Pakistan?*

2. *What are the problems of Pakistan? and what is their solution?*

3. *Who has the authority to decide the issue of Pakistan?*

CHAPTER XIII

MUST THERE BE PAKISTAN?

I

With all that has gone before, the sceptic, the nationalist, the conservative and the old-world Indian will not fail to ask "Must there be Pakistan?". No one can make light of such an attitude. For the problem of Pakistan is indeed very grave and it must be admitted that the question is not only a relevant and fair one to be put to the Muslims and to their protagonists but it is also important. Its importance lies in the fact that the limitations on the case for Pakistan are so considerable in their force that they can never be easily brushed aside. A mere statement of these limitations should be enough to make one feel the force they have. It is writ large on the very face of them. That being so, the burden of proof on the Muslims for establishing an imperative need in favour of Pakistan is very heavy. Indeed the issue of Pakistan or to put it plainly of partitioning India, is of such a grave character that the Muslims will not only have to discharge this burden of proof but they will have to adduce evidence of such a character as to satisfy the conscience of an international tribunal before they can win their case. Let us see how the case for Pakistan stands in the light of these limitations.

II

Must there be Pakistan because a good part of the Muslim population of India happens to be concentrated in certain defined areas which can be easily severed from the rest of India? Muslim population is admittedly concentrated in certain well defined areas and it may be that these areas are severable. But what of that? In considering this question one must never lose sight of the fundamental fact that nature has made India one single geographical unit. Indians are of course quarrelling and no one can prophesy when they will stop quarrelling. But granting the fact, what does it establish? Only that Indians are a quarrelsome people. It does not destroy the fact that India is a single geographical unit. Her unity is as ancient as Nature. Within this geographic unit and covering the whole of it there has been a cultural unity from time immemorial. This cultural unity has defied political and racial divisions. And at any rate for the last hundred and fifty years all institutions — cultural, political, economic, legal and administrative — have been working on a single, uniform spring of action. In any discussion of Pakistan the fact cannot be lost sight of, namely, that the starting point, if not the governing factor, is the fundamental unity of India. For it is necessary to grasp the fact that there are really two cases of partition which must be clearly distinguished. There is a case in which the starting point is a pre-existing state of separation so that partition is only a dissolution of parts which were once separate and which were subsequently joined together. This case is quite different from another in which the starting point at all times is a state of unity. Consequently partition in such a case is the severance of a territory which has been one single whole into separate parts. Where the starting point is not unity of territory, *i.e.*, where there was disunity before there was unity, partition — which is only a return to the original — may not give a mental shock. But in India the starting point is unity. Why destroy its unity now, simply because some Muslims are dissatisfied? Why tear it when the unit is one single whole from historical times?

III

Must there be Pakistan because there is communal antagonism between the Hindus and the Muslims? That the communal antagonism exists nobody can deny. The question however is, is the antagonism such that there is no will to live together in one country and under one constitution? Surely that will to live together was not absent till 1937. During the formulation of the provisions of the Government of India Act, 1935, both Hindus and Musalmans accepted the view that they must live together under one constitution and in one country and participated in the discussions that preceded the passing of the Act. And what was the state of communal feeling in India between—say 1920 and 1935? As has been recorded in the preceding pages, the history of India from 1920 upto 1935 has been one long tale of communal conflict in which the loss of life and loss of property had reached a most shameful limit. Never was the communal situation so acute as it was between this period of 15 years preceding the passing of the Government of India Act, 1935, and yet this long tale of antagonism did not prevent the Hindus and the Musalmans from agreeing to live in a single country and under a single constitution. Why make so much of communal antagonism now?

Is India the only country where there is communal antagonism? What about Canada? Consider what Mr. Alexander Brady * has to say on the relations between the English and the French in Canada :—

> "Of the four original provinces, three, Nova Scotia, New Brunswick and Ontario had populations substantially of the same Anglo-Saxon stock and traditions. Originally a by-product of the American Revolution, these colonies were established by the 50,000 United Empire Loyalists who trekked north from persecution and cut their settlements out of the wilderness. Previous to the American Revolution, Nova Scotia had received a goodly number of Scotch and American settlers, and in all the colonies after the Revolution the Loyalist settlements were reinforced by immigrants from Great Britain and Ireland."

* * * *

> "Very different was the province of Quebec. French Canada in 1867 was a cultural unit by itself, divorced from the British communities, by the barriers of race, language and religion. Its life ran in a different mould. Stirred by a Catholic faith mediaeval in its intensity, it viewed with scant sympathy the mingled Puritanism and other-worldliness of a Protestantism largely Calvinistic. The religious faiths of the two peoples were indeed poles apart. In social, if not always in religious, outlook, English Protestantism tended towards democracy, realism and modernism: the Catholicism of the French leaned to paternalism, idealism and a reverence for the past."

* * * *

> "What French Canada was in 1867 it remains substantially today. It still cherishes beliefs, customs, and institutions which

* *Canada*—Chapter I.

have little hold on the English provinces. It has distinctive thought and enthusiasm, and its own important values. Its attitude, for example, on marriage and divorce is in conflict with the dominant view, not merely of the rest of Canada, but of the remainder of Anglo-Saxon North America."

* * * *

"The infrequency of intercourse between the two peoples is illustrated in Canada's largest city, Montreal. About 63 per cent. of the population is French and 24 per cent. British. Here, if anywhere, is ample scope for association, but in fact they remain apart and distinct except where business and politics force them together. They have their own residential sections; their own shopping centres, and if either is more notable for racial reserve, it is the English."

* * * *

"The English-speaking residents of Montreal, as a whole, have made no effort to know their French-speaking fellow citizens, to learn their language, to understand their traditions and their aspirations, to observe with a keen eye and a sympathetic mind their qualities and their defects. The separation of the two peoples is encouraged by the barrier of language. There is a wealth of significance in the fact revealed by the census of 1921; viz., that about 50 per cent. of the Canadians of French origin were unable to speak English and 95 per cent. of those of British origin were unable to speak French. Even in Montreal, 70 per cent. of the British could not speak French and 34 per cent. of the French could not speak English. The absence of a common language maintains a chasm between the two nationalities and prevents fusion.

"The significance of Confederation is that it provided an instrument of government which enabled the French, while retaining their distinct national life, to become happy partners with the British and attain a Canadian super-nationality, embracing a loyalty extending beyond their own group to that of the Dominion as a whole."

* * * *

"While the federal system successfully opened the path for a wider nationality in Canada, the co-operation which it sponsored has at times been subjected to severe strain by the violent clash of opinion between the French and the British. The super-nationality has indeed often been reduced to a shadow."

What about South Africa? Let those who do not know the relationship between the Boers and the British ponder over what Mr. E. H. Brooks* has to say :—

* *The Political Future of South Africa*, 1927.

"How far is South African nationalism common to both the white races of South Africa? There is, of course, a very real and intense Afrikander nationalism; but it is, generally speaking, a sentiment confined to one of the white races, and characterised, significantly enough, by a love of the Afrikans language, the tongue of the early settlers from Holland, as modified slightly by Huguenot and German influence, and greatly by the passage of time. Afrikander nationalism has a tendency to be exclusive, and has little place for the man who, while in every way a devoted son of South Africa, is wholly or mainly English-speaking."

* * * *

"Is there a South African nation today?

"There are certain factors in South African life which militate against an affirmative answer."

* * * *

"Among English-speaking South Africans there are found many tendencies inclined to hinder the cause of national unity. With all the great virtues of the race they have its one cardinal defect—a lack of imagination, a difficulty in putting one's self in the other man's place. Nowhere does this come out more clearly than in the language question. Until recently comparatively few English-speaking South Africans have studied Afrikans except as a business proposition or (as in the Civil Service) more or less under compulsion; and fewer still have used it conversationally. Many have treated it with open contempt—a contempt in inverse proportion to their knowledge of it—and the majority with mere tolerance, exasperated or amused according to temperament."

Another witness on the same point may be heard. He is Mr. Manfred Nathan.* This is what he has to say on the relations between the Boers and the British in South Africa:—

"They are also, in the main, both of them Protestant peoples—although this is not of too great importance nowadays, when differences of religion do not count for much. They engage freely in commercial transactions with each other."

* * * *

"Nevertheless it cannot with truth be said that hitherto there has been absolutely free social intercourse between these two great sections of the white population. It has been suggested that this is partly due to the fact that in the large urban centres the population is predominantly English, and that the townsfolk know little of the people in the country and their ways of life. But

* *The South African Commonwealth*, p. 365.

> even in the country towns, though there is, as a rule, much greater friendliness, and much hospitality shown by Boers to visitors, there is not much social intercourse between the two sections apart from necessary business or professional relationship, and such social functions, charitable or public, as require co-operation."

Obviously India is not the only place where there is communal antagonism. If communal antagonism does not come in the way of the French in Canada living in political unity with the English, if it does not come in the way of the English in South Africa living in political unity with the Dutch, if it does not come in the way of the French and the Italians in Switzerland living in political unity with the Germans why then should it be impossible for the Hindus and the Muslims to agree to live together under one constitution in India?

IV

Must there be Pakistan because the Muslims have lost faith in the Congress majority? As reasons for the loss of faith Muslims cite some instances of tyranny and oppression practised by the Hindus and connived at by the Congress Ministries during the two years and three months the Congress was in office. Unfortunately Mr. Jinnah did not persist in his demand for a Royal Commission to inquire into these grievances. If he had done it we could have known what truth there was in these complaints. A perusal of these instances, as given in the reports* of the Muslim League Committees, leaves upon the reader the impression that although there may be some truth in the allegations there is a great deal which is pure exaggeration. The Congress Ministries concerned have issued statements repudiating the charges. It may be that the Congress during the two years and three months that it was in office did not show statesmanship, did not inspire confidence in the minorities, nay tried to suppress them. But can it be a reason for partitioning

* On this point, see Report of the Inquiry Committee appointed by the All-India Muslim League to inquire into Muslim grievances in Congress Provinces popularly known as Pirpur Report. Also Report of the Bihar Provincial Muslim League to inquire into some grievances of Muslims in Bihar and the Press Note issued by the Information Officer, Government of Bihar, replying to some of the allegations contained in these reports published in *Amrita Bazar Patrika* of 13-3-39.

India? Is it not possible to hope that the voters who supported the Congress last time will grow wiser and not support the Congress? Or may it not be that if the Congress returns to office it will profit by the mistakes it has made, revise its mischievous policy and thereby allay the fear created by its past conduct?

V

Must there be Pakistan because the Musalmans are a nation? It is a pity that Mr. Jinnah should have become a votary and champion of Muslim Nationalism at a time when the whole world is decrying against the evils of nationalism and is seeking refuge in some kind of international organization. Mr. Jinnah is so obsessed with his new-found faith in Muslim Nationalism that he is not prepared to see that there is a distinction between a society, parts of which are disintegrated, and a society parts of which have become only loose, which no sane man can ignore. When a society is disintegrating—and the two-nation theory is a positive disintegration of society and country—it is evidence of the fact that there do not exist what Carlyle calls "organic filaments"—*i.e.*, the vital forces which work to bind together the parts that are cut asunder. In such cases disintegration can only be regretted. It cannot be prevented. Where, however, such organic filaments do exist, it is a crime to overlook them and deliberately force the disintegration of society and country as the Muslims seem to be doing. If the Musalmans want to be a different nation it is not because they have been but because they want to be. There is much in the Musalmans which, if they wish, can roll them into a nation. But isn't there enough that is common to both Hindus and Musalmans, which if developed, is capable of moulding them into one people? Nobody can deny that there are many modes, manners, rites and customs which are common to both. Nobody can deny that there are rites, customs and usages based on religion which do divide Hindus and Musalmans. The question is, which of these should be emphasized. If the emphasis is laid on things that are common, there need be no two nations in India. If the emphasis is laid on points of difference, it will no doubt give rise to two nations. The view that seems to guide Mr. Jinnah is that Indians are only a people and that they can never be a nation. This follows the line of British writers who make it a point of speaking of Indians as the people of India and avoid speaking of the Indian nation. Granted Indians are not a nation, that they are only a people. What of that? History records that before the rise of nations as great corporate personalities, there were only peoples. There is nothing to be ashamed if Indians are no more than a people. Nor is there any cause for despair that the people of India—if they wish—will not become one nation. For, as Disraeli said, a nation is a work of art and a work of time. If the Hindus and Musalmans agree to emphasize the things that bind them and forget those that separate them there is no reason why in course of time they should not grow into a nation. It may be that their nationalism may not be quite so integrated as that of the French or the Germans. But they can easily produce a common state of mind on common questions which is the sum total which the spirit of nationalism helps to produce and for which it is so much prized. Is it right for the Muslim League to emphasize only differences and ignore altogether the forces that bind? Let it not be forgotten that if two nations come into being it will not be because it is predestined. It will be the result of deliberate design.

The Musalmans of India as I have said are not as yet a nation in the *de jure* or *de facto* sense of the term and all that can be said is that they have in them the elements necessary to make them a nation. But granting that the Musalmans of India are a nation, is India the only country where there are going to be two nations? What about Canada? Everybody knows that there are in Canada two nations, the English and the French. Are there not two nations in South Africa, the English and the Dutch? What about Switzerland? Who does not know that there are three nations living in Switzerland, the Germans, the French and the Italians? Have the French in Canada demanded partition because they are a separate nation? Do the English claim partition of South Africa because they are a distinct nation from the Boers? Has anybody ever heard that the Germans, the French and the Italians have ever agitated for the fragmentation of Switzerland because they are all different nations? Have the Germans, the French and the Italians ever felt that they would lose their distinctive cultures if they lived as citizens of one country and under one constitution? On the contrary, all these distinct nations have been content to live together in one country under one constitution without fear of losing their nationality and their distinctive cultures. Neither have the French in Canada ceased to be French by living with the English, nor have the English ceased to be English by living with the Boers in South Africa. The Germans, the French and the Italians have remained distinct nations notwithstanding their common allegiance to a common country and a common constitution. The case of Switzerland is worthy of note. It is surrounded by countries, the nationalities of which have a close religious and racial affinity with the nationalities of Switzerland. Notwithstanding these affinities the nationalities in Switzerland have been Swiss first and Germans, Italians and French afterwards.

Given the experience of the French in Canada, the English in South Africa and the French and the Italians in Switzerland, the questions that arise are, why should it be otherwise in India? Assuming that the Hindus and the Muslims split into two nations, why cannot they live in one country and under one constitution? Why should the emergence of the two-nation theory make partition necessary? Why should the Musalmans be afraid of losing their nationality and national culture by living with the Hindus? If the Muslims insist on separation, the cynic may well conclude that there is so much that is common between the Hindus and the Musalmans that the Muslim leaders are afraid that unless there is partition whatever little distinctive Islamic culture is left with the Musalmans will eventually vanish by continued social contact with the Hindus with the result that in the end instead of two nations there will grow up in India one nation. If the Muslim nationalism is so thin then the motive for partition is artificial and the case for Pakistan loses its very basis.

VI

Must there be Pakistan because otherwise Swaraj will be a Hindu Raj? The Musalmans are so easily carried away by this cry that it is necessary to expose the fallacies underlying it.

In the first place, is the Muslim objection to Hindu Raj a conscientious objection or is it a political objection? If it is a conscientions objection all one can say is that it is a very strange sort of conscience. There are really millions of Musalmans in India who are living under unbridled and uncontrolled Hindu Raj of Hindu Princes and no objection to it has been raised by the Muslims or the Muslim League. The Muslims had once a conscientious objection to the British Raj. Today not only have they no objection to it but they are the greatest supporters of it. That there should be no objection to British Raj or to undiluted Hindu Raj of a Hindu Prince but that there should be objection to Swaraj for British India on the ground that it is Hindu Raj as though it was not subjected to checks and balances is an attitude the logic of which it is difficult to follow.

The political objections to Hindu Raj rests on various grounds. The first ground is that Hindu society is not a democratic society. True, it is not. It may not be right to ask whether the Muslims have taken any part in the various movements for reforming Hindu society as distinguished from proselytising. But it is right to ask if the Musalmans are the only sufferers from the evils that admittedly result from the undemocratic character of Hindu society. Are not the millions of Shudras and non-Brahmins or millions of the Untouchables, suffering the worst consequences of the undemocratic character of Hindu society? Who benefits from education, from public service and from political reforms except the Hindu governing class—composed of the higher castes of the Hindus—which form not even 10 per cent. of the total Hindu population? Has not the governing class of the Hindus, which controls Hindu politics, shown more regard for safeguarding the rights and interests of the Musalmans than they have for safeguarding the rights and interests of the Shudras and the Untouchables? Is not Mr. Gandhi, who is determined to oppose any political concession to the Untouchables, ready to sign a blank cheque in favour of the

Muslims? Indeed, the Hindu governing class seems to be far more ready to share power with the Muslims than it is to share power with the Shudras and the Untouchables. Surely, the Muslims have the least ground to complain of the undemocratic character of Hindu society.

Another ground on which the Muslim objection to Hindu Raj rests is that the Hindus are a majority community and the Musalmans are a minority community. True. But is India the only country where such a situation exists? Let us compare the conditions in India with the conditions in Canada, South Africa and Switzerland. First, take the distribution of population.* In Canada out of a total population of 10,376,786 only 2,927,990 are French.† In South Africa the Dutch number 1,120,770 and the English are only 783,071.‡ In Switzerland out of the total population of 4,066,400 the Germans are 2,924,313, the French 831,097 and the Italians 242,034.

This shows that the smaller nationalities have no fear of being placed under the Raj of a major community. Such a notion seems to be quite foreign to them. Why is this so? Is it because there is no possibility of the major nationality establishing its supremacy in those centres of power and authority, namely the Legislature and in the Executive? Quite the contrary. Unfortunately no figures are available to show the actual extent of representation which the different major and minor nationalities have in Switzerland, Canada and South Africa. That is because there is no communal reservation of seats such as is found in India. Each community is left to win in a general contest what number of seats it can. But it is quite easy to work out the probable number of seats which each nationality can obtain on the basis of the ratio of its population to the total seats in the Legislature. Proceeding on this basis what do we find? In Switzerland the total representatives in the Lower House is 187. Out of them the German population has a possibility of winning 138, French 42 and Italians only 7 seats. In South Africa out of the total of 153, there is a possibility of the

* *Canada Year Book*, 1936.

† *South Africa Year Book*, 1941.

‡ *Statesman's Year Book*, 1941.

English gaining 62, and the Dutch 94 seats. In Canada the total is 245. Of these the French* have only 65. On this basis it is quite clear that in all these countries there is a possibility of the major nationality establishing its supremacy over the minor nationalities. Indeed, one may go so far as to say that speaking *de jure* and as a mere matter of form in Canada the French are living under the British Raj, the English in South Africa under the Dutch Raj, and the Italians and French in Switzerland under the German Raj. But what is the position *de facto*? Have Frenchmen in Canada raised a cry that they will not live under British Raj? Have Englishmen in South Africa raised a cry that they will not live under Dutch Raj? Have the French and Italians in Switzerland any objection to living under the German Raj? Why should then the Muslims raise this cry of Hindu Raj?

Is it proposed that the Hindu Raj should be the rule of a naked communal majority? Are not the Musalmans granted safeguards against the possible tyranny of the Hindu majority? Are not the safeguards given to the Musalmans of India wider and better than the safeguards which have been given to the French in Canada, to the English in South Africa and to the French and the Italians in Switzerland? To take only one item from the list of safeguards. Haven't the Musalmans got an enormous degree of weightage in representation in the Legislature? Is weightage known in Canada, South Africa or Switzerland? And what is the effect of this weightage to Muslims? Is it not to reduce the Hindu majority in the Legislature? What is the degree of reduction? Confining ourselves to British India and taking account only of the representation granted to the territorial constituencies, Hindu and Muslim, in the Lower House in the Central Legislature under the Government of India Act, 1935, it is clear that out of a total of 187, the Hindus have 105 seats and the Muslims have 82 seats. Given these figures one is forced to ask where is the fear of the Hindu Raj?

If Hindu Raj does become a fact, it will, no doubt, be the greatest calamity for this country. No matter what the Hindus say, Hinduism is a menace to liberty, equality and fraternity. On

*That is for the Province of Quebec.

that account it is incompatible with democracy. Hindu Raj must be prevented at any cost. But is Pakistan the true remedy against it? What makes communal Raj possible is a marked disproportion in the relative strength of the various communities living in a country. As pointed out above, this disproportion is not more marked in India than it is in Canada, South Africa and Switzerland. Nonetheless there is no British Raj in Canada, no Dutch Raj in South Africa, and no German Raj in Switzerland. How have the French, the English and the Italians succeeded in preventing the Raj of the majority community being established in their country? Surely not by partition: What is their method? Their method is to put a ban on communal parties in politics. No community in Canada, South Africa or Switzerland ever thinks of starting a separate communal party. What is important to note is that it is the minority nations which have taken the lead in opposing the formation of a communal party. For they know that if they form a communal political party the major community will also form a communal party and the majority community will thereby find it easy to establish its communal Raj. It is a vicious method of self-protection. It is because the minority nations are fully aware how they will be hoisted on their own petard that they have opposed the formation of communal political parties.

Have the Muslims thought of this method of avoiding Hindu Raj. Have they considered how easy it is to avoid it? Have they considered how futile and harmful the present policy of the League is? The Muslims are howling against the Hindu Maha Sabha and its slogan of Hindudom and Hindu Raj. But who is responsible for this? Hindu Maha Sabha and Hindu Raj are the inescapable nemesis which the Musalmans have brought upon themselves by having a Muslim League. It is action and counter-action. One gives rise to the other. Not partition, but the abolition of the Muslim League and the formation of a mixed party of Hindus and Muslims is the only effective way of burying the ghost of Hindu Raj. It is, of course, not possible for Muslims and other minority parties to join the Congress or the Hindu Maha Sabha so long as the disagreement on the question of constitutional safeguards continues. But this question will be settled, is bound to be settled and there is every hope that the settlement will result in securing to the Muslims and other minorities the safeguards they need. Once this consummation, which we so devoutly wish, takes place nothing can stand in the way of a party re-alignment, of the Congress and the Maha Sabha breaking up and of Hindus and Musalmans forming mixed political parties based on an agreed programme of social and economic regeneration, and thereby avoid the danger of both Hindu Raj or Muslim Raj becoming a fact. Nor should the formation of a mixed party of Hindus and Muslims be difficult in India. There are many lower orders in the Hindu society whose economic, political and social needs are the same as those of the majority of the Muslims and they would be far more ready to make a common cause with the Muslims for achieving common ends than they would with the high caste of Hindus who have denied and deprived them of ordinary human rights for centuries. To pursue such a course cannot be called an adventure. The path along that line is a well trodden path. Is it not a fact that under the Montagu-Chelmsford Reforms in most Provinces, if not in all, the Muslims, the Non-Brahmins and the Depressed Classes united together and worked the reforms as members of one team from 1920 to 1937? Herein lay the most fruitful method of achieving communal harmony among Hindus and Muslims and of destroying the danger of a Hindu Raj. Mr. Jinnah could have easily pursued this line. Nor was it difficult for Mr. Jinnah to succeed in it. Indeed Mr. Jinnah is the one person who had all the chances of success on his side if he had tried to form such a united non-communal party. He has the ability to organize. He had the reputation of a nationalist. Even many Hindus who were opposed to the Congress would have flocked to him if he had only sent out a call for a united party of like-minded Hindus and Muslims. What did Mr. Jinnah do? In 1937 Mr. Jinnah made his entry into Muslim politics and strangely enough he regenerated the Muslim League which was dying and decaying and of which only a few years ago he would have been glad to witness the funeral. However regrettable the starting of such a communal political party may have been, there was in it one relieving feature. That was the leadership of Mr. Jinnah. Everybody felt that with the leadership of

Mr. Jinnah the League could never become a merely communal party. The resolutions passed by the League during the first two years of its new career indicated that it would develop into a mixed political party of Hindus and Muslims. At the annual session of the Muslim League held at Lucknow in October 1937 altogether 15 resolutions were passed. The following two are of special interest in this connection.

Resolution* No. 7:

> "This meeting of the All India Muslim League deprecates and protests against the formation of Ministries in certain Provinces by the Congress parties in flagrant violation of the letter and the spirit of the Government of India Act, 1935, and Instrument of Instructions and condemns the Governors for their failure to enforce the special powers entrusted to them for the safeguards of the interest of the Musalmans *and other important minorities*."

Resolution* No. 8:

> "Resolved that the object of the All India Muslim League shall be the establishment in India of Full Independence in the form of federation of free democratic states in which the rights and interests of the Musalmans *and other minorities* are adequately and effectively safeguarded in the constitution."

Equal number of resolutions were passed at the next annual session of the League held at Patna in December 1938. Resolution* No. 10 is noteworthy. It reads as follows:—

> "The All India Muslim League reiterates its view that the scheme of Federation embodied in the Government of India Act, 1935, is not acceptable, but in view of the further developments that have taken place or may take place from time to time it hereby authorises the President of the All India Muslim League to adopt such course as may be necessary with a view to explore the possibility of a suitable alternative which will safeguard the interests of the Musalmans and *other minorities in India*."

By these resolutions Mr. Jinnah showed that he was for a common front between the Muslims and other non-Muslim minorities. Unfortunately the catholicity and statesmanship that underlies these resolutions did not last long. In 1939 Mr. Jinnah took a somersault and outlined the dangerous and disastrous policy of isolation of the Musalmans by passing that notorious resolution in favour of Pakistan. What is the reason

* Italics not in the original.

for this isolation? Nothing but the change of view that the Musalmans were a nation and not a community!! One need not quarrel over the question whether the Muslims are a nation or a community. But one finds it extremely difficult to understand how the mere fact that the Muslims are a nation makes political isolation a safe and sound policy? Unfortunately Muslims do not realize what disservice Mr. Jinnah has done to them by this policy. But let Muslims consider what Mr. Jinnah has achieved by making the Muslim League the only organization for the Musalmans. It may be that it has helped him to avoid the possibility of having to play the second fiddle. For inside the Muslim camp he can always be sure of the first place for himself. But how does the League hope to save by this plan of isolation the Muslims from Hindu Raj? Will Pakistan obviate the establishment of Hindu Raj in Provinces in which the Musalmans are in a minority? Obviously it cannot. This is what would happen in the Muslim-minority Provinces if Pakistan came. Take an all-India view. Can Pakistan prevent the establishment of Hindu Raj at the centre over Muslim minorities that will remain in Hindustan? It is plain that it cannot. What good is Pakistan then? Only to prevent Hindu Raj in Provinces in which the Muslims are in a majority and in which there could never be Hindu Raj!! To put it differently Pakistan is unnecessary to Muslims where they are in a majority because there, there is no fear of Hindu Raj. It is worse than useless to Muslims where they are in a minority, because Pakistan or no Pakistan they will have to face a Hindu Raj. Can politics be more futile than the politics of the Muslim League? The Muslim League started to help minority Muslims and has ended by espousing the cause of majority Muslims. What a perversion in the original aim of the Muslim League! What a fall from the sublime to the ridiculous! Partition as a remedy against Hindu Raj is worse than useless.

VI

These are some of the weaknesses in the Muslim case for Pakistan which have occurred to me. There might be others which have not struck me. But the list as it is, is quite a formidable one. How do the Muslims propose to meet them? That is a question for the Muslims and not for me. My duty as a student of the subject extends to setting forth these weaknesses. That I have done. I have nothing more to answer for.

There are, however, two other questions of such importance that this discussion cannot be closed with any sense of completeness without reference to them. The purpose of these questions is to clear the ground between myself and my critics. Of these questions, one I am entitled to ask the critics, the other the critics are entitled to ask me.

Beginning with the first question, what I feel like asking the critics is, what good do they expect from a statement of these weaknesses? Do they expect the Musalmans to give up Pakistan if they are defeated in a controversy over the virtues of Pakistan? That of course depends upon what method is adopted to resolve this controversy. The Hindus and the Musalmans may follow the procedure which Christian missionaries had set up in early times in order to secure converts from amongst the Hindus. According to this procedure a day was appointed for a disputation, which was open to public, between a Christian missionary and a Brahmin, the former representing the Christian religion and the latter holding himself out as the protagonist of the Hindu religion with the condition that whoever failed to meet the case against his religion was bound to accept the religion of the other. If such a method of resolving the dispute between the Hindus and the Muslims over the issue of Pakistan was agreed upon there may be some use in setting out this string of weaknesses. But let it not be forgotten that there is another method of disposing of a controversy which may be called Johnsonian after the manner which Dr. Johnson employed in dealing with arguments of Bishop Berkeley. It is recorded by Boswell that when he told Dr. Johnson that the doctrine of Bishop Berkeley that matter was non-existent and that everything in the universe was merely ideal, was only an ingenious sophistry but that it was impossible to refute it, Dr. Johnson with great alacrity answered, striking his foot with mighty force against a large stone, till he rebounded from it saying, "I refute it thus." It may be that the Musalmans will agree, as most rational people do, to have their case for Pakistan decided by the tests of reason and argument. But I should not be surprised if the Muslims decided to adopt the method of Dr. Johnson and say "Damn your arguments! We want Pakistan." In that event the critic must realize that any reliance placed upon the limitations for destroying the case for Pakistan will be of no avail. It is therefore no use being jubilant over the logic of these objections to Pakistan.

Let me now turn to the other question which I said the critic is entitled to put to me. What is my position regarding the issue of Pakistan in the light of the objections, which I have set out? I have no doubts as to my position. I hold firmly that, subject to certain conditions, detailed in the chapters that follow, if the Musalmans are bent on having Pakistan then it must be conceded to them. I know my critics will at once accuse me of inconsistency and will demand reasons for so extraordinary a conclusion—extraordinary because of the view expressed by me in the earlier part of this chapter that the Muslim case for Pakistan has nothing in it which can be said to carry the compelling force which the decree of an inexorable fate may be said to have. I withdraw nothing from what I have said as to the weaknesses in the Muslim case for Pakistan. Yet I hold that if the Muslims must have Pakistan there is no escape from conceding it to them. As to the reasons which have led me to that conclusion I shall not hesitate to say that the strength or weakness of the logic of Pakistan is not one of them. In my judgment there are two governing factors which must determine the issue. First is the defence of India and second is the sentiment of the Muslims. I will state why I regard them as decisive and how in my opinion they tell in favour of Pakistan.

To begin with the first. One cannot ignore that what is important is not the winning of independence but the having of the sure means of maintaining it. The ultimate guarantee of the independence of a country is a safe army—an army on which you can rely to fight for the country at all times and in any eventuality. The army in India must necessarily be a mixed army composed of Hindus and Muslims. If India is invaded by a foreign power, can the Muslims in the army be trusted to defend India? Suppose invaders are their co-religionists. Will the Muslims side with the invaders or will they stand against them and save India? This is a very crucial question. Obviously, the answer to this question must depend upon to what extent the Muslims in the army have caught the infection of the two-nation theory, which is the foundation of Pakistan. If they are infected, then the army in India cannot be safe. Instead of being the guardian of the independence of India, it will continue to be a menace and a potential danger to its independence. I confess I feel aghast when I hear some Britishers argue that it is for the defence of India that they must reject Pakistan. Some Hindus also sing the same tune. I feel certain that either they are unaware as to what the determining factor in the independence of India is or that they are talking of the defence of India not as an independent country responsible for its own defence but as a British possession to be defended by them against an intruder. This is a hopelessly wrong angle of vision. The question is not whether the British will be able to defend India better if there was no partition of India. The question is whether Indians will be able to defend a free India. To that, I repeat, the only answer is that Indians will be able to defend a free India on one and one condition alone—namely, if the army in India remains non-political, unaffected by the poison of Pakistan. I want to warn Indians against the most stupid habit that has grown up in this country of discussing the question of Swaraj without reference to the question of the army. Nothing can be more fatal than the failure to realize that a political army is the greatest danger to the liberty of India. It is worse than having no army.

Equally important is the fact that the army is the ultimate sanction which sustains Government in the exercise of its authority inside the country, when it is challenged by a rebellious or recalcitrant element. Suppose the Government of the day enunciates a policy which is vehemently opposed by a section of the Muslims. Suppose the Government of the day is required to use its army to enforce its policy. Can the Government of the day depend upon the Muslims in the army to obey its orders and shoot down the Muslim rebels? This again depends upon to what extent the Muslims in the army have caught the infection of the two-nation theory. If they have caught it, India cannot have a safe and secure Government.

Turning to the second governing factor the Hindus do not seem to attach any value to sentiment as a force in politics. The Hindus seem to rely upon two grounds to win against the Muslims. The first is that even if the Hindus and the Muslims are two nations, they can live under one state. The other is that the Muslim case for Pakistan is founded on strong sentiment rather than upon clear argument. I don't know how long the Hindus are going to fool themselves with such arguments. It is true that the first argument is not without precedent. At the same time it does not call for much intelligence to see that its value is extremely limited. Two nations and one state is a pretty plea. It has the same attraction which a sermon has and may result in the conversion of Muslim leaders. But instead of being uttered as a sermon· if it is intended to issue it as an ordinance for the Muslims to obey it will be a mad project to which no sane man will agree. It will, I am sure, defeat the very purpose of Swaraj. The second argument is equally silly. That the Muslim case for Pakistan is founded on sentiment is far from being a matter of weakness; it is really its strong point. It does not need deep understanding of politics to know that the workability of a constitution is not a matter of theory. It is a matter of sentiment. A constitution like clothes must suit as well as please. If a constitution does not please, then, however perfect it may be, it will not work. To have a constitution which runs counter to the strong sentiments of a determined section is to court disaster if not to invite rebellion.

It is not realized by the Hindus that, assuming there is a safe army, rule by armed forces is not the normal method of governing a people. Force, it cannot be denied, is the medicine of the body politic and must be administered when the body politic becomes sick. But just because force is the medicine of the body politic it cannot be allowed to become its daily bread. A body politic must work as a matter of course by springs of action which are natural. This can happen only when the different elements constituting the body politic have the will to work together and to obey the laws and orders passed by a duly constituted authority. Suppose the new constitution for a United India contained in it all the provisions necessary to safeguard the interests of the

Muslims. But suppose the Muslims said "Thank you for your safeguards, we don't want to be ruled by you"; and suppose they boycott the Legislatures, refuse to obey laws, oppose the payment of taxes; what is to happen? Are the Hindus prepared to extract obedience from Muslims by the use of Hindu bayonets? Is Swaraj to be an opportunity to serve the people or is it to be an opportunity for Hindus to conquer the Musalmans and for the Musalmans to conquer the Hindus? Swaraj must be a Government of the people by the people and for the people. This is the *raison d'être* of Swaraj and the only justification for Swaraj. If Swaraj is to usher in an era in which the Hindus and the Muslims will be engaged in scheming against each other, the one planning to conquer its rival, why should we have Swaraj and why should the democratic nations allow such a Swaraj to come into existence? It will be a snare, a delusion and a perversion.

The non-Muslims do not seem to be aware that they are presented with a situation in which they are forced to choose between various alternatives. Let me state them. In the first place they have to choose between Freedom of India and the Unity of India. If the non-Muslims will insist on the Unity of India they put the quick realization of India's freedom into jeopardy. The second choice relates to the surest method of defending India, whether they can depend upon Muslims in a free and united India to develop and sustain along with the non-Muslims the necessary will to defend the common liberties of both: or whether it is better to partition India and thereby ensure the safety of Muslim India by leaving its defence to the Muslims and of non-Muslim India by leaving its defence to non-Muslims.

As to the first, I prefer Freedom of India to the Unity of India. The Sinn Feinners who were the staunchest of nationalists to be found anywhere in the world and who like the Indians were presented with similar alternatives chose the freedom of Ireland to the unity of Ireland. The non-Muslims who are opposed to partition may well profit by the advice tendered by the Rev. Michael O'Flanagan, at one time Vice-President of the Feinns to the Irish Nationalists on the issue of the partition of Ireland.* Said the Rev. Father:—

> "If we reject Home Rule rather than agree to the exclusion of the Unionist parts of Ulster, what case have we to put before the world? We can point out that Ireland is an island with a definite geographical boundary. That argument might be all right if we were appealing to a number of Island nationalities that had themselves definite geographical boundaries. Appealing, as we are, to continental nations with shifting boundaries, that argument will have no force whatever. National and geographical boundaries scarcely ever coincide. Geography would make one nation of Spain and Portugal; history has made two of them. Geography did its best to make one nation of Norway and Sweden; history has succeeded in making two of them. Geography has scarcely anything to say to the number of nations upon the North American continent; history has done the whole thing. If a man were to try to construct a political map of Europe out of its physical map, he would find himself groping in the dark. Geography has worked hard to make one nation out of Ireland; history has worked against it. The island of Ireland and the national unit of Ireland simply do not coincide. In the last analysis the test of nationality is the wish of the people."

These words have emanated from a profound sense of realism which we in India so lamentably lack.

On the second issue I prefer the partitioning of India into Muslim India and non-Muslim India as the surest and safest method of providing for the defence of both. It is certainly the safer of the two alternatives. I know it will be contended that my fears about the loyalty of the Muslims in the army to a Free and United India arising from the infection of the two-nation theory is only an imaginary fear. That is no doubt true. That does not militate against the soundness of the choice I have made. I may be wrong. But I certainly can say without any fear of contradiction that, to use the words of Burke, it is better to be ridiculed for too great a credulity than to be ruined by too confident a sense of security. I don't want to leave things to chance. To leave so important an issue, as the defence of India, to chance is to be guilty of the grossest crime.

Nobody will consent to the Muslim demand for Pakistan unless he is forced to do so. At the same time, it would be a

* Quoted by Sir James O'Connor—*History of Ireland*, Vol. II, p. 257.

folly not to face what is inevitable and face it with courage and common sense. Equally would it be a folly to lose the part one can retain in the vain attempt of preserving the whole.

These are the reasons why I hold that if the Musalmans will not yield on the issue of Pakistan then Pakistan must come. So far as I am concerned the only important question is: Are the Musalmans determined to have Pakistan? Or is Pakistan a mere cry? Is it only a passing mood? Or does it represent their permanent aspiration? On this there may be difference of opinion. Once it becomes certain that the Muslims want Pakistan there can be no doubt that the wise course would be to concede the principle of it.

CHAPTER XIV

THE PROBLEMS OF PAKISTAN

I

Among the many problems to which the partition of India into Pakistan and Hindustan must give rise will be the following three problems:—

(1) The problem of the allocation of the financial assets and liabilities of the present Government of India,

(2) the problem of the delimitation of the areas, and

(3) the problem of the transfer of population from Pakistan to Hindustan and *vice versa.*

Of these problems the first is consequential, in the sense, that it would be worth while to consider it only when the partition of India has been agreed to by the parties concerned. The two other problems stand on a different footing. They are conditions precedent to Pakistan in the sense that there are many people who will not make up their mind on Pakistan unless they are satisfied that some reasonable and just solution of them is possible. I will, therefore, confine myself to the consideration only of the last two problems of Pakistan.

II

On the question of the boundaries of Pakistan we have had so far no clear and authoritative statement from the Muslim League. In fact it is one of the complaints made by the Hindus that while Mr. Jinnah has been carrying on a whirlwind campaign in favour of Pakistan, which has resulted in fouling the political atmosphere in the country, Mr. Jinnah has not thought fit to inform his critics of the details regarding the boundaries of his proposed Pakistan. Mr. Jinnah's argument has all along been that any discussion regarding the boundaries of Pakistan is premature and that the boundaries of Pakistan will be a matter for discussion when the principle of Pakistan has been admitted. It may be a good rhetorical answer, but it certainly does not help those who wish to apply their mind without taking sides to offer whatever help they can to bring about a peaceful solution of this problem. Mr. Jinnah seems to be under the impression that if a person is committed to the principle of Pakistan he will be bound to accept Mr. Jinnah's plan of Pakistan. There cannot be a greater mistake than this. A person may accept the principle of Pakistan, which only means the partition of India. But it is difficult to understand how the acceptance of this principle can commit him to Mr. Jinnah's plan of Pakistan. Indeed if no plan of Pakistan is satisfactory to him he will be quite free to oppose any form of Pakistan although he may be in favour of the principle of Pakistan. The plan of Pakistan and the principle of Pakistan are therefore two quite distinct propositions. There is nothing wrong in this view. By way of illustration it may be said that the principle of self-determination is like an explosive substance. One may agree in principle to its use when the necessity and urgency of the occasion is proved. But no one can consent to the use of the dynamite without first knowing the area that is intended to be blown up. If the dynamite is going to blow up the whole structure or if it is not possible to localize its application to a particular part he may well refuse to apply the dynamite and prefer to use some other means of solving the problem. Specifications of boundary lines seem therefore to be an essential preliminary for working out in concrete shape the principle of Pakistan. Equally essential it is for a *bona fide* protagonist of Pakistan not to hide from the public the necessary particulars of the scheme of Pakistan. Such contumacy and obstinacy as shown by Mr. Jinnah in refusing to declare the boundaries of his Pakistan is unforgivable in a statesman. Nevertheless those who are interested in solving the question of Pakistan need not wait to resolve the problems of Pakistan until Mr. Jinnah condescends to give full details. Only one has to carry on the argument on the basis of certain assumptions. In this discussion I will assume that what the Muslim League desires is that the boundaries of the Western Pakistan should be the *present* boundaries of the Provinces of the North-West Frontier, the Punjab, Sind and Baluchistan, and that the boundaries of Eastern Pakistan should be the boundaries of the *present* Province of Bengal with a few districts of Assam thrown in.

III

The question for consideration therefore is: Is this a just claim? The claim is said to be founded on the principle of self-determination. To be able to assess the justice of this claim it is necessary to have a clear understanding of the scope and limitations of the principle of self-determination. Unfortunately, there seems to be a complete lack of such an understanding. It is therefore necessary to begin with the question: What is the *de facto* and *de jure* connotation of this principle of self-determination? The term self-determination has become current since the last few years. But it describes something which is much older. The idea underlying self-determination has developed along two different lines. During the 19th century self-determination meant the right to establish a form of government in accordance with the wishes of the people. Secondly, self-determination has meant the right to obtain national independence from an alien race irrespective of the form of government. The agitation for Pakistan has reference to self-determination in its second aspect.

Confining the discussion to this aspect of Pakistan it seems to me essential that the following points regarding the issue of self-determination should be borne in mind.

In the first place, self-determination must be *by the people*. This point is too simple even to need mention. But it has become necessary to emphasize it. Both the Muslim League and the Hindu Maha Sabha seem to be playing fast and loose with the idea of self-determination. An area is claimed by the Muslim League for inclusion in Pakistan because the people of the area are Muslims. An area is also claimed for being included in Pakistan because the ruler of the area is a Muslim though the majority of the people of that area are non-Muslims. The Muslim League is claiming the benefit of self-determination in India. At the same time the League is opposed to self-determination being applied to Palestine. The League claims Kashmir as a Muslim State because the majority of people are Muslims and also Hyderabad because the ruler is Muslim. In like manner the Hindu Maha Sabha claims an area to be included in Hindustan because the people of the area are non-Muslims. It also comes forward to claim an area to be a part of Hindustan because the ruler is a Hindu though the majority of the people are Muslims. Such strange and conflicting claims are entirely due to the fact that either the parties to Pakistan, namely, the Hindus and the Muslims do not understand what self-determination means or are busy in perverting the principle of self-determination to enable them to justify themselves in carrying out the organized territorial loot in which they now seem to be engaged. India will be thrown into a state of utter confusion whenever the question of reorganization of its territories comes up for consideration if people have no exact notions as to what self-determination involves and have not the honesty to stand by the principle and take the consequences whatever they be. It is, therefore, well to emphasize what might be regarded as too simple to require mention, namely, that self-determination is a determination by the people and by nobody else.

The second point to note is the degree of imperative character with which the principle of self-determination can be said to be invested. As has been said by Mr. O'Connor*:—

> "The doctrine of self-determination is nót a universal principle at all. The most that can be said about it is that generally speaking, it is a sound working rule, founded upon justice, making for harmony and peace and for the development of people in their own fashion, which, again generally speaking, is the best fashion. But it must yield to circumstances, of which size and geographical situation are some of the most important. Whether the rule should prevail against the circumstances or the circumstances against the rule can be determined only by the application of one's common sense or sense of justice, or, as a Benthamite would prefer to put it, by reference to the greatest good of the greatest number—all these three, if properly understood, are really different methods of expressing the same thing. In solving a particular case very great difficulties may arise. There are facts one way and facts another way. Facts of one kind may make a special appeal to some minds, little or none

* *History of Ireland*, Vol. II.

> to others. The problem may be of the kind that is called imponderable, that is to say, no definite conclusion that will be accepted by the generality of the mankind may be possible. There are cases in which it is no more possible to say that a nation is right in its claim to interfere with the self-determination of another nation than that it is to say that it is wrong. It is a matter of opinion, upon which honest and impartial minds may differ."

There are two reasons why this must be so. Firstly, nationality is not such a sacrosanct and absolute principle as to give it the character of a categorical imperative, over-riding every other consideration. Secondly, separation is not quite so essential for the maintenance and preservation of a distinct nationality.

There is a third point to be borne in mind in connection with the issue of self-determination. Self-determination for a nationality may take the form of cultural independence or may take the form of territorial independence. Which form it can take must depend upon the territorial layout of the population. If a nationality lives in easily severable and contiguous areas, other things being equal, a case can be made out for territorial independence. But where owing to an inextricable intermingling the nationalities are so mixed up that the areas they occupy are not easily severable, then all that they can be entitled to is cultural independence. Territorial separation in a case like this is an impossibility. They are doomed to live together. The only other alternative they have is to migrate.

IV

Having defined the scope and limitations of the idea of self-determination we can now proceed to deal with the question of boundaries of Pakistan. How does the claim of the Muslim League for the present boundary to remain the boundaries of Pakistan stand in the light of these considerations? The answer to this question seems to me quite clear. The geographical layout seems to decide the issue. No special pleading of any kind is required. In the case of the North-West Frontier Province, Baluchistan and Sind, the Hindus and the Muslims are intermixed. In these Provinces a case for territorial separation for the Hindus seems to be impossible. They must remain content with cultural independence and such political safeguards as may be devised for their safety. The case of the Punjab and Bengal stands on a different footing. A glance at the map shows that the layout of the population of the Hindus and the Muslims in these two Provinces is totally different from what one finds in the other three Provinces. The non-Muslims in the Punjab and Bengal are not found living in small islands in the midst of and surrounded by a vast Muslim population spread over the entire surface as is the case with the North-West Frontier Province, Baluchistan and Sind. In Bengal and the Punjab the Hindus occupy two different areas contiguous and severable. In these circumstances, there is no reason for conceding what the Muslim League seems to demand, namely, that the present boundaries of the Punjab and Bengal shall continue to be the boundaries of Western Pakistan and Eastern Pakistan.

Two conclusions necessarily follow from the foregoing discussion. One is that the non-Muslims of the Punjab and Bengal have a case for exclusion from Pakistan by territorial severance of the areas they occupy. The other is that the non-Muslims of North-West Frontier Province, Baluchistan and Sind have no case for exclusion and are only entitled to cultural independence and political safeguards. To put the same thing in a different way it may be said that the Muslim League claim for demanding that the boundaries of Sind, North-West Frontier and Baluchistan shall remain as they are cannot be opposed. But that in the case of the Punjab and Bengal such a claim is untenable and that the non-Muslims of these Provinces, if they desire, can claim that the territory they occupy should be excluded by a redrawing of the boundaries of these two Provinces.

V

One should have thought that such a claim by the non-Muslim minorities of the Punjab and Bengal for the redrawing of the boundaries would be regarded by the Muslim League as a just and reasonable claim. The possibility of the redrawing of boundaries was admitted in the Lahore Resolution of the Muslim League passed in March 1940. The Resolution* said:—

> "The establishment of completely independent States formed by demarcating geographically contiguous units into regions

* Italics are mine.

which shall be so constituted, ***with such territorial readjustments as may be necessary***, that the areas in which the Musalmans are numerically in a majority, as in the north-western and eastern zones of India, shall be grouped together to constitute independent States as Muslim free national homelands in which the constituent units shall be autonomous and sovereign."

That this continued to be the position of the Muslim League is clear from the resolution passed by the Muslim League on the Cripps Proposals as anyone who cares to read it will know. But there are indications that Mr. Jinnah has changed his view. At a public meeting held on 16th November 1942 in Jullunder Mr. Jinnah is reported to have expressed himself in the following terms:—

> "The latest trick—I call it nothing but a trick—to puzzle and to mislead the ignorant masses purposely, and those playing the game understand it, is, why should the right of self-determination be confined to Muslims only and why not extend it to other communities? Having said that all have the right of self-determination, they say the Punjab must be divided into so many bits; likewise the North-West Frontier Province and Sind. Thus there will be hundreds of Pakistans.

SUB-NATIONAL GROUPS

> "Who is the author of this new formula that every community has the right of self-determination all over India? Either it is colossal ignorance or mischief and trick. Let me give them a reply, that the Musalmans claim the right of self-determination because they are a national group on a given territory which is their homeland and in the zones where they are in a majority. Have you known anywhere in history that national groups scattered all over have been given a State? Where are you going to get a State for them? In that case you have got 14 per cent. Muslims in the United Provinces. Why not have a State for them? Muslims in the United Provinces are not a national group; they are scattered. Therefore in constitutional language they are characterized as a sub-national group who cannot expect anything more than what is due from any civilized Government to a minority. I hope I have made the position clear. The Muslims are not a sub-national group; it is their birthright to claim and exercise the right of self-determination."

Mr. Jinnah has completely missed the point. The point raised by his critics was not with regard to the non-Muslim

---

* *Eastern Times* (Lahore) of 17th November 1942.

minorities in general. It had reference to the non-Muslim minorities in the Punjab and Bengal. Does Mr. Jinnah propose to dispose of the case of non-Muslim minorities who occupy a compact and an easily severable territory by his theory of a sub-nation? If that is so, then one is bound to say that a proposition cruder than his it would be difficult to find in any political literature. The concept of a sub-nation is unheard of. It is not only an ingenious concept but it is also a preposterous concept. What does the theory of a sub-nation connote? If I understand its implications correctly, it means a sub-nation must not be severed from the nation to which it belongs even when severance is possible: it means that the relations between a nation and a sub-nation are no higher than the relations which subsist between a man and his chattels, or between property and its incidents. Chattels go with the owner, incidents go with property, so a sub-nation goes with a nation. Such is the chain of reasoning in Mr. Jinnah's argument. But does Mr. Jinnah seriously wish to argue that the Hindus of the Punjab and Bengal are only chattels so that they must always go wherever the Muslims of the Punjab and the Muslims of Bengal choose to drive them? Such an argument will be too absurd to be entertained by any reasonable man. It is also the most illogical argument and certainly it should not be difficult for so mature a lawyer as Mr. Jinnah, to see the illogicality of it. If a numerically smaller nation is only a sub-nation in relation to a numerically larger nation and has no right to territorial separation, why can it not be said that taking India as a whole the Hindus are a nation and the Muslims a sub-nation and as a sub-nation they have no right to self-determination or territorial separation?

Already there exists a certain amount of suspicion with regard to the *bona fides* of Pakistan. Rightly or wrongly, most people suspect that Pakistan is pregnant with mischief. They think that it has two motives, one immediate, the other ultimate. The immediate motive, it is said, is to join with the neighbouring Muslim countries and form a Muslim Federation. The ultimate motive is for the Muslim Federation to invade Hindustan and conquer or rather reconquer the Hindus and re-establish Muslim Empire in India. Others think that Pákistan is the culmination of the scheme of hostages which lay behind the demand, put forth by Mr. Jinnah in his fourteen points, for the creation of separate Muslim Provinces. Nobody can fathom the mind of the Muslims and reach the real motives that lie behind their demand for Pakistan. The Hindu opponents of Pakistan if they suspect that the real motives of the Muslims are different from the apparent ones, may take note of them and plan accordingly. They cannot oppose Pakistan because the motives behind it are bad. But they are entitled to ask Mr. Jinnah, Why does he want to have a communal problem within Pakistan? However vicious may be the motives behind Pakistan it should possess at least one virtue. The ideal of Pakistan should be not to have a communal problem inside it. This is the least of virtues one can expect from Pakistan. If Pakistan is to be plagued by a communal problem in the same way as India has been, why have Pakistan at all? It can be welcomed only if it provides an escape from the communal problem. The way to avoid it is to arrange the boundaries in such a way that it will be an ethnic State without a minority and a majority pitched against each other. Fortunately it can be made into an ethnic State if only Mr. Jinnah will allow it. Unfortunately Mr. Jinnah objects to it. Therein lies the chief cause for suspicion and Mr. Jinnah, instead of removing it, is deepening it by such absurd, illogical and artificial distinctions as nations and sub-nations.

Rather than resort to such absurd and illogical propositions and defend what is indefensible and oppose what is just, would it not be better for Mr. Jinnah to do what Sir Edward Carson did in the matter of the delimitation of the boundaries of Ulster? As all those who know the vicissitudes through which the Irish Home Rule question passed know that it was at the Craigavon meeting held on 23rd September 1911 that Sir Edward Carson formulated his policy that in Ulster there will be a government of Imperial Parliament or a Government of Ulster but never a Home Rule Government. As the Imperial Parliament was proposing to withdraw its government, this policy meant the establishment of a provisional government for Ulster. This policy was embodied in a resolution passed at a joint meeting of delegates representing the Ulster Unionist Council, the County Grand Orange Lodges and Unionist Clubs held in Belfast on 25th

September 1911. The Provisional Government of Ulster was to come into force on the day of the passing of the Home Rule Bill. An important feature of this policy was to invest the Provisional Government with a jurisdiction over all "*these districts which they (Ulsterites) could control.*"

The phrase "those districts which they could control" was no doubt meant to include the whole of the administrative division of Ulster. Now this administrative division of Ulster included nine counties. Of these three were overwhelmingly Catholic. This meant the compulsory retention of the three Catholic counties under Ulster against their wishes. But what did Sir Edward Carson do in the end? It did not take long for Sir Edward Carson to discover that Ulster with three overwhelmingly Catholic districts would be a liability, and with all the courage of a true leader he came out with a declaration that he proposed to cut down his losses and make Ulster safe. In his speech in the House of Commons on the 18th of May 1920 he announced that he was content with six counties only. The speech that he made on that occasion giving his reasons why he was content only with six counties is worth quoting. This is what he said*:—

> "The truth is that we came to the conclusion after many anxious hours and anxious days of going into the whole matter, almost parish by parish and townland by townland, that *we would have no chance of successfully starting a Parliament in Belfast which would be responsible for the government of Donegal, Caven and Monaghan.* It would be perfectly idle for us to come here and pretend that we should be in a position to do so. We should like to have the very largest areas possible, naturally. That is a system of land grabbing that prevails in all countries for widening the jurisdiction of the various governments that are set up; but there is no use in our undertaking a government which we know would be a failure if we were saddled with these three counties."

These are wise, sagacious and most courageous words. The situation in which they were uttered has a close parallel with the situation that is likely to be created in the Punjab and Bengal by the application of the principle of Pakistan. The Muslim League and Mr. Jinnah if they want a peaceful Pakistan

* *Hansard* (House of Commons), 1920, Vol. 129, p. 1315. Italics are mine.

should not forget to take note of them. It is no use asking the non-Muslim minorities in the Punjab and Bengal to be satisfied with safeguards. If the Musalmans are not prepared to be content with safeguards against the tyranny of Hindu majority why should the Hindu minorities be asked to be satisfied with the safeguards against the tyranny of the Muslim majority? If the Musalmans can say to the Hindus "Damn your safeguards, we don't want to be ruled by you"—an argument which Carson used against Redmond—the same argument can be returned by the Hindus of the Punjab and Bengal against the Muslim offer to be content with safeguards.

The point is that this attitude is not calculated to lead to a peaceful solution of the problem of Pakistan. Sabre-rattling or show of force will not do. In the first place, this is a game which two can play. In the second place, arms may be an element of strength. But to have arms is not enough. As Rousseau said: "The strongest is never strong enough to be always master, unless he transforms his might into right, and obedience into duty." Only ethics can convert might into right and obedience into duty. The League must see that its claim for Pakistan is founded on ethics.

VI

So much for the problem of boundaries. I will now turn to the problem of the minorities which must remain within Pakistan even after boundaries are redrawn. There are two methods of protecting their interests.

First is to provide safeguards in the constitution for the protection of the political and cultural rights of the minorities. To Indians this is a familiar matter and it is unnecessary to enlarge upon it.

Second is to provide for their transfer from Pakistan to Hindustan. Many people prefer this solution and would be ready and willing to consent to Pakistan if it can be shown that an exchange of population is possible. But they regard this as a staggering and a baffling problem. This no doubt is the sign of a panic-stricken mind. If the matter is considered in a cool and calm temper it will be found that the problem is neither staggering nor baffling.

To begin with consider the dimensions of the problem. On what scale is this transfer going to be? In determining the scale one is bound to take into account three considerations. In the first place, if the boundaries of the Punjab and Bengal are redrawn there will be no question of transfer of population so far as these two Provinces are concerned. In the second place, the Musalmans residing in Hindustan do not propose to migrate to Pakistan nor does the League want their transfer. In the third place, the Hindus in the North-West Frontier Province, Sind and Baluchistan do not want to migrate. If these assumptions are correct, the problem of transfer of population is far from being a staggering problem. Indeed it is so small that there is no need to regard it as a problem at all.

Assuming it does become a problem, will it be a baffling problem? Experience shows that it is not a problem which it is impossible to solve. To devise a solution for such a problem it might be well to begin by asking what are the possible difficulties that are likely to arise in the way of a person migrating from one area to another on account of political changes. The following are obvious enough: (1) The machinery for effecting and facilitating the transfer of population. (2) Prohibition by Government against migration. (3) Levy by Government of heavy taxation on the transfer of goods by the migrating family. (4) The impossibility for a migrating family to carry with it to its new home its immovable property. (5) The difficulty of obviating a resort to unfair practices with a view to depress unduly the value of the property of the migrating family. (6) The fear of having to make good the loss by not being able to realize the full value of the property by sale in the market. (7) The difficulty of realizing pensionary and other charges due to the migrating family from the country of departure. (8) The difficulty of fixing the currency in which payment is to be made. If these difficulties are removed the way to the transfer of population becomes clear.

The first three difficulties can be easily removed by the two States of Pakistan and Hindustan agreeing to a treaty embodying an article in some such terms as follows:—

> "The Governments of Pakistan and Hindustan agree to appoint a Commission consisting of equal number of representa-

tives and presided over by a person who is approved by both and who is not a national of either.

"The expense of the Commission and of its Committees both on account of its maintenance and its operation shall be borne by the two Governments in equal proportion.

"The Government of Pakistan and the Government of Hindustan hereby agree to grant to all their nationals within their territories who belong to ethnic minorities the right to express their desire to emigrate.

"The Governments of the States above mentioned undertake to facilitate in every way the exercise of this right and to interpose no obstacles, directly or indirectly, to freedom of emigration. All laws and regulations whatsoever which conflict with freedom of emigration shall be considered as null and void."

The fourth and the fifth difficulties which relate to transfer of property can be effectually met by including in the treaty articles the following terms:—

"Those who, in pursuance of these articles, determine to take advantage of the right to migrate shall have the right to carry with them or to have transported their movable property of any kind without any duty being imposed upon them on this account.

"So far as immovable property is concerned it shall be liquidated by the Commission in accordance with the following provisions:—

(1) The Commission shall appoint a Committee of Experts to estimate the value of the immovable property of the emigrant. The emigrant interested shall have a representative chosen by him on the Committee.

(2) The Commission shall take necessary measures with a view to the sale of immovable property of the emigrant."

As for the rest of the difficulties relating to reimbursement for loss, for payment of pensionary and charges for specifying the currency in which payments are to be made the following articles in the treaty should be sufficient to meet them:—

"(1) The difference in the estimated value and the sale price of the immovable property of the emigrant shall be paid in to the Commission by the Government of the country of departure as soon as the former has notified it of the resulting deficiency. One-fourth of this payment may be made in the money of the country of departure and three-fourths in gold or short term gold bonds.

"(2) The Commission shall advance to the emigrants the value of their immovable property determined as above.

"(3) All civil or military pensions acquired by an emigrant at the date of the signature of the present treaty shall be capitalized at the charge of the debtor Government, which must pay the amount to the Commission for the account of its owners.

"(4) The funds necessary to facilitate emigration shall be advanced by the States interested in the Commission."

Are not these provisions sufficient to overcome the difficulties regarding transfer of population? There are of course other difficulties. But even those are not insuperable. They involve questions of policy. The first question is: is the transfer of population to be compulsory or is it to be voluntary? The second is: is this right to State-aided transfer to be open to all or is it to be restricted to any particular class of persons? The third is: how long is Government going to remain liable to be bound by these provisions, particularly the provision for making good the loss on the sale of immovable property? Should the provisions be made subject to a time limit or should the liability be continued indefinitely?

With regard to the first point, both are possible and there are instances of both having been put into effect. The transfer of population between Greece and Bulgaria was on a voluntary basis while that between Greece and Turkey was on a compulsory basis. Compulsory transfer strikes one as being *prima facie* wrong. It would not be fair to compel a man to change his ancestral habitat if he does not wish to, unless the peace and tranquillity of the State is likely to be put in jeopardy by his continuing to live where he is or such transfer becomes necessary in his own interest. What is required is that those who want to transfer should be able to do so without impediment and without loss. I am therefore of opinion that transfer should not be forced but should be left open for those who declare their intention to transfer.

As to the second point, it is obvious that only members of a minority can be allowed to take advantage of the scheme of State-aided transfer. But even this restriction may not be sufficient to exclude all those who ought not to get the benefit of this scheme. It must be confined to certain well defined minorities who on account of ethnic or religious differences are sure to be subjected to discrimination or victimization.

The third point is important and is likely to give rise to serious difference of opinion. On a fair view of the matter it can be said that it is quite unreasonable to compel a Government to keep open for an indefinite period the option to migrate at Government cost. There is nothing unfair in telling a person that if he wants to take advantage of the provisions of the scheme of State-aided migration contained in the foregoing articles, he must exercise his option to migrate within a stated period and that if he decides to migrate after the period has elapsed he will be free to migrate but it will have to be at his own cost and without the aid of the State. There is no inequity in thus limiting the right to State-aid. State-aid becomes a necessary part of the scheme because the migration is a resultant consequence of political changes over which individual citizens have no control. But migration may not be the result of political change. It may be for other causes, and when it is for other causes, aid to the emigrant cannot be an obligation on the State. The only way to determine whether migration is for political reasons or for private reasons is to relate it to a definite point of time. When it takes place within a defined period from the happening of a political change it may be presumed to be political. When it occurs after the period it may be presumed to be for private reasons. There is nothing unjust in this. The same rule of presumption governs the cases of civil servants who, when a political change takes place, are allowed to retire on proportionate pensions if they retire within a given period but not if they retire after it has lapsed.

If the policy in these matters is as I suggest it should be, it may be given effect to by the inclusion of the following articles in the treaty :—

> "The right to voluntary emigration may be exercised under this treaty by any person belonging to an ethnic minority who is over 18 years of age.
>
> "A declaration made before the Commission shall be sufficient evidence of intention to exercise the right.

"The choice of the husband shall carry with it that of the wife, the option of parents or guardians that of their children or wards aged less than 18 years.

"The right to the benefit provided by this treaty shall lapse if the option to migrate is not exercised within a period of 5 years from the date of signing the treaty.

"The duties of the Commission shall be terminated within six months after the expiration of the period of five years from the date when the Commission starts to function."

What about the cost? The question of cost will be important only if the transfer is to be compulsory. A scheme of voluntary transfer cannot place a very heavy financial burden on the State. Men love property more than liberty. Many will prefer to endure tyranny at the hands of their political masters than change the habitat in which they are rooted. As Adam Smith said, of all the things man is the most difficult cargo to transport. Cost therefore need not frighten anybody.

What about its workability? The scheme is not new. It has been tried and found workable. It was put into effect after the last European War, to bring about a transfer* of population between Greece and Bulgaria and Turkey and Greece. Nobody can deny that it has worked, has been tried and found workable. The scheme I have outlined is a copy of the same scheme. It had the effect of bringing about a transfer* of population between Greece and Bulgaria and Turkey and Greece. Nobody can deny that it was worked with signal success. What succeeded elsewhere may well be expected to succeed in India.

The issue of Pakistan is far from simple. But it is not so difficult as it is made out to be provided the principle and the ethics of it are agreed upon. If it is difficult it is only because it is heart-rending and nobody wishes to think of its problems and their solutions as the very idea of it is so painful. But once sentiment is banished and it is decided that there shall be Pakistan, the problems arising out of it are neither staggering nor baffling.

* Those who want more information on the question of transfer of population may consult with great advantage *The Exchange of Minorities, Bulgaria, Greece and Turkey* by Stephen P. Ladas (Mac), 1932, where the scheme for the transfer of population between Greece and Bulgaria and Greece and Turkey has been fully set out.

CHAPTER XV

WHO CAN DECIDE?

There are two sides to the question of Pakistan, the Hindu side and the Muslim side. This cannot be avoided. Unfortunately however the attitude of both is far from rational. Both are deeply embedded in sentiment. The layers of this sentiment are so thick that reason at present finds it extremely difficult to penetrate. Whether these opposing sentiments will wither away or they will thicken, time and circumstances alone can tell. How long Indians will have to wait for the melting of the snow no one can prophesy. But one thing is certain that until this snow melts freedom will have to be put in cold storage. I am sure there must be many millions of thinking Indians who are dead opposed to this indefinite postponement of Indian freedom till an ideal and a permanent solution of Pakistan is found. I am one of them. I am one of those who hold that if Pakistan is a problem and not a pose there is no escape and a solution must be found for it. I am one of those who believe that what is inevitable must be faced. There is no use burying one's head in the sand and refusing to take notice of what is happening round about because the sound of it hurts one's sentiments. I am also one of those who believe that one must, if one can, be ready with a solution long before the hour of decision arrives. It is wise to build a bridge if one knows that one will be forced to cross the river.

The principal problem of Pakistan is: who can decide whether there shall or shall not be Pakistan? I have thought over the subject for the last three years, and I have come to some conclusions as to the proper answer to this question. These conclusions I would like to share with others interested in the solution of the problem so that they may be further explored. To give clarity to my conclusions, I have thought that it would serve the purpose better if I were to put them in the form of an Act of Parliament. The following is the draft of the Act which embodies my conclusions :—

Government of India (Preliminary Provisions) Act

Be it enacted by the King's most Excellent Majesty, by and with the advice and consent of the Lords Spiritual and Temporal, and Commons, in this present Parliament assembled, and by the authority of the same as follows:—

I.—(1) *If within six months from the date appointed in this behalf a majority of the Muslim members of the Legislatures of the Provinces of the North-West Frontier, the Punjab, Sind and Bengal pass a resolution that the predominantly Muslim areas be separated from British India, His Majesty shall cause a poll to be taken on that question of the Muslim and the non-Muslim electors of these Provinces and of Baluchistan in accordance with the provisions of this Act.*

(2) *The question shall be submitted to the electors in these Provinces in the following form:—*

(*i*) *Are you in favour of separation from British India?*

(*ii*) *Are you against separation?*

(3) *The poll of Muslim and non-Muslim electors shall be taken separately.*

II.—(1) *If on a result of the poll, a majority of Muslim electors are found to be in favour of separation and a majority of non-Muslim electors against separation, His Majesty shall by proclamation appoint a Boundary Commission for the purpose of preparing a list of such districts and areas in these Provinces in which a majority of inhabitants are Muslims. Such districts and areas shall be called Scheduled Districts.*

(2) *The Scheduled Districts shall be collectively designated as Pakistan and the rest of British India as Hindustan. The Scheduled Districts*

lying in the North-west shall be called the State of Western Pakistan and those lying in the North-east shall be called Eastern Pakistan.

III.—(1) *After the findings of the Boundary Commission have become final either by agreement or the award of an Arbitrator, His Majesty shall cause another poll to be taken of the electors of the Scheduled Districts.*

(2) *The following shall be the form of the questions submitted to the electors:—*

(i) *Are you in favour of separation forthwith?*

(ii) *Are you against separation forthwith?*

IV.—(1) *If the majority is in favour of separation forthwith it shall be lawful for His Majesty to make arrangements for the framing of two separate constitutions, one for Pakistan and the other for Hindustan.*

(2) *The New States of Pakistan and Hindustan shall commence to function as separate States on the day appointed by His Majesty by proclamation issued in that behalf.*

(3) *If the majority are against separation forthwith it shall be lawful for His Majesty to make arrangements for the framing of a single constitution for British India as a whole.*

V.— *No motion for the separation of Pakistan if the poll under the last preceding section has been against separation forthwith and no motion for incorporation of Pakistan into Hindustan if the poll under the last preceding section has been in favour of separation forthwith shall be entertained until ten years have elapsed from the date appointed by His Majesty for putting into effect the new constitution for British India or the two separate constitutions for Pakistan and Hindustan.*

VI.—(1) *In the event of two separate constitutions coming into existence under Section Four it shall be lawful for His Majesty to establish as soon as may be after the appointed day, a Council of India with a view to the eventual establishment of a constitution for the whole of British India, and to bringing about harmonious action between the Legislatures and Governments of Pakistan and Hindustan, and to the promotion of mutual intercourse and uniformity in relation to matters affecting the whole of British India, and to providing for the administration of services which the two parliaments mutually agree should be administered uniformly throughout the whole of British India, or which by virtue of this Act are to be so administered.*

(2) *Subject as hereinafter provided, the Council of India shall consist of a President nominated in accordance with instructions from His Majesty and forty other persons, of whom twenty shall be members representing Pakistan and twenty shall be members representing Hindustan.*

(3) *The members of the Council of India shall be elected in each case by the members of the Lower Houses of the Parliament of Pakistan or Hindustan.*

(4) *The election of members of the Council of India shall be the first business of the Legislatures of Pakistan and Hindustan.*

(5) *A member of the Council shall, on ceasing to be a member of that House of the Legislature of Pakistan or Hindustan by which he was elected a member of the Council, cease to be a member of the Council: Provided that, on the dissolution of the Legislature of Pakistan or Hindustan, the persons who are members of the Council shall continue to hold office as members of the Council until a new election has taken place and shall then retire unless re-elected.*

(6) *The President of the Council shall preside at each meeting of the Council at which he is*

present and shall be entitled to vote in case of an equality of votes, but not otherwise.

(7) *The first meeting of the Council shall be held at such time and place as may be appointed by the President.*

(8) *The Council may act notwithstanding a deficiency in their number, and the quorum of the Council shall be fifteen.*

(9) *Subject as aforesaid, the Council may regulate their own procedure, including the delegation of powers to committees.*

(10) *The constitution of the Council of India may from time to time be varied by identical Acts passed by the Legislature of Pakistan and the Legislature of Hindustan, and the Acts may provide for all or any of the members of the Council of India being elected by parliamentary electors, and determine the constituencies by which the several elective members are to be returned and the number of the members to be returned by the several constituencies and the method of election.*

VII.—(1) *The Legislatures of Pakistan and Hindustan may, by identical Acts, delegate to the Council of India any of the powers of the Legislatures and Governments of Pakistan and Hindustan, and such Acts may determine the manner in which the powers so delegated are to be exercisable by the Council.*

(2) *The powers of making laws with respect to railways and waterways shall, as from the day appointed for the operation of the new constitution, become the powers of the Council of India and not of Pakistan or Hindustan: Provided that nothing in this sub-section shall prevent the Legislature of Pakistan or Hindustan making laws authorising the construction, extension, or improvement of railways and waterways where*

the works to be constructed are situate wholly in Pakistan or Hindustan as the case may be.

(3) *The Council may consider any questions which may appear in any way to bear on the welfare of both Pakistan and Hindustan, and may, by resolution, make suggestions in relation thereto as they may think proper, but suggestions so made shall have no legislative effect.*

(4) *It shall be lawful for the Council of India to make recommendations to the Legislatures of Pakistan and Hindustan as to the advisability of passing identical Acts delegating to the Council of India the administration of any all-India subjects, with a view to avoiding the necessity of administering them separately in Pakistan or Hindustan.*

(5) *It shall be lawful for either Legislature at any time by Act to deprive the delegation to the Council of India of any powers which are in pursuance of such identical Acts as aforesaid for the time being delegated to the Council and thereupon the powers in question shall cease to be exercisable by the Council of India and shall become exercisable in parts of British India within their respective jurisdictions by the Legislatures and Governments of Pakistan and Hindustan and the Council shall take such steps as may be necessary to carry out the transfer, including adjustments of any funds in their hands or at their disposal.*

VIII.—(1) *If at the end of ten years after coming into operation of a constitution for British India as prescribed by Section IV—(3) a petition is presented to His Majesty by a majority of the Muslim members representing the Scheduled Districts in the Provincial and Central Legislatures demanding a poll to be taken with regard to the separation of Pakistan from*

Hindustan, His Majesty shall cause a poll to be taken.

(2) *The following shall be the form of the questions submitted to the electors:—*

(*i*) *Are you in favour of separation of Pakistan from Hindustan?*

(*ii*) *Are you against the separation of Pakistan from Hindustan?*

IX.— *If the result of the poll is in favour of separation it shall be lawful for His Majesty to declare by an Order-in-Council that from a day appointed in that behalf Pakistan shall cease to be a part of British India, and dissolve the Council of India.*

X.—(*1*) *Where two constitutions have come into existence under circumstances mentioned in Section IV it shall be lawful for His Majesty to declare by an Order-in-Council that Pakistan shall cease to be a separate State and shall form part of Hindustan.*

Provided that no such order shall be made until ten years have elapsed from the commencement of the separate constitution for Pakistan.

Provided also that no such declaration shall be made unless the Popular Legislatures of Pakistan and Hindustan have passed Constituent Acts as are provided for in Section X—(2).

(2) *The popular Legislatures of Pakistan and Hindustan may, by identical Acts agreed to by an absolute majority of members at the third reading (hereinafter referred to as Constituent Acts), establish, in lieu of the Council of India, a Legislature for United India, and may determine the number of members thereof and the manner in which the members are to be appointed or elected and the constituencies for which the several elective members are to be returned, and the number of members to be*

returned by the several constituencies, and the method of appointment or election, and the relations of the two Houses if provided for to one another.

XI.—(1) *On the date of the union of Pakistan and Hindustan the Council of India shall cease to exist and there shall be transferred to the Legislature and Government of India all powers then exercisable by the Council of India.*

(2) *There shall also be transferred to the Legislature and Government of British India all the powers and duties of the Legislatures and Governments of Pakistan and Hindustan, including all powers as to taxation, and those Legislatures and Governments shall cease to exist.*

XII.—(1) *A poll under this Act shall be taken by ballot in the same manner so far as possible as a poll of electors for the election of a member to serve in a Legislature and His Majesty may make rules adopting the election laws for the purpose of the taking of the poll.*

(2) *An elector shall not vote more than once at the poll, although registered in more than one place.*

(3) *Elector means every adult male and female residing in the Provinces of North-West Frontier, the Punjab, Sind, and Bengal and in Baluchistan.*

XIII.—*This Act may be called the Indian Constitution (Preliminary Provisions) Act, 194 .*

I do not think that any detailed explanation is necessary for the reader to follow and grasp the conclusions I have endeavoured to embody in this skeleton Act. Perhaps it might be advantageous if I bring out some of the salient features of the proposals to which the projected statute of Parliament is intended to give effect by comparing them with the Cripps proposals.

Who Can Decide?

In my opinion it is no use for Indians to ask and the British Parliament to agree to proceed forthwith to pass an Act conferring Dominion Status or Independence without first disposing of the issue of Pakistan. The Pakistan issue must be treated as a preliminary issue and must be disposed of one way or the other. This is why I have called the proposed Act "The Government of India (Preliminary Provisions) Act." The issue of Pakistan being one of self-determination must be decided by the wishes of the people. It is for this that I propose to take a poll of the Muslims and non-Muslims in the predominantly Muslim Provinces. If the majority of the Muslims are in favour of separation and a majority of non-Muslims are against separation, steps must be taken to delimit the areas wherever it is possible by redrawing provincial boundaries on ethnic and cultural lines by separating the Muslim majority districts from the districts in which the majority consists of non-Muslims. A Boundary Commission is necessary for this purpose. So a Boundary Commission is provided for in the Act. It would be better if the Boundary Commission could be international in its composition.

The scheme of separate referenda of Muslims and non-Muslims is based on two principles which I regard as fundamental. The first is that a minority can demand safeguards for its protection against the tyranny of the majority. It can demand them as a condition precedent. But a minority has no right to put a veto on the right of the majority to decide on questions of ultimate destiny. This is the reason why I have confined the referendum on the establishment of Pakistan to Muslims only. The second is that a communal majority cannot claim a communal minority to submit itself to its dictates. Only a political majority may be permitted to rule a political minority. This principle has been modified in India where a communal minority is placed under a communal majority subject to certain safeguards. But this is as regards the ordinary question of social, economic and political importance. It has never been conceded and can never be conceded that a communal majority has a right to dictate to a communal minority on an issue which is of a constitutional character. That is the reason why I have provided a separate referendum of non-Muslims only, to decide whether they prefer to go in Pakistan or come into Hindustan.

After the Boundary Commission has done its work of delimiting the areas, various possibilities can arise. The Musalmans may stop with the delimitation of the boundaries of Pakistan. They may be satisfied that after all the principle of Pakistan has been accepted—which is what delimitation means. Assuming that the Musalmans are not satisfied with mere delimitation but want to move in the direction of establishing Pakistan there are two courses open to them. They may want to establish Pakistan forthwith or they may agree to live under a common Central Government for a period of say ten years and put the Hindus on their trial. Hindus will have an opportunity to show that the minorities can trust them. The Muslims will learn from experience how far their fears of Hindu Raj are justified. There is another possibility also. The Musalmans of Pakistan having decided to separate forthwith may after a period become so disgusted with Pakistan that they might desire to come back and be incorporated in Hindustan and be one people subject to one single constitution.

These are some of the possibilities I see. These possibilities should in my judgment be kept open for time and circumstances to have their effect. It seems to me to be wrong to say to the Musalmans if you want to remain as part of India then you can never go out or if you want to go then you can never come back. I have in my scheme kept the door open and have provided for both the possibilities in the Act (1) for union after a separation of ten years, (2) for separation for ten years and union thereafter. I personally prefer the second alternative although I have no strong views either way. It would be much better that the Musalmans should have the experience of Pakistan. A union after an experience of Pakistan is bound to be stable and lasting. In case Pakistan comes into existence forthwith, it seems to me necessary that the separation should not altogether be a severance, sharp and complete. It is necessary to maintain live contact between Pakistan and Hindustan so as to prevent any estrangement growing up and preventing the chances of re-union. A Council of India is accordingly provided for in the Act. It cannot be mistaken for a federation. It is not even a confederation. Its purpose is to do nothing more than to serve as a coupling to link Pakistan to Hindustan until they are united under a single constitution.

Such is my scheme. It is based on a community-wise plebiscite. The scheme is flexible. It takes account of the fact that the Hindu sentiment is against it. It also recognizes the fact that the Muslim demand for Pakistan may only be a passing mood. The scheme is not a divorce. It is only a judicial separation. It gives to the Hindus a term. They can use it to show that they can be trusted with authority to rule justly. It gives the Musalmans a term to try out Pakistan.

It might be desirable to compare my proposals with those of Sir Stafford Cripps. The proposals were given out as a serial story in parts. The draft Declaration issued on 29th March 1943 contained only the following:—

> "His Majesty's Government therefore make the following terms:—
>
> (a) Immediately upon cessation of hostilities steps shall be taken to set up in India in manner described hereafter an elected body charged with the task of framing a new constitution for India.
>
> (b) Provision shall be made, as set out below, for participation of Indian States in the constitution-making body.
>
> (c) His Majesty's Government undertake to accept and implement forthwith the constitution so framed subject only to:
>
> (i) The right of any province of British India that is not prepared to accept the new constitution to retain its present constitutional position, provision being made for its subsequent accession if it so decides.
>
> With such non-acceding provinces should they so desire, His Majesty's Government will be prepared to agree upon a new constitution giving them the same full status as the Indian Union and arrived at by a procedure analogous to that here laid down."

Particulars of accession and secession were given in his broadcast. They were in the following terms:—

> "That constitution-making body will have as its object the framing of a single constitution for the whole of India—that is, of British India, together with such of the Indian States as may decide to join in.
>
> "But we realize this very simple fact. If you want to persuade a number of people who are inclined to be antagonistic to enter the same room, it is unwise to tell them that once they go in there is no way out, they are to be forever locked in together.
>
> "It is much wiser to tell them they can go in and if they find they can't come to a common decision, then there is nothing to prevent those who wish, from leaving again by another door. They are much more likely all to go in if they have knowledge that they can by their free will go out again if they cannot agree.
>
> "Well, that is what we say to the provinces of India. Come together to frame a common constitution — if you find after all your discussion and all the give and take of a constitution-making assembly that you cannot overcome your differences and that some provinces are still not satisfied with the constitution, then such provinces can go out and remain out if they wish and just the same degree of self-government and freedom will be available for them as for the Union itself, that is to say complete self-government."

To complete the picture further details were added at the Press Conference. Explaining the plan for accession or secession of provinces Sir Stafford Cripps said:—

> "If at the end of the Constituent Assembly proceedings, any province or provinces did not wish to accept the new constitution and join the Union, it was free to keep out—provided the Provincial Assembly of that province, by a substantial vote say not less than 60 per cent., decided against accession. If it was less than 60 per cent., the minority could claim a plebiscite of the whole province for ascertaining the will of the people. In the case of the plebiscite, a bare majority would be enough. Sir Stafford explained that for completing accession there would have to be a positive vote from the Provincial Assembly concerned. The non-acceding province could, if they wanted, combine into a separate union through a separate Constituent Assembly, but in order to make such a Union practicable they should be geographically contiguous."

The main difference between my plan and that of Sir Stafford Cripps is quite obvious. For deciding the issue of accession or secession which is only another way of saying, will there be or will there not be Pakistan, Sir Stafford Cripps took the Province as a deciding unit. I have taken community as the deciding unit. I have no doubt that Sir Stafford adopted a wrong basis. The Province can be a proper unit if the points of dispute were inter-provincial. For instance, if the points of dispute related to questions such as distribution of taxation, of water, etc., one could understand the Province as a whole or a particular majority in that Province having the right to decide. But the dispute regarding Pakistan is an inter-communal problem which has involved two communities in the same Province. Further the issue in the dispute is not on what terms the two communities will agree to associate in a common political life. The dispute goes deeper and raises the question whether the communities are prepared at all to associate in a common political life. It is a communal difference in its essence and can only be decided by a community-wise plebiscite.

IV

I do not claim any originality for the solution I have proposed. The ideas which underlie it are drawn from three sources, from the Irish Unity Conference at which Horace Plunket presided, from the Home Rule Amending Bill of Mr. Asquith and from the Government of Ireland Act of 1920. It will be seen that my solution of the Pakistan problem is the result of pooled wisdom. Will it be accepted? There are four ways of resolving the conflict which is raging round the question of Pakistan. First is that the British Government should act as the deciding authority. Second is that the Hindus and the Muslims should agree. Third is to submit the issue to an International Board of Arbitration and the fourth is to fight it out by a Civil War.

Although India today is a political mad-house there are I hope enough sane people in the country who would not allow matters to reach the stage of Civil War. There is no prospect of an agreement between political leaders in the near future. The A.I.C.C. of the Indian National Congress at a meeting in Allahabad held in April 1942 on the motion of Mr. Jagat

Narayan Lal resolved* not to entertain the proposal for Pakistan. Two other ways are left to have the problem solved. One is by the people concerned; the other is by international arbitration. This is the way I have suggested. I prefer the former. For various reasons this seems to me the only right course. The leaders having failed to resolve the dispute it is time it was taken to the people for decision. Indeed, it is inconceivable how an issue like that of partition of territory and transference of peoples' allegiance from one government to another can be decided by political leaders. Such things are no doubt done by conquerors to whom victory in war is sufficient authority to do what they like with the conquered people. But we are not working under such a lawless condition. In normal times when constitutional procedure is not in abeyance the views of political leaders cannot have the effect which the *fiats* of dictators have. That would be contrary to the rule of democracy. The highest value that can be put upon the views of leaders is to regard them as worthy to be placed on the agenda. They cannot replace or obviate the necessity of having the matter decided by the people. This is the position which was taken by Sir Stafford Cripps. The stand taken by the Muslim League was, let there be Pakistan because the Muslim League has decided to have it. That position has been negatived by the Cripps proposals and quite rightly. The Muslim League is recognized by the Cripps proposals only to the extent of having a right to propose that Pakistan as a proposition be considered. It has not been given the right to decide. Again it does not seem to have been realized that the decision of an All-India body like the Congress which does not carry with it the active consent of the majority of the people, immediately affected by the issue of Pakistan, cannot carry the matter to solution. What good can it do if Mr. Gandhi or Mr. Rajagopalachariar agreeing or the All-India Congress Committee resolving to concede Pakistan, if it was opposed by the Hindus

---

* The text of the resolution is as follows :—

"The A.I.C.C. is of opinion that any proposal to disintegrate India by giving liberty to any component State or territorial unit to secede from the Indian Union or Federation will be highly detrimental to the best interests of the people of the States and Provinces and the country as a whole and the Congress, therefore, cannot agree to any such proposal."

of the Punjab, or Bengal. Really speaking it is not the business of the people of Bombay or Madras to say, 'let there be Pakistan'. It must be left to be decided by the people who are living in those areas and who will have to bear the consequences of so violent, so revolutionary and so fundamental a change in the political and economic system with which their lives and fortunes have been closely bound up for so many years. A referendum by people in the Pakistan Provinces seems to me the safest and the most constitutional method of solving the problem of Pakistan.

But I fear that solving the question of Pakistan by a referendum of the people howsoever attractive may not find much favour with those who count. Even the Muslim League may not be very enthusiastic about it. This is not because the proposal is unsound. Quite the contrary. The fact is that there is another solution which has its own attractions. It calls upon the British Government to establish Pakistan by the exercise of its sovereign authority. The reason why this solution may be preferred to that which rests on the consent of the people is that it is simple and involves no such elaborate procedure as that of a referendum to the people and has none of the uncertainties involved in a referendum. But there is another ground why it is preferred, namely, that there is a precedent for it. The precedent is the Irish precedent and the argument is that if the British Government by virtue of its sovereign authority divided Ireland and created Ulster why cannot the British Government divide India and create Pakistan?

The British Parliament is the most sovereign legislative body in the world. De L'home, a French writer on English Constitution, observed that there is nothing the British Parliament cannot do except make man a woman and woman a man. And although the sovereignty of the British Parliament over the affairs of the Dominions is limited by the Statute of Westminster it is still unlimited so far as India is concerned. There is nothing in law to prevent the British Parliament from proceeding to divide India as it did in the case of Ireland. It can do it, but will it do it? The question is not one of power but of will.

Those who urge the British Government to follow the

precedent in Ireland should ask what led the British Government to partition Ireland. Was it the conscience of the British Government which led them to sanction the course they took or was it forced upon them by circumstances to which they had to yield? A student of the history of Irish Home Rule will have to admit that the partition of Ireland was not sanctioned by conscience but by the force of circumstances. It is not often clearly realized that no party to the Irish dispute wanted partition of Ireland. Not even Carson, the Leader of Ulster. Carson was opposed to Home Rule but he was not in favour of partition. His primary position was to oppose Home Rule and maintain the integrity of Ireland. It was only as a second line of defence against the imposition of Home Rule that he insisted on partition. This will be quite clear from his speeches both inside and outside the House of Commons. Asquith's Government on the other side was equally opposed to partition. This may be seen from the proceedings in the House of Commons over the Irish Home Rule Bill of 1912. Twice amendments were moved for the exclusion of Ulster from the provisions of the Bill, once in the Committee stage by Mr. Agar-Roberts and again on the third reading by Carson himself. Both the times the Government opposed and the amendments were lost.

Permanent partition of Ireland was effected in 1920 by Mr. Lloyd George in his Government of Ireland Act. Many people think that this was the first time that partition of Ireland was thought of and that it was due to the dictation of the Conservative—Unionists in the Coalition Government of which Mr. Lloyd George was the nominal head. It may be true that Mr. Lloyd George succumbed to the influence of the predominant party in his coalition. But it is not true that partition was thought of in 1920 for the first time. Nor is it true that the Liberal Party had not undergone a change and shown its readiness to favour partition as a possible solution. As a matter of fact partition as a solution came in 1914 six years before Mr. Lloyd George's Act when the Asquith Government, a purely Liberal Government, was in office. The real cause which led to the partition of Ireland can be understood only by examining the factors which made the Liberal Government of Mr. Asquith change its mind. I feel certain that the factor which brought about this change in the viewpoint of the Liberal Government was the Military crisis which took place in March 1914 and which is generally referred to as the "Curragh Incident". A few facts will be sufficient to explain what the "Curragh Incident" was and how decisive it was in bringing about a change in the policy of the Asquith Government.

To begin at a convenient point the Irish Home Rule Bill had gone through all its stages by the end of 1913. Mr. Asquith who had been challenged that he was proceeding without a mandate from the electorate had however given an undertaking that the Act would not be given effect to until another general election had been held. In the ordinary course there would have been a general election in 1915 if the War had not supervened. But the Ulstermen were not prepared to take their chance in a general election and started taking active steps to oppose Home Rule. They were not always very scrupulous in choosing their means and their methods and under the seductive pose that they were fighting against the Government which was preventing them from remaining loyal subjects of the King they resorted to means which nobody would hesitate to call shameless and nefarious. There was one Maginot Line on which the Ulstermen always depended for defeating Home Rule. That was the House of Lords. But by the Parliament Act of 1911 the House of Lords had become a Wailing Wall neither strong nor high. It had ceased to be a line of defence to rely upon. Knowing that the Bill might pass notwithstanding its rejection by the House of Lords, feeling that in the next election Asquith might win, the Ulstermen had become desperate and were searching for another line of defence. They found it in the Army. The plan was twofold. It included the project of getting the House of Lords to hold up the Annual Army Act so as to ensure that there would be no Army in existence to be used against Ulster. The second project was to spread their propaganda—That Home Rule will be Home Rule—in the Army with a view to preparing the Army to disobey the Government in case Government decided to use the Army for forcing Home Rule on Ireland. The first became unnecessary as they succeeded easily in bringing about the second. This became clear in March 1914 when there occurred the Curragh Incident. The Government had reasons to suspect that certain Army depots in Ireland were likely to be raided by the Unionist Volunteers. On March 20th, orders were sent to Sir Arthur Paget, Commander-in-Chief of the Forces in Ireland, to take steps to safeguard these depots. His reply was a telegram to the effect that officers were not prepared to obey and were resigning their commissions and it was feared that men would refuse to move. General Sir Hubert Gough had refused to serve against the Ulster Unionists and his example had been followed by others. The Government realized that the Army had become political,* nay, partisan. It took fright and decided in favour of partition acting on the wellk-nown maxim that wisdom is the better part of valour. What made Asquith change his position was not conscience but the fright of the Army rebelling. The fright was so great that no one thereafter felt bold enough to challenge the Army and enforce Home Rule without partition.

Can His Majesty's Government be depended upon to repeat in India what it did in Ireland? I am unable to answer the question. But two things I will say. The first thing is that His Majesty's Government knows full well what have been the consequences of this partition of Ireland. The Irish Free State has become the most irreconcilable enemy of Great Britain. The enmity knows no limits. The wound caused by partition will never be healed so long as partition remains a settled fact. The Partition of Ireland cannot but be said to be morally indefensible inasmuch as it was the result not of the consent of the people but of superior force. It was as bad as the murder of Duncan by Macbeth. The blood stains left on His Majesty's Government are as deep as those on Lady Macbeth and of which Lady Macbeth said that "All the perfumes of Arabia" had failed to remove the stink. That His Majesty's Government does not like to be responsible for the execution of another deed

* On this point see *Life of Field-Marshal Sir Henry Wilson* by Major General Sir C. E. Callwell, Vol. I, Chapter IX; also Parliamentary Debates (House of Lords), 1914, Vol. 15, pp. 998-1017, on Ulster and the Army. This shows that the Army had been won over by the Ulsterites long before the Curragh Incident. It is possible that Mr. Asquith decided in 1913 to bring in an Amending Bill to exclude Ulster from Home Rule for six years because he had become aware that the Army had gone over to Ulster and that it could not be used for enforcing Home Rule.

of partition is quite clear from its policy with the Jew-Arab problem in Palestine. It appointed the Peel Commission to investigate. The Commission recommended partition of Palestine. The Government accepted it in principle as the most hopeful line of solving the deadlock. Suddenly the Government realized the gravity of forcing such a solution on the Arabs and appointed another Royal Commission called the Woodhead Commission which condemned partition and opened an easy way to a Government which was anxious to extricate itself from a terrible position. The partition of Ireland is not a precedent worthy to be followed. It is an ugly incident which requires to be avoided. It is a warning and not an example. I doubt very much if His Majesty's Government will partition India on its own authority at the behest of the Muslim League.

And why should His Majesty's Government oblige the Muslim League? In the case of Ulster there was the tie of blood which made a powerful section of the British politicians take the side of Ulster. It was this tie of blood which made Lord Curzon say "You are compelling Ulster to divorce her present husband, to whom she is not unfaithful and you are compelling her to marry someone else who she cordially dislikes, with whom she does not want to live." There is no such kinship between His Majesty's Government and the Muslim League and it would be a vain hope for the League to expect His Majesty's Government to take her side.

The other thing I would like to say is that it would not be in the interests of the Muslim League to achieve its object by invoking the authority of His Majesty's Government to bring about the partition of India. In my judgment more important than getting Pakistan is the procedure to be adopted in bringing about Pakistan if the object is that after partition Pakistan and Hindustan should continue as two friendly States with goodwill and no malice towards each other.

What is the procedure which is best suited for the realization of this end? Everyone will agree that the procedure must be such that it must not involve victory to one community and

* See Parliamentary Debates (Commons), 1938-39, Vol. 341, pp. 1987-2107; also Lords) 1936-37, Vol. 106, pp. 599-674.

humiliation to the other. The method must be of peace with honour to both sides. I do not know if there is another solution better calculated to achieve this end than the decision by a referendum of the people. I have made my suggestion as to which is the best course. Others also will come forth with theirs. I cannot say that mine is the best. But whatever the suggestion be unless good sense as well as a sense of responsibility is brought to bear upon the solution of this question it will remain a festering sore.

EPILOGUE

Here I propose to stop. For I feel that I have said all that I can say about the subject. To use legal language I have drawn the pleadings. This I may claim to have done at sufficient length. In doing so, I have adopted that prolix style so dear to the Victorian lawyers, under which the two sides plied one another with plea and replication, rejoinder and rebutter, sur-rejoinder and surrebutter and so on. I have done this deliberately with the object that a full statement of the case for and against Pakistan may be made. The foregoing pages contain the pleadings. The facts contained therein are true to the best of my knowledge and belief. I have also given my findings. It is now for Hindus and Muslims to give theirs.

To help them in their task it might be well to set out the issues. On the pleadings the following issues seem to be necessary issues:

(1) Is Hindu-Muslim unity necessary for India's political advancement? If necessary, is it still possible of realization notwithstanding the new ideology of the Hindus and the Muslims being two different nations?

(2) If Hindu-Muslim unity is possible, should it be reached by appeasement or by settlement?

(3) If it is to be achieved by appeasement, what are the new concessions that can be offered to the Muslims to obtain their willing co-operation, without prejudice to other interests?

(4) If it is to be achieved by a settlement, what are the terms of that settlement? If there are only two alternatives, (i) Division of India into Pakistan and Hindustan, or (ii) Fifty-fifty share in Legislature, Executive and the Services, which alternative is preferable?

(5) Whether India, if she remained one integral whole, can rely upon both Hindus and Musalmans to defend her independence, assuming it is won from the British?

(6) Having regard to the prevailing antagonism between Hindus and Musalmans and having regard to the new ideology demarcating them as two distinct nations and postulating an

opposition in their ultimate destinies, whether a single constitution for these two nations can be built in the hope that they will show an intention to work it and not to stop it?

(7) On the assumption that the two-nation theory has come to stay, will not India as one single unit become an incoherent body without organic unity, incapable of developing into a strong united nation bound by a common faith in a common destiny and therefore likely to remain a feeble and sickly country, easy to be kept in perpetual subjection either of the British or of any other foreign power ?

(8) If India cannot be one united country, is it not better that Indians should help India in the peaceful dissolution of this incoherent whole into its natural parts, namely, Pakistan and Hindustan ?

(9) Whether it is not better to provide for the growth of two independent and separate nations, a Muslim nation inhabiting Pakistan and a Hindu nation inhabiting Hindustan, than pursue the vain attempt to keep India as one undivided country in the false hope that Hindus and Muslims will some day be one and occupy it as the members of one nation and sons of one motherland ?

Nothing can come in the way of an Indian getting to grips with these issues and reaching his own conclusions with the help of the material contained in the foregoing pages except three things: (1) A false sentiment of historical patriotism, (2) a false conception of the exclusive ownership of territory and (3) absence of willingness to think for oneself. Of these obstacles, the last is the most difficult to get over. Unfortunately thought in India is rare and free thought is rarer still. This is particularly true of Hindus. That is why a large part of the argument of this book has been addressed to them. The reasons for this are obvious. The Hindus are in a majority. Being in a majority, their viewpoint must count. There is not much possibility of peaceful solution if no attempt is made to meet their objections rational or sentimental. But there are special reasons which have led me to address so large a part of the argument to them and which may not be quite so obvious to others. I feel that those Hindus who are guiding the destinies of their fellows have lost what Carlyle calls "the Seeing Eye" and are walking in the glamour of certain vain illusions, the consequences of which must, I fear, be terrible for the Hindus. The Hindus are in the grip of the Congress and the Congress is in the grip of Mr. Gandhi. It cannot be said that Mr. Gandhi has given the Congress the right lead. Mr. Gandhi first sought to avoid facing the issue by taking refuge in two things. He started by saying that to partition India is a moral wrong and a sin to which he will never be a party. This is a strange argument. India is not the only country faced with the issue of partition or shifting of frontiers based on natural and historical factors to those based on national factors. Poland has been partitioned three times and no one can be sure that there will be no more partition of Poland. There are very few countries in Europe which have not undergone partition during the last 150 years. This shows that the partition of a country is neither moral nor immoral. It is unmoral. It is a social, political or military question. Sin has no place in it.

As a second refuge Mr. Gandhi started by protesting that the Muslim League did not represent the Muslims and that Pakistan was only a fancy of Mr. Jinnah. It is difficult to understand how Mr. Gandhi could be so blind as not to see how Mr. Jinnah's influence over the Muslim masses has been growing day by day and how he has engaged himself in mobilizing all his forces for battle. Never before was Mr. Jinnah a man for the masses. He distrusted them.* To exclude them from political power he was always for a high franchise. Mr. Jinnah was never known to be a very devout, pious or a professing Muslim. Besides kissing the Holy Koran as and when he was sworn in as an M.L.A., he does not appear to have bothered much about its contents or its special tenets. It is doubtful if he frequented any mosque either out of curiosity or religious fervour. Mr. Jinnah was never found in the midst of Muslim mass congregations, religious or political. Today one finds a complete change in Mr. Jinnah. He has become a man of the masses. He is no longer above them. He is among them. Now they have raised him above themselves and call him their Qaid-e-Azam. He has not only become a believer in Islam, but is prepared to die for Islam. Today, he knows more of Islam than mere *Kalama*. Today, he goes to the mosque to hear *Khutba* and takes delight in joining the *Id* congregational prayers. Dongri and Null Bazaar once knew Mr. Jinnah by name. Today they know him by his presence. No Muslim

* Pandit Jawaharlal Nehru in his autobiography says that Mr. Jinnah wanted the Congress to restrict its membership to matriculates.

meeting in Bombay begins or ends without Allah-ho-Akbar and Long Live Qaid-e-Azam. In this Mr. Jinnah has merely followed King Henry IV of France—the unhappy father-in-law of the English King Charles I. Henry IV was a Huguenot by faith. But he did not hesitate to attend mass in a Catholic Church in Paris. He believed that to change his Huguenot faith and go to mass was an easy price to pay for the powerful support of Paris. As Paris became worth a mass to Henry IV, so have Dongri and Null Bazaar become worth a mass to Mr. Jinnah and for similar reason. It is strategy; it is mobilization. But even if it is viewed as the sinking of Mr. Jinnah from reason to superstition, he is sinking with his ideology which by his very sinking is spreading into all the different strata of Muslim society and is becoming part and parcel of its mental make-up. This is as clear as anything could be. The only basis for Mr. Gandhi's extraordinary view is the existence of what are called Nationalist Musalmans. It is difficult to see any real difference between the communal Muslims who form the Muslim League and the Nationalist Muslims. It is extremely doubtful whether the Nationalist Musalmans have any real community of sentiment, aim and policy with the Congress which marks them off from the Muslim League. Indeed many Congressmen are alleged to hold the view that there is no difference between the two and that the Nationalist Muslims inside the Congress are only an outpost of the communal Muslims. This view does not seem to be quite devoid of truth when one recalls that the late Dr. Ansari, the leader of the Nationalist Musalmans, refused to oppose the Communal Award although it gave the Muslims separate electorates in teeth of the resolution passed by the Congress and the Nationalist Musalmans. Nay, so great has been the increase in the influence of the League among the Musalmans that many Musalmans who were opposed to the League have been compelled to seek for a place in the League or make peace with it. Anyone who takes account of the turns and twists of the late Sir Sikandar Hyat Khan and Mr. Fazlul Huq, the late Premier of Bengal, must admit the truth of this fact. Both Sir Sikandar and Mr. Fazlul Huq were opposed to the formation of branches of the Muslim League in their Provinces when Mr. Jinnah tried to revive it in 1937. Notwithstanding their opposition, when the branches of the League were formed in the Punjab and in Bengal within one year both were compelled to join them. It is a case of those coming to scoff remaining to pray. No more cogent proof seems to be necessary to prove the victory of the League.

Notwithstanding this Mr. Gandhi instead of negotiating with Mr. Jinnah and the Muslim League with a view to a settlement, took a different turn. He got the Congress to pass the famous Quit India Resolution on the 8th August 1942. This Quit India Resolution was primarily a challenge to the British Government. But it was also an attempt to do away with the intervention of the British Government in the discussion of the Minority question and thereby securing for the Congress a free hand to settle it on its own terms and according to its own lights. It was in effect, if not in intention, an attempt to win independence by bypassing the Muslims and the other minorities. The Quit India Campaign turned out to be a complete failure. It was a mad venture and took the most diabolical form. It was a scorch-earth campaign in which the victims of looting, arson and murder were Indians and the perpetrators were Congressmen. Beaten, he started a fast for twenty-one days in March 1943 while he was in gaol with the object of getting out of it. He failed. Thereafter he fell ill. As he was reported to be sinking the British Government released him for fear that he might die on their hand and bring them ignominy. On coming out of gaol, he found that he and the Congress had not only missed the bus but had also lost the road. To retrieve the position and win for the Congress the respect of the British Government as a premier party in the country which it had lost by reason of the failure of the campaign that followed up the Quit India Resolution, and the violence which accompanied it, he started negotiating with the Viceroy. Thwarted in that attempt, Mr. Gandhi turned to Mr. Jinnah. On the 17th July 1944 Mr. Gandhi wrote to Mr. Jinnah expressing his desire to meet him and discuss with him the communal question. Mr. Jinnah agreed to receive Mr. Gandhi in his house in Bombay. They met on the 9th September 1944. It was good that at long last wisdom dawned on Mr. Gandhi and he agreed to see the light which was staring him in the face and which he had so far refused to see.

The basis of their talks was the offer made by Mr. Rajagopalachariar to Mr. Jinnah in April 1944 which, according to the somewhat incredible* story told by Mr. Rajagopalachariar, was discussed by him with Mr. Gandhi in March 1943 when he (Mr. Gandhi) was fasting in gaol and to which Mr. Gandhi had given his full approval. The following is the text of Mr. Rajagopalachariar's formula popularly spoken of as the C. R. Formula :—

(1) *Subject to the terms set out below as regards the constitution for Free India, the Muslim League endorses the Indian demand for Independence and will co-operate with the Congress in the formation of a provisional interim government for the transitional period.*

(2) *After the termination of the war, a commission shall be appointed for demarcating contiguous districts in the north-west and east of India, wherein the Muslim population is in absolute majority. In the areas thus demarcated, a plebiscite of all the inhabitants held on the basis of adult suffrage or other practicable franchise shall ultimately decide the issue of separation from Hindustan. If the majority decide in favour of forming a sovereign State separate from Hindustan, such decision shall be given effect to, without prejudice to the right of districts on the border to choose to join either State.*

(3) *It will be open to all parties to advocate their points of view before the plebiscite is held.*

(4) *In the event of separation, mutual agreements shall be entered into for safeguarding defence, and commerce and communications and for other essential purposes.*

(5) *Any transfer of population shall only be on an absolutely voluntary basis.*

(6) *These terms shall be binding only in case of transfer by Britain of full power and responsibility for the governance of India.*

* The formula was discussed with Mr. Gandhi in March 1943 but was not communicated to Mr. Jinnah till April 1944.

Epilogue

The talks which began on the 9th September were carried on over a period of 18 days till 27th September when it was announced that the talks had failed. The failure of the talks produced different reactions in the minds of different people. Some were glad, others were sorry. But as both had been, just previous to the talks, worsted by their opponents in their struggle for supremacy, Gandhi by the British and Jinnah by the Unionist Party in the Punjab, and had lost a good deal of their credit the majority of people expected that they would put forth some constructive effort to bring about a solution. The failure may have been due to the defects of personalities. But it must however be said that failure was inevitable having regard to certain fundamental faults in the C. R. Formula. There are many faults in the C. R. Formula. In the first place, it tied up the communal question with the political question in an indissoluble knot. No political settlement, no communal settlement, is the strategy on which the formula proceeds. The formula did not offer a solution. It invited Mr. Jinnah to enter into a deal. It was a bargain—"If you help us in getting independence, we shall be glad to consider your proposal for Pakistan." I don't know from where Mr. Rajagopalachariar got the idea that this was the best means of getting independence. It is possible that he borrowed it from the old Hindu kings of India who built up alliances for protecting their independence against foreign enemies by giving their daughters to neighbouring princes. Mr. Rajagopalachariar forgot that such alliances brought neither a good husband nor a permanent ally. To make communal settlement depend upon help rendered in winning freedom is a very unwise way of proceeding in a matter of this kind. It is a way of one party drawing another party into its net by offering communal privileges as a bait. The C. R. Formula made communal settlement an article for sale.

The second fault in the C. R. Formula relates to the machinery for giving effect to any agreement that may be arrived at. The agency suggested in the C. R. Formula is the Provisional Government. In suggesting this Mr. Rajagopalachariar obviously overlooked two difficulties. The first thing he overlooked is that once the Provisional Government was established, the promises of the contracting parties, to use legal phraseology, did not remain concurrent promises. The case became one of an executed promise against an executory promise. By consenting to the establishment of a Provisional Government, the League would have executed its promise to help the Congress to win independence. But the promise of the Congress to bring about Pakistan would remain executory. Mr. Jinnah who insists, and quite rightly, that the promises should be concurrent could never be expected to agree to place himself in such a position. The second difficulty which Mr. Rajagopalachariar has overlooked is what would happen if the Provisional Government failed to give effect to the Congress part of the agreement. Who is to enforce it? The Provisional Government is to be a sovereign government, not subject to any superior authority. If it was unwilling to give effect to the agreement, the only sanction open to the Muslims would be rebellion. To make the Provisional Government the agency for forging a new Constitution, for bringing about Pakistan, nobody will accept. It is a snare and not a solution. The only way of bringing about constitutional changes will be through an Act of Parliament embodying provisions agreed upon by the important elements in the national life of British India. There is no other way.

There is a third fault in the C. R. Formula. It relates to the provision for a treaty between Pakistan and Hindustan to safeguard what are called matters of common interests such as Defence, Foreign Affairs, Customs, etc. Here again Mr. Rajagopalachariar does not seem to be aware of obvious difficulties. How are matters of common interest to be safeguarded? I see only two ways. One is to have a Central Government vested with Executive and Legislative authority in respect of these matters. This means Pakistan and Hindustan will not be sovereign States. Will Mr. Jinnah agree to this? Obviously he does not. The other way is to make Pakistan and Hindustan sovereign States and to bind them by a treaty relating to matters of common interests. But what is there to ensure that the terms of the treaty will be observed? As a sovereign State Pakistan can always repudiate it even if it was a Dominion. Mr. Rajagopalachariar obviously drew his inspiration in drafting this clause from the Anglo-Irish Treaty of 1922. But he forgot the fact that the treaty lasted so long as Ireland was not a Dominion and that as soon as it became a Dominion it repudiated the treaty and the British Parliament stood silent and grinned, for it knew that it could do nothing.

One does not mind very much that the talks failed. What one feels sorry for is that the talks failed without giving us a clear idea of some of the questions about which Mr. Jinnah has been observing discreet silence in his public utterances, though he has been quite outspoken about them in his private talks. These questions are—(1) Is Pakistan to be conceded because of the Resolution of the Muslim League? (2) Are the Muslims, as distinguished from the Muslim League, to have no say in the matter? (3) What will be the boundaries of Pakistan? Whether the boundaries will be the present administrative boundaries of the Punjab and Bengal or whether the boundaries of Pakistan will be ethnological boundaries? (4) What do the words "subject to such territorial adjustments as may be necessary" which occur in the Lahore Resolution mean? What were the territorial adjustments the League had in mind? (5) What does the word "finally" which occurs in the last part of the Lahore Resolution mean? Did the League contemplate a transition period in which Pakistan will not be an independent and sovereign State? (6) If Mr. Jinnah's proposal is that the boundaries of Eastern and Western Pakistan are to be the present administrative boundaries, will he allow the Scheduled Castes, or, if I may say so, the non-Muslims in the Punjab and Bengal to determine by a plebiscite whether they wish to be included in Mr. Jinnah's Pakistan and whether Mr. Jinnah would be prepared to abide by the results of the plebiscite of the non-Muslim elements in the Punjab and Bengal? (7) Does Mr. Jinnah want a corridor running through U. P. and Bihar to connect up Eastern Pakistan to Western Pakistan? It would have been a great gain if straight questions had been put to Mr. Jinnah and unequivocal answers obtained. But instead of coming to grips with Mr. Jinnah on these questions, Mr. Gandhi spent his whole time proving that the C. R. Formula is substantially the same as the League's Lahore Resolution—which was ingenious if not nonsensical and thereby lost the best opportunity he had of having these questions clarified.

After these talks Mr. Gandhi and Mr. Jinnah have retired to their pavilions as players in a cricket match do after their game is over, as though there is nothing further to be done. There is no indication whether they will meet again and if so when. What next? is not a question which seems to worry them. Yet it is difficult to see how India can make any political advance without a solution of the question of Pakistan. The question of Pakistan is not an academic question which one may refuse to discuss. It does not belong to that class of questions about which people can agree to differ. It is a question for which solution will have to be found. How? It must be by agreement or by arbitration. If it is to be by agreement, it must be the result of negotiations—of give and take and not of surrender by one side to the other. That is not agreement. It is dictation. Good sense may in the end prevail and parties may come to an agreement. But agreement may turn out to be a very dilatory way. It may take long before good sense prevails. How long one cannot say. The political freedom of India is a most urgent necessity. It cannot be postponed and yet without a solution of the communal problem it cannot be hastened. To make it dependent on agreement is to postpone its solution indefinitely. Another expeditious method must be found. It seems to me that arbitration by an International Board is the best way out. The disputed points in the minorities problem including that of Pakistan should be remitted to such a Board. The Board should be constituted of persons drawn from countries outside the British Empire. Each statutory minority in India—Muslims, Scheduled Castes, Sikhs, Indian Christians—should be asked to select its nominee to this Board of Arbitration. These minorities as also the Hindus should appear before the Board in support of their demands and should agree to abide by the decision given by the Board. The British should give the following undertakings:—

(1) That they will have nothing to do with the communal settlement. It will be left to agreement or to a Board of Arbitration.

(2) They will implement the decision of the Board of Arbitration on the communal question by embodying it in the Government of India Act.

(3) That the award of the International Board of Arbitration would be regarded by them as a sufficient discharge of their obligations to the minorities in India and would agree to give India Dominion Status.

The procedure has many advantages. It eliminates the fear of British interference in the communal settlement which has been offered by the Congress as an excuse for its not being able to settle the communal problem. It is alleged that, as there is always the possibility of the minorities getting from the British something more than what the Congress thinks it proper to give, the minorities do not wish to come to terms with the Congress. The proposal has a second advantage. It removes the objection of the Congress that by making the constitution subject to the consent of the minorities, the British Government has placed a veto in the hands of the minorities over the constitutional progress of India. It is complained that the minorities can unreasonably withhold their consent or they can be prevailed upon by the British Government to withhold their consent as the minorities are suspected by the Congress to be mere tools in the hands of the British Government. International arbitration removes completely every ground of complaint on this account. There should be no objection on the part of the minorities. If their demands are fair and just no minority need have any fear from a Board of International Arbitration. There is nothing unfair in the requirement of a submission to arbitration. It follows the well known rule of law, namely, that no man should be allowed to be a judge in his own case. There is no reason to make any exception in the case of a minority. Like an individual it cannot claim to sit in judgment over its own case. What about the British Government? I cannot see any reason why the British Government should object to any part of this scheme. The Communal Award has brought great odium on the British. It has been a thankless task and the British should be glad to be relieved of it. On the question of the discharge of their responsibilities for making adequate provision for the safety and security of certain communities in respect of which they have regarded themselves as trustees before they relinquish their sovereignty what more can such communities ask than the implantation in the constitution of safeguards in terms of the award of an International Board of Arbitration? There is only one contingency which may appear to create some difficulty for the British Government in the matter of enforcing the award of the Board of Arbitration. Such a contingency can arise if any one of the parties to the dispute is not prepared to submit its case to arbitration. In that case the question will be : will the British Government be justified in enforcing the award against such a party? I see no difficulty in saying that the British Government can with perfect justice proceed to enforce the award against such a party. After all what is the status of a party which refuses to submit its case to arbitration? The answer is that such a party is an aggressor. How is an aggressor dealt with? By subjecting him to sanctions. Implementing the award of the Board of Arbitration in a constitution against a party which refuses to go to arbitration is simply another name for the process of applying sanctions against an aggressor. The British Government need not feel embarrassed in following this process if the contingency should arise. For it is a well recognized process of dealing with such cases and has the imprimatur of the League of Nations which evolved this formula when Mussolini refused to submit to arbitration his dispute with Abyssinia. What I have proposed may not be the answer to the question : What next ? I don't know what else can be. All I know is that there will be no freedom for India without an answer. It must be decisive, it must be prompt and it must be satisfactory to the parties concerned.

LIST OF APPENDICES

MAPS

APPENDIX I

Population of India by Communities

Communities	British India	Indian States and Agencies	Total
1. Hindus	150,890,146	55,227,180	206,117,326
2. Muslims	79,398,503	12,659,593	92,058,096
3. Scheduled Castes* ...	39,920,807	8,892,373	48,813,180
4. Tribal	16,713,256	8,728,233	25,441,489
5. Sikhs	4,165,097	1,526,350	5,691,447
6. Christians :			
(*i*) Indian Christians ...	1,655,982	1,413,808	3,069,790
(*ii*) Anglo-Indians ...	113,936	26,486	140,422
(*iii*) Others	75,751	7,708	83,459
7. Jains	578,372	870,914	1,449,286
8. Buddhists	167,413	64,590	232,003
9. Parsees	101,968	12,922	114,890
10. Jews	19,327	3,153	22,480
11. Others	371,403	38,474	409,877
Total ...	294,171,961	89,471,784	383,643,745

* This is a statutory designation given to the untouchables by the Government of India Act, 1935.

NOTE.—The figures for the Scheduled Castes both for British India and Indian States do not give the correct totals. The figures for Ajmer-Merwara in British India and for Gwalior State are not included in the totals. The Census Reports for 1940 fail to give these figures.

APPENDIX II

COMMUNAL DISTRIBUTION OF POPULATION BY MINORITIES IN THE PROVINCES OF BRITISH INDIA

Provinces	Total Population	Muslims Population	Muslims Per-centage	Scheduled Castes Popula-tion	Scheduled Castes Per-centage	Indian Christians Popula-tion	Indian Christians Per-centage	Sikhs Popula-tion	Sikhs Per-centage
1. Ajmere-Merwara	583,693	89,899	15·4	Nil (?)	..	3,895	·8	867	·15
2. Andaman Nicobar	33,768	8,005	23·7	Nil	..	779	2·3	744	2·2
3. Assam	10,204,733	3,442,479	33·7	676,291	6·6	37,750	·4	3,464	·03
4. British Baluchistan	501,631	438,930	87·5	5,102	1·0	2,633	·5	11,918	2·3
5. Bengal	60,306,525	33,005,434	54·7	7,878,970	13·0	110,923	·2	16,281	·03
6. Bihar*	36,340,151	4,716,314	12·9	4,840,379	13·3	24,693	·07	13,213	·04
7. Bombay	20,849,840	1,920,368	9·2	1,855,148	8·9	338,812	1·6	8,011	·04
8. Central Provinces & Berar† ...	16,813,584	783,697	4·7	3,051,413	18·1	48,260	·3	14,996	·09
9. Coorg	168,726	14,780	8·8	25,740	15·3	3,309	2·0	Nil	..
10. Delhi	917,939	304,971	33·2	121,693	13·3	10,494	1·1	16,157	1·8
11. Madras	49,341,810	3,896,452	7 9	8,068,492	16·4	2,001,082	4·06	418	·001
12. N.-W. F. P.	3,038,067	2,788,797	91·8	Nil	..	5,426	·2	57,989	1·9
13. Orissa	8,728,544	146,301	1·7	1,238,171	14·2	26,584	·3	232	·003
14. Punjab	28,418,819	16,217,242	57·0	1,248,635	4·4	486,038	1.7	3,757,401	13·2
15. Panth Piploda	5,267	251	4·8	918	17·4	216	4·1	Nil	..
16. Sind	4,229,221	3,054,635	72·2	191,634	4·5	13,232	·3	31,011	·7
17. United Provinces @ ...	55,020,617	8,416,308	15.3	11,717,158	21·3	131,327	·2	232,445	·4
Total ...	295,502 935	79,344,863	26·9	40,919,744	13·9	3,245,453	1·0	4,155,147	1·0
* Bihar	28,823,802	4,168,470	14·4	3,919,619	13·6	12,651	·04	3,204	·01
Chota Nagpur	7,516,349	547,844	7·3	420,760	5·6	12,042	·2	10,009	·1
+ C. P.	13,208,718	448,528	3·4	2,359,836	17·9	42,135	·3	12,766	·1
Berar	3,604,866	335,169	9·3	691,577	19·2	6,125	·2	2,230	·05
@ Agra	40,903,147	6,231,062	15·2	8,018,803	19·6	120,549	·3	226,096	·5
Oudh	14,114,470	2,185,246	15.5	3,698,355	26·2	10,778	·08	6,349	·05

APPENDIX III

COMMUNAL DISTRIBUTION OF POPULATION BY MINORITIES IN INDIAN STATES

	States and Agencies	Total Population	Muslims		Scheduled Castes		Indian Christians		Sikhs	
			Population	Per-centage	Population	Per-centage	Population	Per-centage	Population	Per-centage
1.	Assam	725,655	31,662	4·4	265	0·04	25,913	3.6	381	·05
2.	Baluchistan	356.204	346,251	97·2	65	0·02	40	·01	126	·04
3.	Baroda	2,855,010	223,610	7·8	230,794	8·1	9,182	·3	566	·02
4.	Bengal	2,144,829	372,113	17·3	269,729	12·6	564	·03	28	·001
5.	Central India	7,506,427	439,850	5·9	1,027,009	13·7	7,582	·1	2,731	·04
6.	Chattisgarh	4,050,000	28,773	0·7	483,132	11·9	11,820	·3	507	·01
7.	Cochin	1,422,875	109,188	7·7	141,154	9·9	399,394	28·1	9	..
8.	Deccan (and Kolhapur) ...	2,785,428	182,036	6·5	306,898	11·0	17,236	·6	22	·001
9.	Gujarat	1,458,702	58,000	3·9	55,204	3·8	4,215	·3	182	·01
10.	Gwalior	4,006,159	240,903	6·0	..	..	1,352	·03	2,342	·06
11.	Hyderabad	16,338,534	2,097,475	12·8	2,928,048	17·9	215,989	1·3	5,330	·03
12.	Kashmir and Feudatories	4,021,616	3,073,540	76·4	113,464	2·8	3,079	·08	65,903	1·6
13.	Madras	498,754	30,263	6.0	83,734	16·8	20,806	4·2	5	..
14.	Mysore	7,329,140	485,230	6·6	1,405,067	19·2	98,580	1·3	269	·004
15.	N.-W.F.P.	46,267	22,069	47·7	Nil	..	571	1·2	4,472	9·1
16.	Orissa	3,023,731	14,355	0·47	352,088	11·6	2,249	·07	151	·005
17.	Punjab	5,503,554	2,251,459	40·9	349,962	6·4	6,952	·1	1,342,685	24·4
18.	Punjab Hill	1,090,644	46,678	4·3	238,774	21·9	188	·02	17,739	1·6
19.	Rajputana	13,670,208	1,297,841	9·5	..	..	4,349	·03	81,896	·6
20.	Sikkim	121,520	83	0·07	76	·06	34	·03	1	..
21.	Travancore	6,070,018	434,150	7·2	395,952	6·5	1,958,491	32·3	31	..
22.	U.P.	928,470	273,625	29·5	152,927	16·5	1,281	·1	731	·08
23.	Western India	4,904,156	600,440	12·2	358,038	7·3	3,105	·06	239	·005
	Total ...	91,310,571	15,733,133	16·59	8,892,373	9·7	2,794,959	3·1	1,526,350	1·7

APPENDIX IV

Communal Distribution of Population in the Punjab by Districts

	Districts	Total Population	Muslims Population	Muslims Percentage	Scheduled Castes Population	Scheduled Castes Percentage	Indian Christians Population	Indian Christians Percentage	Sikhs Population	Sikhs Percentage	Hindus Population	Hindus Percentage
1.	Hissar	1,006,709	285,208	28·3	128,240	12·7	1,235	·1	60,731	6·0	524,602	52·1
2.	Rohtak	956,399	166,569	17·4	135,103	14·1	1,026	·1	1,466	·2	645,371	57·5
3.	Gurgaon	851,458	285,992	33·6	119,250	14·0	1,457	·2	637	·07	441,287	51·8
4.	Karnal	994,575	304,346	30·6	136,713	13·7	1,223	·1	19,887	2·0	529,588	53·2
5.	Ambala	847,745	268,999	31·7	124,006	14·6	4,892	·6	153,543	18·1	288,652	34·0
6.	Simla	38,576	7,022	18·2	7,092	18·4	508	1·3	1,032	2·7	22,374	58·0
7.	Kangra	899,377	43,249	4·8	121,622	13·5	590	·07	4,809	·5	725,909	80·7
8.	Hoshiyarpur ...	1,170,323	380,759	32·5	170 855	14·6	6,060	·5	198,194	16·9	413,837	35·4
9.	Jullundar ...	1,127,190	509,804	45·2	154,431	13·7	5,971	·5	298,744	26·5	156,579	13·9
10.	Ludhiana	818,615	302,482	36·9	68,469	8·4	1,632	·2	341,175	41·7	106,246	12·9
11.	Ferozpore	1,423,076	641,448	45·1	73,504	5·1	11,031	·8	479,486	33·7	216,229	15·2
12.	Lahore	1,695,375	1,027,772	60·6	32,735	1·9	67,686	4·0	310,648	18·3	252,004	14·9
13.	Amritsar	1,413,876	657,695	46·5	22,750	1·6	25,330	1·8	510,845	36·1	194,727	13·8
14.	Gurdaspur	1,153,511	589,923	51·1	45,839	4·0	40,262	4·4	221,251	19·2	244,935	21·2
15.	Sialkot	1,190,497	739,218	62·1	65,354	5·5	73,846	6·2	139,409	11·7	165,965	13·9
16.	Gujranwalla ...	912,235	642,706	70·5	7,485	·8	60,380	6·6	99,139	10·9	100,630	11·0
17.	Shakhupura ...	852,508	542,344	63.6	22,438	2·6	59,985	7.0	160,706	18·9	66,744	7·8
18.	Gujarat	1,104,[illegible]52	945,609	85·6	4,621	·4	4,391	·4	70,233	6·3	80,022	7·2
19.	Shahapur	998,921	835,918	83·7	9,693	1·0	12,690	1·3	48,046	4·8	92,479	9·2
20.	Jhealam	629,658	563,033	89·4	771	·1	730	·1	24,680	3·9	40,117	6·4
21.	Rawalpindi .	785,231	628,193	80·0	4,233	·5	4,212	·5	64,127	8·2	78,245	10·0
22.	Attock	675,875	611,128	90·4	1,015	·1	504	·09	20,102	3·0	42,194	6·2
23.	Mianwali	506,321	436,260	86·2	1,008	·2	324	·06	6,865	1·3	61,806	12·2
24.	Montgomery ...	1,329,103	918,564	69·1	43,456	3·2	24,101	1·9	175,064	13·2	167,510	12·6
25.	Lyallpore	1,396,305	877,518	62·8	68,222	4·9	51,694	3·7	262,737	18·8	135,637	9·7
26.	Jhang	821,631	678,736	82·6	1,943	·2	744	·1	12,238	1·5	127,946	15·6
27.	Multan	1,484,333	1,157,911	78·0	24,530	1·7	13,270	·9	61,628	4·1	225,342	15·2
28.	Muzaffargarh ...	712,849	616,074	86·4	2,691	·4	218	·03	5,882	·8	87,952	12·3
29.	Dera Gazi Khan ...	581,350	512,678	88·1	1,059	·2	46	·01	1,072	·2	66,348	11·4
30.	Transfrontier Tract	40,246	40,084	99·6	Nil	..	Nil	..	2	..	160	·4
	Total ...	28,418,820	16,217,242	57·1	1,592,320	5·6	486,038	1·7	3,757,401	13·2	6,301,737	22·2

APPENDIX V

Communal Distribution of Population in Bengal by Districts

Districts	Total Population	Muslims Population	Muslims Per-centage	Scheduled Castes Population	Scheduled Castes Per-centage	Hindus Population	Hindus Per-centage	Indian Christians Population	Indian Christians Per-centage
1. Burdwan	1,890,732	336,665	17·8	430,300	22·8	963,520	51·0	3,280	·2
2. Birbhum	1,048,317	287,310	27·4	280,254	26·7	406,182	38·8	344	·03
3. Bankura	1,289,640	55,564	4·3	355,290	27·5	723,269	56·1	1,216	·1
4. Midnapore	3.190,647	246.559	7·7	339,066	10·6	2,342,897	73·4	3,834	·1
5. Hooghly	1,377,729	207,077	15·0	245,810	17·8	853,734	61·9	543	·04
6. Howrah	1 490,304	296,325	19·9	184,318	12·4	1,000,548	67·1	994	·06
7. 24-Parganas	3,536,386	1,148,180	32·5	743,397	21·0	1,566,599	44·3	20,823	·6
8. Calcutta	2,108,891	497,535	23·6	55,228	2·6	1,476,284	70·0	16,431	·8
9. Nadia	1,759,846	1,078,007	61·3	143,682	8·2	514,268	29·2	10,749	·6
10. Murshidabad	1,640,530	927,747	56·6	167,184	10·2	517,803	31·6	394	·02
11. Khulna	1,943,218	959,172	49·4	470,550	24·2	507,143	26·1	3,538	·2
12. Rajashahi	1,571,750	1,173,285	74·6	75,650	4·8	253,580	16·1	1,166	·07
13. Dinajpur	1,926,833	967,246	50·2	399,410	20·7	375,212	19·5	1,448	·07
14. Jalpaiguri	1,089,513	251,460	23·1	325,504	29·9	226,143	20·8	2,589	·2
15. Darjeeling	376,369	9,125	2·4	28,922	7 7	149,574	39·7	2,599	·7
16. Raugpur	2,877,847	2,055,186	71·4	495,462	17·2	307,387	10·7	389	·01
17. Bogra	1,260,463	1,057,902	83·9	61,303	4·9	126,229	10·0	286	·02
18. Pabna	1,705,072	1,313,968	77·1	114,738	6·7	269,017	15·8	285	·02
19. Malda	1,232,618	699,945	56·7	75,535	6·1	390,143	31·6	466	·04
20. Dacca	4,222,143	2,841,261	67·3	409,905	9·7	950,227	22·5	15,846	·4
21. Mymensingh	6,023,758	4,664,548	77·4	340,676	5·7	955,962	15·9	2,322	·04
22. Faridpur	2,888,803	1,871,336	64·4	527,496	18·3	478,742	16·6	9,549	·3
23. Bakargunj	3,549,010	2,567,027	72·3	427,667	12·1	480,962	13·6	9,357	·2
24. Tippera	3,860,139	2,975,901	77·1	227,643	5·9	652,318	16·9	428	·01
25. Naokhali	2,217,402	1,803,937	81·3	81,817	3·7	330,494	14·9	535	·02
26. Chittagong	2,153,296	1,605,183	74·5	57,024	2·6	401,050	18·6	395	·02
27. Chittagong Hill Tracts	247,053	7,270	2,9	283	·1	4,598	1·9	60	·02
28. Jessore	1,828,216	1,100,713	60·2	314,856	17·2	406,223	22·2	1,057	·06
Total ..	60,306,525	33,005,434	54·7	7,378,970	12·2	17,630,054	29·3	110,923	·2

APPENDIX VI

Communal Distribution of Population in Assam by Districts

Districts	Total Population	Muslims		Scheduled Castes		Indian Christians		Sikhs		Hindus	
		Population	P. C.	Popula-tion	P. C.	Popula-tion	P. C.	Popula-tion	P. C.	Popula-tion	P. C.
Surma Valley											
1. Kachahar ..	641,181	232,950	36·3	51,961	8·1	3,744	·6	..	..	173,855	27·1
2. Sylhet ..	3,116,602	1,892,117	60·7	364,510	11·7	2,590	·08	..	..	785,004	25·2
3. Khasi and Jantia Hills ..	118,665	1,555	1·3	63	·05	120	·1	..	..	12,676	10·7
4. Naga Hills ..	189,641	531	·2	45	·02	9	..	..	..	4,153	2·2
5. Lushai Hills ..	152,786	101	·06	22	·01	Nil	..	..	..	2,425	1·6
Assam Valley											
6. Goalpara ..	1,014,285	468,924	46·2	23,434	2·3	269	·03	..	..	282,789	27·9
7. Kamrup ..	1,264,200	361,522	39·1	59,092	4·7	1,038	·08	..	..	637,457	50·4
8. Darang ..	736,791	120,995	16·4	19,475	2·6	6,367	·8	..	..	328,283	44·6
9. Nowgong ..	710,800	250,113	35·2	59,214	8·3	4,049	·6	..	..	229,137	32·2
10. Sibsagar ..	1,074,741	51,769	4·8	50,184	4·7	15,268	1·4	..	..	593,007	55·2
11. Lakmipur ..	894,842	44,579	5·0	43,527	4·9	3,786	·4	..	..	457,509	51·1
12. Garo Hills ..	233,569	10,398	4·5	789	·3	1	..	..	..	13,518	5·8
13. Sadiya Frontier Tract ..	60,118	864	1·4	3,991	6·6	486	·8	..	..	14,605	24·3
14. Balipara Frontier Tract ..	6,512	61	·9	74	1·1	23	·4	..	..	2,514	38·6
Total ..	10,204,733	3,442,479	33·7	676,291	6·6	37,750	·4	3,464	·03	3,536,932	34·6

APPENDIX VII

N.-W. F. Province

Proportion of Muslim Population by Districts

Districts	Total Population	Total Muslim Population	P. C. of Muslim Population to Total	Total Non-Muslim Population	P. C. of Non-Muslim to Total
Hazara	796,230	756,004	94·9	40,226	5·1
Mardan	506,539	483,575	96·5	22,964	4·5
Peshawar	851,833	769,589	90·4	82,244	9·6
Kohat	289,404	266,224	92·0	23,180	8·0
Bannu	295,930	257,648	87·1	38,282	12·9
D. I. Khan	298,131	255,757	85·8	42,374	14·2

APPENDIX VIII

N.-W. F. PROVINCE

Proportion of Muslim to Non-Muslim Population in Towns

C = Cantonment. M = Municipality. N.A. = Notified Area.

Towns by Districts			Total Population	Total Muslim Population	Percentage of Muslims to Total	Total Non-Muslim Population	Percentage of Non-Muslims to Total
	Hazara						
1.	Abbottabad ...	C.	13,866	3,331	24	10,535	7·6
2.	Abbottabad ...	M.	13,558	8,861	66·1	4,697	33·9
3.	Haripur ...	M.	9,322	5,174	55·5	4,148	44·5
4.	Baffa ...	N.A.	7,988	7,166	89·7	822	10·3
5.	Nawanshehr ...	N.A.	6,414	5,075	79·1	1,339	20·9
6.	Kot Najibullah	...	5,315	4,228	79·5	2,087	20·5
7.	Mansehra ...	...	10,217	8,141	79·7	1,076	20·3
	Mardan						
8.	Mardan ...	M.	39,200	28,994	73·9	10,206	26·1
9.	Mardan ...	C.	3,294	1,307	39·7	1,987	60·3
	Peshawar						
10.	Peshawar ...	M.	1,30,967	1,04,650	79·9	26,317	20·1
11.	Peshawar ...	C.	42,453	18,322	43·2	24,131	56·8
12.	Nowshera ...	N.A.	17,491	16,976	97	515	3
13.	Nowshera ...	C.	26,531	11,256	42·4	15,275	57·6
14.	Risalpur ...	C.	9,009	3,506	38·9	5,503	61·1
15.	Cherat ...	C.	337	270	80·1	67	19·9
16.	Charsada ...	...	16,945	15,747	92·9	1,198	7·1
17.	Utamanzai ...	...	10,129	9,768	96·4	361	3·6
18.	Tangi ...	...	12,906	12,456	96·5	450	3·5
19.	Parang ...	...	13,496	13,494	99·9	2	...
	Kohat						
20.	Kohat ...	M.	34,316	27,868	81·2	6,448	18·8
21.	Kohat ...	C.	10,661	4,243	39·8	6,418	60·2
	Bannu						
22.	Bannu ...	M.	33,210	8,507	25·6	24,703	74·4
23.	Bannu ...	C.	5,294	2,189	41·4	3,105	58·6
24.	Lakki ...	N.A.	10,141	5,883	58	4,258	42
	Dera Ismail Khan						
25.	D. I. Khan ...	M.	49,238	25,443	51·7	23,795	48·3
26.	D. I. Khan ...	C.	2,068	981	47·4	1,087	52·6
27.	Kulachi ...	N.A.	8,840	6,610	74·8	2,230	25·2
28.	Tauk ...	N.A.	9,089	5,531	60·8	3,558	39·2

APPENDIX IX

SIND

DISTRIBUTION OF MUSLIM POPULATION BY DISTRICTS

Districts	Total Population	Total Muslim Population	P. C. of Muslims to Total	Total Non-Muslims	P. C. of Non-Muslims to Total
1	2	3	4	5	6
1. Dadu	389,380	329,991	84·7	59,389	15·3
2. Hyderabad ...	758,748	507,620	66·9	251,128	33·1
3. Karachi... ...	713,900	457,035	64·0	256,865	36·0
4. Larkana ...	511,208	418,543	81·9	92,665	18·1
5. Nawabshah ...	584,178	436,414	74·7	147,764	25·3
6. Sukkur	692,556	491,634	71·0	200,922	29·0
7. Thar Parkar ...	581,004	292,025	50·3	288,979	49·7
8. Upper Sind Frontier	304,034	275,063	90·5	28,971	9·5
Total * ...	4,553,008	3,208,325	70·7	1,326,683	29·3.

* This is exclusive of the population of Khairpur State.

APPENDIX X

SIND

Proportion of Muslim to Non-Muslim Population in Towns

M=Municipality; Cl. C.=Civil Cantonment; Mily. C.=Military Cantonment

Towns by Districts	Total Population	Total Muslim Population	P. C. of Muslims to Total	Total Non-Muslim Population	P.C. of Non-Muslims to Total
1	2	3	4	5	6
Dadu					
1. Dadu ... M.	10,996	5,279	48	5,717	52·0
2. Kotri ... M.	9,979	5,137	51·5	4,842	48·5
3. Manjhand ... M.	3,025	1,053	34·8	1,972	65·2
4. Sehwan ... M.	4,364	2,218	50·8	2,146	49·2
Hyderabad					
5. Hala ... M.	7,960	5,042	63·3	2,918	36·7
6. Hyderabad ... M.	1,27,521	31,983	25·1	95,538	74·9
7. Hyderabad ... Cl. C.	5,255	2,667	50·7	2,588	49·3
8. Hyderabad ..Mily. C.	1,917	1,419	74	498	26
9. Matiari ... M.	5,910	4,339	73·4	1,571	26·6
10. Nasarpur ... M.	3,810	2,331	61·2	1,479	38·8
11. Tando Allahyar M.	8,406	1,690	20·1	6,716	79·9
12. Tando Mahomed Khan ... M.	8,718	2,902	33·3	5,816	66·7
Karachi					
13. Karachi ... M.	3,58,492	1,52,365	42·5	2,06,127	57·5
14. Karachi ... Cl. C.	5,854	895	15·3	4,959	84·7
15. Daigh Road ... Cl. C.	2,881	1,172	40·7	1,709	59·3
16. Manora ... Cl. C.	2,533	932	36·8	1,601	63·2
17. Karachi ..Mily. C.	15,895	7,063	44·4	8,832	5·56
18. Tatta ... M.	8,262	4,198	50·8	4,064	49·2
Larkana					
19. Kambar ... M.	11,681	6,297	53·1	5,384	46·9
20. Larkana ... M.	20,390	7,834	38·4	12,556	61·6
21. Ratedero ... M.	9,925	2,393	24·1	7,532	75·9
Nawabshah					
22. Nawabshah ... M.	17,509	4,420	25·3	13,089	74.7
23. Shahabadpur ... M.	11,786	1,898	16·1	9,888	83·9
24. Tando Adam ... M.	17,233	2,994	17·4	14,239	82·6
Sukkur					
25. Ghari Yasin ... M.	8,397	2,895	34·5	5,502	65·5
26. Ghotki ... M.	5,236	1,533	29·3	3,703	70·7
27. Rohri ... M.	14,721	4,132	28·7	10,589	71·9
28. Shikarpur ... M.	67,746	21,775	32·1	45,971	67·9
29. Sukkur ... M.	66,466	18,152	27·3	48,314	72·7
Thar Parkar					
30. Mirpurkhas ... M.	19,591	5,086	25·9	14,505	74·1
31. Umarkot ... M.	4,275	986	22·9	3,289	77·1
Upper Sind Frontier					
32. Jacobabad ... M.	21,588	9,774	45·3	11,814	54·7

APPENDIX XI

LANGUAGES USED IN INDIA BY MUSLIMS IN ORDER OF IMPORTANCE

(*According to Census of 1921*)

Urdu (Western Hindi)	20,791,000
Bengali	23,995,000
Punjabi	7,700,000
Sindhi	2,912,000
Kashmiri (and allied languages) ...	1,500,000
Pushtu	1,460,000
Gujarati	1,400,000
Tamil	1,250,000
Malayalam	1,107,000
Telugu	750,000
Oriya	400,000
Baluchi	224,000
Brahui	122,000
Arabic	42,000
Persian	22,000
Other languages...	5,060,000
Total ...	68,735,000

APPENDIX XII

Address* presented to H. E. Lord Minto, Viceroy and Governor-General of India

by

A Deputation of the Muslim Community of India on 1st October 1906 at Simla

ADDRESS

"May it please your Excellency,—Availing ourselves of the permission accorded to us, we, the undersigned nobles, jagirdars, taluqdars, lawyers, zemindars, merchants and others representing a large body of the Mahomedan subjects of His Majesty the King-Emperor in different parts of India, beg most respectfully to approach your Excellency with the following address for your favourable consideration.

* This document has a great importance and significance in the history of India. It marks the beginning of the British Government's policy of giving favourable treatment to the Muslims in the administration of India which, it is alleged, was intended to wean them away from the Congress and to create a breach and disunity between the Hindus and the Musalmans. It has also acquired a certain amount of notoriety in the minds of the Indians in view of the statement made by late Maulana Mohammad Ali in his address as President of the Congress, stating that "it was a command performance", meaning thereby that the address was arranged by the British Government. On this account there has been a great deal of curiosity on the part of many Indians to know the text of the address and the reply given by Lord Minto. I had made a long search to obtain the same. I had even approached elderly Muslim politicians prominent in those days for a copy but none of them had it or knew where it was available. Newspapers of that day do not appear to have carried the text of the address and the reply. I was however lucky to get a copy of it from my friend Sir Raza Ali, M.L.A. (Central), who happened to have kept a cutting of the *Indian Daily Telegraph*—a paper then published from Lucknow but had long ago become defunct, in which the full text of the address as well as of the reply was printed. I am grateful to Sir Raza Ali for a loan of the cutting. As the document marks a historic event in the political history of British administration in India, it might be of some interest to reproduce details about the function which the Simla correspondent of the *Indian Daily Telegraph* had published in its issue of October 3rd, 1906. Says the correspondent:—

We fully realise and appreciate the incalculable benefits conferred by British rule on the teeming millions belonging to diverse races and professing diverse religions who form the population of the vast continent of India, and have every reason to be grateful for the peace, security, personal freedom and liberty of worship that we now enjoy. Further, from the wise and enlightened character of the Government, we have every reasonable ground for anticipating that these benefits will be progressive, and that India will in the future occupy an increasingly important position in the comity of nations.

"The representatives of the Mahomedan community who were to present the address to His Excellency the Viceroy this morning at Viceregal Lodge collected in the Ballroom at 11 A.M. They numbered thirty-five and were seated in a horse-shoe facing His Excellency's chair. Precisely at 11 A.M. Lord Minto, preceded by his staff, entered the room, all standing to receive him. His Excellency was taken round and personally introduced to each member by the Aga Khan. The Khalifa from Patiala then asked permission for the presentation of the address and the Aga Khan then advanced and facing His Excellency read the petition given below, all the representatives standing."

Those who formed the deputation were: His Highness Aga Sir Sultan Mahomed Shah Aga Khan, G.C.I.E., (Bombay), Shahzadah Bakhtiar Shah, O.I.E., Head of the Mysore family, Calcutta; Hon'ble Malik Omar Hayat Khan, C.I.E., Lieutenant 17th Prince of Wales' Tiwana Lancers, Tiwana, Shahpur (Punjab); Hon'ble Khan Bahadur Mian Mohomed Shah Din, Bar.-at-Law, Lahore; Hon'ble Maulvi Sharfuddin, Bar.-at-Law, Patna; Khan Bahadur Syed Nawab Ali Chowdhury, Mymensingh (Eastern Bengal); Nawab Bahadur Syed Amir Husan Khan, C.I.E., Calcutta; Naseer Hussain Khan Khayal, Calcutta; Khan Bahadur Mirza Shujaat Ali Beg; Persian Consul-General, Murshidabad, Calcutta (Bengal); Syed Ali Imam, Bar.-at-Law, Patna (Behar); Nawab Sarfraz Husain Khan, Patna (Behar); Khan Bahadur Ahmad Mohiuddin Khan, Stipendiary of the Carnatic family (Madras); Maulvi Rafiuddin Ahmed, Bar.-at-Law (Bombay); Ebrahimbhoy Adamji Peerbhoy, General Merchant (Bombay); Mr. Abdur Rahim, Bar.-at-Law, Calcutta; Syed Allahdad Shah, Special Magistrate and Vice-President, Zamindars' Association, Khairpore (Sindh); Maulana H. M. Malak, Head of Mehdi Bazh Bohras, Nagpur (Central Provinces); Mushir-ud-Doula Mumtazal-ul-Mulk Khan Bahadur Khalifa Syed Mohamed Hussain, Member of the State Council of Patiala (Punjab); Khan Bahadur Col. Abdul Majid Khan, Foreign Minister, Patiala (Punjab); Khan Bahadur Khwaja Kusuf Shah, Hony. Magistrate, Amritsar (Punjab); Mian Mahomed Shafi, Bar.-at-Law, Lahore (Punjab); Shaikh Ghulam Sadik, Amritsar (Punjab); Hakim Mohamed Ajmul Khan, Delhi (Punjab); Munshi Ihtisham Ali, Zamindar and Rais, Kakori (Oudh); Syed Nabi Ullah, Bar.-at-Law, Rais Kara, Dist. Allahabad; Maulvi Syed Karamat Husain, Bar.-at-Law, Allahabad; Syed Abdulraoof, Bar.-at-Law, Allahabad; Munshi Abdur Salam Khan, retired Sub-Judge, Rampur; Khan Bahadur Mohamad Muzammil Ullah Khan, Zamindar, Secretary, Zamindars' Association, United Provinces, and Joint

One of the most important characteristics of British policy in India is the increasing deference that has so far as possible been paid from the first to the views and wishes of the people of the country in matters affecting their interests, with due regard always to the diversity of race and religion which forms such an important feature of all Indian progress.

Claims of the Community

Beginning with the confidential and unobtrusive method of consulting influential members of important communities in different parts of the country, this principle was gradually extended by the recognition of the right of recognised political or

---

Secretary, M. A. O. College Trustees, Aligarh; Haji Mohamed Ismail Khan, Zamindar, Aligarh; Sahabzadas Aftab Ahmad Khan, Bar.-at-Law, Aligarh; Maulvi Mushtaq Hussain, Rais, Amroha, United Provinces; Maulvi Habibul Rahaman Khan, Zamindar, Bhikhanpur, United Provinces; Nawab Syed Sirdar Ali Khan, son of the late Nawab Sirdar Diler-Ul-mulk Bahadur, C.I.E., Hyderabad (Deccan); Maulvi Syed Mahdee Ally Khan (Muhsin-ul-Mulk), Hony. Secretary, M. A. O. College, Aligarh, Etawah, United Provinces.

The following gentlemen intended to have attended the presentation of the address to the Viceroy, but were prevented by illness or other causes:— Hon'ble Nawab Khwaja Salimulla, Nawab of Dacca, Hon'ble Nawab Haji Mohamed Fateh Ali Khan, Qazelbash, Lahore; Hon'ble Syed Zainul-Edros, Surat, Khan Bahadur Kasim Mir Ghayasuddin Peerzadah of Broach; Khan Bahadur Raja Jahandad of Hazara and Shaik Shahid Hussain of Lucknow.

The correspondent of the *Telegraph* adds:—

Lady Minto, the Ladies Elliot and the Hon. Mrs. Hewett were present at the function.

At the presentation of the address today most of the deputies wore ordinary European dress with a fez as distinguishing head-dress, but the Patiala representatives, Lieut. Hon. Malik Omar Hayat Khan, Khan Bahadur Ali Choudhary, Khan Bahadur Ahmad Mohiuddin Khan and a few others, were in Indian dress, while a few others wore uniforms with gold lace. His Excellency the Viceroy was in morning dress with the Order of the Star of India on his frock coat.

GARDEN PARTY AT VICEREGAL LODGE

This afternoon a garden party was held in the Viceregal Lodge grounds when the Mahomedan representatives were received by the Viceroy, who spoke with each deputy individually.

The Hon. Mr. Baker, Financial Secretary, has invited the following Bengal gentlemen of the Mahomedan deputation to lunch tomorrow:—

Nawab Amir Hosein, Mirza Shujat Ali, Nawab Nasar Hossein, Hon. Shurfuddin and Ali Imam.

commercial organisations to communicate to the authorities their criticisms and views on measures of public importance, and finally by the nomination and election of direct representatives of the people in Municipalities, District Boards, and above all in the Legislative Chambers of the country. This last element is, we understand, about to be dealt with by the Committee appointed by your Excellency with the view of giving it further extension, and it is with reference mainly to our claim to a fair share in such extended representation and some other matters of importance affecting the interests of our community, that we have ventured to approach your Excellency on the present occasion.

Past Traditions

The Mahomedans of India number, according to the census taken in the year 1901, over sixty-two millions or between one-fifth and one-fourth of the total population of His Majesty's Indian dominions, and if a reduction be made for the uncivilised portions of the community enumerated under the heads of animist and other minor religions, as well as for those classes who are ordinarily classified as Hindus but properly speaking are not Hindus at all, the proportion of Mahomedans to the Hindu majority becomes much larger. We therefore desire to submit that under any system of representation extended or limited a community in itself more numerous than the entire population of any first class European power except Russia may justly lay claim to adequate recognition as an important factor in the State.

We venture, indeed, with your Excellency's permission to go a step further, and urge that the position accorded to the Mahomedan community in any kind of representation, direct or indirect, and in all other ways affecting their status and influence should be commensurate, not merely with their numerical strength, but also with their political importance and the value of the contribution which they make to the defence of the empire, and we also hope that your Excellency will in this connection be pleased to give due consideration to the position which they occupied in India a little more than hundred years ago and of which the traditions have naturally not faded from their minds.

The Mahomedans of India have always placed implicit reliance on the sense of justice and love of fair dealing that have characterised their rulers, and have in consequence abstained from pressing their claims by methods that might prove at all embarrassing, but earnestly as we desire that the Mahomedans of India should not in the future depart from that excellent and time-honoured tradition, recent events have stirred up feelings, especially among the younger generation of Mahomedans, which might, in certain circumstances and under certain contingencies easily pass beyond the control of temperate counsel and sober guidance.

We therefore pray that the representations we herewith venture to submit, after a careful consideration of the views and wishes of a large number of our co-religionists in all parts of India, may be favoured with your Excellency's earnest attention.

European representative institutions

We hope your Excellency will pardon our stating at the outset that representative institutions of the European type are new to the Indian people; many of the most thoughtful members of our community in fact consider that the greatest care, forethought and caution will be necessary if they are to be successfully adapted to the social, religious and political conditions obtaining in India, and that in the absence of such care and caution their adoption is likely, among other evils, to place our national interests at the mercy of an unsympathetic majority. Since, however, our rulers have, in pursuance of the immemorial instincts and traditions, found it expedient to give these institutions an increasingly important place in the Government of the country, we Mahomedans, cannot any longer in justice to our own national interests hold aloof from participating in the conditions to which their policy has given rise. While, therefore, we are bound to acknowledge with gratitude that such representation as the Mahomedans of India have hitherto enjoyed has been due to a sense of justice and fairness on the part of your Excellency and your illustrious predecessor in office and the heads of Local Governments by whom the Mahomedan members of Legislative Chambers have almost without exception been nominated, we cannot help observing that the representation thus accorded to us has necessarily been inadequate to our requirements, and has not always carried with it the approval of those whom the nominees were selected to represent. This state of things was probably under existing circumstances unavoidable, for while on the one hand the number of nominations reserved to the Viceroy and Local Governments has necessarily been strictly limited, the selection on the other hand of really-representative men, has, in the absence of any reliable method of ascertaining the direction of popular choice, been far from easy.

The Results of Election

As for the results of election, it is most unlikely that the name of any Mahomedan candidate will ever be submitted for the approval of Government by the electoral bodies as now constituted unless he is in sympathy with the majority in all matters of importance. Nor can we in fairness find fault with the desire of our non-Muslim fellow-subjects to take full advantage of their strength and vote only for members of their own community, or for persons who, if not Hindus, are expected to vote with the Hindu majority on whose goodwill they would have to depend for their future re-election. It is true that we have many and important interests in common with our Hindu fellow-countrymen and it will always be a matter of the utmost satisfaction to us to see these interests safeguarded by the presence in our Legislative Chambers of able supporters of these interests, irrespective of their nationality.

A DISTINCT COMMUNITY

Still, it cannot be denied that we Mahomedans are a distinct community with additional interests of our own which are not shared by other communities, and these have hitherto suffered from the fact that they have not been adequately represented. Even in the provinces in which the Mahomedans constitute a distinct majority of the population, they have too often been treated as though they were inappreciably small political factors that might without unfairness be neglected. This has been the case, to some extent, in the Punjab, but in a more marked degree in Sind and in Eastern Bengal.

Before formulating our views with regard to the election of representatives, we beg to observe that the political importance of a community to a considerable extent gains strength or suffers detriment according to the position that the members of that community occupy in the service of the State. If, as is unfortunately the case with the Mahomedans, they are not adequately represented in this manner, they lose in the prestige and influence which are justly their due.

Employment in Government Service

We therefore pray that Government will be graciously pleased to provide that both in the gazetted and the subordinate and ministerial services of all Indian provinces a due proportion of Mahomedans shall always find place. Orders of like import have at times been issued by Local Governments in some provinces, but have not, unfortunately, in all cases been strictly observed on the ground that qualified Mahomedans were not forthcoming. This allegation, however well founded it may have been at one time, is, we submit, no longer tenable now, and wherever the will to employ them is not wanting the supply of qualified Mahomedans, we are happy to be able to assure your Excellency, is equal to the demand.

The Competitive Element

Since, however, the number of qualified Mahomedans has increased, a tendency is unfortunately perceptible to reject them on the ground of relatively superior qualifications having to be given precedence. This introduces something like the competitive element in its worst form, and we may be permitted to draw your Excellency's attention to the political significance of the monopoly of all official influence by one class. We may also point out in this connection that the efforts of Mahomedan educationists have from the very outset of the educational movement among them been strenuously directed towards the development of character, and this we venture to think is of greater importance than mere mental alertness in the making of good public servants.

Mahomedans on the Bench

We venture to submit that the generality of Mahomedans in all parts of India feel aggrieved that Mahomedan Judges are not more frequently appointed to the High Courts and Chief Courts of Judicature. Since the creation of these Courts only three Mahomedan lawyers have held these honourable appointments, all of whom have fully justified their elevation to the Bench. At the present moment there is not a single Mahomedan Judge sitting on the Bench of any of these Courts, while there are three Hindu Judges in the Calcutta High Court, where the proportion of Mahomedans in the population is very large, and two in the Chief Court of the Punjab, where the Mahomedans form the majority of the population. It is not, therefore, an extravagant request on our part that a Mahomedan should be given a seat on the Bench of each of the High Courts and Chief Courts. Qualified Mahomedan lawyers eligible for these appointments can always be found, if not in one province then in another. We beg permission further to submit that the presence on the Bench of these Courts of a Judge learned in the Mahomedan Law will be a source of considerable strength to the administration of justice.

Municipal Representation

As Municipal and District Boards have to deal with important local interests affecting to a great extent the health, comfort, educational needs and even the religious concerns of the inhabitants, we shall, we hope, be pardoned if we solicit for a moment your Excellency's attention to the position of Mahomedans thereon before passing to higher concerns. These institutions form, as it were, the initial rungs in the ladder of self-government, and it is here that the principle of representation is brought home intimately to the intelligence of the people, yet the position of Mahomedans on these Boards is not at present regulated by any guiding principle capable of general application, and practice varies in different localities. The Aligarh Municipality, for example, is divided into six wards and each ward returns one Hindu and one Mahomedan Commissioner, and the same principle we understand is adopted in a number of Municipalities in the Punjab and elsewhere, but in a good many places the Mahomedan tax-payers are not adequately represented. We would, therefore, respectfully suggest that the local authority should in every case be required to declare the number of Hindus and Mahomedans entitled to seats on Municipal and District Boards, such proportion to be determined in accordance with the numerical strength, social status, local influence and special requirements of either community. Once their relative proportion is authoritatively determined, we would suggest that either community should be allowed severally to return their own representatives as is the practice in many towns in the Punjab.

Fellows of Universities

We would also suggest that the Senates and Syndicates of Indian Universities might be similarly dealt with, that is to say, there should, so far as possible, be an authoritative declaration of the proportion in which Mahomedans are entitled to be represented in either body.

Nomination to Provincial Councils

We now proceed to the consideration of the question of our representation in the Legislative Chambers of the country. Beginning with the Provincial Councils, we would most respectfully suggest that as in the case of Municipalities and District Boards the proportion of Mahomedan representatives entitled to seats should be determined and declared with due regard to the important considerations which we have ventured to point out in paragraph 5 of this address, and that the important Mahomedan landowners, lawyers, merchants and representatives of other important interests, the Mahomedan members of District Boards and Municipalities and the Mahomedan graduates of universities of a certain standing, say five years, should be formed into Electoral Colleges and be authorised, in accordance with such rules of procedure as your Excellency's Government may be pleased to prescribe in that behalf, to return the number of members that may be declared to be eligible.

The Viceroy's Council

With regard to the Imperial Legislative Council whereon the due representation of Mahomedan interests is a matter of vital importance, we crave leave to suggest (1) that in the cadre of the Council the proportion of Mahomedan representatives should not be determined on the basis of the numerical strength of the community, and that in any case the Mahomedan representatives should never be an ineffective minority; (2) that as far as possible, appointment by election should be given preference over nomination; (3) that for the purposes of choosing Mahomedan members, Mahomedan landowners, lawyers, merchants and representatives of other important interests of a status to be subsequently determined by your Excellency's Government, Mahomedan members of the Provincial Councils and Mahomedan fellows of universities should be invested with electoral powers to be exercised in accordance with such procedure as may be prescribed by your Excellency's Government in that behalf.

The Executive Council

An impression has lately been gaining ground that one or more Indian Members may be appointed on the Executive Council of the Viceroy. In the event of such appointment being made we beg that the claims of Mahomedans in that connection may not be overlooked. More than one Mahomedan, we venture to say, will be found in the country fit to serve with distinction in that august chamber.

A Mahomedan University

We beg to approach your Excellency on a subject which must closely affect our national welfare. We are convinced that our aspirations as a community and our future progress are largely dependent on the foundation of a Mahomedan University which will be the centre of our religious and intellectual life. We therefore most respectfully pray that your Excellency will take steps to help us in an undertaking in which our community is so deeply interested.

In conclusion, we beg to assure your Excellency that in assisting the Mahomedan subjects of His Majesty at this stage in the development of Indian affairs in the directions indicated in the present address, your Excellency will be strengthening the basis of their unswerving loyalty to the Throne and laying the foundation of their political advancement and national prosperity, and your Excellency's name will be remembered with gratitude by their posterity for generations to come, and we feel confident that your Excellency will be gracious enough to give due consideration to our prayers. We have the honour to subscribe ourselves, Your Excellency's most obedient and humble servants.

LORD MINTO'S REPLY

Appreciation of Mahomedan aspirations

After the address, His Excellency rose and delivered a most sympathetic reply, which was frequently punctuated with cheers and cries of "Hear, hear" from the members of the deputation, particularly when his Excellency declared that he was entirely in accord with the views of the deputation that any electoral system must take cognizance of the various religious beliefs of this great Empire and that the British Government would always in the future as in the past safeguard the political rights of the different communities entrusted to their charge. The Viceroy concluded by thanking the deputation for affording him the unique opportunity of meeting so many representative men.

The Viceroy said :—

Your Highness and Gentlemen, Allow me before I attempt to reply to the many considerations your address embodies, to welcome you heartily to Simla. Your presence here to-day is very full of meaning. To the document which you have presented me are attached the signatures of nobles, of Ministers of various States, of great landowners, of lawyers, of merchants and of many others of His Majesty's subjects. I welcome the representative character of your deputation as expressing the views and aspirations of the enlightened Muslim community of India. I feel that all you have said emanates from a representative body basing its opinions on a matured consideration of the existing political conditions of India, totally apart from the small personal or political sympathies and antipathies of scattered localities, and I am grateful to you for the opportunity you are affording me of expressing my appreciation of the just aims of the followers of Islam and their determination to share in the political history of our Empire.

As your Viceroy, I am proud of the recognition you express of the benefits conferred by British rule on the diverse races of many creeds who go to form the population of this huge continent. You yourselves, the descendants of a conquering and ruling race, have told me to-day of your gratitude for the personal freedom, the liberty of worship, the general peace and the hopeful future which British administration has secured for India.

Help in the Past

It is interesting to look back on early British efforts to assist the Mahomedan population to qualify themselves for the public service. In 1782 Warren Hastings founded the Calcutta Madrassah with the intention of enabling its students to compete on more equal terms with the Hindus for employment under Government. In 1811 my ancestor, Lord Minto, advocated improvements in the Madrassah and the establishment of Mahomedan Colleges at other places throughout India. In later years the efforts of the Mahomedan Association led to the Government resolution of 1885 dealing with the educational position of the Mahomedan community and their employment in the public service, whilst Mahomedan educational effort has culminated in the College of Aligarh that great institution which the noble and broad-minded devotion of Sir Syed Ahmed Khan has dedicated to his co-religionists.

The Aligarh College

It was in July 1877 that Lord Lytton laid the foundation-stone of Aligarh, when Sir Syed Ahmed Khan addressed these memorable words to the Viceroy: "The personal honour which you have done me assures me of a great fact and fills me with feelings of a much higher nature than mere personal gratitude. I am assured that you, who upon this occasion represent the British rule, have sympathies with our labours and this assurance is very valuable and a source of great happiness. At my time of life it is a comfort to me to feel that the undertaking which has been for many years, and is now the sole object of my life has roused on the one hand the energies of my own countrymen, and on the other has won the sympathy of our British fellow-subjects and the support of our rulers, so that when the few years I may still be spared are over, and when I shall be no longer amongst you, the College will still prosper and succeed in educating my countrymen to have the same affection for their country, the same feelings of loyalty for the British rule, the same appreciation of its blessings, the same sincerity of friendship with our British fellow-subjects as have been the ruling feelings of my life."

Sir Syed's Influence

Aligarh has won its laurels. Its students have gone forth to fight the battle of life strong in the tenets of their own religion, strong in the precepts of loyalty and patriotism, and now when there is much that is critical in the political future of India the inspiration of Sir Syed Ahmed Khan and the teachings of Aligarh shine forth brilliantly in the pride of Mahomedan history, in the loyalty, commonsense and sound reasoning so eloquently expressed in your address. But, gentlemen, you go on to tell me that sincere as your belief is in the justice and fair dealings of your rulers, you cannot but be aware that "recent events" have stirred up feelings amongst the younger generation of Mahomedans which might "pass beyond the control of temperate counsel and sober guidance."

Policy in Eastern Bengal

Now I have no intention of entering into any discussion upon the affairs of Eastern Bengal and Assam, yet I hope that without offence to anyone I may thank the Mahomedan community of the new Province for the moderation and self-restraint they have shown under conditions which were new to them, and as to which there has been inevitably much misunderstanding, and that I may at the same time sympathise with all that is sincere in Bengalee sentiments. But above all, what I would ask you to believe is that the course the Viceroy and the Government of India have pursued in connection with the affairs of the new Province, the future of which is now I hope assured, has been dictated solely by a regard for what has appeared best for its present and future populations as a whole, irrespective of race or creed, and that the Mahomedan community of Eastern Bengal and Assam can rely as firmly as ever on British justice and fairplay for the appreciation of its loyalty and the safeguarding of its interests.

The unrest in India

You have addressed me, gentlemen, at a time when the political atmosphere is full of change. We all feel it would be foolish to attempt to deny its existence, hopes and ambitions new to India are making themselves felt. We cannot ignore them — we should be wrong to wish to do so — but to what is all this unrest due? Not to the discontent of misgoverned millions — I defy anyone honestly to assert that — not to say uprising of a disaffected people.

Fruits of Western Education

It is due to that educational growth in which only a very small portion of the population has as yet shared, of which British rule first sowed the seed and the fruits of which British rule is now doing its best to foster and to direct. There may be many tares in the harvest we are now reaping. The Western grain which we have sown may not be entirely suitable to the requirements of the people of India but the educational harvest will increase as years go on, and the healthiness of the nourishment it gives will depend on the careful administration and distribution of its products. You need not ask my pardon, gentlemen, for telling me that "Representative institutions of the European type are entirely new to the people of India" or that their introduction here requires the most earnest thought and care. I should be very far from welcoming all the political machinery of the Western world amongst the hereditary instincts and traditions of Eastern races. Western breadth of thought, the teachings of Western civilisation, the freedom of British individuality can do much for the people of India, but I recognise with you that they must not carry with them an impracticable insistence of the acceptance of political methods.

Political Future of Mahomedans

And now, gentlemen, I come to your own position in respect to the political future; the position of the Mahomedan community for whom you speak. You will, I feel sure, recognise that it is impossible for me to follow you through any detailed consideration of the conditions and the share that the community has a right to claim in the administration of public affairs. I can at present only deal with generalities. The points which you have raised are before the Committee, which, as you know, I have lately appointed to consider the question of presentation (? representation), and I will take care that your address is submitted to them, but at the same time I hope I may be able to reply to the general tenor of your remarks without in any way forestalling the Committee's report.

The Question of Representation

The pith of your address, as I understand it, is a claim that in any system of representation whether it affects a Municipality, a District Board or a Legislative Council, in which it is proposed to introduce or increase an electoral organisation, the Mahomedan community should be represented as a community. You point out that in many cases electoral bodies, as now constituted, cannot be expected to return a Mahomedan candidate, and that if by chance they did so it could only be at the sacrifice of such a candidate's view to those of a majority opposed to his own community whom he would in no way represent, and you justly claim that your numerical strength both in respect to the political importance of your community and the service it has rendered to the Empire entitle you to consideration. I am entirely in accord with you; please do not misunderstand me. I make no attempt to indicate by what means the representation of communities can be obtained, but I am as firmly convinced as I believe you to be that any electoral representation in India would be doomed to mischievous failure which aimed at granting a personal enfranchisement regardless of the beliefs and traditions of the communities composing the population of this continent. The great mass of the people of India have no knowledge of representative institutions. I agree with you, gentlemen, that the initial rungs in the ladder of self-government are to be found in the Municipal and District Boards and that it is in that direction that we must look for the gradual political education of the people.

An Assurance

In the meantime I can only say to you that the Mahomedan community may rest assured that their political rights and interests as a community will be safeguarded in any administrative reorganization with which I am concerned and that you and the people of India may rely upon the British Raj to respect, as it has been its pride to do, the religious beliefs and the national traditions of the myriads composing the population of His Majesty's Indian Empire.

Your Highness and Gentlemen, I sincerely thank you for the unique opportunity your deputation has given me of meeting so many distinguished and representative Mahomedans. I deeply appreciate the energy and interest in public affairs which have brought you here from great distances, and I only regret that your visit to Simla is necessarily so short.

APPENDIX XIII

Allocation of Seats under the Government of India Act, 1935, for the Lower House in each Provincial Legislature

Province.	Total Seats.	General Seats: Total of General Seats.	General Seats: General Seats reserved for Scheduled Castes.	Seats for representatives of backward areas and tribes.	Sikh Seats.	Mahomedan Seats.	Anglo-Indian Seats.	European Seats.	Indian Christian Seats.	Seats for representatives of commerce, industry, mining and planting.	Land-holders Seats.	University Seats.	Seats for representatives of labour.	Seats for Women: General.	Seats for Women: Sikh.	Seats for Women: Mahomedan.	Seats for Women: Anglo-Indian.	Seats for Women: Indian Christian.
1	2	3	4	5	6	7	8	9	10	11	12	13	14	15	16	17	18	19
Madras	215	146	30	1	..	28	2	3	8	6	6	1	6	6	..	1	..	1
Bombay	175	114	15	1	..	29	2	3	3	7	2	1	7	5	..	1	..	..
Bengal	250	78	30	..	..	117	3	11	2	19	5	2	8	2	..	2	1	..
United Provinces	228	140	20	..	..	64	1	2	2	3	6	1	3	4	..	2	..	..
The Punjab	175	42	8	..	31	84	1	1	2	1	5	1	3	1	1	2	..	..
Bihar	152	86	15	7	..	39	1	2	1	4	4	1	3	3	..	1	..	..
Central Provinces and Berar ..	112	84	20	1	..	14	1	1	..	2	3	1	2	3	..	..	..	..
Assam	108	47	7	9	..	34	..	1	1	11	..	..	4	1	..	..	..	..
North-West Frontier Province ..	60	9	..	..	3	36	..	..	..	..	2	..	..	..	..	..	..	..
Orissa	60	44	6	5	..	4	..	..	1	1	2	..	1	2	..	..	..	..
Sind	60	18	..	..	..	33	..	2	..	2	2	..	1	1	..	1	..	..

In Bombay seven of the general seats shall be reserved for Marathas.
In the Punjab one of the Land-holders seats shall be a seat to be filled by a Tumandar.
In Assam and Orissa the seats reserved for women shall be non-communal seats.

APPENDIX XIV

Allocation of Seats under the Government of India Act, 1935, for the Upper House in each Provincial Legislature

Province. 1	Total of Seats. 2	General Seats. 3	Mahomedan Seats. 4	European Seats. 5	Indian Christian Seats. 6	Seats to be filled by Legislative Assembly. 7	Seats to be filled by Governor
Madras	Not less than 54 Not more than 56	35	7	1	3	..	Not less than 8 Not more than 10
Bombay	Not less than 29 Not more than 30	20	5	1	..	..	Not less than 3 Not more than 4
Bengal	Not less than 63 Not more than 65	10	17	3	..	27	Not less than 6 Not more than 8
United Provinces	Not less than 58 Not more than 60	34	17	1	..	..	Not less than 6 Not more than 8
Bihar	Not less than 29 Not more than 30	9	4	1	..	12	Not less than 3 Not more than 4
Assam	Not less than 21 Not more than 22	10	6	2	..	..	Not less than 3 Not more than 4

APPENDIX XV

Allocation of Seats under the Government of India Act, 1935, for the Lower House of the Federal Legislature for British India

Province.	Total Seats.	General Seats.		Sikh Seats.	Mahomedan Seats.	Anglo-Indian Seats.	European Seats.	Indian Christian Seats.	Seats for representatives of commerce and industry.	Landholders Seats.	Seats for representatives of labour.	Women's Seats.
		Total of General Seats.	General Seats reserved for Scheduled Castes.									
1	2	3	4	5	6	7	8	9	10	11	12	13
Madras	37	19	4	..	8	1	1	2	2	1	1	2
Bombay	30	13	2	..	6	1	1	1	3	1	2	2
Bengal	37	10	3	..	17	1	1	1	8	1	2	1
United Provinces	37	19	3	..	12	1	1	1	..	1	1	1
The Punjab	30	6	1	6	14	..	1	1	..	1	..	1
Bihar	30	16	2	..	9	..	1	1	..	1	1	1
Central Provinces and Berar ..	15		2	..	3	..	..	..	..	1	1	1
Assam	10	4	1	..	3	..	1	1	..	..	1	..
North-West Frontier Province	5	1	..	..	4	..	..	..	..	..	..	..
Orissa	5	4	1	..	1	..	..	..	..	..	..	..
Sind	5	1	..	..	3	..	1	..	..	..	..	..
British Baluchistan	1	..	..	..	1	..	..	..	..	..	..	..
Delhi	2	1	..	..	1	..	..	..	..	..	..	..
Ajmer-Merwara	1	1	..	..	..	..	..	..	..	..	..	..
Coorg	1	1	..	..	..	..	..	..	..	..	..	..
Non-Provincial Seats ..	4	..	..	..	..	..	..	..	3	..	1	..
Total ..	250	105	19	6	82	4	8	8	11	7	10	9

APPENDIX XVI

ALLOCATION OF SEATS UNDER THE GOVERNMENT OF INDIA ACT, 1935, FOR THE UPPER CHAMBER OF THE FEDERAL LEGISLATURE FOR BRITISH INDIA

Province or Community.	Total Seats.	General Seats.	Seats for Scheduled Castes	Sikh Seats	Mahomedan Seats.	Women's Seats.
1	2	3	4	5	6	7
Madras	20	14	1	..	4	1
Bombay	16	10	1	..	4	1
Bengal	20	8	1	..	10	1
United Provinces	20	11	1	..	7	1
The Punjab	16	3	..	4	8	1
Bihar	16	10	1	..	4	1
Central Provinces and Berar ..	8	6	1	..	1	..
Assam	5	3	..	..	2	..
North-West Frontier Province ..	5	1	..	..	4	..
Orissa	5	4	..	..	1	..
Sind	5	2	..	..	3	..
British Baluchistan	1	..	..	..	1	..
Delhi	1	1	..	..	..	..
Ajmer-Merwara	1	1	..	..	..	..
Coorg	1	1	..	..	..	..
Anglo-Indians	1	..	..	..	..	..
Europeans	7	..	..	..	..	..
Indian Christians	2	..	..	..	..	..
Total ..	150	75	6	4	49	6

APPENDIX XVII

ALLOCATION OF SEATS UNDER THE GOVERNMENT OF INDIA ACT, 1935, FOR THE LOWER AND UPPER HOUSE OF THE FEDERAL LEGISLATURE FOR INDIAN STATES

States and Groups of States.	Number of seats in the Council of State.	States and Groups of States.	Number of Seats in the Federal Assembly.	Population
1	2	3	4	5
DIVISION I		DIVISION I		
Hyderabad	5	Hyderabad	16	14,436,142
DIVISION II		DIVISION II		
Mysore	3	Mysore	7	6,557,302
DIVISION III		DIVISION III		
Kashmir	3	Kashmir	4	3,646,243
DIVISION IV		DIVISION IV		
Gwalior	3	Gwalior	4	3,523,070
DIVISION V		DIVISION V		
Baroda	3	Baroda	3	2,443,007
DIVISION VI		DIVISION VI		
Kalat	2	Kalat	1	342,101
DIVISION VII		DIVISION VII		
Sikkim	1	Sikkim	..	109,808
DIVISION VIII		DIVISION VIII		
1. Rampur	1	1. Rampur	1	465,225
2. Benares	1	2. Benares	1	391,272
DIVISION IX		DIVISION IX		
1. Travancore	2	1. Travancore	5	5,095,973
2. Cochin	2	2. Cochin	1	1,205,016
3. Pudukkottai .. Banganapalle .. Sandur	1	3. Pudukkottai .. Banganapalle .. Sandur	1	400,694 39,218 13,583
DIVISION X		DIVISION X		
1. Udaipur	2	1. Udaipur	2	1,566,910
2. Jaipur	2	2. Jaipur	3	2,631,775
3. Jodhpur	2	3. Jodhpur	2	2,125,982
4. Bikaner	2	4. Bikaner	1	936,218
5. Alwar	1	5. Alwar	1	749,751
6. Kotah	1	6. Kotah	1	685,804
7. Bharatpur	1	7. Bharatpur	1	486,954
8. Tonk	1	8. Tonk	1	317,360

APPENDIX XVII—(*Contd.*)

States and Groups of States.	Number of seats in Council of State	States and Groups of States.	Number of seats in the Federal Assembly	Population.
1	2	3	4	5
DIVISION X—(Continued)		DIVISION X—(Continued)		
9. Dholpur	1	9. Dholpur	1	254,986
10. Karauli	1	Karauli		140,525
11. Bundi	1	10. Bundi	1	216,722
12. Sirohi	1	Sirohi		216,528
13. Dungarpur	1	11. Dungarpur	1	227,544
14. Banswara	1	Banswara		260,670
15. Partabgarh	1	12. Partabgarh	1	76,539
Jhalawar		Jhalawar		107,890
16. Jaisalmer	1	13. Jaisalmer	1	76.255
Kishengarh		Kishengarh		85,744
DIVISION XI		DIVISION XI		
1. Indore	2	1. Indore	2	1,325,089
2. Bhopal	2	2. Bhopal	1	729,955
3. Rewa	2	3. Rewa	2	1,587,445
4. Datia	1	4. Datia	1	158,834
5. Orchha		Orchha		314,661
6. Dhar	1	5. Dhar	1	243,430
7. Dewas (Senior)	1	Dewas (Senior)		83,321
Dewas (Junior)		Dewas (Junior)		70,513
8. Jaora	1	6. Jaora	1	100,166
Ratlam		Ratlam		107,321
9. Panna	1	7. Panna	1	212,130
Samthar		Samthar		33,307
Ajaigarh		Ajaigarh		85,895
10. Bijawar	1	8. Bijawar	1	115,852
Charkhari		Charkhari		120,351
Chhatarpur		Chhatarpur		161,267
11. Baoni	1	9. Baoni	1	19,132
Nagod		Nagod		74,589
Maihar		Maihar		68,991
Baraundha		Baraundha		16,071
12. Barwani	1	10. Barwani	1	141,110
Ali Rajpur		Ali Rajpur		101,963
Shahpura		Shahpura		54,233
13. Jhabua	1	11. Jhabua	1	145,522
Sailana		Sailana		35,223
Sitamau		Sitamau		28,422
14. Rajgarh	1	12. Rajgarh	1	134,891
Narsingarh		Narsingarh		113,873
Khilchipur		Khilchipur		45,583

APPENDIX XVII—(*Contd.*)

States and Groups of States	Number of seats in Council of State.		States and Groups of States	Number of seats in the Federal Assembly.	Population.
1	2		3	4	5
DIVISION XII			DIVISION XII		
Cutch	1	1	Cutch	1	514,307
Idar	1	2.	Idar	1	262,660
Nawanagar	1	3	Nawanagar	1	409,192
Bhavnagar	1	4.	Bhavnagar	1	500 274
Junagadh	1	5	Junagadh	1	545,152
Rajpipla	1	6	Rajpipla	1	206,114
Palanpur			Palanpur		264,179
Dhrangadhra	1	7	Dhrangadhra	1	88,961
Gondal			Gondal		205,846
Porbandar	1	8.	Porbandar	1	115,673
Morvi			Morvi		113,023
Radhanpur	1	9.	Radhanpur	1	70,580
Wankaner			Wankaner		44,259
Palitana			Palitana		624,150
Cambay	1	10.	Cambay	1	87,701
Dharampur			Dharampur		112,031
Balasinor			Balasinor		52,527
Baria	1	11	Baria	1	159,429
Chhota Udepur			Chhota Udepur		144,640
Sunt			Sunt		83,531
Lunawada			Lunawada		95,162
Bansda	1	12.	Bansda	1	48,839
Sachin			Sachin		22,107
Jawhar			Jawhar		57,261
Danta			Danta		26,196
Dhrol	1		Dhrol		27,639
Limbdi			Limbdi		40,088
Wadhwan			Wadhwan		42,602
Rajkot			Rajkot ..		75,540
DIVISION XIII			DIVISION XIII		
Kolhapur	2	1.	Kolhapur	1	957,137
Sangli	1	2.	Sangli	1	258,442
Savantvadi			Savantvadi		230,589
Janjira	1	3.	Janjira ..	1	110,379
Mudhol			Mudhol		62,832
Bhor			Bhor ...		141,546
Jamkhandi	1	4.	Jamkhandi ...	1	114,270
Miraj (Senior)			Miraj (Senior) ..		93,938
Miraj (Junior)			Miraj (Junior) ..		40,684
Kurundwad (Senior)			Kurundwad (Senior) ..		44,204
Kurundwad (Junior)			Kurundwad (Junior)...		75,540

APPENDIX XVII—(*Contd.*)

States and Groups of States.	Number of seats in Council of State.	States and Groups of States	Number of seats in the Federal Assembly.	Population
1	2	3	4	5
DIVISION XIII—(Continued)		DIVISION XIII—(Continued)		
5. Akalkot ..		5 Akalkot .. .		92,605
Phaltan ...		Phaltan . ..		58,761
Jath	1	Jath .	1	91,099
Aundh . .		Aundh ...		76,507
Ramdurg .		Ramdurg . .		35 454
DIVISION XIV		DIVISION XIV		
1 Patiala . ..	2	1 Patiala	2	1,625,520
2 Bhawalpur	2	2. Bhawalpur	1	984,612
3. Khairpur .	1	3 Khairpur . .	1	227,183
4. Kapurthala	1	4 Kapurthala . ..	1	316,757
5. Jind	1	5. Jind . ..	1	324,676
6 Nabha	1	6 Nabha ...	1	287,574
		7 Tehri-Garhwal ...	1	349,573
7 Mandi		8 Mandi...		207,465
Bilaspur	1	Bilaspur ..	1	100,994
Suket		Suket ..		58,408
8. Tehri-Garhwal ...		9. Sirmur		
Sirmur	1	Chamba ..	1	148,568
Chamba				146,870
9. Faridkot		10. Faridkot ...		164,364
Malerkotla	1	Malerkotla	1	83,072
Loharu . ..		Loharu .		23,338
DIVISION XV		DIVISION XV		
1 Cooch Behar...	1	1. Cooch Behar	1	590,886
2. Tripura	1	2 Tripura	1	382,450
Manipur		3 Manipur	1	445,606
DIVISION XVI		DIVISION XVI		
1 Mayurbhanj	1	1 Mayurbhanj	1	889,603
Sonepur		2. Sonepur	1	237,920
2. Patna	1	3. Patna	1	566,924
Kalahandi		4. Kalahandi	1	513,716
3. Keonjhar ...		5 Keonjhar	1	460,609
Dhenkanal		6. Gangpur	1	356,674
Nayagarh	1	7. Bastar	1	524,721
Talcher		8. Surguja	1	501,939
Nilgiri				

APPENDIX XVII—(*Contd.*)

States and Groups of States.	Number of seats in Council of State.	States and Groups of States.	Number of seats in the Federal Assembly.	Population.
1	2	3	4	5
DIVISION XVI—(Continued)		DIVISION XVI—(Continued)		
4. Gangpur ... ... Bamra ... ... Seraikela ... ... Baud ... ... Bonai	1	9. Dhenkanal ... ... Nayagarh ... ... Seraikela ... ... Baud ... ... Talcher ... ... Bonai ... ... Nilgiri ... ... Bamra	3	284,326 142,406 148,525 185,248 69,702 80,186 68,594 151,047
5. Bastar ... .. Surguja ... .. Raigarh ... .. Nandgaon	1			
6. Khairgarh ... .. Jashpur ... .. Kanker ... ... Korea ... ... Sarangarh	1	10. Raigarh .. ... Khairagarh ... ... Jashpur Kanker Sarangarh Korea .. Nandgaon	3	277,569 157,400 193,698 186,101 128,967 90,886 182,380
DIVISION XVII		DIVISION XVII		
States not mentioned in any of the preceding Divisions, but described in paragraph 12 of this Part of this Schedule.	2	States not mentioned in any of the preceding Divisions but described in paragraph 12 of this Part of this Schedule.	5	8,047,129
Total Population of the States in this Table			...	78,996,844

APPENDIX XVIII

COMMUNAL AWARD BY HIS MAJESTY'S GOVERNMENT—1932

In the statement made by the Prime Minister on 1st December last on behalf of His Majesty's Government at the close of the second session of the Round Table Conference, which was immediately afterwards endorsed by both Houses of Parliament, it was made plain that if the communities in India were unable to reach a settlement acceptable to all parties on the communal questions which the Conference had failed to solve His Majesty's Government were determined that India's constitutional advance should not on that account be frustrated, and that they would remove this obstacle by devising and applying themselves a provisional scheme.

2. On the 19th March last His Majesty's Government, having been informed that the continued failure of the communities to reach agreement was blocking the progress of the plans for the framing of a new Constitution, stated that they were engaged upon a careful re-examination of the difficult and controversial questions which arise. They are now satisfied that without a decision of at least some aspects of the problems connected with the position of minorities under the new Constitution, no further progress can be made with the framing of the Constitution.

3. His Majesty's Government have accordingly decided that they will include provisions to give effect to the scheme set out below in the proposals relating to the Indian Constitution to be laid in due course before Parliament. The scope of this scheme is purposely confined to the arrangements to be made for the representation of the British Indian communities in the Provincial Legislatures, consideration of representation in the Legislature at the Centre being deferred for the reason given in paragraph 20 below. The decision to limit the scope of the scheme implies no failure to realise that the framing of the Constitution

* Parliamentary Paper (Command 4147) of 1932. Officially it is spoken of as *Communal Decision.*

will necessitate the decision of a number of the problems of great importance to minorities, but has been taken in the hope that once a pronouncement has been made upon the basic questions of method and proportions of representation the communities themselves may find it possible to arrive at a *modus vivendi* on other communal problems, which have not as yet received the examination they require.

4. His Majesty's Government wish it to be most clearly understood that they themselves can be no parties to any negotiations which may be initiated with a view to the revision of their decision, and will not be prepared to give consideration to any representation aimed at securing the modification of it which is not supported by all the parties affected. But they are most desirous to close no door to an agreed settlement should such happily be forthcoming. If, therefore, before a new Government of India Act has passed into law, they are satisfied that the communities who are concerned are mutually agreed upon a practicable alternative scheme, either in respect of any one or more of the Governors' Provinces or in respect of the whole of the British India, they will be prepared to recommend to Parliament that that alternative should be submitted for the provisions now outlined.

5. Seats in the Legislative Councils in the Governors' Provinces, or in the Lower House if there is an Upper Chamber, will be allocated as shown in the annexed table.*

6. Election to the seats allotted to Muhammadan, European and Sikh constituencies will be by voters voting in separate communal electorates covering between them the whole area of the Province (apart from any portions which may in special cases be excluded from the electoral area as "backward").

Provision will be made in the Constitution itself to empower a revision of this electoral arrangement (and the other similar arrangements mentioned below) after 10 years with the assent of the communities affected, for the ascertainment of which suitable means will be devised.

7. All qualified electors, who are not voters either in a Muhammadan, Sikh, Indian Christian (see paragraph 10 below),

* See page 370.

Anglo-Indian (see paragraph 11 below) or European constituency, will be entitled to vote in a general constituency.

8. Seven seats will be reserved for Mahrattas in certain selected plural member general constituencies in Bombay.

9. Members of the "depressed classes" qualified to vote will vote in a general constituency. In view of the fact that for a considerable period these classes would be unlikely, by this means alone, to secure any adequate representation in the Legislature, a number of special seats will be assigned to them as shown in the table. These seats will be filled by election from special constituencies in which only members of the "depressed classes" electorally qualified will be entitled to vote. Any person voting in such a special constituency will, as stated above, be also entitled to vote in a general constituency. It is intended that these constituencies should be formed in selected areas where the Depressed Classes are most numerous, and that, except in Madras, they should not cover the whole area of the Province.

In Bengal it seems possible that in some general constituencies a majority of the voters will belong to the Depressed Classes. Accordingly, pending further investigation, no number has been fixed for the members to be returned from the special Depressed Class constituencies in that Province. It is intended to secure that the Depressed Classes should obtain not less than 10 seats in the Bengal Legislature.

The precise definition in each Province of those who (if electorally qualified) will be entitled to vote in the special Depressed Class constituencies has not yet been finally determined. It will be based as a rule on the general principles advocated in the Franchise Committee's Report. Modification may, however, be found necessary in some Provinces in Northern India where the application of the general criteria of untouchability might result in a definition unsuitable in some respects to the special conditions of the Province.

His Majesty's Government do not consider that these special Depressed Class constituencies will be required for more than a limited time. They intend that the Constitution shall provide that they shall come to an end after 20 years if they have not previously been abolished under the general powers of electoral revision referred to in paragraph 6.

10. Election to the seats allotted to Indian Christians will be by voters voting in separate communal electorates. It seems almost certain that practical difficulties will, except possibly in Madras, prevent the formation of Indian Christian constituencies covering the whole area of the Province, and that accordingly special Indian Christian constituencies will have to be formed only in one or two selected areas in the Province. Indian Christian voters in these areas will not vote in a general constituency. Indian Christian voters outside these areas will vote in a general constituency. Special arrangements may be needed in Bihar and Orissa, where a considerable proportion of the Indian Christian community belongs to the aboriginal tribes.

11. Election to the seats allotted to Anglo-Indians will be by voters voting in separate communal electorates. It is at present intended, subject to investigation of any practical difficulties that may arise, that the Anglo-Indian constituencies shall cover the whole area of each Province, a postal ballot being employed; but no final decision has yet been reached.

12. The method of filling the seats assigned for representatives from backward areas is still under investigation, and the number of seats so assigned should be regarded as provisional pending a final decision as to the constitutional arrangements to be made in relation to such areas.

13. His Majesty's Government attach great importance to securing that the new Legislatures should contain at least a small number of women members. They feel that at the outset this object could not be achieved without creating a certain number of seats specially allotted to women. They also feel that it is essential that women members should not be drawn disproportionately from one community. They have been unable to find any system which would avoid this risk, and would be consistent with the rest of the scheme for representation which they have found it necessary to adopt, except that of limiting the electorate for each special women's seat to voters from one community.* The special women's seats have accordingly been specifically

* Subject to one exception, see note (e) to Table, Appendix XVI .

divided, as shown in the table, between the various communities. The precise electoral machinery to be employed in these special constituencies is still under consideration.

14. The seats allotted to "Labour" will be filled from non-communal constituencies. The electoral arrangements have still to be determined, but it is likely that in most Provinces the Labour constituencies will be partly trade union and partly special constituencies as recommended by the Franchise Committee.

15. The special seats allotted to Commerce and Industry, Mining and Planting will be filled by election through Chambers of Commerce and various Associations. The details of the electoral arrangements for these seats must await further investigation.

16. The special seats allotted to Land-holders will be filled by election by special Land-holders' constituencies.

17. The method to be employed for election to the University seats is still under consideration.

18. His Majesty's Government have found it impossible in determining these questions of representation in the Provincial Legislatures to avoid entering into considerable detail. There remains, nevertheless, the determination of the constituencies. They intend that this task should be undertaken in India as early as possible.

It is possible that in some instances delimitation of constituencies might be materially improved by slight variations from the numbers of seats now given. His Majesty's Government reserve the right to make such slight variations, for such purpose, provided that they would not materially affect the essential balance between communities. No such variations will, however, be made in the case of Bengal and Punjab.

19. The question of the composition of Second Chambers in the Provinces has so far received comparatively little attention in the constitutional discussions and requires further consideration before a decision is reached as to which Provinces shall have a Second Chamber or a scheme is drawn up for their composition.

His Majesty's Government consider that the composition of the Upper House in a Province should be such as not to disturb in any essential the balance between the communities resulting from the composition of the Lower House.

20. His Majesty's Government do not propose at present to enter into the question of the size and composition of the Legislature at the Centre, since this involves among other questions that of representation of the Indian States which still needs further discussion. They will, of course, when considering the composition, pay full regard to the claims of all communities for adequate representation therein.

21. His Majesty's Government have already accepted the principle that Sind should be constituted a separate Province, if satisfactory means of financing it can be found. As the financial problems involved still have to be reviewed in connection with other problems of federal finance, His Majesty's Government have thought preferable to include, at this stage, figures for a Legislature for the existing Province of Bombay, in addition to the schemes for separate Legislatures for Bombay Presidency proper and Sind.

22. The figures given for Bihar and Orissa relate to the existing Province. The question of constituting a separate Province of Orissa is still under investigation.

23. The inclusion in the table of figures relating to a Legislature for the Central Provinces including Berar does not imply that any decision has yet been reached regarding the future constitutional position of Berar.

London,
4th August, 1932.

APPENDIX XVIII — (*contd.*)

ALLOCATION OF SEATS IN PROVINCIAL LEGISLATURES (LOWER HOUSE ONLY)

Province.	General.	Depressed Classes	Represen-tatives from Backward Areas.	Sikh.	Muham-madan.	Indian Christ-ian.	Anglo-Indian.	European.	Commerce and Industry, Mining and Planting, Special. (a)	Land-holders, Special.	University, Special.	Labour, Special	Total.
Madras	134 (including 6 women)	18	1	0	29 (including 1 woman)	9 (inc. 1 woman)	2	3	6	6	1	6	215
Bombay (including Sind	97 (b) (including 5 women)	10	1	0	63 (including 1 woman)	3	2	4	8	3	1	8	200
Bengal	80 (c) (including 2 women	[illegible]	0	0	119 (including 2 women,	2	4 (inc 1 woman)	11	19	5	2	8	250
United Provinces	132 (including 4 women)	12	0	0	66 (including 2 women)	2	1	2	3	5	1	3	228
Punjab	43 (including 1 woman	0	0	32 (Including 1 woman)	86 (including 2 women)	2	1	1	1	5(d)	1	3	175
Bihar and Orissa	99 (including 3 women	7	8	0	42 (including 1 woman)	2	1	2	4	4	1	4	175
Central Provinces (including Berar).	77 (including 3 women)	10	1	0	14	0	1	1	2	3	1	2	112
Assam	44 (including 1 woman e	4		0	34	1	0	1	11		0	4	108

APPENDIX XVIII—(*contd.*)

Province.	General.	Depressed Classes.	Representatives from Backward Areas.	Sikh.	Muhammadan.	Indian Christian.	Anglo-Indian.	European.	Commerce and Industry, Mining and Planting, Special. (a)	Land-holders, Special.	University, Special.	Labour, Special.	Total.
North-West Frontier Province.	9	0	0	3	36	0	0	0	0	2	0	0	50
Bombay (without Sind)	109 (b) (including 5 women)	10	1	0	30 (including 1 woman)	3	2	3	7	2	1	7	175
Sind	19 (including 1 woman)	0	0	0	34 (including 1 woman)	0	0	2	2	2	0	1	60

(a) The composition of the bodies through which election to these seats will be conducted, though in most cases neither predominantly European or predominantly Indian, will not be statutorily fixed. It is, accordingly, not possible in each Province to state with certainty how many Europeans and Indians respectively will be returned. It is, however, expected that, initially, the numbers will be approximately as follows:—Madras, 4 Europeans, 2 Indians; Bombay (including Sind), 5 Europeans, 3 Indians; Bengal, 14 Europeans, 5 Indians; United Provinces, 2 Europeans, 1 Indian; Punjab, 1 Indian; Bihar and Orissa, 2 Europeans, 2 Indians; Central Provinces including Berar, 1 European, 1 Indian; Assam, 8 Europeans, 3 Indians; Bombay without Sind, 4 Europeans, 3 Indians; Sind, 1 European, 1 Indian.

(b) Seven of these seats will be reserved for Mahrattas.

(c) As explained in paragraph 9 of the statement, the number of special Depressed Class seats in Bengal—which will not exceed 10—has not yet been fixed. The number of General seats will be 80, less the number of special Depressed Class seats.

(d) One of these seats is a Tumandar's seat. The four Land-holder's seats will be filled from special constituencies with joint electorates. It is probable, from the distribution of the electorate, that the members returned will be one Hindu, one Sikh, and two Muhammadans.

(e) This woman's seat will be filled from a non-communal constituency at Shillong.

APPENDIX XIX

SUPPLEMENTARY COMMUNAL AWARD*

"Then there was the question of the representation of communities in the Centre, particularly of the Muslim community. There, I think, I can say definitely—I think I have said it indirectly very often before—that the Government consider that the Muslim community should have a representation 33⅓ per cent. in the Federal Centre. As far as Indian India is concerned that must be a matter for arrangement between the communities affected and the princes, but, so far as the British Government has any part in the question we will, at any time, give our good offices to making it as easy as possible for the arrangement between those parties with regard to the future allocation of seats."

* The Communal Award of His Majesty's Government (Appendix XVIII) did not give any decision regarding the Muslim claim for 33⅓ per cent. representation in the Central Government. The decision of His Majesty's Government on this claim was announced by the Secretary of State for India on 24th December 1932 in the course of his statement to the Third Round Table Conference.

APPENDIX XX

POONA PACT*

(1) There shall be seats reserved for the Depressed Classes out of the general electorate seats in the Provincial Legislatures as follows:—

Madras 30: Bombay with Sind 15; Punjab 8; Bihar and Orissa 18; Central Provinces 20; Assam 7; Bengal 30; United Provinces 20; Total 148.

These figures are based on the total strength of the Provincial Councils, announced in the Prime Minister's decision.

(2) Election to these seats shall be by joint electorates subject, however, to the following procedure:

All the members of the Depressed Classes registered in the general electoral roll in a constituency will form an electoral college, which will elect a panel of four candidates belonging to the Depressed Classes for each of such reserved seats, by the method of the single vote; the four persons getting the highest number of votes in such primary election, shall be candidates for election by the general electorate.

(3) Representation of the Depressed Classes in the Central Legislature shall likewise be on the principle of joint electorates and reserved seats by the method of primary election in the manner provided for in Clause two above, for their representation in the Provincial Legislatures.

(4) In the Central Legislature, eighteen per cent. of the seats allotted to the general electorate for British India in the said Legislature shall be reserved for the Depressed Classes.

(5) The system of primary election to a panel of candidates for election to the Central and Provincial Legislatures, as hereinbefore mentioned, shall come to an end after the first ten years, unless terminated sooner by mutual agreement under the provision of Clause six below.

(6) The system of representation of the Depressed Classes by reserved seats in the Provincial and Central Legislatures as

* Signed on 25th September 1932.

provided for in Clauses 1 and 4 shall continue until determined by mutual agreement between the communities concerned in the settlement.

(7) Franchise for the Central and Provincial Legislatures for the Depressed Classes shall be as indicated in the Lothian Committee Report.

(8) There shall be no disabilities attaching to anyone on the ground of his being a member of the Depressed Classes in regard to any elections to local bodies or appointment to the Public Services. Every endeavour shall be made to secure fair representation of the Depressed Classes in these respects, subject to such educational qualifications as may be laid down for appointment to the Public Services.

(9) In every province, out of the educational grant an adequate sum shall be earmarked for providing educational facilities to the members of the Depressed Classes.

APPENDIX XXI

Minority Representation under the Government of India Act of 1935 in Provincial Legislatures

I. LOWER HOUSE

PROVINCE.	Total Seats.	Muslims: Seats Allotted under the Act.	Muslims: Seats due according to Population.	Muslims: Excess + or Deficit —	Scheduled Castes: Seats Allotted under the Act.	Scheduled Castes: Seats due according to Population.	Scheduled Castes: Excess + or Deficit	Indian Christians: Seats Allotted under the Act.	Indian Christians: Seats due according to Population.	Indian Christians: Excess + or Deficit —	Sikhs: Seats Allotted under the Act	Sikhs: Seats due according to Population.	Sikhs: Excess + or Deficit —
Madras	215	29	17	+12	30	35	—5	9	9	...	Nil	Nil	...
Bombay	175	30	16	+14	15	16	—1	3	3	...	Nil	Nil	...
Bengal	250	119	137	—18	30	33	—3	3	Nil	+3	Nil	Nil	...
U. P.	228	66	35	+31	20	49	—29	2	Nil	+2	Nil	1	—1
Punjab	175	86	100	—14	8	8	...	2	3	—1	32	23	+9
Bihar	152	40	20	+20	15	20	—5	1	Nil	+1	Nil	Nil	...
C.P. & Berar	112	14	5	+9	20	20	..	Nil	Nil	...	Nil	Nil	...
Assam	108	34	36	—2	7	7	..	1	Nil	+1	Nil	Nil	...
N.-W.F.P.	50	36	46	—10	Nil	...	..	Nil	Nil	...	3	1	+2
Orissa	60	4	1	—3	6	9	—3	1	Nil	—1	Nil	Nil	...
Sind	60	34	43	—9	Nil	3	—3	Nil	Nil	...	Nil	Nil	...
Total ...	1585	492	456	+36	151	200	—49	22	15	—7	35	25	+10

II. UPPER HOUSE

PROVINCE.	Total Seats.	Muslims: Seats Allotted under the Act.	Muslims: Seats due according to Population.	Muslims: Excess + or Deficit —	Scheduled Castes: Seats Allotted under the Act.	Scheduled Castes: Seats due according to Population.	Scheduled Castes: Excess + or Deficit	Indian Christians: Seats Allotted under the Act.	Indian Christians: Seats due according to Population.	Indian Christians: Excess + or Deficit —	Sikhs: Seats Allotted under the Act	Sikhs: Seats due according to Population.	Sikhs: Excess + or Deficit —
Madras	56	7	4	+3	Nil	9	—9	3	2	+1	Nil	Nil	...
Bombay	30	5	3	+2	Nil	3	—3	Nil	Nil	...	Nil	Nil	...
Bengal	65	17	36	—19	Nil	8	—8	Nil	Nil	...	Nil	Nil	...
United Provinces ...	60	17	9	+8	Nil	13	—13	Nil	Nil	...	Nil	Nil	...
Bihar	30	4	4	...	Nil	4	—4	Nil	Nil	..	Nil	Nil	...
Assam	22	10	7	+3	Nil	1	—1	Nil	Nil	...	Nil	Nil	...
Total ...	263	60	63	—3	Nil	38	—38	3	2	+1	Nil	Nil	...

APPENDIX XXII

Minority Representation under the Government of India Act of 1935 in the Central Legislature

—	Total seats for British India.	Muslims.			Scheduled Castes.			Indian Christians.			Sikhs.		
		Seats allotted under the Act.	Seats due according to population.	Excess+ or deficit—	Seats allotted under the Act.	Seats due according to population.	Excess+ or deficit—	Seats allotted under the Act.	Seats due according to population.	Excess+ or deficit—	Seats allotted under the Act.	Seats due according to population.	Excess+ or deficit—
I. Lower House ..	250	82	67	—15	19	35	—16	8	3	+5	6	3	+3
II. Upper House ..	150	49	40	—9	6	21	—15	Nil	2	—2	4	2	+2

APPENDIX XXIII

COMMUNAL REPRESENTATION IN SERVICES

GOVERNMENT OF INDIA RESOLUTION*

Establishments

the 4th July 1934

SECTION I—GENERAL

No. F. 14/17-B./33.—In accordance with undertakings given in the Legislative Assembly the Government of India have carefully reviewed the results of the policy followed since 1925 of reserving a certain percentage of direct appointments to Government service for the redress of communal inequalities. It has been represented that though this policy was adopted mainly with the object of securing increased representation for Muslims in the public services, it has failed to secure for them their due share of appointments and it has been contended that this position cannot be remedied unless a fixed percentage of vacancies is reserved for Muslims. In particular, attention has been drawn to the small number of Muslims in the Railway services, even on those railways which run through areas in which Muslims form a high percentage of the total population.

The review of the position has shown that these complaints are justified, and the Government of India are satisfied by the enquiries they have made that the instructions regarding recruitment must be revised with a view to improving the position of Muslims in the services.

2. In considering this general question the Government of India have also to take into account the claims of Anglo-Indians and Domiciled Europeans and of the depressed classes. Anglo-Indians have always held a large percentage of appointments in certain branches of the public service and it has been recognised that, in view of the degree to which the community has been dependent on this employment, steps must be taken to prevent in the new conditions anything in the nature of a rapid displacement of Anglo-Indians from their existing positions, which might occasion a violent dislocation of the economic structure of the com-

* *Gazette of India*, Part I, July 7, 1934.

munity. The instructions which follow in regard to the employment of Anglo-Indians and Domiciled Europeans in certain departments are designed to give effect to this policy.

3. In regard to the depressed classes it is common ground that all reasonable steps should be taken to secure for them a fair degree of representation in the public services. The intention of caste Hindus in this respect was formally stated in the Poona Agreement of 1932 and His Majesty's Government in accepting that agreement took due note of this point. In the present state of general education in these classes the Government of India consider that no useful purpose will be served by reserving for them a definite percentage of vacancies out of the number available for Hindus as a whole, but they hope to ensure that duly qualified candidates from the depressed classes are not deprived of fair opportunities of appointment merely because they cannot succeed in open competition.

4. The Government of India have also considered carefully the position of minority communities other than those mentioned above and are satisfied that the new rules will continue to provide for them, as at present, a reasonable degree of representation in the services.

SECTION II—SCOPE OF RULES

5. The Government of India propose to prescribe annual returns in order to enable them to watch the observance of the rules laid down below.

6. The general rules which the Government of India have with the approval of the Secretary of State adopted with the purpose of securing these objects are explained below. They relate only to direct recruitment and not to recruitment by promotion which will continue to be made as at present solely on merit. They apply to the Indian Civil Service, the Central Services, Class I and Class II, and the Subordinate Services under the administrative control of the Government of India with the exception of a few services and posts for which high technical or special qualifications are required, but do not apply to recruitment for these Services in the province of Burma. In regard to the Railways, they apply to all posts other than those of inferior

servants or labourers on the four State-managed Railways, and the administrations of the Company-managed Railways will be asked to adopt similar rules for the services on these Railways.

SECTION III—RULES FOR SERVICES RECRUITED ON AN ALL-INDIA BASIS

7. (1) For the Indian Civil Service and the Central and Subordinate Services to which recruitment is made on an All-India basis, the following rules will be observed:—

(i) 25 per cent. of all vacancies to be filled by direct recruitment of Indians, will be reserved for Muslims and 8 1/3 per cent. for other minority communities.

(ii) When recruitment is made by open competition, if Muslims or the other minority communities obtain less than these percentages, these percentages will be secured to them by means of nomination: if, however, Muslims obtain more than their reserved percentage in open competition, no reduction will be made in the percentage reserved for other minorities, while if the other minorities obtain more than their reserved percentage in open competition, no reduction will be made in the percentage reserved for Muslims.

(iii) If members of the other minority communities obtain less than their reserved percentage in open competition and if duly qualified candidates are not available for nomination, the residue of the 8 1/3 per cent. will be available for Muslims.

(iv) The percentage of 8 1/3 reserved for the other minorities will not be distributed among them in any fixed proportion.

(v) In all cases a minimum standard of qualification will be imposed and the reservations are subject to this condition.

(vi) In order to secure fair representation for the depressed classes duly qualified members of these classes may be nominated to a public service, even though recruitment to that service is being made by competition. Members of these classes, if appointed by nomination, will not count against the percentages reserved in accordance with clause (i) above.

(2) For the reasons given in paragraph 2 of this Resolution, the Government of India have paid special attention to the question of Anglo-Indians and Domiciled Europeans in the gazetted posts on the Railways for which recruitment is made on an All-India basis. In order to maintain approximately their present representation in these posts the Anglo-Indian and Domiciled

European community will require to obtain about 9 per cent. of the total vacancies available to members of Indian communities. The Government of India have satisfied themselves that at present the community is obtaining by promotions to these gazetted posts and by direct recruitment to them more than 9 per cent. of these vacancies. In these circumstances, it has been decided that no special reservation is at present required. If and when the community is shown to be receiving less than 9 per cent. of the vacancies, it will be considered what adjustments in regard to direct recruitment may be required to safeguard their legitimate interests.

SECTION IV—RULES FOR SERVICES RECRUITED LOCALLY

(3) In the case of all services to which recruitment is made by local areas and not on an All-India basis, e.g., subordinate posts in the Railways, Posts and Telegraphs Department, Customs Service, Income-tax Department, etc., the general rules prescribed above will apply subject to the following modifications:—

> (1) The total reservation for India as a whole of 25 per cent. for Muslims and of 8 1/3 per cent. for other minorities will be obtained by fixing a percentage for each Railway or local area or circle having regard to the population ratio of Muslims and other minority communities in the area and the rules for recruitment adopted by the local Government of the area concerned;
>
> (2) In the case of the Railways and Posts and Telegraphs Department and Customs Service in which the Anglo-Indian and Domiciled European community is at present principally employed special provisions described in the next paragraph are required in order to give effect to the policy stated in paragraph 2 above.

9. (1) (a) The Anglo-Indian and Domiciled European community at present holds 8·8 per cent. of the subordinate posts on the Railways. To safeguard their position 8 per cent. of all vacancies to be filled by direct recruitment will be reserved for members of this community. This total percentage will be obtained by fixing a separate percentage (i) for each Railway having regard to the number of members of this community at present employed, (ii) for each branch or department of the Railway service, so as to ensure that Anglo-Indians continue to be employed in those branches in which they are at present

principally employed, e.g., the Mechanical Engineering, Civil Engineering and Traffic Departments. No posts in the higher grades of the subordinate posts will be reserved, and promotion to these grades will be made, as at present, solely on merit.

(b) The reservation of 25 per cent. for Muslims and 8 per cent. for Anglo-Indians makes it necessary to increase the reservation of 33⅓ per cent., hitherto adopted for all minority communities, in order to safeguard the interests of minorities other than Muslims and Anglo-Indians. It has been decided, therefore, to reserve for them 6 per cent. of vacancies filled by direct recruitment, which is approximately the percentage of posts held by members of these communities at present. This total reservation will be obtained in the manner prescribed in paragraph 8 (1) of this Resolution and will not be further sub-divided among the minority communities.

(2) In the Posts and Telegraphs Department the same principles will be followed as in the case of the Railways for safeguarding the interests of the Anglo-Indian and Domiciled European community which at present holds about 2·2 per cent. of all subordinate posts. It has been ascertained that if a reservation is made for this community of 5 per cent. of the vacancies in the branches, departments or categories which members of this community may reasonably be expected to enter, it will result in securing for them a percentage equal to slightly less than the percentage of subordinate posts which they at present hold. In the departments or branches in which a special reservation is made for Anglo-Indians the reservation of vacancies for other minorities will be fixed so as to be equal approximately to the percentage of subordinate posts at present held by them. The total reservation for Anglo-Indians and other minority communities, other than Muslims, will in any case be not less than 8⅓ per cent.

(3) Anglo-Indians are at present largely employed in subordinate posts in the Appraising Department and in the Superior Preventive Service at the major ports. For the former department special technical qualifications are required, and in accordance with the general principles indicated in paragraph 6 of this Resolution it will be excluded from the operation of these rules.

In the Preventive Service special qualifications are required, and the present system of recruitment whereby posts are reserved for Anglo-Indians will be maintained.

ORDER.—Ordered that this Resolution be communicated to all Local Governments and Administrations and the several Departments of the Government of India, for information (and guidance) and that it be also published in the *Gazette of India*.

M. G. HALLET,
Secretary to the Government of India.

APPENDIX XXIV

GOVERNMENT OF INDIA RESOLUTION OF 1943 ON COMMUNAL REPRESENTATION OF SCHEDULED CASTES IN THE SERVICES

HOME DEPARTMENT

RESOLUTION

New Delhi, the 11th August 1943

No. 23/5/42-Ests(S).—In pursuance of the undertaking given in the Central Legislative Assembly in 1942, the Government of India have carefully reviewed the policy which they have followed since 1934 in regard to the representation of Depressed Classes, since described in the Government of India Act, 1935 as 'Scheduled Castes', in services under their administrative control. In their Resolution No. F. 14/17-B/33, dated the 4th July 1934, the Government of India stated that in the then state of general education among these classes they did not consider that any useful purpose would be served by reserving for them a definite percentage of vacancies. In order, however, to secure fair representation for Scheduled Castes they directed that duly qualified members of these classes might be nominated to a public service even though recruitment to that service was being made by competition. Various measures have been taken since then to secure increased representation of the Scheduled Castes in the public services. The results obtained so far have, however, not been substantial. While the Government of India recognize that this is mainly due to the difficulty of getting suitably qualified candidates, they now consider that the reservation of a definite percentage of vacancies might provide the necessary stimulus to candidates of these castes to obtain better qualifications and thus make themselves eligible for various Government posts and services. It is believed that the grant of age concessions and the reduction of prescribed fees might also help to secure qualified candidates from among members of the Scheduled Castes. The Government of India have accordingly decided to prescribe the rules mentioned in paragraph 4 below.

2. On the basis of the proportion which the population of the Scheduled Castes bears to the population of the other communities entitled to a share in the present unreserved vacancies, the Scheduled Castes would be entitled to 12.75 per cent. out of the total number of such vacancies. It is, however, not likely that sufficient number of candidates from the Scheduled Castes would be forthcoming to fill the full number of vacancies to which they are entitled on a population basis. The Government of India have, therefore, come to the conclusion that for the present it will be sufficient to reserve a somewhat smaller percentage, *viz.*, 8 1/3. They propose to consider the question of raising this percentage as soon as a sufficient number of qualified candidates from these classes are found to be available.

3. The rules mentioned below will apply only to direct recruitment and not to recruitment by promotion which will continue to be made as at present without reference to communal considerations. They will apply to Central Services (Class I and Class II) and the Subordinate Services under the administrative control of the Government of India with the exception of a few services and posts for which highly technical or special qualifications are required and which have been excluded from the purview of the communal representation orders contained in their Resolution No. F. 14/17-B/33, dated the 4th July 1934. In regard to the Railways, the rules will apply to all posts other than those of inferior servants and labourers. The administrations of the Company-managed Railways will be asked to adopt similar rules for the services on those Railways.

4. The following rules will therefore be observed in future in order to secure better representation of the Scheduled Castes in public services:—

(1) 8 1/3 per cent. of all vacancies to be filled by direct recruitment of Indians in the Central and Subordinate Services to which recruitment is made on an all-India basis will be reserved for Scheduled Castes candidates.

(2) In the case of services to which recruitment is made by local areas or circles and not on an all-India basis, *e.g.*, subordinate posts in the Railways, Posts and Telegraphs Department, the Customs Services, the Income-Tax Department, etc., the total

reservation for India as a whole of 8 1/3 per cent. of vacancies for Scheduled Castes candidates will be obtained by fixing a percentage for each local area or circle having regard to the population of Scheduled Castes in the area or circle concerned and the rules for recruitment adopted by the Provincial Government of the area or circle concerned.

(3) When recruitment is made by open competition and Scheduled Castes candidates obtain fewer vacancies than are reserved for them, the difference will, if possible, be made up by the nomination of duly qualified candidates of those castes.

(4) If Scheduled Castes candidates obtain less than the number of vacancies reserved for them in open competition and duly qualified candidates of these castes are not available, or not available in sufficient numbers, for nomination, the remaining vacancies reserved for such candidates will be treated as unreserved; but a corresponding number of vacancies will be reserved for them in that year under clause (1) or clause (2) above.

(5) If duly qualified candidates of the Scheduled Castes are again not available to fill the vacancies carried forward from the previous year under clause (4), the vacancies not filled by them will be treated as unreserved.

(6) In all cases, a minimum standard of qualification will be prescribed and the reservation will be subject to this condition.

(7) The maximum age limit prescribed for appointment to a service or post will be increased by three years in the case of candidates belonging to the Scheduled Castes.

(8) The fees prescribed for admission to any examination or selection will be reduced to one-fourth in the case of candidates belonging to the Scheduled Castes.

(9) The orders contained in the foregoing rules will also apply to temporary vacancies lasting three months or longer, including vacancies in permanent posts filled temporarily by persons not permanently employed in Government service.

(10) For the purposes of these rules a person shall be held to be a member of the Scheduled Castes if he belongs to a caste which under the Government of India (Scheduled

Castes) Order, 1936, has been declared to be a Scheduled Caste for the area in which he and his family ordinarily reside.

Order.—Ordered that a copy of this Resolution be communicated to all Chief Commissioners, the several Departments of the Government of India, the Director, Intelligence Bureau, and the Federal Public Service Commission for information and guidance; to the Political Department, the Crown Finance Department, the Secretary to the Governor-General (Public), the Secretary to the Governor-General (Reforms), the Secretary to the Governor-General (Personal), the Legislative Assembly Department, the Federal Court, the Military Secretary to His Excellency the Viceroy, and all Provincial Governments for information, and also that the Resolution be published in the *Gazette of India*.

E. CONRAN-SMITH, Secy.

APPENDIX XXV

CRIPPS PROPOSALS

Published on March 29, 1941

DRAFT DECLARATION FOR DISCUSSION WITH INDIAN LEADERS

His Majesty's Government having considered the anxieties expressed in this country and in India as to the fulfilment of promises made in regard to the future of India have decided to lay down in precise and clear terms the steps which they propose shall be taken for the earliest possible realisation of self-government in India. The object is the creation of a new Indian Union which shall constitute a Dominion associated with the United Kingdom and other Dominions by a common allegiance to the Crown but equal to them in every respect, in no way subordinate in any aspect of its domestic or external affairs.

His Majesty's Government, therefore, make the following Declaration:

(a) Immediately upon cessation of hostilities steps shall be taken to set up in India in manner described hereafter an elected body charged with the task of framing a new Constitution for India.

(b) Provision shall be made, as set out below, for participation of Indian States in the Constitution-making body.

(c) His Majesty's Government undertake to accept and implement forthwith the Constitution so framed subject only to:—

(i) The right of any Province of British India that is not prepared to accept the new Constitution to retain its present constitutional position, provision being made for its subsequent accession if it so decides.

With such non-acceding Provinces, should they so desire, His Majesty's Government will be prepared to agree upon a new Constitution giving them the same full status as the Indian Union and arrived at by a procedure analogous to that here laid down.

(ii) The signing of a Treaty which shall be negotiated between His Majesty's Government and the Constitution-making body. This Treaty will cover all necessary matters arising out of the complete transfer of responsibility from British to Indian hands; it will make provision, in accordance with undertakings given by His Majesty's Government, for the protection of racial and religious minorities; but will not impose any restriction on the power of the Indian Union to decide in future its relationship to other Member States of the British Commonwealth.

Whether or not an Indian State elects to adhere to the Constitution it will be necessary to negotiate a revision of its Treaty arrangements so far as this may be required in the new situation.

(d) The Constitution-making body shall be composed as follows unless the leaders of Indian opinion in the principal communities agree upon some other form before the end of hostilities:—

Immediately upon the result being known of Provincial Elections which will be necessary at the end of hostilities, the entire membership of the Lower Houses of Provincial Legislatures shall as a single electoral college proceed to the election of the Constitution-making body by the system of provincial representation. This new body shall be in number about 1/10th of the number of the electoral college.

Indian States shall be invited to appoint representatives in the same proportion to their total population as in the case of representatives of British India as a whole and with the same powers as British Indian members.

(e) During the critical period which now faces India and until the New Constitution can be framed His Majesty's Government must inevitably bear the responsibility for and retain the control and direction of the defence of

India as part of their world war effort, but the task of organising to the full the military, moral and material resources of India must be the responsibility of the Government of India with the co-operation of the people of India. His Majesty's Government desire and invite the immediate and effective participation of the leaders of the principal sections of the Indian people in the counsels of their country, of the Commonwealth and of the United Nations. Thus they will be enabled to give their active and constructive help in the discharge of a task which is vital and essential for the future freedom of India.

INDEX

INDEX—(*Continued*)